W9-CJY-390

MEASURING
HUMAN
BEHAVIOR

**Tools for the Assessment
of Social Functioning**

DALE G. LAKE
Severna Park, Maryland

MATTHEW B. MILES
Program in Humanistic Education
State University of New York at Albany

RALPH B. EARLE, JR.
Massachusetts Institute of Technology

TEACHERS COLLEGE PRESS

Teachers College, Columbia University
New York and London

Copyright © 1973 by Teachers College, Columbia University
Library of Congress Catalogue Card Number 72–82083

Cover Photograph: Teachers College, Office of Public Information

Manufactured in the United States

155.28
L14m

Contents

201266

Introduction

Tools have always been a crucial aspect of human culture: the knife, the plow, the whip, the abacus, the telescope, the hypodermic syringe have each emerged as needs grew, and have in turn transformed the way people lived, changed their knowledge of "what was so," and created new and unforeseen problems, for which new tools were needed.

Measuring tools are an interesting special case. To have a yardstick, to be able to map precisely the extent of one's land, to agree on what a gram is, to make something that shows the same number whenever water freezes, to know how many decibels an SST will produce are not trivial matters. Shared public agreement on how big, hot, loud, wide, or empty something is is crucial for coherence, predictability, and confidence—and for invention, growth, change, and development. For it is only by credible contrast with the old that we know what the new may be, and whether we should resist or embrace it. So, to have a common metric (and accepted devices for employing it) is a part of our common language, essential both for stability and for change.

Over history, measuring tools were centrally and always devoted to scaling the environment of *things*. Humans came late to the systematic measuring of each other, their configurations, their inner states. Something like social science has existed for less then a hundred years, if we mean by science something more than the words of the *I Ching* or Plato's views of the social system, or Machiavelli's advice to his prince. If science means systematically knowing, predicting, replicating, building, then common metrics are needed. Numbers must be attached to elusive, "non-thing" ephemeral states—numbers in which we have confidence. So if we want to understand, explain, predict, or change such matters as why citizens do not vote, or what "madness" is, or why certain leaders achieve remarkable results, or how children learn to tell the truth—in any way more cumulative than that involved in folk wisdom or day-to-day coping —agreed-on measuring tools are essential.

All this is more or less obvious. Yet it is equally obvious that social scientists, and social practitioners concerned with improved social functioning, have succeeded in building very few jointly-accepted measuring tools. Even such widely used tools as the IQ tests begun by Binet in the first decade of the century, the Rorschach developed in the twenties, Murray's Thematic Apperception Test (1935), or the well-known F-Scale

(1950) can hardly be said to enjoy the confidence any good measuring tool must have.

A good measuring tool must give the same results when used by different operators. It must not change its properties over time. It must address itself to some aspect of the real world which is important and relevant to decisions real people must make. And the user must have confidence that the numbers produced bear a precise relationship to the real-world phenomena being "measured."

When such criteria are employed, it must be said immediately that most of the thousands of social-science measuring instruments developed in the past seventy years fare very poorly indeed in comparison to rulers, thermometers, and analytical balances. Some of this weakness is inherent in the difference between measuring the net behavior of billions of molecules, and the net behavior of a single person; some of it follows from the fact that attempting to measure the behavior of a self-aware organism alters that behavior far, far more than does attempting to measure the flow of current in a circuit. But much of that weakness, we believe, stems from the way in which social science is organized and operated. Specifically, the high degree of specialization within the various social sciences, their placement in the university, detached from the day-to-day demands of social practice, the "publish or perish" reward system which encourages "original," short-range projects rather than sustained inquiry, and the generally low level of public financial support for the social sciences all lead to a state of affairs in which:

> Thoroughgoing instrument development and standardization is relatively rare;
>
> Most investigators either develop measures *de novo* or uncritically adopt an easily-available tool, without knowing its merits;
>
> Information on the operating properties of existing instruments is widely scattered through journal articles, technical reports, preprints, books, papers read at meetings, and research memoranda;
>
> Instruments which are apparently simple (and perhaps ideologically attractive) are faddishly used in hundreds of studies, while others with far more validity and stability languish unseen; and
>
> Few researchers are willing to expend energy on the systematic compilation and critique of measuring instruments that is essential for scientific progress and science-based improvement in daily life.

The rapid growth of interest in the application of the behavioral sciences, and planned social change in general, during the past two decades (cf. Bennis, Benne, and Chin, 1961, 1969) has begun to alter this state of affairs somewhat. As human relations training, group psychotherapy, organizational improvement, rehabilitative programs, educational innovation, curriculum development, and similar fields of what might be called "social engineering" have developed, the interaction between social practitioners and social scientists has deepened and extended considerably. Pressure has mounted for the creation of reliable measuring devices which are relevant to real-world problems, and on the basis of which valid knowledge about the processes and outcomes of planned change efforts can be accumulated. Such measuring tools are needed for (1) diagnosing the existing state of affairs in systems, prior to change efforts; (2) evaluating the results of change attempts; (3) explaining and understanding the reasons for the success of such attempts. Many useful tools were developed from the 1920's onward in relation to the assessment of ability and achievement in schools. We are now seeing a similar growth in the availability of instruments for the assessment of social functioning, more generally viewed.

We use the term "social functioning" to refer to the properties of the individual (cognitive/perceptual, motivational, and overt behavioral) as he or she takes part in social interaction, and to the properties of the immediate social system involved (dyads, small groups, organizations).

PURPOSE OF THE BOOK

This book aims at remedying the less-than-satisfactory state of affairs in relation to tools for measuring social functioning which has been reviewed above. In it we bring together systematic reviews of 84 different instruments (38 oriented to personal variables (of which 13 are cognitive-perceptual, 19 are affective-motivational, and 6 deal with overt behavior), 24 interpersonal, 10 group, and 12 organizational) which seemed to us to deserve critical attention as measuring tools in these domains. Secondly, we present reviews of 20 other existing compendia of instruments (most of them developed in the last decade), explaining what variables they cover, and what the adequacy of information presented in them is.

Our audiences for the book are several: the social-science researcher, whether principal investigator or graduate student, who wants to study some aspect of social functioning; the applied behavioral scientist who wishes to diagnose a system, evaluate a program, or explain planned-change processes; and the program-based manager, practitioner, or researcher in educational, governmental, voluntary, or industrial settings who needs tools to monitor the progress and effectiveness in his organization.

CRITERIA FOR INSTRUMENT INCLUSION

Given the proliferation of dispersed, diverse measurement efforts in the social sciences, we chose instruments with certain criteria in mind. To be included, an instrument should:

> Be in the general domain of normal "social functioning" as defined above. Intra-personal measures with little apparent relevance to social functioning, and those usable only with abnormal, special, or pathological populations were excluded. That is, we chose instruments directly related to properties of organization, groups, or interpersonal relationships—or to properties of normal persons directly relevant to their participation in such social situations.
>
> Be based on some underlying theory or conceptual scheme.
>
> Have required a non-trivial amount of developmental work. Brief, one-shot instruments such as rating scales, indices, activity counts, etc., are by and large not included.
>
> Be interesting, promising, potentially useful—though not necessarily well known.
>
> By and large, not have been reviewed or discussed elsewhere in the recent literature.
>
> Be available for use by responsible researchers.
>
> Be supported by some reasonably current information on reliability and validity.

In the pool of the 300-odd instruments we considered for inclusion—and undoubtedly outside it as well—there are certainly more than 84 instruments meeting these criteria. We hope that the appearance of this book encourages the appearance of more like it.

FORMAT FOR INSTRUMENTS

Each instrument is presented in the following manner.

TITLE.   Instruments are alphabetized through book by title.

AUTHORS.   Those responsible for instrument design and development.

AVAILABILITY.   Where and how the instrument can be obtained, as of June 1971. We deliberately chose *not* to include instruments verbatim, not only because of copyright problems, but because we believe that a decision to use an instrument should be based on a careful review, and the energy required of a responsible researcher to obtain it—not on an arbitrary exercise of whim or expedient copying of what's easily available.

VARIABLES.   What the instrument claims to be measuring, and the conceptual scheme behind it.

DESCRIPTION.   What the instrument looks like, its format. Items similar to those in the actual instrument are presented.

ADMINISTRATION AND SCORING.   How the instrument is used, time involved, supervision required if any, manner in which numbers or scores are generated; availability of machine scoring services if any; availability of norms.

DEVELOPMENT.   The history of the instrument, and what operations the authors went through to produce the present version. Usually includes early reliability and validity findings.

CRITIQUE.   The presently-known properties of the instrument. Ordinarily includes comments on reliability (internal consistency and stability), and any available validity evidence (face, construct, predictive, concurrent). The adequacy of norms is discussed. Possible difficulties such as item transparency, fakeability, and various response sets (acquiescence, extremes, social desirability) are reviewed.

GENERAL COMMENT.   An over-all statement about the usefulness of the instrument, cautions to be observed, its future promise, and any final observations not covered earlier.

REFERENCES.   All published and unpublished work referred to in the body of the review.

UNITERMS.   A list of key words referring to the variables tapped by the measure, or relevant to it in some important way. These Uniterms (such as "abasement," "ability," "acceptance") appear in the Uniterm Index (pp. 389–414) and can be used by the reader to gain access to instruments (or compendia of instruments) measuring variables he or she is concerned with (e.g., "abasement").

Initials appearing at the end of the review indicate who took primary responsibility for producing it.

FORMAT OF COMPENDIA REVIEWS

The second section of this book reviews other published collections of instruments in the broad domain of the social sciences, primarily psychology, sociology, and political science. Each review follows this format:

TITLE.

AUTHORS.

AVAILABILITY.   Publisher, location, date. Access methods if they are other than purchasing the publication.

TESTING AREAS COVERED.   A list of Uniterms characterizing the variables covered by instruments which are covered in the collection. Such Uniterm-ing is necessarily less thorough than that made for the instruments in our volume, but is detailed enough to send the reader to the right compendium for a variable he or she is interested in.

DESCRIPTION.   An overview of the nature and approach of the compendium; criteria for inclusion; nature of information presented on each instrument.

CRITIQUE.   Comments on the adequacy of the approach taken, similarities to and differences from the present volume.

GENERAL COMMENT.   Summary reactions, advice to the user.

HOW TO USE THIS BOOK

Uniterm Index. As indicated above, this index enables the reader to locate instruments bearing on variables in which he is interested, either in the present volume, or in the other compendia which are reviewed here.

Author Index. This lists all instrument authors, and all authors of studies cited in reviews.

Instrument Reviews. Instruments in this volume are listed alphabetically by title.

In sum, three modes of access to instruments are possible. If a *variable* is of interest, consult the Uniterm Index, which sends the reader to one or more instruments reviewed in this book, or to one or more other compendia. If an *author* is of interest, consult the Author Index, which will refer the reader to authors of studies reviewed in this volume (and to authors of compendia). If a particular *instrument* is of interest, the 84 instrument reviews in this book are arranged in alphabetical sequence by title.

ACKNOWLEDGEMENTS

The idea for this book dates back to 1957. At that time, Miles began a comprehensive reference file of abstracts (eventually totaling over 3500 items) of social-psychological studies dealing with behavior change induced through small group experiences. Support for this work was provided through 1963 by the Horace Mann-Lincoln Institute of School Experimentation of Teachers College, Columbia University. We are grateful to Arthur W. Foshay, Institute director during that period, for his continuing interest. Francine N. Lang did much of the early work on the file, and was followed by Thomas M. Harris and Alvin Atkins. Irvin Cohen was instrumental in setting up the Uniterm system used for storage and retrieval of abstracts. During early stages of the book's planning (1964–67), Louis Jones, Ella Lasky, and Eugene Hittleman were extremely helpful in organizing available materials and locating more, filling information gaps, and developing a format for describing instruments; they also aided with preliminary decisions about instruments to be included. Leslie J. Rifkind, Morton Elfenbein, and James L. Midwinter, Jr. did first drafts of many instrument write-ups. During final editing stages, Paul Ruffer was helpful in locating needed information in the material files, and Katherine Garner did extremely thorough library search work.

For project financial support, we are indebted to the Horace Mann-Lincoln Institute; to the Kettering Foundation, which supplied full support for the years 1965 through 1967; to the American Society for Training and Development, which supplied a grant to aid the final process of writing and editing; and to the United States Office of Education, through its grant for the Cooperative Project for Educational Development, which enabled the development and testing of several new instruments included here. Charles Seashore and Dorothy Mial of the NTL Institute for Applied Behavioral Science were especially helpful in aiding with obtaining support through ASTD and USOE.

The division of labor among the authors has varied over the life of the book's preparation. Miles initiated the project, and did much of the original planning, and supervision of search and abstracting. Beginning in 1964, Lake took central responsibility for raising additional funds, and for supervision of search and abstracting, first at Teachers College, then at Boston University, and at the Program in Humanistic Education at the State University of New York at Albany. During the final stages of the project (1968–70), Earle, then a Ph.D. candidate in Political Science at Massachusetts Institute of Technology, was responsible for over half of semi-final drafts of write-ups, and shared the writing of reviews of compendia with Miles. Semi-final editing was by Lake, with Miles completing the finally-edited manuscript.

Finishing an enterprise of this sort naturally produces mixed feelings: satisfaction and relief; gnawing worry that some crucial instrument, variable, or study has been somehow overlooked (of *course* that must be the case, given the development in the domain we are concerned with); and pleasure in having produced what we feel is a useful assemblage of tools for users who need them. The appearance of other compendia during the preparation of this one lends weight to our diagnosis that this sort of book is—and will continue to be—much needed. We look forward to seeing many more similar enterprises by others.

D. G. L.

M. B. M.

R. B. E.

Instrument Reviews

1
Activities Index

AUTHOR.   George G. Stern

AVAILABILITY.   Psychological Research Center, Syracuse University, Syracuse, New York 13210.

VARIABLES.   The Activities Index (Form 957) is the revision of a scale designed to measure 42 "psychogenic needs" adopted with some modifications from Murray (1938). The booklet contains definitions and item examples of each need. The following are some of the better-known and used needs and their respective definitions as given by Stern: *Abasement,* Self-depreciation and devaluation; acknowledgment of mistakes, failures, and humiliation; *Achievement,* Surmounting obstacles (physical, personal, or interpersonal) and proving personal worth; *Adaptiveness,* Defendance, acceptance of advice and criticism versus concealment or justification of failure or humiliation; *Affiliation,* Close, friendly, reciprocal associations with others; *Aggression,* Blame-avoidance; overt or covert hostility towards others versus the denial of such impulses; *Change,* Unroutinized, changeable behavior versus repetitive, perseverative action patterns; *Emotionality,* Intensive, active emotional expression versus calm, serene, restrained responsiveness or placidity; *Energy,* Intense, sustained, vigorous effort versus sluggish inertia or passivity; *Nurturance,* Supporting others by providing love, assistance, and protection; *Scientism,* Manipulation of external physical objects through empirical analysis, reflection, and discussion; and *Succorance,* Dependence on others for love, assistance, and protection versus detachment or autonomy.

Stern states that needs are functional and that a need is revealed in the modes of behavior employed by the individual. In this sense the list of needs is a taxonomy of interaction processes. The Index has been considered a research tool, but studies are being done concerning diagnostic possibilities. The form has been used with persons from 13 to 63 years of age in various social and educational strata. An additional index, called College Characteristics Index (see Pace and Stern, 1970), has been constructed as a direct complement to the Activities Index; it measures Murray's concept of "environmental press." Similar procedures are used, although there is not yet definite evidence to indicate direct relationship.

DESCRIPTION.   The form contains 30 subscales of 10 items each. Respondents answer either "like" or "dislike" to each item, which is a statement of a means of manifesting a particular need. Items of this type are:

Doing something crazy occasionally just for the fun of it.

Listening to music that makes me feel sad.

ADMINISTRATION AND SCORING.   The Activities Index is self-administering, following instructions on the cover of a reusable question booklet, and requires from thirty to ninety minutes to complete, depending on the age and reading ability of the subject. Answers are recorded on a special sheet, using an electrographic pencil. There is no time limit, but subjects are encouraged to work quickly. It is essential that every item be answered. In accordance with a key given in the manual, the index may be hand-scored with a single stencil, or machine-scored in five runs on a standard IBM test-scoring machine. Methods for computation of scores are indicated both on the key and on the Diagnostic Summary form. All scores are plotted as arcs, which taken together form a circular profile diagram for each individual.

DEVELOPMENT.   The prototype for the Activities Index was constructed in 1950–51, in the Examiner's Office of the University of Chicago. It was called the Interest Index, after an inventory by Sheviakov (Sheviakov and Friedberg, 1939) which suggested the format for a needs measure. It differed from other inventories of activities and interests in being designed as a systematic representation of variables stemming from an explicit personality theory.

The Index was developed from over 1,000 items describing commonplace daily activities and feelings which appeared to represent unambiguous manifestations of need processes. Eight psychologists independently coded these items, and the Index was assembled from those items unanimously considered to be diagnostic of specific elements in the need taxonomy.

In its original form, the Index consisted of 400 items distributed unequally among 41 overlapping needs categories. The author states that the Index went through several revisions and assessment studies, but does not give any information, other than a reference to Stern (1956). The report lacks information concerning the samples originally used, and description of the population from which samples were chosen.

CRITIQUE.   The author states in his manual that the *reliability* of a multivariate test is best estimated in terms of the stability of the profile pattern, and has conducted scale and cluster reliabilities for 122 school teachers retested after seven months of participation in a workshop program. Stern says the pre-post correlations were underestimated, but coefficients for the 10-item scales ranged from .47 to .93, with an average of .69. A smaller sample of 11 social workers involved in a two-week workshop yielded product—moment test—retest coefficients ranging from .67 to .94, with a mean of .88, based on cluster scales only. At the time of the printing of the manual in 1958, studies were still being done.

Stern states that the most convincing proof of the *validity* of the Activities Index has come from the positive recognition of unidentified descriptions of subjects by psychiatrists, supervisors, and colleagues. The author has given an extensive reference list in which he says many of the validity studies have been discussed, but there is a definite lack of statistically valid information given in the manual. There have been *concurrent validity* studies done with other tests, including Strong Vocational, Rorschach, TAT, Edwards Personal Preference Scale, MMPI, Cattell 16 Personality Factor, and California Personality Inventory.

No statistics are given for *predictive validity*, but Stern lists some of the applications made that now have results. A multiple *r* of .63 cross-validated between a 23-item subscale from the Activities Index and first-year comprehensive examination average in general education programs was found. There were significant differences found on Index subscales between extreme scorers on a positivity—negativity index for TAT protocols.

The Index has many items which are *fakeable*.

GENERAL COMMENT. The Stern Activities Index is an important attempt to demonstrate empirically the validity of Murray's theoretical constructs. And despite the fact that there is, at the time of this writing, little statistical information concerning the reliability and validity of the test, it is felt that this is a useful test, and one which can be of benefit to many, including school personnel, clinical diagnosticians, and psychological researchers. It seems to do a good job of limiting and defining needs, and the results of an individual's profile can be nicely descriptive of extreme feelings and needs. It is recommended that the user of this test be aware of the lack of statistics, and keep an eye open for further validational studies.

REFERENCES

Murray, H. A. *Explorations in personality.* New York: Oxford University Press, 1938.

Naugle, F. W., Stern, G. G., and Eschenfelder, W. The derivation of quantitative personality models for the assessment and prediction of performance. *American Psychologist,* 1956, *11,* 356.

Pace, C. R. and Stern, G. G. *College Characteristics Index, Form 457.* Syracuse University Psychological Research Center, 1957.

Scanion, J. The Activities Index: an inquiry into validity. Unpublished doctoral dissertation, Syracuse University, 1958.

Sheviakov, G. V. and Friedberg, J. Evaluation of personal and social adjustment. Progressive Education Association: *Evaluation in the Eight-Year Study.* Chicago: University of Chicago Press, 1939.

Stern, G. G., Stein, H. I., and Bloom, B. S. *Methods in personality assessment.* Glencoe, Illinois: Free Press, 1956.

Tatham, D. F., Stellwagen, W., and Stern, G. G. The Stern Activities Index as a measure of differences among vocational and academic groups. *American Psychologist,* 1957, *12,* 457.

UNITERMS. Abasement; achievement; activity; adaptiveness; affiliation; aggression; audacity; change; egoism; emotionality; energy; expressiveness; intellectual interests; motivation; need; nurturance; orderliness; scientism; self-assertion; sensuousness; succorance.

—R. B. E.

2
Adjective Check List (ACL)

AUTHORS.   Harrison G. Gough and Alfred B. Heilbrun

AVAILABILITY.   Consulting Psychologists Press, 577 College Avenue, Palo Alto, California 94306.

VARIABLES.   The Adjective Check List produces 24 scales. In addition to three counts (total number of adjectives checked, the number of favorable adjectives checked, and the number of unfavorable adjectives checked), measures are obtained of *Defensiveness; Self-Confidence; Self-Control; Lability* (spontaneity, flexibility, need for change, rejection of convention, assertive individuality); *Personal Adjustment;* 15 of Murray's needs (*Achievement, Dominance, Endurance, Order, Intraception, Nurturance, Affiliation, Heterosexuality, Exhibition, Autonomy, Aggression, Change, Succorance, Abasement, Deference*); and *Counseling Readiness.*

DESCRIPTION.   The ACL is a list of 300 adjectives which can be descriptive of personality attributes (simulated items: trustworthy, courteous, brave, obedient, reverent).

ADMINISTRATION AND SCORING.   The ACL can be filled out in about ten to fifteen minutes, singly or in groups. Ss merely check adjectives which they believe are descriptive of the subject, whether that subject be themselves, someone known personally by them, a historical figure, or an archetype ("the typical banker" or "most Canadians"). Two scoring forms are available, a four-page hand-scored folder and a single answer sheet which may be hand-scored or machine-scored by National Computer Systems, 1015 South Sixth Street, Minneapolis, Minnesota. Completed lists are scored first on the basis of the number of adjectives checked. For each of four frequency groups, the manual gives standard scores by sex for the conversion of raw frequency scores for adjectives keyed to other scales. Because of the large number of scales, machine scoring is recommended.

DEVELOPMENT.   The nucleus for the ACL was Cattell's (1943) compilation of 171 personality traits from his factorial studies of personality structure. To these were added words suggested by the theoretical work of persons such as Freud, Jung, Mead, and Murray to form a first

7

list of 279 items. Two years of testing resulted by 1952 in the current form of 300 words.

CRITIQUE.   Test—retest *reliability* of the 300-word list is not high. For 100 males over a six–month interval, *phi*-coefficients for adjectives checked both times, neither time, the first but not the second, and the second but not the first ranged from .01 to .86, with a mean of .54 and a standard deviation of .19. The test–retest reliabilities for the 24 scales over ten weeks for 56 college males ranged from .54 (Succorance) to .85 (Nurturance) with a median of .76, and for 23 college females scales ranged from .45 (Succorance) to .90 (Aggression), with a median of .76. For two sets of five judges of five males, intergroup reliability coefficients (corrected for all ten judges by the Spearman–Brown formula) were (for each S) .70, .63, .61, .75, and .61.

Heilbrun's 1958 study of *validity* correlated the 15 Murray need scales with their counterparts on the Edwards Personal Preference Schedule (Edwards, 1954). Although the rank orders of needs correlated at $rho = .60$, the between-scale correlations were low. Ten of the 15 were significant at the .01 level; the median correlation coefficient for all 15 needs was $r = .31$, the range, .01 (Achievement) to .48 (Aggression). A correlation of all 24 scales with 8 tests of intellectual ability and functioning for 100 males produced (out of a total of 192 rs) 23 correlations significant at $p < .05$ and 15 significant at $p < .01$. The largest was that between Lability and the Bennett Mechanical Comprehension Test, where $r = .36$, $p < .01$. The Lability scale correlated significantly most often with the General Information Survey and the Terman Concept Mastery Test, also at the .01 level, and with the Gottschaldt Figures Test and the Wesman Personnel Classification Test ($p < .05$). Other comparisons, such as those with the California Personality Inventory and the Minnesota Multiphasic Personality Inventory, yielded similarly inconclusive results.

The authors used as an *acquiescence* measure the total number of adjectives checked. Raw scores from a sample of 100 males for Affiliation and Heterosexuality correlated with the total number of words checked at .78 and .64. The 23 scales range in raw score correlations from −.48 (Counseling Readiness) through .01 (Succorance) to .78 (Affiliation). The absolute value of the median "acquiescence" correlation is .44. However, converted standard scores correlate from −.19 to .26, with the median at .04, which represents a considerable improvement. Standard score tables are available separately for each quartile on "total words checked" by males and females.

The impact of *social desirability* is evident in the correlations with the Edwards Social Desirability Scale of .41 for Achievement, .45 for Dominance, and −.41 for Succorance.

The scales show a fair degree of independence, but there is a correlation of .64 for 400 males, and .79 for 400 females between Personal Adjustment and number of favorable adjectives checked (the Fav score). Also, a correlation of .72 exists between Endurance and Order (.61 for males, .88 for females), and of .76 between Fav and total words checked. These relationships are in part due to the presence of overlapping items.

The *norms* are based on samples of 1,364 college men and 642 college women.

GENERAL COMMENT.   The ease with which the ACL may be administered is counterbalanced by the laboriousness of scoring it. The validity data are spotty and unreassuring. As is generally true of self-report measures, agreement response sets and social desirability effects are present, although it should be remembered that the standard score method, which controls roughly for total number of adjectives checked, reduces the effects of agreement sets.

Although Gough and Heilbrun have devised several indices to measure subject versus observer discrepancies, it is not clear that the Adjective Check List is appropriate for use as a measure of independent variables. The low correlations, for example, between Edwards' measures of Murray's needs and those of the ACL warn against using the Adjective Check List for other than exploratory or supplementary research.

REFERENCES

Cattell, R. B. The description of personality: 2. Basic traits resolved into clusters. *Journal of Abnormal and Social Psychology*, 1943, 38, 476–507.

Edwards, A. L. *Manual: Edwards Personal Preference Schedule.* New York: The Psychological Corp., 1954.

Gough, H. G. The Adjective Check List as a personality assessment research technique. *Psychological Reports*, 1960, 6, 107–122.

Heilbrun, A. B. Relationships between the Adjective Check List, Personal Preference Schedule and desirability factors under varying defensiveness conditions. *Journal of Clinical Psychology*, 1958, 14, 237–238.

UNITERMS.   Abasement; acquiescence; achievement; affiliation; aggression; autonomy; change; counseling readiness; defensiveness; deference; dominance; endurance; exhibition; heterosexuality, intraception; lability; nurturance; order; personal adjustment; self-confidence; self-control; succorance.

—R. B. E.

3
Altruism Scale

AUTHOR.   Jack Sawyer

AVAILABILITY.   Sawyer, J. The Altruism Scale: a measure of cooperative, individualistic, and competitive interpersonal orientation. *American Journal of Sociology*, 1966, 71 (4), 407–416.

VARIABLES.   This scale is designed to measure *altruism*, the value one person places upon the welfare of another in relation to his own. The author conceives of altruism as a characteristic that may vary within individuals as a function of the object of the altruism, the commodity involved, and the situation in which it is expressed. Altruism is conceptualized as occurring in an interaction situation involving two individuals, labeled Person and Other. The values of the situation to each individual are imperfectly correlated (as in non-zero-sum games). If Person is purely cooperative, he will try to maximize his own welfare, *and* that of Other. If he is individualistic, he will maximize his own welfare without regard to Other's welfare. If he is purely competitive, he will maximize his own welfare at Other's expense. Positive altruism exists in the cooperative orientation, no altruism exists in the individualistic orientation, and "negative" values of altruism exist in the competitive orientation.

DESCRIPTION.   The Altruism Scale consists of two instruments. The first is a three-by-three matrix with the row entries being the outcomes of a two-person situation for the self and the column entries being those same outcomes for an Other. The outcomes depend upon the facts hypothesized; Sawyer has used academic grades, yearly or monthly salaries, degrees of physical intimacy with girl friend (single males), and frequencies of dating (single females). The second instrument is a scale for the direct estimation of altruism. The scale contains 21 points, ranging from −1.0 to +1.0 by tenths and anchored at five points:

1.0 I am *equally* interested in how *good* his grade (salary, etc.) is and in how *good* my grade is.

0.5 I am *half* as interested in how *good* his grade is than in how *good* my grade is.

0.0 I am *only* interested in how good my grade is; how good or poor his grade is makes no difference to me.

0.5 I am *equally* interested in how much *better* my grade is than his and in how *good* my grade is *per se.*

−1.0 I am *only* interested in how much *better* my grade is than his; I do not care how good my grade is *per se*.

ADMINISTRATION AND SCORING. The scale is not an observational measure (although the author indicates that observation would be the best method of measuring), but rather a response measure. The subject is asked to respond to two instruments. The first instrument is a three-by-three matrix in which the subject ranks desired outcomes. For example:

> Imagine yourself in the following situation. It is the beginning of the term and you are taking, among other courses, an important seminar in your area of specialization. It so happens that there is only one other student in the seminar. You are both taking the course for credit, however, and each of you will receive one of the grades, A, B, or C. Since there are three possible outcomes for each of you, and the instructor assigns grades independently, there exist nine possible combinations of outcomes, ranging from both A's to both C's. Rank your preference for these nine outcomes in the following situation. Place the numbers 1 (first choice) to 9 in the cells of the accompanying table, indicating your preference for each of the combinations of grades for you and the other student. If you have absolutely no preference between the combinations indicate this by placing the same number in both of the cells.

The scoring of the allocation of the nine ranks is accomplished in such a way that the three defining orientations produce altruism values of 1.0, 0.0, and −1.0.

$$a = \frac{\text{Summed ranks for C to other minus summed ranks for A to other}}{\text{Summed ranks for C to self minus summed ranks for A to self}}$$

The second measure is taken by having the subject respond to the scale; the score is taken directly from the scale.

For both tests the subject is instructed that Other is a friend, a stranger, or an antagonist.

DEVELOPMENT. Sawyer's examination of the few previous attempts to measure altruism objectively as a stable characteristic convinced him of the futility of such a line of experimentation.

CRITIQUE. To assess *reliability*, Sawyer considered his two instruments equivalent to one 12-item scale involving two measures of three Others, in two situations (grades and salaries). For a composite sample of 62 YMCA social service students, 32 business graduate students, and 28 social science students, the Cronbach (1951) alpha coefficient was .79. Considering his two measures of two situations as four scales of altruism, Sawyer calculated scale intercorrelations for the three Others and found that altruism involving a stranger correlates at .63 with a corresponding composite for friends and .57 with one involving antagonists. Similarly, the two 6-item composites measuring the grades and salaries correlate at .75. But the two composites obtained by combining the results for grades and salaries and comparing instruments (matrix versus scale) correlate at only .32.

The major findings of Sawyer's *validity* studies were that t-tests at the .01 level indicated significant and large differences between altruism toward friend, stranger, and antagonist. The mean scores for each category were .42, .12, and —.18. These results, however, can be interpreted as contraindicative of *construct validity* insofar as altruism has been defined as "affection and concern for others" and "where the goal of conduct (of the ego) is exterior to itself" (Sawyer, 1965). Sawyer's conception, however (as well as his results), specifically includes a concern for Person as well as for the Other. Pure altruism would produce equal scores for friend, stranger, and antagonist; the *absolute* score on Sawyer's or any other scale could vary from subject to subject. In this regard, the absolute differences in altruism toward friend and antagonist were, for the YMCA sample .54, business students .62, and social science students .91. The social science students were by far the *least* altruistic.

Sawyer has shown that YMCA college students score generally higher toward all others (mean = .21) than do social science students (.07) and business students (.02), a result more nearly supporting construct validity. Sex differences showed up in the sample of YMCA students, where women were generally more altruistic toward all three Others (level of significance unreported). Among the social science students, women differed only in showing less negative altruism (—.22) than men (—.42). (The business students sample contained no women.)

No *norms* are presented and, more seriously, Sawyer does not discuss the Altruism Scales' susceptibility to *social desirability*, which may be considerable, particularly in view of the instrument's transparency.

GENERAL COMMENT.   The test does not really measure "altruism" as usually construed. As the author notes, the three orientations could be conceived of as cooperation, competition, and individualism. In a sense, Person's fate is tied to Other's. The relationship between them is negotiable. "Altruism" usually implies that Person helps Other, independently of his own outcome. If altruism is to be a meaningful term, it must be distinguished logically and behaviorally from cooperation. However, the test does appear to be a moderately good indicator of a cooperative orientation. It is easy to administer and score, and does differentiate between groups.

REFERENCE

Sawyer, J. The Altruism Scale: a measure of cooperative, individualistic, and competitive interpersonal orientation. *American Journal of Sociology*, 1966, *71*, 407–416.

UNITERMS.   Altruism; competition; cooperation; game; individualism; interpersonal.

—L. J. R.

4
The Anxiety Differential (AD)

AUTHORS.   Sheldon Alexander and Theodore R. Husek

AVAILABILITY.   Alexander, S. and Husek, T. R. The Anxiety Differential: initial steps in the development of a measure of situational anxiety. *Educational and Psychological Measurement*, 1962, 22, 325–348.

VARIABLES.   The Anxiety Differential is a verbal-response measure of *situational anxiety*, or anxiety as a momentary motivational state. The measurement is made in terms of cognitive changes in meanings of "various events, persons, objects, and ideas" as affected by anxiety states. Anxiety is conceptualized as specifically relating to bodily harm.

DESCRIPTION.   At this point in the development of the instrument the AD is best suited for research purposes. It consists of 6 scales which vary according to which of 28 items are scored. The 28 items consist of concepts which are rated on a seven-point semantic differential scale. For example, a simulated item:

MYSELF

happy __:__:__:__:__:__: sad

Four different forms of the test are suggested, their use depending on research design (whether a control group is available, whether the design is directed toward identifying incremental anxiety, or whether an after-only design is used). In addition, a fifth, all-purpose test is suggested.

ADMINISTRATION AND SCORING.   The test can be administered individually or in groups, and takes an estimated five to ten minutes to complete. Scoring can be done by machine on the basis of keys. Scoring for high anxiety is indicated for each item. A number of different kinds of analyses can be done. Pre–post changes on individual items can be calculated; selected items (based on criteria above) can be summed for a total anxiety score. No special training is required for administration or scoring.

While separate norming information is not presented exclusive of the reliability samples, means and standard deviations for males and females are presented in Alexander and Husek (1962), and in Husek and Alexander (1963).

14

DEVELOPMENT.   Alexander and Husek proposed the AD format for measuring situational anxiety as offering a number of advantages over existing measures. Theoretically, the AD was chosen to measure cognitive changes, especially the connotative or affective meanings which accompany the anxiety state. The authors began with a 68-item semantic differential test which was administered to 247 male college freshmen. 119 subjects were then shown a color film involving a surgical operation, after which they were given the post-test. At this time, they also received the Nowlis–Green Adjective Check List. Controls were run for the effect of the film and for faking. A factor analysis of items produced an anxiety factor (the first and largest factor) and other smaller and uninterpretable factors. A number of scales involving combinations of items showing differences among control groups were constructed. The items in these scales provided the greatest number of items on the anxiety factor, 18 out of 25. In addition, these scales correlated significantly (between .48 and .63) with the Nowlis–Green Check List. Further studies were done for male–female differences and a palmar sweating index. Male–female differences were significant in only one out of 12 of the comparisons made. Palmar sweating was not significantly related to scale scores.

Cross validation of the scale was achieved by using a filmstrip involving an automobile accident, viewed by a sample of 41 males and 59 females. Internal consistency estimates using alpha coefficients were obtained for the various forms of the scales; the coefficients ranged from .42 to .82. Four scales were derived which indicate the best items to be used for pre–post group difference designs, experimental–control group difference designs, experimental and control for post-test only designs, and finally, an all-purpose test.

An extension of the generality of the scale from the domain of bodily harm anxiety to anxiety related to test-taking was also examined. All four forms of the new test showed significant differences between the experimental group and the control. From the items used in this study, 18 were chosen to constitute a new AD measure of examination anxiety. Twelve of the items had been used in the tests 1 to 4 described above, four were chosen from other research, and two were new.

CRITIQUE.   Some *reliability* data beyond those reported above are available. In a later study involving 124 female and 76 male students, the odd–even split-half reliability estimate was .68; in a second study involving 248 students, the figure was .64. The authors do indicate a concern for sex differences on the scale. They suggest that male and female test results be examined separately.

Construct validity of the AD has been examined through some cross-situational testing. The utility of the instrument for predicting both bodily-harm anxiety and test-taking anxiety has been established. Husek and Alexander (1963) found consistent, significant differences in AD scores between control and pre-examination samples of both males and females. The authors suggested the need for work in the area of other varieties of anxiety. The AD was found to have significantly low correlations with measures of general characterological anxiety: *rs* of .15 and .28 with Taylor Manifest Anxiety Scale, and .29 with the Sarason Anxiety Test (Husek, Schaefer, and Alexander, undated). The AD was not found to relate significantly with palmar sweating.

With respect to *concurrent validity*, the AD was found to correlate significantly with the Nowlis–Green Check List as a measure of momentary mood.

Norms for this test in the form of anxiety level difference for different situations are not clearly presented; that is, different, incomparable test forms were used for various situations. The authors also indicate that parts of the tests are differentially sensitive to the bodily harm versus examination anxiety situations.

The AD is not appreciably affected by *social desirability;* it correlates at .29 with the Edwards SD scale. A similar low correlation of .13 is reported for *acquiescence.* The authors suggest that faking does not appreciably alter the test scores.

GENERAL COMMENT.   The Anxiety Differential scales appear to be living up to their authors' initial criteria of imperviousness to faking or response sets; objective, nonjudgmental scoring; easy administration; short duration; and low cost. As Alexander and Husek note, the scales require further studies of their applicability to other types of anxiety, such as those associated with failure, guilt, rejection, or aggression, and should be primarily employed for research, not clinical purposes. Within the areas of bodily harm and examination anxiety, they can adequately distinguish both individuals and groups.

REFERENCES

Alexander, S. and Husek, T. The Anxiety Differential: initial steps in the development of a measure of situational anxiety. *Educational and Psychological Measurement,* 1962, *22,* 325–348.

Alexander, S. and McHose, J. The Anxiety Differential: task difficulty and sex in verbal learning. Paper presented at the annual meeting of the Midwestern Psychological Association, St. Louis, May 1964.

Husek, T. and Alexander, S. The effectiveness of the Anxiety Differential in examination stress situations. *Educational and Psychological Measurement,* 1963, *23,* 309–318.

Husek, T., Schaefer, S., and Alexander, S. The relationship of the Anxiety Differential to other anxiety scales and to test-taking habits. Unpublished mimeographed paper, undated.

UNITERMS.   Achievement; aggression; anxiety; examination; failure; harm; semantic differential; test anxiety.

—M. E.

5
Attitude–Belief Scales (AB Scales)

AUTHORS.   Martin Fishbein and Bertram H. Raven

AVAILABILITY.   Fishbein, M. and Raven, B. H. The AB scales. *Human Relations*, 1962, *15*, 35–44.

VARIABLES.   The AB Scales were adapted from Osgood's Semantic Differential (1957) and are designed to measure the attitudes and beliefs of an individual toward a concept, or a relation between two concepts. Attitudes and beliefs are conceived as two independent variables relatively uncorrelated with each other. *Attitude* is defined as the "evaluative component" of the individual's perception of a concept or a relation between concepts. Thus, attitude refers to the good–bad quality of the concept. *Belief* involves the individual's perception of the likelihood of the existence of the concept or of a relation between two concepts. Thus, belief refers to the probability of the existence of a particular concept (e.g., extrasensory perception (ESP)).

DESCRIPTION.   The AB Scales are a paper-and-pencil test comprised of 20 adjective pairs. The technique follows standard semantic differential technique, with 7-point scales balanced to prevent response bias. Five scales measure attitude; five scales measure belief; ten scales are fillers. Some examples are:

> dirty/clean   (attitude)
>
> impossible/possible   (belief)
>
> cruel/kind   (filler)

ADMINISTRATION AND SCORING.   An individual's score is derived by summing his score on each of the five scales aimed at his belief or attitude. Scoring of a single scale is accomplished by assigning the numbers 1 through 7 to the possible responses. Change is measured by subtracting the score on the first administration from the score on the second administration. No weighting or normative data are provided.

DEVELOPMENT.   The scales comprising the final instrument were developed empirically. Twenty-two pairs of polar adjectives, selected *a priori*, were administered to 15 graduate psychology students who had been randomly assigned to four experimental groups. Group I "role-played" a person who strongly believed in ESP and who was strongly in favor of such a phenomenon's existence. The role players filled out the scales as if they were that person. Group II role-played non-belief and positive attitude. Group III role-played belief and negative attitude. Group IV role-played negative belief and negative attitude. The 22 pairs of adjectives were administered using the standard semantic differential directions (Osgood, Suci, and Tannenbaum, 1957). In analyzing the data, adjective pairs which did not clearly distinguish between attitude and belief were eliminated. Scales which yielded high or low scores in three or more groups were also eliminated. The procedure was then repeated with two groups of introductory psychology students. The first group consisted of 19 students; the second group consisted of 20 students. Items were eliminated until five scales for belief and five for attitude were selected. Ten filler scales were added to disguise the purpose of the instrument. The test was then administered to a number of introductory psychology students twice, with a one-month interval between administrations.

To determine the applicability of the test to other concepts than ESP, 121 subjects were asked to rate the concepts "extrasensory perception," "atomic fallout," and "racial prejudice." The tests were able to discriminate between attitude and belief for all three concepts: correlations between attitude and belief were $-.17$, $-.07$, and $.12$, respectively.

CRITIQUE.   Fishbein and Raven felt that the *reliability* of the semantic differential technique was already established. They also give test–retest figures of .61 for attitude and .66 for belief.

Validity has been measured in two ways. First, the test has detected predictable changes in both attitude and cognitive dissonance studies (Fishbein and Raven, 1962). Second, Fishbein (1963) conducted a study in which 125 subjects were asked to give word associations to the stimulus word "Negro." The ten most frequently given characteristics were used to construct ten belief statements (e.g., Negroes have dark skin). Two weeks later, 50 subjects returned for a second session in which each subject rated each of the concepts (characteristic statements) on the AB Scales. Then they rated the same concepts on the B scale. Finally, they rated the concept Negro on the A scale. The rank–order correlation between obtained scores and the frequency of the responses for each concept during the nomination part of the experiment was .94 ($N = 10$, $p < .001$).

The scales are relatively *transparent* and, therefore, if the subject wishes to bias his results, he may do so easily. No *norms* are given.

GENERAL COMMENT.   This is a simple and clearly worked-out instrument, usable, apparently, for measuring attitudes and beliefs regarding a range of objects/subjects. The absence of norms means that its primary use must be in experimental attitude or belief change studies.

REFERENCES

Fishbein, M. An investigation of the relationships between beliefs about an object and the attitude toward that object. *Human Relations*, 1963, *16*, 233–239.

Osgood, C. E., Suci, G. J., and Tannenbaum, P. H. *The measurement of meaning.* Urbana: University of Illinois Press, 1957.

UNITERMS.   Attitude; belief; change; cognitive dissonance; concept; evaluation; prejudice; semantic differential.

—D. G. L.

6

Audience Sensitivity Inventory (ASI) and Children's Audience Sensitivity Inventory (CASI)

AUTHOR.   Allan Paivio

AVAILABILITY.   Allan Paivio, Department of Psychology, University of Western Ontario, London, Ontario, Canada.

VARIABLES.   The Audience Sensitivity Inventory conceptualizes audience sensitivity as an experientially determined predisposition to be anxious before observers. The children's form contains 3 subscales: *Audience Anxiety* (AA); *Exhibitionism,* the need for public exposure of the self or a self-product (Exh); and *Self-Consciousness,* a negative attitude towards public exposure (S-C).

DESCRIPTION.   The adult form contains 21 items which evoke a True or False response depending upon whether the subject feels they describe him. An item might be: I am usually active rather than passive in a discussion group. A modified adult form uses a five-category response.

The children's form contains 35 items, 16 for AA, 13 for Exh, and 6 for S-C. Items are similar to those of the adult form, but are rephrased to suit a classroom situation. The following are simulated items:

I like to be called on to recite.

I get scared when I know I am going to be asked a question by the teacher.

ADMINISTRATION AND SCORING.   The inventories are self-administering, and require about twenty minutes to complete. Scores are raw agreement frequencies ("True" responses), adjusted for negatively worded items. No norms or standard scores were indicated in the material for this review.

DEVELOPMENT.   The adult form contains items taken from the Bernreuter Personality Inventory and the Minnesota Multiphasic Personality Inventory as well as items added by the author. The original 31-item children's form was revised after factor studies to include 6 additional items to increase the reliability of the Exh scale. Some items from the original form were reworded to include specific reference to fear before an audience; these items form the AA scale.

CRITIQUE.   The uncorrected, split-half, odd–even reliability of the modified (five-category) adult form is .83 ($N = 76$). For the CASI, split-half reliabilities for the three scales, corrected by the Spearman–Brown formula, are .80 (AA), .67 (Exh), and .66 (S-C), all for a sample of 223 third, fourth, and fifth graders. Six-month test–retest reliabilities are .54 (AA), .62 (Exh), and .45 (S-C) ($N = 209$).

Concurrent validity studies for the ASI have shown the inventory to correlate at .67 with stage fright items on Gilkinson's PRCS, at .48 with the Test Anxiety Scale (Sarason, Davidson, Lighthall, and Waite, 1958), and .58 with a short form of the Manifest Anxiety Scale (Taylor, 1953). Murray's (1938) need Exhibitionism questionnaire correlated with the ASI at —.35.

Similar studies of the CASI produced intercorrelations with the children's form of the TAS of .74 (AA), —.40 (Exh), and .59 (S-C) and with the children's form of the MAS of .62 (AA), —.27 (Exh), and .61 (S-C). The sample of 421 third through tenth graders was divided into three male and three female subgroups; the rs are averages and are not true of every subgroup.

Using the earlier, 31-item form of the CASI as a single "scale," Paivio (1964) obtained a biserial r of —.56 between CASI scores and choosing to write a composition either on "Why I like to recite in front of the class" or "Why I do not like to recite. . . ," from 189 third and fourth grade children. Correlations of CASI scores, teachers' ratings of shyness, and parents' ratings of shyness were .25 and .30, respectively.

Biserial correlations between CASI scale scores and willingness to participate in a "skit night" at a summer camp were significant on two scales for boys, —.35 (AA) and .31 (Exh). Girls correlated only on AA, but the r was —.45. The CASI scales show intercorrelations of —.55 (AA and Exh), .58 (AA and S-C), and —.21 (Exh and S-C).

The problem of agreement response sets is not discussed; only four CASI items are negatively worded. The absence of norms is a substantial shortcoming.

GENERAL COMMENT.   The adult form appears to be less well researched or tested than the children's form. The absence of norms is sufficient reason to relegate ASI and CASI to the status of research instruments, though the concurrent validity results are encouraging. Its easy administration and scoring should make it a helpful adjunct to more general investigations of anxiety-provoking situations, especially if the distributions of responses are used dichotomously.

REFERENCES

Paivio, A. Child-rearing antecedents of audience sensitivity. *Child Development*, 1964, *35*, 397–416.

Paivio, A. and Lambert, W. E. Measures and correlates of audience anxiety ("stage fright"). *Journal of Personality*, 1959, *27*, 1–17.

Paivio, A., Baldwin, A. L., and Berger, S. M. Measurements of children's sensitivity to audiences. *Child Development*, 1961, *32*, 721–730.

Saranson, S. B., Davidson, K., Lighthall, F., and Waite, R. A. test anxiety scale for children. *Child Development*, 1958, *29*, 105–113.

Taylor, J. A. A personality scale of manifest anxiety. *Journal of Abnormal and Social Psychology*, 1953, *48*, 285–290.

UNITERMS.   Anxiety; audience; child; exhibitionism; fear; self-consciousness.

—R. B. E.

7
Barratt Impulsiveness Scale (BIS)

AUTHOR.   Ernest S. Barratt

AVAILABILITY.   Ernest S. Barratt, Behavioral Science Laboratory, Medical Branch, University of Texas, Galveston, Texas 77550

VARIABLES.   *Impulsiveness* has been empirically identified as orthogonal to anxiety, and as related to predispositional "oscillation of behavior," intra-individual variability, extraversion, and rhathymia (carefree, happy-go-lucky disposition). Conceptually, this variable has been viewed by Barratt as a "function of central nervous system mechanisms, primarily the limbic system." Impulsivity is viewed as the bipolar opposite of restraint. A typical impulsive subject makes up his mind easily, acts on the spur of the moment, and has quick interest changes.

DESCRIPTION.   At this point in the development of the BIS, use is restricted to research purposes. The BIS comes in several "forms," depending upon the particular items scored. The BIS-I is the basic questionnaire, and consists of 85 true–false items (40 of which are "fillers") such as the following:

I always like to be on time.

I make decisions quickly.

The BIS-II contains the same 85 items, and is based on a study by Twain (1957) which isolated 5 subfactors: Lack of Persistence; Social Optimism; Lack of Motor Inhibition; Aggression–Autonomy; and Action Oriented. The BIS-V scores only 26 of the 85 items; it correlates .86 with the BIS-I.

ADMINISTRATION AND SCORING.   The test can be administered individually or in groups and takes an estimated five to ten minutes. Since the statements are of the true–false variety, machine scoring can be used. The score is computed on the number of items chosen true or false, as keyed. A high score means high impulsivity. No norms are presented, although means and standard deviations for the 5 subscales of the test (BIS-II) are given. No indication, however, is given regarding which items relate to which subscales.

DEVELOPMENT.   The BIS items were derived from a number of sources. Originally, in a study examining the relationship between impulsiveness and anxiety, the impulsiveness scale of the Thurstone Temperament Schedule (1953) was utilized. In a following study (Barratt, 1959) a new impulsiveness scale (IS) was constructed which included new items plus some chosen from other scales and rewritten. This scale consisted of 45 impulsiveness items and 35 filler items. Test–retest reliability was .87 with a one-month interval between testings, using 300 subjects. Item *phi* coefficients using the top and bottom 27% with respect to the total score were calculated; the author noted that the IS was not factorially homogeneous. It did not correlate with the Taylor Manifest Anxiety Scale (Taylor, 1953), although both relate to the Guilford–Zimmerman Temperament Survey (1953) variables.

CRITIQUE. Concerning internal *reliability*, it can be said that the BIS is *not* homogeneous. For the 45 impulsiveness items in the 85-item form the *phi* coefficients ($N = 300$) range from —.01 to .68, with a median of .32. Thirty coefficients are significant at the .01 level; ten, at the .05 level; five are nonsignificant. Three-year test–retest reliability of the BIS was .84 for 150 medical students. With shorter time periods it has been as high as .94 for 60 subjects.

Construct validity looks plausible, especially as to the proposed orthogonal relationship between impulsiveness and anxiety. In 50 studies not once has the BIS correlated with the Taylor Manifest Anxiety Scale.

In relation to the Guilford–Zimmerman and the Cattell 16 Personality Factors (Cattell, Saunders, and Stice, 1957) Barratt (1959) reports that for a sample of 120 general psychology students at Texas Christian University the BIS-I correlates negatively with the Guilford–Zimmerman Restraint (—.65) and Thoughtfulness (—.26) subscales, and with the Emotional Stability (—.22), Objectivity (—.23), and Cooperativeness (—.23) subscales. The BIS correlates positively with the General Activity subscale (.23). For 126 male and 97 female general psychology students (Barratt, 1965), the BIS-I correlates —.66 with G–Z scores of Restraint, .39 with General Activity, .21 with Ascendance, —.16 with Emotional Stability, and —.17 with Objectivity. For this sample of 223 the BIS-I correlates .63 with the Enthusiastic–Glum, —.42 with the Conscientious–Casual, and —.36 with the Controlled–Uncontrolled subscales of the Cattell 16 Personality Factors.

Similar correlations were found for the 5 factors of the BIS-II. With Guilford–Zimmerman Restraint the correlations were: Lack of Persistence, —.46; Social Optimism, —.67; Lack of Motor Inhibition, —.49; Aggression–Autonomy, —.29, and Action Oriented, —.59. With Cattell Enthusiastic–Glum the respective *r*s were .28, .63, .41, .29, and .62. With Cattell Conscientious–Casual the *r*s ranged from —.21 to —.33; with Cattell Controlled–Uncontrolled, from —.16 to —.36.

Barratt views impulsiveness as in part a measure of behavior oscillation which has its basis in specific central nervous system centers. It has been related to perceptual motor tasks and differential eyelid conditioning (Barratt, 1963) and in an exploratory study to adjustment in medical school (Barratt and White, undated).

While specific *norms* are not available, Barratt (1965) has reported means and standard deviations for the population of 223 general psychology students mentioned above.

No data are reported concerning response sets; *social desirability* could be particularly worrisome. And for the 45 scored items in the BIS-I, 32 are scored "impulsive" if checked True; only 13 require a False response. Thus, *acquiescence set* can be a biasing factor.

GENERAL COMMENT.   The clearly orthogonal relationship of Barratt's Impulsiveness Scale to measures of anxiety and its construct validity are the BIS's major strengths. Also in its favor are its ease of administration and scoring, particularly the BIS-V (short) form, which is balanced to minimize the effects of acquiescence. Social desirability remains unknown, and is potentially a problem; "impulsiveness" in the form of "get-up-and-go" might be seen as desirable. On balance, however, the BIS appears to be a useful instrument.

REFERENCES

Barratt, E. S. Anxiety and impulsiveness related to psychomotor efficiency. *Perceptual and Motor Skills*, 1959, *9*, 191–198.

Barratt, E. S. Intra-individual variability of performance: ANS and psychometric correlates. *Texas Reports on Biology and Medicine*, 1963, *21*, 496–504.

Barratt, E. S. Factor analysis of some psychometric measures of impulsiveness and anxiety. *Psychological Reports*, 1965, *16*, 547–554.

Barratt, E. S. and White, R. Impulsiveness and anxiety related to medical students' performance and attitudes. Unpublished mimeographed report. University of Texas, Medical Branch, undated.

Cattell, R., Saunders, D. R., and Stice, G. *Handbook for the Sixteen Personality Factors Questionnaire.* Champaign, Illinois: Institute for Personality and Ability Testing, 1957.

Guilford, J. P. and Zimmerman, W. S. *The Guilford–Zimmerman Temperament Survey (Manual).* Beverly Hills, California: Sheridan Supply Co., 1949.

Taylor, J. A. A personality scale of manifest anxiety. *Journal of Abnormal and Social Psychology*, 1953, *48*, 285–290.

Thurstone, L. L. *Examiner Manual for the Thurstone Temperament Schedule*. Chicago: Science Research Associates, 1953.

Twain, D. C. Factor analysis for particular aspects of behavioral control: impulsivity. *Journal of Clinical Psychology*, 1957, *13*, 133–136.

UNITERMS.   Anxiety; autonomic nervous system (ANS); control; impulsiveness; restraint.

—M. E.
—R. B. E.

8

Behavior Interpretation Inventory (BII)

AUTHOR.   George Moeller and Mortimer H. Applezweig

AVAILABILITY.   Mortimer H. Applezweig, Dean of the Graduate School, University of Massachusetts, Amherst, Massachusetts 01002

VARIABLES.   The Behavior Interpretation Inventory is designed to measure four dimensions of human motivation: *Escape from Present Pain or Discomfort* (Esc); *Avoidance of Future Pain or Discomfort* (Avoid); *Social Approval,* or Belongingness (SocApp); Self-Realization, or *Self-Approval* (SelfApp).

DESCRIPTION.   The BII is a forced-choice projective questionnaire of 59 items which contains a sampling of 26 behavior modes. Ss are presented with statements describing real behavior, followed by four alternative explanations of that behavior, like these simulated items:

A. He takes on the most difficult job because:
   1. his values are set up that way.
   2. he knows people value someone who puts his back into it.
   3. he'll become indispensable.
   4. he can keep busy and forget his troubles.

B. He expects his life to be a restless, exploring one because:
   1. his identity is really that of a pioneer.
   2. staying in the same place feels oppressive.
   3. his friends like his accounts of adventures.
   4. his searching will pay off big some day.

ADMINISTRATION AND SCORING.   The BII is self-administering. Ss are asked to rank the alternative explanations from 1 through 4 in the order of likelihood for the behavior described. No time limit is imposed, but thirty-five to forty minutes should be sufficient if Ss are urged to complete their Inventories as rapidly as possible.

   Four scoring stencils, one for each scale, can be constructed from unused answer sheets by punching out the appropriate response to each item for a given scale. Three scoring modes are possible: 1) most–least, whereby the first and fourth choices of S are tabulated separately and the difference in number between first and fourth choices is S's score (equivalent to assigning the value +1 to a first choice, −1 to a fourth choice, and summing); 2) sum of ranks, whereby S's responses (1, 2, 3, or 4) are summed for each scale (and therefore translating low scores into high standings); and 3) first choices, whereby the number of alternatives ranked first for each scale is S's score on that scale (and the remaining second, third, and fourth choices are ignored). On the basis of scale intercorrelations and coefficients of internal consistency (scale reliabilities) the authors recommend the scoring modes in the order given. Norms are available, including percentiles, T-scores, and frequency polygons, for all three scoring methods (Moeller and Applezweig, 1957a).

DEVELOPMENT. Starting with a distinction between modes as being particular behavior sequences directed toward particular goals, and motives as being generalized goal orientations, Moeller and Applezweig from uncontrolled observation constructed sets of motivators and reinforcers to correspond to each of the four behavior motives (Esc, Avoid, SocApp, SelfApp). Items were revised and modified until the investigators were unanimously agreed that each of the four completion alternatives (A, B, C, D) for each item was an instance of a single motive class. Measures of internal consistency, measures of predictive value, and an empirical study of the utility of the four motive categories in the scoring of a sentence completion form of the BII convinced the authors of the empirical validity of the four classes.

Four populations were used in the development of the BII: 1) USN enlisted men entering the submarine school at New London, Connecticut, in June 1955 ($N = 134$); 2) U.S. Coast Guard Cadets entering the Coast Guard Academy in June 1955 ($N = 216$); 3) women undergraduates, primarily sophomores, enrolled in a general psychology course at Connecticut College in May 1955 ($N = 102$); and 4) freshmen women entering Connecticut College in September 1955 ($N = 263$). All Ss were in their early twenties or late teens; all groups were above average either in verbal intelligence as measured by armed services examinations, or in measures of scholastic aptitude.

CRITIQUE. Scale *reliabilities* based on the correlation of odd–even items, corrected by the Spearman–Brown formula, were computed for the four scales for all four populations for all three scoring methods. For most–least scoring, the 16 scale reliabilities ranged from .41 (freshmen, Avoid) to .87 (sophomores, SelfApp), and had a median of .75. For the combined norm groups ($N = 715$) and most–least scoring, the scale reliabilities were .68 (Esc), .50 (Avoid), .79 (SocApp), and .80 (SelfApp).

The BII originally contained 72 items. Test–retest *reliabilities* have been obtained only for the 72-item form. Over a one-month interval and under the first-choice scoring system, 139 submariners showed correlations of .72 (Esc), .57 (Avoid), .61 (SocApp), and .71 (SelfApp). Two hundred forty freshmen entering in September 1956 (the norm group had entered in 1955) produced first-choice correlations of .62, .60, .56, and .72; for most–least scoring their respective correlations were .63, .51, .64, and .86.

In a separate report, Applezweig and Moeller (1956) report a summary of *item analyses* which shows which items discriminate between persons with high and low scores on the four BII scales, as indicated by a significance level of .10 (*chi* square). "High" and "low" scores represent the upper and lower 27%; for the 59-item form (scored by first choices) two populations were sampled: 134 submariners, and 263 freshmen entering in September 1955. The percentages of discriminating items for each scale and group were: 50%, 74% (Esc); 61%, 69% (Avoid); 52%, 54% (SocApp); and 81%, 79% (SelfApp).

Several studies have been undertaken to establish *construct validity*. In Moeller and Applezweig (1957b), 41 women students were selected from a sample of 263 for equality on the scales Esc and Avoid and divided into three groups: above the median on the SocApp scale; above the median on the SelfApp scale; and above the medians on both the SocApp and the SelfApp scale. The Ss were then subjected to an Asch-type (1956) conformity situation with the expectation that the first two groups would differ significantly in compromise behavior and that the third group would be conflicted. The high SocApp group did differ (p approached .05) in frequency of yielding to the majority.

To test the construct validity of the Esc and Avoid scales, students in a classroom situation viewed a film which showed the more extreme physical deformities associated with mental deficiency. The degree to which students were upset by the film (on a 7-choice Likert scale) was expected to be positively correlated with their scores on the Esc scale. The correlation, −.38, was not significantly different from zero. In addition, the sample means on the BII differed significantly from the parent population, and comparison was therefore invalidated.

Again to test the Esc and Avoid scales, Ss completed the portion of the Sarason Test Anxiety Questionnaire (1953) which relates specifically to examinations in an academic setting on two occasions: one week before, and one day after the beginning of the final examination period at Connecticut College. It was hypothesized that at the first testing Avoid but not Esc should be positively related to anxiety. At the second testing, with Ss now in a presumably unpleasant situation, the anxiety scores of Ss having a high Esc score should increase. They decreased, possibly due to Ss' familiarity with the anxiety questionnaire itself. Avoid was correlated with anxiety scores (−.45, significant at $p < .05$), but in the wrong direction.

The BII was correlated with three standard published personality inventories, the Edwards Personal Preference Schedule, the Gough California Psychological Inventory, and the Gordon Personal Profile, as well as with self-ratings on the four scales. For 194 women freshmen tested in the fall of 1955, only 9 out of a total of 168 correlations were significant at the .05 level or better (and note that one would expect about 8 significant correlations on the basis of chance alone). The absence of overlap can be interpreted as indicating that the BII does measure distinctive dimensions of motivation.

The data on *norms* are thorough, but the groups themselves are relatively narrow populations from which to generalize. The sample means differ significantly ($p < .05$) for the male and female groups. Whether this is a generalizable sex-related difference is not clear. It may be related, for example, to the fact that the males were all voluntarily associated with the military, and submariner training in particular. One might expect that males with either potential SocApp–SelfApp conflicts or high Esc or Avoid scores would be weeded out in the selection process.

The manual notes that, if asked, the administrator should stress that S should respond on the basis of what he thinks motivates the person described, and not by what motivates the S himself. This procedure risks exposing the BII as a projective measure and thereby triggering *response set*. Also it should be noted that all the items have a definite masculine flavor, and it is difficult to imagine a young college woman identifying with the situations sufficiently to be able to project into them.

GENERAL COMMENT.   The construct validity of the Esc and Avoid scales has yet to be established. Respondent difficulties for females should be considerable. Norm groups are highly specific. The actions do not appear to be equally ambiguous for all four alternative motives. Many behaviors could be said to relate objectively to one motive more strongly than to others. In the absence of equal plausibility for the motives, the anticipated projection by Ss will be interfered with. The SocApp and SelfApp scales appear to have some value.

REFERENCES

Applezweig, M. H. and Moeller, G. *Motivation and psychological stress: third annual report.* ONR Contract 996 (02), NR 172–228, Connecticut College, November, 1956.

Applezwieg, M. H. and Moeller, G. Conforming behavior and personality variables in college women. *Journal of Abnormal and Social Psychology,* 1963, *66,* 284–290.

Asch, S. E. Studies of independence and conformity: 1. A minority of one against a unanimous majority. *Psychological Monographs,* 1956, 70, No. 8 (Whole No. 416).

Edwards, A. L. *Manual: Edwards Personal Preference Schedule,* New York: The Psychological Corp., 1954.

Gordon, L. V. *Manual: Gordon Personal Profile.* Yonkers: World Book Co., 1953.

Gough, H. G. *Manual: California Psychological Inventory.* Palo Alto: Consulting Psychologists Press, Inc., 1956.

Moeller, G. and Applezweig, M. H. *Manual: The Behavior Interpretation Inventory.* Technical Report No. 2, ONR Contract 996 (02), NR 172–228, Connecticut College, November, 1957a.

Moeller, G. and Applezweig, M. H. A. motivational factor in conformity. *Journal of Abnormal and Social Psychology,* 1957b, 55, 114–120.

Sarason, S. B. and Gordon, E. M. The Test Anxiety Questionnaire: scoring norms. *Journal of Abnormal and Social Psychology,* 1953, 48, 447–448.

UNITERMS.   Approval; avoidance; conflict; escape; flight; mode; motive; projective; self-approval.

—R. B. E.

9
Bristol Social Adjustment Guides

AUTHORS.   Dennis H. Stott and E. G. Sykes

AVAILABILITY.   University of London Press Ltd., Warwick Lane, London E. C. 4, England

VARIABLES.   The four Bristol Social Adjustment Guides—The Child in School, The Child in Residential Care, The Child in the Family, and the Delinquency Prediction Instrument—record a variety of behaviors collectively described as *"maladjustment."*

The Child in School and The Child in Residential Care Guides measure sixteen behavioral aspects: *Unforthcomingness* (U), a lack of confidence with people or unfamiliar situations (shyness); *Depression* (D); *Withdrawal* (W); *Anxiety about Adult Interest and Affection* (XA); *Hostility toward Adults* (HA); *Anxiety for Approval of and Acceptance by Other Children* (XC); *Knavery* (K), an attitude of unconcern for adult approval and a "writing-off" of adults; *Hostility toward other Children* (HC); *Restlessness* (R); *Miscellaneous Symptoms of Emotional Tension, Strain, or Disturbance* (M); *Miscellaneous Nervous Symptoms* (MN); *Environmental or Other Disadvantage* (E); *Backwardness* (intellectual capacity) (B); *Sexual Development* (S); *Psychosomatic Ailments* (PS); and *Physical Defects* (PD).

The Child in the Family Guide covers each parent's attitude towards the child, the child's attitude towards each parent, the child's general family insecurity, and stress symptoms in the child. Attitudes are measured on three dimensions: *Anxious Over-Concern; Hostility— Anxiety Conflict;* and *Lack of Maternal/Paternal Feeling,* or (in the child) *Estrangement.* General family insecurity has four components: *Seeking a Parent-Substitute; Anxiety for Approval or Acceptance by Other Children; Avoidance;* and *Miscellaneous Symptoms of Insecurity.* Stress symptoms include: *Nervousness and Unforthcomingness; Depression; Flight from the Situation* (removal); and *Somatic Conditions.*

The Delinquency Prediction Instrument combines items from the other guides in the areas of *Knavery, Withdrawal, Hostility to Children,* and miscellaneous items.

DESCRIPTION.   The form guides are checklists of behavior items. The "School" guide contains 210 items; the "Family" guide, 213 items; the Delinquency Prediction Instrument, 98 items. Some simulated items are:

Becomes angry when provoked.
Often daydreams.
Fights "dirty" with other children.
Takes foolhardy risks.
Lies artfully, without compunction.

ADMINISTRATION AND SCORING.   Essentially observation schedules, the
guides require about twenty minutes for the administrator to check off
those items which pertain to a particular child or family situation. Most
items are proportionately weighted, many are listed in order of severity.
Transparent scoring guides (Diagnostic Forms) are available; the
Delinquency Prediction Instrument is actually a special form to be
placed over the Child in School guide. Computer-scoring forms are
available from Dr. D. H. Stott, Psychology Department, University of
Glasgow, Glasgow, W.2, Scotland.

    Raw data norms are included in the manual. These raw scores rep-
resent the simple sum of items checked (all items are "unfavorable")
despite Stott's repeated warning that unitary scores of maladjustment
should not be derived from his scales.

DEVELOPMENT.   From his studies of delinquent boys and youths, Stott
compiled a list of possible items—over 200 behaviors in 18 categories
which he felt indicated maladjustment. One hundred sixty-eight school
children were grouped as being maladjusted, unsettled or stable. Items
were then selected for their discriminating ability among these three
groups. (The manual, however, does not indicate what criteria were
used to distinguish these three groups. It also reports only the development of the Child in School Guide.) Presumably in this and later
revisions, teachers familiar with the children did the sorting. After two
revisions, 195 items were retained. Of these, 111 discriminated between
maladjusted and stable children at $p = .001$ or less, 22 discriminated at
$p = .01$ or less, 22 discriminated at $p = .05$ or less, and the remaining
40 items did not discriminate at statistically significant levels.

CRITIQUE.   The only evidence of *reliability* presented in the manual are
Spearman *rho's* of .49, .58, and .55 for the intercorrelations of three
nurses' ratings of 45 inmates of a psychopathic unit, using the Residential Guide. The Residential Guide shows a test–retest reliability of
.77 after nine months. Elsewhere, correlations between pairs of observations by teachers have been reported at .78 for "unsettled" children and
.76 for "maladjusted" children for the School Guide.

    Some of the better *validity* evidence lies in the fact that combined
mean scores on the Residential and School Guides distinguished

($p < .02$) among "most seriously disturbed," "moderately disturbed," and "least disturbed" of 23 maladjusted children, aged four to twelve. The criteria, however, are not indicated; it should also be noted that the Guides distinguished among maladjusted children and did not differentiate between the maladjusted and the stable. A study of 64 delinquent boys who had previously been in correctional school showed their mean scores on the School Guide to be more than twice that of non-delinquent classmates.

The Delinquency Prediction Instrument has been shown capable of differentiating degrees of truancy, regardless of the specific reasons for particular acts of truancy. IQ and school attainment are not related to guide scores; reading, English, arithmetic, and total attainment scores are negatively correlated with combined XA/HA scores at about $-.34$.

No comprehensive *norms* are avaliable. The norms in the manual are raw scores for small populations. Norms for the individual dimensions (W, R, D, HA, etc.) are not presented. The Delinquency Prediction Instrument is based solely upon a small sample ($N = 403$) of Glasgow boys, aged nine to fourteen years.

GENERAL COMMENT. The profusion of named but completely non-validated subscales, the contradiction between Stott's injunction against a total "maladjustment" score and his use of one, plus the absence of norms are major and serious handicaps. Interested users in the United States will have to develop their own norms. Ease of administration and moderate face validity mitigate these drawbacks. The manual is often abstruse and self-centered; validity data are often less than pertinent. Data on the Child in the Family Guide are almost non-existent. Finally, the user should keep in mind: 1) that the original instrument was conceived fifteen years ago, which is a long time as youth culture shifts go these days; and 2) that many behaviors categorized by the authors as "delinquent" or "maladjusted" may in fact be rational child responses to oppressive school environments. We include the Bristol Social Adjustment Guides primarily as an example of an apparently straightforward instrument beset with weaknesses.

REFERENCES

Lunzer, E. A. Aggressive and withdrawing children in the normal school: I. Patterns of behavior. *British Journal of Educational Psychology*, 1960, *30*, 1–10.

Stott, D. H. *The social adjustment of children: manual to the Bristol Social Adjustment Guides.* Third edition. London: University of London Press, 1966.

Stott, D. H. *Unsettled children and their families.* London: University of London Press, 1956.

UNITERMS.   Behavior; child; delinquency; family; home; maladjustment; school.

—R. B. E.

10
California Psychological Inventory (CPI)

AUTHOR.   Harrison G. Gough

AVAILABILITY.   Consulting Psychologists Press, Inc., 577 College Avenue, Palo Alto, California 94306

VARIABLES.   Eighteen variables are grouped under four a priori classifications: Class I, measures of poise, ascendancy, and self-assurance; Class II, measures of socialization, maturity, and responsibility; Class III, measures of achievement potential and intellectual efficiency; and Class IV, measures of personal orientation and attitudes toward life. Each of the 18 scales is intended to measure an important facet of interpersonal behavior. According to Gough, however, each scale is best understood and interpreted in light of the total battery. The scales are as follows:

Class I: Poise, Ascendancy, and Self-Assurance

1. *Dominance* (Do): indicating dominance, leadership, initiative, and the tendency to behave in a forthright and resolute manner.
2. *Capacity for Status* (Cs): reflecting the personal qualities which underlie and lead to status and social attainment; being ambitious, forceful, and interested in success; the kind of person who will get ahead in the world.
3. *Sociability* (Sy): indicating a liking for and interest in social life and activity, being outgoing and sociable; the kind of person who enjoys group activities and likes to be with and work with others.
4. *Social Presence* (So): indicating factors such as poise, spontaneity, self-confidence, and vivaciousness in personal and social interaction.
5. *Self-Acceptance* (Sa): reflecting one's sense of personal worth and satisfaction with one's self; relative freedom from self-doubt and critical attitudes about one's self.
6. *Sense of Well-Being* (Wb): indicating a sense of physical and emotional well-being and comfort; the feeling of being able to enjoy life.

Class II: Socialization, Maturity, and Social Responsibility

7. *Responsibility* (Re): indicating seriousness of thought and manner, conscientiousness, dependability and uprightness; being the kind of person that others tend to trust and to rely upon.
8. *Socialization* (So): indicating a strong sense of probity and

propriety; acceptance of rules, proper authority, and custom; a person who seldom if ever gets into trouble.

9. *Self-Control* (Sc): indicating the degree and adequacy of self-regulation and self-control; not impulsive, or given to acting on the spur of the moment.

10. *Tolerance* (To): indicating attitudes of permissiveness, tolerance, and acceptance of others; being open-minded and unprejudiced about beliefs and values quite different from one's own.

11. *Good Impression* (Gi): indicating an interest in making a good impression and being concerned about how others will react to oneself.

12. *Communality* (Cm): indicating a fitting-in with the crowd, having the same reactions and feelings as everyone else, seeing things the way most people see them.

Class III: Achievement Potential and Intellectual Efficiency

13. *Achievement via Conformance* (Ac): indicating someone with a strong need for achievement, and who is at his best in situations having definite rules and structure.

14. *Achievement via Independence* (Ai): indicating the kind of person who has a strong need for achievement and who is at his best in new or untried situations where he must work on his own and without external guidance.

15. *Intellectual Efficiency* (Ie): indicating the efficiency with which one uses intellectual and personal resources; the ability to start working quickly without need to delay or procrastinate, and to keep working on intellectual tasks over long periods of time.

Class IV: Personal Orientation and Attitudes toward Life

16. *Psychological-Mindedness* (Py): indicating the degree to which one is interested in and responsive to the inner needs, motives, and feelings of others; being introceptive, sensitive to others; having a knack for understanding how others feel and react inwardly.

17. *Flexibility* (Fx): indicating the degree of flexibility and adaptability of a person's thinking and social behavior; the liking for change and innovation and even a preference for things new and untried.

18. *Femininity* (Fe): indicating the tendency to help and support others through patience and loving kindness; being in general gentle and sympathetic (low scorers tend to be more decisive, robust, and action oriented).

DESCRIPTION.   The CPI consists of 480 items. The respondent is required to indicate whether each item is true or false. Sample items are:

31. I doubt whether I would make a good leader.

226. Most people worry too much about sex.

ADMINISTRATION AND SCORING.   The 18 scales are normative and are made up of 480 statements, which are essentially self-administering to literate subjects. Three types of answer sheets are available: one for hand scoring and two for machine scoring. The 18 raw scores are easily converted to profile forms which provide graphic representations of standard scores. The norms are based on over 6,000 males and 7,000 females. The samples include a wide range of ages, socio-economic groups, and geographical areas.

DEVELOPMENT.   Eleven of the 18 scales in the Inventory were developed by utilizing empirically derived scoring weights assigned to responses found to differentiate defined criterion groups such as high school drop-outs and juvenile delinquents. Four of the scores are based on weights originally judged by the author as indicating a designated variable and refined by internal consistency checks. The remaining three scores are also derived empirically to detect tendencies to fake or to respond in a manner which makes the other scores of doubtful validity.

CRITIQUE.   Very little more can be added to the existing excellent reviews of this inventory in Buros (1959, 1965) by Kelly, Thorndike, and Cronbach. These reviewers have pointed out that convincing evidence exists to validate each of the 18 scales. Even for the scales developed on the basis of a priori weights such as the Self-Acceptance scale, scores significantly differentiate between high school students rated as high and low on self-acceptance by staff assessment ratings. These same authors do criticize the development of the Inventory in regard to: 1) using only extreme groups (i.e., top and bottom 10%) in population samples as evidence of the ability to distinguish between groups; 2) ignoring empirical intercorrelations among scales in favor of logical scale relations; and 3) not discussing the high correlations of some of the scales with other standard inventories, such as the Bernreuter.

Only test–retest *reliabilities* are reported, but these are sufficiently high for both group and individual use. For instance, on a sample of 200 prisoners retested after one to three weeks reliabilities range from .49 to .87, with a median of .80. For high school subjects tested after one year, the median test–retest correlation is .65 for males and .68 for females.

A large number of studies present an impressive array of *validity* data. For instance, Gough (1966) presents data which show that, using a combined score from seven of the scales, drop-outs could be predicted more accurately than by either an ability measure or a grade-point average. Another study utilizing the Socialization scale discriminated between delinquent and non-delinquent boys. In his review, Kelly's major reservation, however, is that the 18 scales are not entirely independent and may not be measuring as many separate traits as the names would suggest. Megargee (1972) has assembled a handbook devoted solely to the development and characteristics of the CPI; it reviews the 18 basic scales, plus selected scales developed subsequently, reviews the published CPI literature, and discusses CPI uses in assessment and research.

GENERAL COMMENT.   This instrument is standardized more than many of the instruments in this collection; it has been included because of its relatively solid research base, and its importance as a measure of *social* functioning (as contrasted with the clinical tone of many personality inventories).

One cannot resist commenting, though, on the probable datedness of many of the personality constructs, especially in the Class II domain. Given the shifts in values (and interpersonal styles) occurring currently in America, it seems likely that scales such as those measuring responsibility, socialization, self-control, good impression, and achievement via conformance are rapidly becoming "irrelevant." The Femininity scale is a striking case in point; its male chauvinism would be insulting to most women (and many men) today.

REFERENCES

Buros, O. K. (Ed.) *The fifth mental measurements yearbook*. Highland Park, N.J.: Gryphon Press, 1959.

Buros, O. K. (Ed.) *The sixth mental measurements yearbook*. Highland Park, N. J.: Gryphon Press, 1965.

Gough, H. G. *Manual for the California Psychological Inventory*. Palo Alto: Consulting Psychologists Press, 1957.

Gough, H. G. Graduation from high school as predicted from the California Psychological Inventory. *Psychology in the Schools*, 1966, 3, (3) 208–216.

Megargee, E. I. *The California Psychological Inventory Handbook*. San Francisco: Jossey-Bass, 1972.

UNITERMS. Achievement; conformity; dominance; empathy; femininity; flexibility; good impression; independence; intellectual efficiency; nurturance; personality; propriety; responsibility; self-acceptance; self-control; sensitivity; similarity to others; sociability; socialization; spontaneity; status; tolerance; well-being.

—D. G. L.

11
California Q-Set (CQ-Set)

AUTHOR.   Jack Block

AVAILABILITY.   Consulting Psychologists Press, 577 College Avenue, Palo Alto, California 94306.

VARIABLES.   The California Q-Set seeks to provide a comprehensive description of an individual's personality in terms of the relative *salience of personality dimensions,* rather than measure the strength of specific dimensions of personality.

DESCRIPTION.   The CQ-Set consists of 100 2¼″ × 3½″ cards, on each of which is printed a descriptive statement such as the following:

Is fastidious.
Is subtly negativistic; tends to undermine and obstruct or sabotage.
Responds to humor.
Is physically attractive; good-looking.
Tends to proffer advice.

ADMINISTRATION AND SCORING.   Personality descriptions are obtained by one person's sorting the cards into 9 groups according to salience, most to least, on the basis of whatever information the observer may possess concerning the S. A fixed number of statements is assigned to each group in order to simulate a normal distribution. Sorts generally require about thirty minutes to complete. Criterion sorts may be obtained by combining clinical sorts made by several competent observers. An individual's Q-sort can then be correlated with the criterion to provide a score relative to that criterion. (Block's manual gives a simple formula for transforming discrepancy scores into correlation coefficients.) Clearly, then, a variety of criterion sorts can be readily created. The manual includes criterion sorts for the optimally adjusted individual, the male paranoid, and the female hysteric, each based upon judgments by nine clinical psychologists.

DEVELOPMENT.   The 100 items are the result of editing, selection, and testing, and incorporate the suggestions of over 50 clinicians who experimented with earlier versions of the sort.

CRITIQUE.   The CQ-Set is not a test, but a systematic mode for expressing individual judgments, which naturally vary from observer to observer. Test–retest *reliabilities* have been repeatedly found to be between .80 and .90.

Correlation with a criterion Q-sort does not provide *construct validity*. Edwards reports that for nine judges a criterion sort for "optimal adjustment" correlated with a criterion sort of *social desirability* at .88, but he does not indicate the clinical capabilities of his nine judges.

GENERAL COMMENT.   While improvable, the California Q-Set is a useful instrument, thoroughly researched, of good quality and considerable flexibility. That the items are sorted with respect to the *salience,* and not the strength, of a dimension, is one of its strongest points. The fact that the establishment of criteria depends solely upon the competency of the judges is another. The large number of possible constellations of traits is a third. In addition, the manual presents an excellent review of the theory and development of Q-sorts generally. The California Q-Set commends itself to all concerned with personality assessment.

REFERENCE

Block, J. *The Q-sort method in personality assessment and psychiatric research.* Springfield, Illinois: Charles C Thomas, 1961.

UNITERMS.   Personality; Q-sort; salience.

—R. B. E.

12
Caring Relationship Inventory (CRI)

AUTHOR.   Everett L. Shostrom

AVAILABILITY.   Educational and Industrial Testing Service, Box 7234, San Diego, California 92107

VARIABLES.   The Caring Relationship Inventory measures five aspects of caring or loving in human relationships: *Affection*, a helping, nurturing form of love; *Friendship*, a peer love based on a common interest and respect for each other's equality; *Eros*, the romantic form of love, including inquisitiveness, jealousy, exclusiveness, and sexual drive; *Empathy*, a charitable, altruistic love expressed by compassion, tolerance, and appreciation of another person as a unique human being; and, *Self-Love*, the ability to accept one's own weaknesses and strengths. In addition, Shostrom, after Maslow's (1962) distinction, has devised two subscales: *Being Love*, the ability to have and accept the other person as he or she is; and *Deficiency Love*, the love of another for what they can do for the person.

DESCRIPTION.   The CRI consists of 83 true/false descriptive statements similar to the following:

> I am very demanding of her.
> My feeling for her is characterized by patience.
> I am afraid to weep in front of her.

The inventory comes in two forms; the female form to be used by a woman in rating her relationship with a man contains the same items, with the appropriate gender changes, as the form used by a male in rating his relationship with a woman.

ADMINISTRATION AND SCORING.   The inventory is self-administering. The test booklet is so designed that it may be completed twice, once for an actual partner (girl friend, fiancée, wife, divorced spouse) and once for an ideal marriage partner. The inventory has no time limit for completion; fifteen minutes should be sufficient.

Five overlay stencils are available for the scoring of the main variables; two additional keys are included for scoring the Being Love and Deficiency Love subscales. Scoring of all 7 scales can usually be accomplished in less than two minutes.

In addition, Shostrom suggests four additional scores based on: 1) differences between "ideal" and "other" responses; 2) differences between two members of the same dyad; 3) the ratio of outward love to self love; and 4) the ratio of Deficiency Love to Being Love. Aside from giving median scores from a sample of 75 couples, he does not elaborate these experimental scores.

For the 5 main scales and 2 subscales, norms and a profile chart with standard scores are included in the manual.

DEVELOPMENT.   The manual, the only source of information on the CRI available for this review, does not present a history of the inventory.

CRITIQUE.   The split-half *reliability* (corrected by the Spearman–Brown formula) of the five scales and two subscales ranges from .66 (Deficiency Love) to .87 (Eros), with a median of .80.

The only evidence of *validity* (predictive) presented in the manual is the consistency of differences in mean scores on the five scales and 2 subscales between (self-described) successfully married couples and couples seeking marital counseling, and between successfully married couples and divorced couples. Of 14 differences (two comparisons of 5 scales and 2 subscales) 12 are significant at the .01 confidence level, one is significant at the .05 level, and one was not significant (Deficiency Love for successful versus troubled couples). In addition, the scores are everywhere lower for divorced couples than for troubled couples, which are in turn everywhere lower than for successful couples.

This evidence of the monotonic quality of the scales and subscales is implicitly challenged, however, by Shostrom's hypothesis in the manual that ". . . excessively high scores on the CRI may be indicative of unrealistic caring in that particular category. More evidence will be needed before differential interpretation of scores at various levels above the 50th percentile is possible. . . ." If high scores *are* indicative of "unrealistic caring," then the scales which provide those scores are not valid for the full range of subjects completing them.

Discussion of the interpretation of scores is meager. No examination is attempted of what differences between partners' scores are practically significant in pointing to discord in the relationship, nor is any theory presented dealing with the desirable balance among the five basic elements of caring.

The norms are based on 75 successfully married couples, 50 couples seeking counseling, and 54 divorced couples. No norms for single or engaged persons are available.

GENERAL COMMENT.   The Caring Relationship Inventory appears to be a plausible and probably useful instrument. At its current state of limited development, however, it can be recommended for research purposes only, as the manual appropriately specifies.

REFERENCES

Maslow, A. H. *Motivation and personality.* New York: Harper and Row, 1962.

Shostrom, E. L. *Manual: The Caring Relationship Inventory.* San Diego: Educational and Industrial Testing Service, 1966.

UNITERMS.   Acceptance; affection, being; caring; deficiency; dyad; empathy; eros; friendship; interpersonal; love; marriage; relationship; self-acceptance; self-love; sexuality.

—R. B. E.

13
Category-Width (C-W) Scale

AUTHOR.   Thomas F. Pettigrew

AVAILABILITY.   Thomas F. Pettigrew, Department of Social Relations, Harvard University, Cambridge, Massachusetts 02138

VARIABLES.   The Category-Width Scale measures a subject's typical *equivalence range for classifying objects,* and may tap a dimension of *risk-taking.*

DESCRIPTION.   The scale contains 20 items, each of which states an average estimate of some quantifiable phenomenon and then asks for the S's choice of alternative estimates as to the upper and lower bounds of that phenomenon. For example, a simulated item might be:

The average mean altitude of states in the United States is 1,790 feet. What do you think:
  (a) is the mean altitude of the highest state . . .
      1. 6,700 feet
      2. 4,100 feet
      3. 5,700 feet
      4. 7,300 feet
  (b) is the mean altitude of the lowest state . . .
      1. 630 feet
      2. 100 feet
      3. 240 feet
      4.   30 feet

ADMINISTRATION AND SCORING.   The scale is self-administering in about thirty minutes. The score for each response ranges from 0 to 3, from the smallest to the largest alternative for the upper bound, and vice versa. Scores for the *a* and *b* questions of all items are summed and range therefore from 0 to 120, with the higher scores indicating broader category widths. The norms for college males and females are quite abbreviated.

DEVELOPMENT.   The first form of the C-W Scale contained 14 items and solicited open-end responses. A test by Kendall's W showed that rank orders of respondents from five college and high school samples were significantly correlated, with Ss proving to be reliably consistent in delimiting broad, medium, or narrow estimated ranges. The final form was devised with fixed alternatives; the alternatives were those which fell at the 10th, 35th, 65th, and 90th percentile for the 750 college students who replied to the open-ended forms.

CRITIQUE.   The corrected Spearman–Brown *reliability* coefficient for a sample of 281 college students is .90. Six-week test–retest reliability for 97 University of North Carolina undergraduates is .72.

In a study of *criterion validity,* 26 undergraduates were presented with drawn lines on a blackboard of the average lengths of pheasants and turtles and were asked to choose from among other lines the longest and shortest instances of these categories. They also estimated the weight extremes of ostrich eggs with fixed sets of weights and the pitch extremes of women's singing voices and factory whistles from fixed alternatives generated by an audio-oscillator. An item analysis of the ability of C-W items to correctly distinguish between broad and narrow categories showed one-tailed t-tests of $p = .10$ or less for 11 items, of $p = .20$ or less for a total of 14 items. The rank-order correlation between C-W items and the criterion was .57 ($p < .01$).

Tests of *concurrent validity* show a correlation with the ACE (American Council on Education) quantitative score of .26 ($p < .01$) for 200 college undergraduates. "Comprehensive" categorizers in Rokeach's "narrow-mindedness" test (1951) scored significantly higher ($p < .05$) on the C-W than did Rokeach's "narrow" and "isolated" categorizers. (Rokeach's "comprehensive" categorizers group all of his ten political and religious labels under one concept; "narrows" use more than one; "isolateds" omit labels.) The C-W Scale does not correlate either with the California F-Scale of authoritarianism nor with Rokeach's D-Scale of dogmatism (1956).

Factor analysis has revealed the C-W Scale to be two-dimensional. One factor consists of 4 time or speed items; the other is more general and least related to quantitative ability.

The absence of *norms* is a major drawback.

GENERAL COMMENT.   Only 11 items have sufficient criterion validity. Pettigrew himself has not researched this instrument since 1958. Just what the significance of category width is in relation to other cognitive phenomena (e.g., extreme response set) remains intriguing but unexplored. The Category-Width Scale is recommended for research purposes only.

REFERENCES

Pettigrew, T. F. The measurement and correlates of category width as a cognitive variable. *Journal of Personality,* 1958, *26,* 523–544. Also reprinted in Harper, R. H. C., Anderson, C. C., Christensen, C. M., and

Hunka, S. M. *The cognitive process: readings.* Englewood Cliffs: Prentice-Hall, 1964, 450–460.

Rokeach, M. A method for studying individual differences in "narrow-mindedness." *Journal of Personality,* 1951, *20,* 219–233.

Rokeach, M. Political and religious dogmatism: an alternative to the authoritarian personality. *Psychological Monographs,* 1956, *70,* No. 18 (Whole No. 425).

UNITERMS.   Categorizing; cognition; flexibility; perception.

—R. B. E.

14
Coping Operations Preference Enquiry (COPE)

AUTHORS.   William C. Schutz and Nancy Waxler

AVAILABILITY.   Counsulting Psychologists Press, Inc., 577 College Avenue, Palo Alto, California 94306

VARIABLES.   The Coping Operations Preference Enquiry measures a subject's relative preference for five types of defense mechanisms: *Denial*, the refusal to recognize feeling toward an object; *Isolation*, the recognition of the discrepancy between ideal and actual behavior, accompanied by a refusal to admit the anxiety which this discrepancy creates; *Projection*, the reversal of the subject with the object of the feeling; *Regression*, the recognition of the anxiety accompanied by the need to be helped by a parent figure; and *Turning against the Self*, the substitution of the self for the object of the feeling.

DESCRIPTION.   The COPE contains 6 items, all of which describe self-to-other behavior anxieties. Following Schutz's (1958, 1967) FIRO theory of interpersonal behavior, each of 3 items reflects too much Inclusion, too much Control, or too much Affection; the other 3 items represent too little Inclusion, Control, or Affection. Each item consists of a short paragraph which for a hypothetical subject establishes the existence of a problem, states the usual actual behavior, indicates its discrepancy from an ideal, expresses the subject's dissatisfaction with that discrepancy, and presents the problem to the respondent. The respondent rank-orders alternative expressions of coping behavior, presumably in a projective manner, thereby revealing his own preferences for defense mechanisms. Here is a simulated item:

> Yesterday Gregory noticed something disturbing about himself. Ordinarily he thinks of himself as an independent person who gets along fine by himself and doesn't need to tell other people his troubles.
>
> Yesterday, however, during a talk with an acquaintance he found himself wanting very much to talk about his just ended relationship with a girl. Suddenly he began to doubt his own ability to handle his problems independently.
>
> Today, Gregory is apparently still upset by the feeling that his independence is not as strong as he always thought it was. How would you guess he really feels now?

The five coping mechanisms (Denial, Isolation, Projection, Regression, Turning against the Self) are then presented in somewhat the following manner:

a. He's not worried. This isn't really an important problem.
b. He feels he may not be as independent as he once thought, but that has little to do with how much he enjoys other people.
c. Although he may be too independent, nevertheless he feels that others expect this of him.
d. He feels that he may be too independent, but with help from someone more experienced, he could change.
e. He realizes that the fault for being too independent lies entirely within himself and has nothing to do with anyone else.

ADMINISTRATION AND SCORING. The coping mechanisms are ranked from most likely (1) to least likely (5) by the respondents. Scores for each of the five types of defense mechanisms are simply the sum of the ranks across the 6 items and therefore range from a high of 6 to a low of 30. The COPE should take no more than twenty minutes to administer. Profile charts for a sample of 5,847 adults are available.

DEVELOPMENT. The COPE grew out of Waxler's dissertation work (1960) on substructing the full theoretical set of interpersonal feelings, including their direction and intensity, all based on Schutz's FIRO theory of interpersonal needs. Only self-to-other behavior was instrumentalized. Other-to-self behavior anxieties were being formulated in a separate instrument (current status unknown). The manual does not indicate what revision, if any, items underwent before emerging in their present form.

CRITIQUE. The manual provides no *reliability* or *validity* data. The COPE was tested on a sample of 3,750 teachers, 445 school administrators, 231 school board members, and 1,421 parents, but all that is published of these data are the means and standard deviations for the raw scores and the decile scores.

One datum on *item transparency* is presented: only one of a sample of 554 subjects perceived that all the responses were of a defensive nature and that no nondefensive alternative was offered. No discussion is offered of the possibility of varying degrees of *social desirability* being attached to the responses.

GENERAL COMMENT. The COPE limits itself to a small subset of interpersonal behavior–focused, self-to-other anxieties. It is bound tightly to the FIRO theory, which may or may not be an asset. The mere self-classification of a subject's preferences from among a subset of defense mechanisms has limited utility, especially in predicting his interpersonal behavior. The absence of any reliability or validity data in the manual is incomprehensible as well as unprofessional. The reason for including it here is that Schutz's FIRO theory continues to receive recognition by those who study and work in small groups; and the COPE might be useful in developing a broader research base for the FIRO theory.

REFERENCES

Schutz, W. C. *FIRO: a three-dimensional theory of interpersonal behavior.* New York: Holt, Rinehart and Winston, 1958.

Schutz, W. C. *Manual: the FIRO scales.* Palo Alto: Consulting Psychologists Press, 1967.

Waxler, Nancy. Defense mechanisms and interpersonal behavior. Unpublished doctoral dissertation, Harvard University, 1960.

UNITERMS.   Affection; behavior; control; defense mechanism; denial; inclusion; introversion; isolation; projection; projective; regression.

—R. B. E.

15
Core Culture Inventory

AUTHOR.   Walter Gruen

AVAILABILITY.   Gruen, W. The composition and some correlates of the American core culture. Document No. 8749, ADI Auxiliary Publications Project, Photoduplication Service, Library of Congress, Washington, D.C. 20540

VARIABLES.   The Core Culture Inventory aims at measuring value areas presumably relevant to American culture. Seventeen such areas, divided among four major variables, are ostensibly tapped.

1. Vigorous pursuit of status change
   a. Preferences for upward mobility and role change as criteria for success (versus stable role development)
   b. Postponement of gratification for the future (versus hedonistic, immediate enjoyment)
   c. Optimism in one's own efforts

2. Preference for external rather than personality attributes of people and social relationships
   a. Preferring extroversion to the cultivation of a few intimate friends
   b. External, stereotyped expression rather than genuine expression of feeling
   c. Idolization of youth and beauty instead of respect for age and experience
   d. Lack of interest in reading and books

3. Standardized behavior
   a. Conformity to community standards rather than tolerance for individualistic ones
   b. Desire to work for a stable, well-known organization

4. Impulse restriction and control
   a. Tight control of emotion instead of freedom
   b. Regularity in scheduling rather than spontaneity
   c. Extreme instead of functional concern over cleanliness
   d. Preference for bland rather than spicy food
   e. Romantic love rather than love as a developing process
   f. Prevention rather than enjoyment of sensual experiences
   g. Keeping busy instead of enjoying idle time
   h. Relaxation for health rather than enjoyment

DESCRIPTION.   The inventory consists of 40 items, each stating a value supposedly relevant to one of the seventeen areas described above. Six statements are reverse-scored, and thus describe values presumably more often held by those who are relatively more resistant to enculturation. Examples follow, simulating statements of both core and reverse values found on the instrument.

A. (Core value) When a woman starts to age, she should take advantage of all cosmetic devices available that help her maintain an appearance of youth and beauty, lest she become unhappy.

B. (Reverse value) A woman who knows what age she is and acts it will realize herself most fully.

The scale was not intended to measure a linear dimension. Thus low scores do not necessarily indicate adherence to the value opposite the ones in question. A 6-point Likert scale, ranging from strongly agree to strongly disagree, was used. Low scores presumably indicate deviation (in an unspecified direction) from adherence to American core culture as defined by the seventeen value preferences described above.

ADMINISTRATION AND SCORING.   Items are scaled on a 7-point continuum, the theoretical midpoint being defined as zero. No indication of time limit has been given by the author of the Inventory, and there is no mention of scoring keys. Presumably, total core culture scores are tabulated by simply summing Likert ratings for all items. However, scoring procedures have not been fully elaborated in any material available at the time of this review.

DEVELOPMENT.   The author believed that a cluster of core culture values, including most of those recognized as middle-class American by Loeb, Mead, Lewin, Erikson, and others, occurs as the accepted or rejected standard of most Americans. The instrument originally devised to test this supposition contained 76 items intended to express 24 value areas considered by Loeb et al. as typically American. Two items for each value area were included, half of the total being worded positively, the remainder negatively, to control for response set. Five items from McClelland (1958) were included. The scale was administered to an original population of 114 college undergraduates and 101 upper-middle class adults (only 25% of whom returned the inventory mailed to them). Item analysis revealed 28 items significantly correlated with the total score.

New items were added to these 28, creating a revised 59-item scale. It was administered by mail to 255 adult non-profesional employees in a large mental hospital (50% return); 40 items correlated significantly with total score.

To pursue validity studies, the author postulated that lower-middle class and upper-lower class persons should exhibit core culture values—a "common man" complex—more strongly than upper-middle class persons. Data from the upper-middle sample ($N = 101$), and from 139 lower-middle class and 195 upper-lower class persons supported this expectation; variance was also larger in the upper-middle sample.

Scores from foreign samples (71 Australian college students, 105 Irish upper middle class adults, and 54 middle class German adults) differed significantly from those of the American sample, supposedly supporting the "American" nature of the values measured.

The author also expected that core culture acceptance and conformity should correlate positively. For 34 students, inventory scores correlated .29 ($p = .07$) with the Crutchfield version of the Asch conformity measure. An index of preference for popularly chosen items (e.g., cars, clothing, silverware) correlated .35 with inventory scores ($N = 98$ students, $p = .05$).

Gruen also proposed that those strongly adhering to core culture values should more often expose themselves to mass media—magazines, T.V. programs, and movies—which serve as "culture carriers." Further, those who deviate from these values were expected to "turn more to para-popular sources of reading and entertainment." These theses provided a further opportunity to check on criterion validity. The original upper-lower and lower-middle class samples ($N = 255$) indicated their preferred leisure time activities. Significant differences were obtained, though not in the expected direction for frequency of T.V. viewing. However, those deviating from core culture were more likely to report preferences for drama and educational T.V. Similar differences were also obtained between content of movies seen and magazines read, and core culture scores, as predicted. Thus both *predictive* and *concurrent validity* are partially demonstrated.

Finally, it was predicted that the core culture syndrome should be a visible part of the value system of public schools. Those Core Culture Inventory items presumed to measure the 17 value areas of the cluster names were recast as paragraphs, paired with opposing paragraphs, and administered to 90 teachers, who were asked to indicate which values they wished to impart to their students. However, in 11 of the 17 value areas, the majority preferred *anti*-core culture values. Older teachers (as with the earlier sample of adults) tended to subscribe to core values more often than younger ones.

CRITIQUE.   Split-half *reliabilities* are reported by Gruen as .86, .78, and .84 for three successive samples (N's unspecified). Intercorrelations among the items (original or revised version not specified) for the sample of 255 middle and lower class adults ranged from −.16 to +.36, average *r* obtained being .12. Scale reliability, based solely upon the above figures, appears adequate for group, not individual assessment. No other reliability studies have, to the writer's knowledge, been completed.

As for the *validity* of the instrument, it too has been only partially demonstrated. Although it appears that separate value areas are being assessed, much more validational evidence is needed before confidence in individual Inventory scores can be justified.

Norms were drawn from samples too small to permit generalization about any of the populations tested. Moreover, these were obtained for only 28 of the items in the final 40-item scale.

GENERAL COMMENT.   Individual diagnostic and prognostic usage of the Core Culture Inventory should not be attempted on the basis of the available validity and reliability information. Though the scale does appear promising as a measure of degree of enculturation in "mid-American" terms, *much* more widespread and current data collection is needed before the a priori item clusters—or, indeed, the over-all score—can be considered useful. Rapid changes are supposedly occurring in American values (viz. Gruen's teacher data), and it must be shown empirically that a scale developed even as recently as 1966 accurately represents the existing state of affairs. Data from a national probability sample would seem indicated before confidence should be placed in this instrument.

REFERENCES

Gruen, W. The composition and some correlates of the American core culture value configuration. Unpublished mimeographed paper, undated.

Gruen, W. Composition and some correlates of the American core culture. *Psychological Reports*, 1966, *18*, 483–486.

UNITERMS.   Attitude; belief; class; conformity; control; culture; enculturation; mobility; norm; socio-economic status; societal; value.

—R. B. E.
—M. B. M.

16
Cultural Awareness Scales

AUTHOR.   Jack Danielian

AVAILABILITY.   Jack Danielian, Human Resources Research Office, 300 N. Washington Street, Alexandria, Virginia 22314

VARIABLES.   Danielian has developed four separate tests of cultural awareness, intended primarily for members of U.S. advisory and assistance missions stationed in non-Western countries. Cultural awareness has been conceptualized as an *appreciation of the impact of cultural values on psychological processes.*

DESCRIPTION.   Test A is an attitudinal-level multiple-choice test of idealized non-Western values and assumptions. The 30 items ask questions about an hypothesized counterpart (advisee) "most different from an American," such as:

> A (foreign) counterpart probably reacts best to advice
> (a) which stresses facts and figures about concrete issues
> (b) which is well-embedded in a discussion
> (c) which is carefully offered in terms of "opinion" rather than "fact"
> (d) which clearly indicates the direction in which he is to move.

Test B, developed by M. Steinin and titled "Counterpart Response Prediction Index," contains 16 multiple-choice items embedded in a continuing dialogue such as:

> Foreign counterpart: Well, you see our training comes from the instructors. The instructors know everything.
>
> American: If the people have any questions while they're being trained, do they ask the instructor?
>
> Foreign counterpart: (a) No, the instructors ask the questions. When the people are giving good answers, they know it's time to give more instruction.
> (b) We take care to select our people properly. We see to it that what they have done before makes them already familiar with the kind of work we are training them to do.
> (c) You see, we have only a limited time to give them instruction. With these conditions it is more important to dispense information than to answer questions.

(d) I don't think they would have any questions because the instructors tell them all they need to know. The instructors give them all the training they need. Why should there be any questions?

Test C asks the respondent to check each of 29 adjectives on a 6-point Likert scale from "very like" to "very unlike" a "typical" American. Sixteen adjectives are keyed "American;" the remainder, "non-American." Some examples of each are:

(American)	*(non-American)*
analytical	theoretical
optimistic	abstract
explicit	idealistic
casual	harmonizing

Test D contains 20 nine-point Likert items which posit an individual who holds a particular belief (ten keyed "American" and ten "non-American") and ask the respondent 17 questions about how he would behave toward such a person. An example:

A person who holds that . . .

What is true for oneself in his deepest heart is true for all men.

would   : 1 : 2 : 3 : 4 : 5 : 6 : 7 : 8 : 9 :   would not talk to him

would not   : 1 : 2 : 3 : 4 : 5 : 6 : 7 : 8 : 9 :   would be partners with this person in an athletic game

ADMINISTRATION AND SCORING.   All the tests are self-administering without a time limit, although respondents are urged to give their first impression on Tests C and D and not to linger over items. The battery probably requires up to two hours to complete.

Scores for tests A and B are simply the number of correct items (see below for derivation of correct response). For Test C the score is the number of keyed "American" items checked as being "very," "rather," or "a little" like a "typical" American plus the number of "non-American" items checked as being "a little," "rather," or "very" unlike a "typical" American. Test D, being a self-descriptive inventory, wants no "right" answers, except for the presumed approach/avoidance dimension; it was used by Danielian to measure changes in attitudes after sensitivity training.

DEVELOPMENT.   The items for Test A were chosen empirically by Danielian to reflect, so to speak, a mirror image of Western society. Communalities (h^2) were determined from a factor analysis of a sample of 119 Army advisors in training. These communalities, in conjunction with the requirement that four of five cross-cultural experts agree on the best (most culturally aware) response, were used to refine the score to 12 items. Test B was developed similarly with the embedding protocol being taken from a real dialogue. The adjectives chosen for Test C came from Gulick (1963). Danielian's (1965) paper contains no information on the development of Test D.

CRITIQUE. The split-half *reliability* of Test A ($N = 119$) is .27, corrected by Spearman–Brown to .43. Its three-week test–retest reliability ($N = 63$ military advisors in training), is, surprisingly, .67. As of 1967, no further psychometric data on any of the four tests were available. Danielian (1965) has done pre- and post-sensitivity-training studies and has shown that significant score changes accompany such training, but these results cannot be interpreted as attesting to the *validity* of any of the tests. No *norms* are yet available.

GENERAL COMMENT. These four tests were developed specifically to assess the training of military assistance officials in cultural awareness. In a private communication, Danielian has indicated that the instruments "may eventually find more use as selection instruments than as measures to assess change." In the state of development reported here, they can only suggest an area of study—particularly the evocation of the problems involved in intercultural contacts between Americans and others. The instruments are reviewed here for information purposes only.

REFERENCES

Danielian, J. Assessing the training impact of a simulated (role-playing) cross-cultural exercise. Alexandria, Va.: Division of Human Resources Research Office, George Washington University, unpublished staff paper, 1965.

Gulick, S. L. *The East and West.* Rutland, Vermont and Tokyo: Charles E. Tuttle Co., 1963.

UNITERMS. Attitude; awareness; culture; intercultural contact; society; values.

—R. B. E.

17
Do's and Don'ts

AUTHOR.   Matthew B. Miles

AVAILABILITY.   Educational Resources Information Center (ERIC), Microfiche No. ED 042266 (Dale G. Lake, Final Report, Cooperative Project for Educational Development, Appendix, 1970), U.S. Office of Education, 400 Maryland Avenue, S.W., Washington, D.C. 20202

VARIABLES.   This instrument contains 27 items designed to measure the *perceived interpersonal norms* of a system and an individual's own *attitudes* toward the behaviors regulated by the same norms. The norms are: *Awareness; Authenticity; Trust; Inquiry; Objectivity; Collaboration; Changefulness; Altruistic Concern; Consensual Decision-Making; Competence-Based Power; Emotionality as Data;* and *Individuality.* In addition, various derived scores for *conformity* and *deviation* can be obtained.

DESCRIPTION.   Each item contains a statement of something a person might say or do. The respondent is asked to estimate the percentage of people in the system of which he is a member who would feel that you should or should not do or say the thing in question. The following is a sample item:

Ask others who seem upset to express their feelings:	Percent who think you should	Percent who think you should not	Percent who have no opinion	
	_____% +	_____% +	_____%	= 100%

After making such estimations across all 27 items, the respondent is asked to go through the items again, and indicate by a check mark whether he thinks he himself should engage in the behavior, should not engage in it, or has no opinion.

ADMINISTRATION AND SCORING.   The instrument is self-administering. However, since the individual must complete the instrument both as he perceives the rest of his colleagues would fill it out and for himself, the directions are complex and may even lead to a kind of self-contamination. Some work has been done with an alternate form which asks the subject to simply indicate how the majority feels rather than to estimate a percentage. This simplifies the instrument considerably, but normative data are not currently available for the revised form.

Several different scoring formats are available. One can simply sum the various items which make up a particular norm. For instance, three items are asserted to comprise the norm of Trust; these are summed to derive the Trust score. Detailed scoring directions are given in the appendix of the ERIC document for each norm. Also, a scoring system has been devised by Callahan (1970) to measure Perceived Conformity, the extent to which an individual endorses the prescriptions (across all items) which he perceives the majority of others to have endorsed. Perceived Deviance is the extent to which the individual's endorsement contravenes that of the perceived majority. For instance, an individual perceives himself to be more deviant if he sees himself opposed to a 95% majority than if he were opposed to only a 55% majority.

DEVELOPMENT.   This instrument is one of 20 created for the Cooperative Project for Educational Development (COPED). As such, it was field-tested on a small number of teachers and principals ($N = 150$), revised slightly, and then inserted in the package of 20 and administered to more than 3,000 adults—largely principals and teachers—in 21 school systems ranging from rural to metropolitan in makeup. The entire package was administered at two points in time during one school year. Some correlational work was carried out with these data (see Callahan, 1970 and Hilfiker, 1970).

CRITIQUE.   A number of *reliability* studies have been conducted with Ns ranging from 21 to 100. In one study by Callahan (1970) with a one-week testing interval and a sample of 34 superintendents, 6 items were discovered not to have sufficient reliability in that their r_{tt} values did not depart significantly from zero. Overall, reliabilities tended to be low even when significant, with a range of .57 to .75. Test–retest reliabilities were also obtained for the Conformity and Deviance measures. These data were collected from 74 school system employees, including teachers, principals, directors, curriculum workers, and administrators. The testing interval was two weeks. The reliabilities for Perceived Conformity and Perceived Deviance were .82 and .58 respectively.

The major evidence for *validity* comes from Callahan (1970) and Hilfiker (1970). Hilfiker's study demonstrates concurrent validity for the norms of Openness and Trust by showing that they are significantly correlated (each at .79) with innovativeness in nine school systems. Callahan provides *predictive validity* information regarding the derived scores for Actual Conformity and Deviation by showing that females are more conforming than males, as has been shown in numerous other studies. He also found that females scored significantly lower on

Perceived Deviance ($p < .01$) and significantly higher on the Perceived Conformity index ($p < .01$). Callahan also showed that Perceived Conformity and Deviance were positively and negatively related to morale, suggesting *construct validity*.

Benedict (1970) has shown that the instrument is *fakeable* in a *socially desirable* direction. Both human relations trainers and school administrators were able to predict the "good" direction of the norms measured.

GENERAL COMMENT. While caution must be exercised in using this instrument, due to its low reliabilities and easy fakeability, Do's and Don'ts does attempt to measure important dimensions of interest both to human relations trainers and more generally to those interested in the normative system or culture of large organizations. Enough evidence is presented to warrant use of this instrument in a diagnostic package designed to examine an organization's (or a subsystem's) health, though individual scores probably mean little.

REFERENCES

Benedict, B. Cooperative Project for Educational Development: *Research outcomes*. Contract OEG 3-8-080069-43(010), project No. 8-0069, 1970.

Callahan, D. M. Conformity, deviation, and morale among educators in school systems. In Cooperative Project for Educational Development: *Research outcomes*, Contract OEG 3-8-080096-43(010), project No. 8-0069, 1970.

Hilfiker, L. The relationships of school system innovativeness to selected dimensions of interpersonal behavior in eight school systems. Cooperative Project for Educational Development: *Research outcomes*. Contract OEG 3-8-080069-43(010), Project No. 8-0069, 1970.

Lake, D. G. Final Report, Cooperative Project for Educational Development, Project No. 8-0069. Grant No. OEG-3-8-080069-43(010). Appendix, ERIC Microfiche No. ED 042266. Volume I, Research Outcomes, ERIC Microfiche No. ED 042268. Washington: National Training Laboratories, 1970.

UNITERMS. Altruism; authenticity; awareness; changefulness; collaboration; conformity; consensus; competence; decision-making; deviation; emotionality; individuality; inquiry; norms; objectivity; power; trust.

—D. G. L.

18
The Dogmatism Scale

AUTHOR. Milton Rokeach

AVAILABILITY.   Rokeach, M. *The open and closed mind.* New York: Basic Books, Inc., 1960.

VARIABLES.   Rokeach's primary area of interest in constructing the Dogmatism Scale was to devise a measure of general authoritarianism (regardless of ideological content) and general intolerance of those with differing belief systems. Individuals are seen as having a "belief system" (things believed, accepted as true) and a "disbelief system" (things rejected, disbelieved, seen as false). The major variable measured by the scale is the *openness—closedness of belief systems of individuals,* conceptualized as relatively antithetical traits organized in terms of belief—disbelief, centrality—peripherality, and certain aspects of time perspective.

Open systems are characterized by a low degree of rejection of disbelief systems, and full communication within and between belief and disbelief systems. Open systems are also conceptualized as showing little discrepancy in degree of differentiation (richness of detail) between belief and disbelief, and relatively high differentiation of disbelief. Conversely, closed systems are hypothesized to show greater rejection of disbelief, isolation of parts within and between belief and disbelief subsystems, greater discrepancy in differentiation between these, and little differentiation of the disbelief system.

The determining factors of degree of openness vs. closedness are seen as two opposing sets of motives—the need to know and the need to defend against threat. Prevalence of the former theoretically leads to openness; that of the latter, to closedness. Time orientation is presumably broader for those with open systems, and narrower and more future-oriented for those with closed ones.

No limitations in populations to be tested have been stipulated, and the author (1960) considered cross-cultural usage a possibility.

DESCRIPTION.   The final version, Form E, contains 40 negatively-worded items based on a 6-point Likert rating scale. Each item is a statement of opinion. No neutral response category is provided, and alternatives range from "I agree a little" to "I disagree very much." A simulated example:

It is necessary to censor the ideas to which we expose youths, in order
that they may learn important moral precepts handed down from the past.

Basically, items are categorized as involving one of three aspects of
belief systems: "belief–disbelief," "central–peripheral," and "time–
perspective." The first has already been discussed. Items relevant to it
presumably measure isolation within and between belief and disbelief
systems, and relative degrees of their differentiation. Items relevant to
the central–peripheral dimension may refer to primitive or pre-ideologi-
cal beliefs (such as percepts of the world as being, in general, hostile
or friendly); to attitudes toward authority, causes, believers, or dis-
believers; or to interrelations among primitive, intermediate, and
peripheral beliefs. Finally, items involving the time dimension are
intended to tap attitudes toward past, present, future, knowing the
future, and belief in force as a method for changing present situations.

ADMINISTRATION AND SCORING.   For all items, agreement is scored as
closed-mindedness, and disagreement as open-mindedness. Each Likert
category is assigned a weight, from $+3$ ("agree very much") to -3
("disagree very much"). Respondents are instructed to write $+1$, $+2$,
$+3$, etc. in accord with how much they agree or disagree with each
item. For scoring, the administrator converts the scale to a 1-to-7 scale
by adding 4 to each item score. Scores are summed to compute a total
Dogmatism score. Normative data in terms of means and standard
deviations for the original reliability samples (see below) are available
in Rokeach (1960).

DEVELOPMENT.   While most of the items were constructed by Rokeach,
a few were incorporated "with or without modification" from the work
of others (Rokeach, 1960). Item 21 is from Hoffer (1951), items 14
and 24 are from Berger (1952), and those numbered 22, 23, 27, 31, 33,
and 34 are from the MMPI.

Various American and English groups containing both students and
workers constituted the original samples used by Rokeach. Sampling
methods are not specified.

Form A was composed of 57 items from which item analysis eliminated 14, yielding Form B. Further item analyses eliminated 26
more items, eventually yielding the final Form E. These item analyses
reportedly revealed consistent, statistically significant differences between those scoring in the first and fourth quartile of the obtained
frequency distribution on most items. Odd–even *reliabilities* for 12
college student samples (Ns 21 to 207) from both the United States
and England ranged from .68 to .91, with a median of .74. For 60

English workers, odd–even *r* was .78. Test–retest reliabilities were .71 for 58 Ohio State University students (five- to six-month intervals), and .93 for 24 VA employees (one-month interval).

Rokeach was interested in developing a relatively ideology-free measure of general authoritarianism and intolerance. It has been pointed out by many observers that the California F-Scale (which see) is heavily loaded with right-wing political content. Thus Rokeach, to check construct validity, built a measure of "opinionation," a series of scales devoted to political right and left orientations. If Rokeach has succeeded in developing a Dogmatism Scale relatively free of ideological slant, then the Scale results ought to correlate well with those measuring right and left opinionation (that is, ardent Communists, who were included in Rokeach's English samples, should show up as high dogmatic, though they typically score low on the F-Scale). Rokeach (1960) reports the reliability of his right and left opinionation scales (20 items each, containing opinionated phrases directed at political and religious issues) as .75. He administered the scales, and a 5-item political—economic conservativism scale (Adorno et al., 1950), to seven samples (*N*s 135 to 207) in Michigan, New York, and England, along with the D Scale and the F-Scale. In general, the F-Scale correlated from .15 to .40 with the two measure of right (conservative) orientation, and the Dogmatism Scale correlations were negligible (.03 to .17 for the right–left opinionation index, and .11 to .28 for the political—economic conservatism scale). The evidence is encouraging, but far from decisive, especially since the D and F-Scales correlated at .54 to .77 in the same samples.

CRITIQUE.   Additional *reliability* studies have been conducted by Roberts (1962) who found a corrected split-half reliability of .81 with 100 undergraduates, and by Hough (undated) who found .86 with 50 student teachers. Test–retest figures of .70 were found for a fifteen-week interval by Zagona and Zurcher (1965) who tested 517 freshmen and sophomores. Shupe and Wolfer (1966) found twelve to twenty-eight-day retest correlations of .74 to .86, and also discovered that an agree–disagree response mode was as reliable as the original 6-point one. In general, the reliability seems reasonable, but marginal for the study of individuals.

Rokeach, Gladin, and Trumbo (Rokeach, 1960) completed two *construct validity* studies using known high and low dogmatic groups. In one of these, graduate students were nominated by their college professors for inclusion in one or the other of the groups. No differences nearing significance were found. However, in the second study, using subjects nominated by psychology graduate students as *most* and *least* dogmatic, significant differences were obtained. Additionally, differences between these groups' Ethnocentrism and F-Scale scores also reached significance. All these were in the direction expected.

Further studies of political and religious group members in England and America were interpreted as providing stronger (but still somewhat inconclusive) evidence for the validity of the instrument in measuring general authoritarianism and general intolerance. In one experiment by Rokeach, 54 Conservatives, 22 Liberals, 27 Attleeites, 19 Bevanites and 13 Communists, all from England, were given the Dogmatism Scale. The only nearly significant difference ($p = .16$) among group mean comparisons was that between Communists and Liberals, the latter having the lower mean of the two groups. None of the other differences was significant.

A comparison study of Michigan State University groups of 42 Catholics, 145 Protestants, and 15 non-believers yielded significant differences among groups on Dogmatism, Ethnocentrism, F, and Opinionation Scales: Catholics showed significantly higher mean Dogmatism scores than Protestants and non-believers. Finally, in a study of New York college students grouped as 46 Catholics, 24 Protestants, 131 Jews, and 6 non-believers, the only difference in Dogmatism group means approaching statistical significance was that between Catholics and Jews ($p = .10$).

In another construct validity study, Zagona and Zurcher (1964) observed the behavior of 60 introductory psychology students (taken from the high- and low-scoring ends of a group of 517), in classroom and experimental settings. High dogmatics were found to be more leader-oriented, to have a greater need for structure, and to react to challenges by authority figures with reduced confidence in solutions and reduced cohesiveness.

Haiman and Duns (1964) attempted a *predictive validity* study with moderate success, notably with high dogmatics. Observers were asked to predict subjects' D scores from observed interaction behavior in public speaking courses.

Korn and Giddan (1964) found moderate *concurrent validity* evidence: for 195 Stanford freshmen, correlations of from $-.24$ to $-.38$ were found between the D scale and the California Personality Inventory scales measuring Well-Being, Tolerance, and Flexibility.

In another validity study by Hough (undated), the only significant relationship between Dogmatism scores and growth in human relations skill was in the area of empathy. Those scoring in the lower and middle thirds of the sample ($N = 156$) on Dogmatism tended to score significantly higher on Empathy after human relations training, as measured by the Relationship Inventory (which see). Effects on the other subtests of the Inventory were in the expected direction but did not reach significance.

Lefcourt (1962) also found that among 272 drug addicts Dogmatism Scale scores were higher in those changing less as a result of counseling.

In a *criterion validity* study by Hough and Amidon (1965), six student teachers had scored low on the Dogmatism Scale. They were found to have changed significantly as a result of interaction analysis training, as measured by a pre-to-post-training comparison of their scores on an instrument presumably assessing attitudes toward appropriate teacher role behavior.

Norms are based on limited (primarily college student) samples, and cannot be considered to represent the general or normal adult population.

The likelihood that a substantial proportion of variance in scores flows from *acquiescence* seems high. It can be argued that acquiescence is naturally associated with closed-mindedness, but the opposite seems plausible as well.

GENERAL COMMENT.   The Dogmatism Scale is based on careful conceptualization, has moderate reliability, and the beginnings of good validity support. Recommended for non-clinical use. Use of a concurrent acquiescence measure would be wise; development of a form not subject to yea-saying response set is needed. Norms for non-student populations are much needed if the instrument is to be widely useful.

REFERENCES

Adorno, T. W., Frenkel-Brunswik, E., Levinson, D. J., and Sanford, R. N. *The authoritarian personality.* New York: Harper, 1950.

Berger, E. M. The relation between expressed acceptance of performance and expressed acceptance of others. *Journal of Abnormal and Social Psychology,* 1952, *47,* 778–782.

Haiman, F. S. and Duns, D. F. Validations in communicative behavior of attitude scale measures of dogmatism. *Journal of Social Pychology,* 1964, *64* (2), 287–297.

Hoffer, E. *The true believer.* New York: Harper, 1951.

Hough, J. A study of the use of Human Development Institute programs for improving the human relations skills of pre-service teachers. Unpublished mimeographed paper, undated.

Hough, J. and Amidon, E. The relationship of personality structure and training in interaction analysis to attitude change during student teaching. Paper presented to American Educational Research Association, Chicago, February, 1965.

Korn, H. A. and Giddan, N. S. Scoring methods and construct validity of the Dogmatism Scale. *Educational and Psychological Measurement*, 1964, *24* (4), 867–874.

Lefcourt, H. M. Clinical correlates of dogmatism. *Journal of Clinical Psychology*, 1962, *18* (3), 327–328.

Roberts, A. H. Intra-test variability as a measure of generalized response set. *Psychological Reports*, 1962, *11* (3), 793–799.

Rokeach, M. *The open and closed mind.* New York: Basic Books, 1960.

Shupe, D. R. and Wolfer, J. A. Comparative reliability of Dogmatism Scale with 2 and 6 scale points. *Psychological Reports*, 1966, *19* (1), 284–286.

Zagona, S. V. and Zurcher, L. A., Jr. Participation, interaction and role behavior in groups selected from the extremes of the open–closed cognitive continuum. *Journal of Psychology*, 1964, *58*, 255–264.

Zagona, S. V. and Zurcher, L. A., Jr. Notes on the reliability and validity of the Dogmatism Scale. *Psychological Reports*, 1965, *16* (3, Pt. 2), 1234–1236.

UNITERMS.   Acquiescence; authoritarianism; authority; belief; cognition; dogmatism; ethnocentrism; ideological; intolerance; openness; opinionation; political; prejudice; rigidity; time perspective.

—L. J. R.
—M. B. M.

19
Edwards Personal Preference Schedule (EPPS)

AUTHOR.   Allen L. Edwards

AVAILABILITY.   The Psychological Corporation, 304 East 45th Street, New York, New York 10007

VARIABLES.   The Edwards Personal Preference Schedule measures the relative strengths of 15 of Murray's needs: *Abasement; Achievement; Affiliation; Aggression; Autonomy; Change; Deference; Dominance; Endurance; Exhibition; Heterosexuality; Intraception; Nurturance; Order;* and *Succorance.*

DESCRIPTION.   The EPPS is a 225-item, forced-choice inventory. Each item consists of a pair of statements which represents two needs at the same average level of social desirability rating. Fifteen pairs are repeated to provide a consistency score. Pair-items are of the following type:

A. I like to tell amusing stories and jokes at parties.
B. I would like to write a great novel or play.

The need scores are ipsative, reflecting the relative strengths of the needs within an individual, not the strengths of those needs relative to needs of other individuals.

ADMINISTRATION AND SCORING.   The EPPS is self-administering without a time limit; Ss normally require forty to fifty-five minutes to complete the schedule. Hand-scoring keys, IBM answer sheets, and NCS (National Computer Systems) answer sheets are available from The Psychological Corporation. Centile rank norms for both college students and adults, and T-score norms for college students (only), both based on large samples, are presented for males and females separately.

DEVELOPMENT.   A sample of 140 college students was given an inventory of self-descriptive items previously scaled for social desirability. The percent Yes responses correlated with the social desirability values at .87. Pairs of statements of presumed approximately equal social desirability were selected using these results.

CRITIQUE.   Internal consistency *reliabilities* range from .60 to .87, with a median of .78; item overlap, however, inflates these estimates.

(Overlap stems from the fact that endorsement of one alternative both increases that scale's score and decreases the others'.) One-week test–retest reliabilities range from .74 to .87, with a median of .83; three-week test–retest reliabilities range from .55 to .87, with a median of .73, suggesting that memory effects might have influenced the one-week data.

The *validity* data in the manual are sparse. The EPPS has received considerable criticism for its insufficient validation, to which Edwards in his revised manual has not replied. The implications of the ipsative nature of the scores have not been investigated. For example, in utilizing the centile norms, the user should be aware that the person with an average rank profile (50th percentile) on all needs would *not* be a person in whom all needs have equal strength.

Tests for *concurrent validity* involving the Guilford–Martin Personnel Inventory, the Guilford–Zimmerman Temperament Survey, the California Test of Personality, and the MMPI have produced low correlations with EPPS scores. *Construct validity* studies have not been convincing. The EPPS Achievement scale was not significantly related to McClelland's measure of need achievement (n Ach) in five of six studies (the single significant correlation was .26). The same scale was significantly related to the French Test of Insight in but one of four studies ($r = .51$). The means of the EPPS scores and the means of the Adjective Check List scores correlated at .60 for the ACL real self and at .57 and .64 for the ACL ideal self. Academic achievement was related to Achievement scores in seven of ten studies.

As to *content validity*, no evidence is presented which demonstrates the comparability of items measuring a particular need. Even if each item's content did reflect a particular need, there is no reason to believe that the strengths of the needs represented are equal. Correlations between the proportion of A responses chosen under normal instructions and under instructions to make a good impression have been reported at both .69 and .88, despite Edwards' attempt to minimize *social desirability* effects. It has not been established that group-defined social desirability coincides with individual social desirability. Heilbrun and Goodstein (1961) found that the alternative rated as more individually socially desirable was chosen (on the average) 67% of the time, while the group-defined socially desirable alternative was chosen 56% of the time.

Norms are presented in the manual for 760 college males and for 749 college females and for 4031 male and for 4932 female heads of households.

Experiments in instructing college students to make a favorable impression suggest easy *fakeability* for the EPPS towards Deference,

Endurance, Order, and Achievement, and away from Autonomy, Heterosexuality, Aggression, Change, Succorance, and Exhibition (Dicken, 1959). These results reinforce the evidence that the EPPS remains extremely vulnerable to social desirability response sets.

GENERAL COMMENT. Though the EPPS is built around a systematic set of needs, and is more interpersonally/socially oriented than most personality measures, there is insufficient ground for belief that the schedule measures the needs it purports to measure. It is still plagued by the effects of item transparency and social desirability. The ipsative scores it generates make comparisons among individuals tentative. The revised manual is not responsive to criticism of the EPPS. The instrument is recommended only as a research tool.

REFERENCES

Dicken, C. F. Simulated patterns on the Edwards Personal Preference Schedule, *Journal of Applied Psychology,* 1959, 43, 372–378.

Heilbrun, A. B., Jr. and Goodstein, L. D. The relationships between individually-defined and group-defined social desirability and performance on the Edwards Personal Preference Schedule. *Journal of Counsulting Psychology,* 1961, 25, 200–204.

UNITERMS. Abasement; achievement; affiliation; autonomy; change; deference; dominance; endurance; exhibition; heterosexuality; inception; need; nurturance; order; personality; succorance.

—R. B. E.

20
Embedded Figures Test (EFT)

AUTHOR.   Herman A. Witkin

AVAILABILITY.   Consulting Psychologists Press, Inc., 577 College Avenue, Palo Alto, California 94306

VARIABLES.   The Embedded Figures Test measures *field-independence/dependence*. Witkin defines this dimension of perceptual functioning: "The person with a more field-independent way of perceiving tends to experience his surroundings analytically, with objects experienced as discrete from their backgrounds. The person with a more field-dependent way of perceiving tends to experience his surroundings in a relatively global fashion, passively conforming to the influence of the prevailing field or context" (Witkin et al., 1962). The test is intended for use with persons above the age of ten. A special children's form is available for ages five through nine.

DESCRIPTION.   The EFT consists of 24 complex, colored figures, in each of which one of eight simple geometric figures is embedded. The eight simple figures are also printed on separate cards so that they can be presented to the respondent independent of the embedding context. A shortened form using only the first twelve items of the series has been shown to correlate in the mid-.90s with the total test. In addition, a group form of the test has been copyrighted by the Educational Testing Service. The group form contains 16 figures, with the complex figures falling on one page and the simple figures on the other. Special instructions for children are also available.

ADMINISTRATION AND SCORING.   The 24-item test is administered by the experimenter, who first shows the subject a complex figure for fifteen seconds and asks him to describe its overall pattern. Next he presents the simple figure for ten seconds. The subject is then required to find the simple figure as it is embedded in the complex one. The simple figure must be found in the upright position and in the size it appears alone. As soon as the subject begins his search, a stopwatch is started. When the subject says he has found the simple figure, the watch is stopped but not reset and the time noted. If the subject can trace the simple figure within the complex one, his score is the time noted. If he cannot, the time is noted and marked as incorrect, the watch is started up from that time and the subject continues to try to find the simple figure. The time limit for each of the 24 items is five minutes. For the short form of 12 items, the time limit is three minutes per item. The group form imposes a total time limit of fifteen minutes for its 16 figures; the response format is a multiple choice among five alternative simple figures. The score on the group form is the number of simple figures successfully found within the fifteen minute time limit.

DEVELOPMENT. The impetus for Witkin's adaptation of Gottschaldt's figures was his dissatisfaction with the interpretations offered by the universal visual Gestalt view of the part–whole relation, or Gibson's view of the effects of postural factors in explaining the perceptual property of "uprightness." Witkin instead developed the ideas of field-independence and field-dependence to account for differences in individual perceptions, and devised the test to measure these cognitive phenomena.

CRITIQUE. Five studies of the *reliability* of the 24-item test have shown a median coefficient of .92, with a three-year test–retest reliability of .89 for both young adult men and women. The corrected odd–even reliability of the short form is .88.

As to *construct validity,* there is some question whether a distinction exists between embedding fields and merely distracting fields. For example, Longenecker (1956) compared the EFT with two forms of the Holtzman Form-Recognition Test (Holtzman, 1955), an achromatic one which requires the identification of incomplete line drawings of animal and human figures, and a chromatic one in which the subject is distracted from identifying figures by a transparent overlay of colored inkblots. These correlated at .54 and .46, respectively, with the EFT. Jackson (1955) has reported for men a correlation of .46 between EFT scores and performance in a test of ability to distinguish words against a background of noise. The correlation for women (.21) was not significant. These studies suggest that the ability to lift figures from an embedding context is a specific manifestation of a more general ability to overcome distracting contexts. Karp (1962) tested this hypothesis with a series of four tests which were specifically distraction-oriented, and compared the results with the EFT, as well as with Witkin's other embedded figure tests—the Body Adjustment Test and the Rod-and-Frame Test. A factor analysis of the scores showed Witkin's three tests clearly defining one factor, with the four distracting tests loading on another factor.

Concurrent validity is suggested by the correlations of .46, .77, and

.69 in three separate comparisons of the EFT with the Thurstone Gottschaldt test of flexibility and closure (Thurstone's "freedom from Gestalt binding").

In the manual, Witkin refers to studies relating EFT scores to social behavior which "demonstrate that the tendency for the perception of an item to be dominated by the organization of the surrounding context in the EFT is associated with a tendency for attitudes, beliefs, sentiments, or self-view to be strongly influenced by standards derived from the prevailing social context." He does not, however, identify this study. Witkin also says that more analytic ability on the EFT is related to the defenses of intellectualization and isolation; and that less analytic ability, to those of massive repression and primitive denial.

The chief *respondent difficulty* of the EFT is its length, which, in the extreme, can run over two hours; hour-long sessions are not unusual, particularly with children. The short form (items 1–12) is an answer to this problem as well as to the problem of learning which may occur during the test. Figures 13 through 24 may be used as a parallel form to items 1 through 12.

The *norms* are scanty; item-intercorrelation analysis and correlations with measures of academic performance or job success are yet to be seen.

GENERAL COMMENT.   The Embedded Figures Test has been generally recognized as tapping important dimensions of cognition and perception. Its current state of development does not allow its use for diagnostic purposes, but the test is adequate for research in a field of fundamental significance.

REFERENCES

Holtzman, W. H. *Tentative manual: the Holtzman Form-Recognition Test.* Austin: University of Texas, 1955 (mimeo).

Jackson, D. N. Stability in resistance to field forces. Unpublished doctoral dissertation, Purdue University, 1955.

Karp, S. A. Field dependence and overcoming embeddedness. *Journal of Consulting Psychology,* 1963, *27,* 294–302.

Longenecker, E. D. Form perception as a function of anxiety, motivation, and the testing situation. Unpublished doctoral dissertation, University of Texas, 1956.

Witkin, H. A. Individual differences in ease of perception of embedded figures. *Journal of Personality,* 1950, *19,* 1–15.

Witkin, H. A. Cognitive development and the growth of personality. *Acta Psychologica,* 1961, *18,* 245–257.

Witkin, H. A., Dyk, R. B., Faterson, H. F., Goodenough, D. R., and Karp, S. A. *Psychological differentiation: studies of development.* New York: Wiley, 1962.

UNITERMS.   Cognition; field-dependence; Gestalt; Gottschaldt figures; graphic.

—R. B. E.

21
The Family Concept Q-Sort

AUTHOR. Ferdinand van der Veen

AVAILABILITY. Ferdinand van der Veen, Dane County Mental Health Center, Madison, Wisconsin 53705

VARIABLES. The author defines *family concept* as the way an individual perceives his family as a functioning unit; such concepts are believed to result from patterns of interaction.

DESCRIPTION. The Family Concept Q-Sort is composed of 80 items that are descriptive of the family unit, both the ideal family concept and the real family concept. Examples of the items are:

We get along very well in the community.
There is not enough discipline in our family.

The items are not concerned with individual relationships within the family, but rather with the entire family unit.

ADMINISTRATION AND SCORING. The instrument is an interval scale test with a stack of 80 cards presented to the subject; on each card is a printed item. On a table before the subject are nine large cards, on one of which he will place each of the 80 cards. The large cards are in sequence from "least like my family" (position 0) to "most like my family" (position 8). A forced distribution of 3, 6, 9, 13, 18, 13, 9, 6, 3 is required. The instructions are clear enough and simple enough to make the test applicable to most literate individuals.

The mechanics of scoring are simple (cards in a pile on a large card receive the weight (0 through 8) of that large card). The test is not long (thirty to forty-five minutes) and would appear to hold the attention and interest of subjects. Cumulative scoring is used with the Q-Sort. The sum of items rated plus and minus by the subject compared to those rated by a group of professionals (see below) determines the score for the various family perceptions. There are 27 plus-scored items, and 21 minus-scored items which when converted yield a maximum score of 48.

Several global scores have been developed for the Q-Sort along with the specific item scores. Among these are a *family adjustment* score, a *family satisfaction* score, a *family congruence* score, and a *family compatibility* score.

DEVELOPMENT.　　The author begins with the following assumptions: 1) The family concept influences behavior (i.e., a breakdown in family interaction may be the result of discrepant family concepts rather than a product of intrapsychic conflicts); 2) it can be referred to and shared; and 3) it can change as a result of experience (e.g., group psychotherapy). The instrument was developed to determine how an individual's actual family concept and his ideal family-concept are related to adjustments or changes in his family.

The author began with 200 items which were descriptive of the family and had been formulated by three professionals in the family treatment field; 136 of these were presented to 11 other professionals, who rated the value of each item. The surviving 80 items were agreed upon by 75% of the professionals. A second sample of 17 professionals was combined with the first group to determine the present items. The agreement was high for the two groups, as shown by a product–moment correlation of .95. The present form of the Q-Sort contains these 80 items.

Five families on a clinic waiting list were selected as the original population, but the instrument has been applied to well and maladjusted groups, to parents as well as adolescents.

CRITIQUE.　　*Reliabilities* determined by a median test–retest correlation for ten clinic waiting list parents over a four-week time were .71 and .80 for real and ideal family concepts, respectively. The test–retest correlations were .51, .39, .66, and .63 for the family adjustment, family satisfaction, family congruence, and family compatibility scores of the lower adjustment group. The subjects used were clinic and low adjustment groups. The professional adjustment criterion of the first sample of ten clinicians correlated at .95 with that of a subsequent sample of 17 clinicians.

Three *validity* studies (van der Veen, 1960–65) showed that parents of children higher in social and emotional school adjustment scored higher on family adjustment than parents of low adjusted children, or than parents of clinic children.

In another study Ayers (1965) showed that in a clinical group receiving treatment, seven of eight families moved toward greater family compatibility. Whether this was actually a function of treatment is undetermined.

In a concurrent validity study (van der Veen et al., 1964) three Q-Sort scores (for adjustment, congruence, and satisfaction) were found to be associated with the Locke–Wallace test of marital adjustment. In another study (Fike and van der Veen, 1966) the family adjustment score of adolescents was positively related to their perception of their parents' attitudes toward them, as measured by the Relationship Inventory (which see).

In an item analysis, using three groups of 10 parents (clinic, non-clinic low adjustment, and non-clinic high adjustment), significant item differences between groups were found on 34 items. It was concluded that the clinic parents were more likely to perceive conflict and to feel a greater inability to deal with their difficulties than were the other two groups.

In another sample of 25 adolescents used to test *social desirability* of the items, the Q-Sort was compared with two California Personality Inventory scales (Good Impression and Self Control). The Good Impression scale was related to 13 of the 80 items and the Self Control scale to 22. Of these, 18 are in the 47 items used to compute the family adjustment score. So social desirability is a factor, but degree of influence is undetermined.

GENERAL COMMENT.   Though the sample of subjects is varied, and the test reliable and valid for these groups, the sample sizes have not been large enough to determine how general the usefulness of the Family-Concept Q-Sort might be. The need for instruments which relate to family functioning is obvious. This instrument represents an important attempt to meet the need; it is worthy of further consideration and research.

REFERENCES

Ayers, E. G. A Study of conflict between parents in clinic and non-clinic families. Unpublished doctoral dissertation, University of Kansas, 1965.

Barrett-Lennard, G. T. Dimensions of therapist response as causal factors in therapeutic change. *Psychological Monographs*, 1962, 76, 7 (Whole No. 562).

Berkowitz, N. Perceived family relationships in families differing in adjustment level. Unpublished master's thesis, University of Wisconsin, 1963.

Crandall, V. C. Personality characteristics, and social and achievement behaviors associated with children's social desirability response tendencies. *Journal of Personality and Social Psychology*, 1966, 4 (5), 477–486.

Fike, C., and van der Veen, F. Untitled pilot study, 1966.

Hamilton, R. B., Hunter, J. B., and Rentmiester, J. A. Changes in family perceptions due to psychotherapy. Unpublished master's thesis, University of Wisconsin, 1966.

Huebner, B., Jorgens, B., and Neja, P., Jr. A research study of the individual's perception of his family and its influence on the functioning of the family. Unpublished master's thesis, University of Wisconsin, 1961.

van der Veen, F. The Family-Concept Q-Sort. Dane County Mental Health Center, Madison, Wisconsin, 1960 (mimeo).

van der Veen, F. The parent's concept of the family unit and child adjustment. *Journal of Counseling Psychology,* 1956, *12,* 196–200.

van der Veen, F., Huebner, B., Jorgens, B., and Neja, P., Jr. Relationships between the parents' concept of the family and family adjustment. *American Journal of Orthopsychiatry,* 1964, *34,* 45–55.

van der Veen, F., Ostrander, K., and van der Veen, M. Some results of the first study of clinic families using the Family-Concept Q-Sort. Dane County Mental Health Center, Madison, Wisconsin, 1961 (mimeo).

van der Veen, M. and Ostrander, K. Development and initial use of a family-concept Q-Sort with clinicians and clients of the Dane County Guidance Center. Unpublished master's thesis, University of Wisconsin, 1961.

UNITERMS.   Adjustment; compatibility; congruence; family; marital and family roles; Q-Sort; satisfaction.

—D. G. L.

22
Fascism (and Reversed Fascism) Scales

AUTHORS.   Theodor W. Adorno, Else Frenkel-Brunswik, Daniel J. Levinson, and R. Nevitt Sanford

AVAILABILITY.   Adorno, T. W., Frenkel-Brunswik, E., Levinson, D. J., and Sanford, R. N. *The Authoritarian Personality.* New York: Harper, 1950.

VARIABLES.   The F-Scale was devised to measure *pre-fascist anti-democratic,* or, later, *authoritarian* syndromes. The authoritarian personality as hypothesized is notable for rigidity in interpersonal situations, discomfort in situations conducive to introspection, general hostility, and pessimism regarding the future. Theoretically, authoritarians are expected to show cynicism; anti-intraception; authoritarian submission (the propensity to demur to superiors and authority); conventionalism; authoritarian aggression (that which is directed toward violators of conventional values); concern with power and toughness; destructiveness; superstitiousness; stereotypy; overconcern with sex; projectivity; dichotomization of complex issues; and acceptance of traditional authoritarian figures—in sum, the attitude that one lives in a hostile, jungle-like milieu (Christie and Jahoda, 1954), and should behave accordingly.

DESCRIPTION.   The F-Scale as constituted has three forms. Form 78 contains 38 Likert-type items. The respondent indicates his degree of agreement or disagreement on a +3 to −3 scale, with the neutral point eliminated. Form 60 contains 34 items, 15 of which are new to this form. The remaining 19 were the best from Form 78. Form 45-40 contains 30 items, and is meant to improve on the shorter versions of the F-Scale. Items resemble the following simulated examples:

The world is made up of two kinds of people—the weak and the strong.

Most people have only their self-interest at heart.

ADMINISTRATION AND SCORING.   The scale is self-administering; no time limit is specified. Scoring is the usual Likert summation.

DEVELOPMENT.   The F-Scale, from its initial development, was the subject of widespread, even faddish, use and vigorous methodological critique. The methodological issues cannot be fully explored in a brief

80

review; see Christie and Jahoda (1954) for thorough and thoughtful commentary. See also Christie and Cook (1958) for a listing of studies about and with the F-Scale through 1956.

About 2,000 middle-class people comprised the original population. Minority group members were excluded; the average educational level was twelfth grade. All were members of some formally organized group (e.g., church, union) and had volunteered to take the questionnaire.

Items were chosen for the F-Scale with two aims in mind: 1) to tap minority group prejudice without explicitly referring to specific ethnic groups, and 2) to measure "potentially anti-democratic tendencies at the personality level" (Adorno et al., p. 233). Items were developed from "remarks made by prejudiced interviewees, from newspapers and magazines, and from previous research" (Christie and Jahoda, 1954). Initially, items were included which bore a theoretical relationship to the variables hypothesized to be of importance. Items finally retained had to discriminate high and low total scorers on the F-Scale as a whole, be relevant to current world affairs, have rational or logical justification for inclusion, and discriminate high from low scorers on two associated scales measuring Anti-Semitism and Ethnocentrism. Successive forms of the F-Scale show increasing correlations with Ethnocentrism scores: Form 78, $r = .65$; Form 60, $r = .69$; Form 45, $r = .73$; Form 40 (the final version), $r = .77$.

Some energy was put during the developmental phases into validation, via analysis of depth interviews with persons who (unknown to the interviewers) had scored high or low on the F-Scale. However, H. H. Hyman and P. B. Sheatsley, writing in Christie and Jahoda (1954) suggest that systematic bias may have entered the interview coding, the analysis of projective questions and Thematic Apperception Test results.

All original F-Scale items are worded so that endorsement increases scale scores. This naturally led to efforts to produce "reversed" F-Scale items, on the theory that acquiescence response set should be separated, analytically, from authoritarianism as conceived by the original developers of the scale. The results of such attempts were uneven: Bass' (1955) reversed scale correlated $+.20$ with the original version; Chapman and Campbell's (1957), .17 and $-.01$ for two samples; Jackson, Messick, and Solley's (1957), $-.35$; and Leavitt, Hax, and Roche's (1955), rs from $-.66$ to $+.42$ in five small samples.

Christie, Havel, and Seidenberg (1958) took account of these efforts in building their reversed F-Scale. In constructing items, they considered the following: logical opposition to the original items, avoidance of extreme wording, and psychological opposition to the original items. Two 30-item subscales were assembled, each containing one half of the original F-Scale items and reversals of the remaining original items; items were randomly assigned. The usual Likert response mode was employed. Both forms were used with university summer session samples in the Southwest ($N = 75$) and Northeast ($N = 40$). "Of the 30 reversals, 22 discriminated in the appropriate direction between high and low quartiles on the F-Scale on both samples . . . the attempt to find workable reversals is thus viewed as moderately successful."

A 20-item scale containing 10 original and 10 reversed items was given to eight samples of students and teachers ($N = 702$); original items correlated with reversed items at from .10 to .58, median .45 (corrected for attenuation). The reliabilities of the 10 reversed items ranged from .18 to .72, with a median of .42. The authors concluded from analysis of another national sample of college-educated adults that no significant degree of acquiescence set existed in responses to the reversed scale.

CRITIQUE.   The F-Scale has been used in hundreds of studies since its development; to cover them even representatively here would be impossible.

The *reliability* of the instrument is quite reasonable. Adorno et al. (1950) report (apparently split-half) mean reliabilities for Form 78 as .74 ($N = 295$); Form 60, .87 ($N = 286$); Form 45, .90 ($N = 290$); Form 40, .91 ($N = 779$), and Form 45-40, .85 ($N = 449$). The Form 40 reliability sample included students, service club members, and middle class and working class persons, so the figures seem trustworthy. It is not clear whether the authors conducted any retest reliability studies.

Four *concurrent validity* studies were summarized by Christie and Jahoda (1954):

> [these] utilized some behavior other than another attitude scale or report of own beliefs or activities. . . . Counselors accepting authoritarian statements were judged to have behaved in a punitive and condescending manner to social inferiors (Eager and Smith, 1952); high scorers were reluctant to serve as experimental subjects, reflecting anti-intraceptiveness (Rosen, 1951); low scorers tended to be better at estimating preferences of peers and high scorers those of superiors, which suggests differential preoccupation with the role of authority (Christie, 1952); and high scorers tended to attribute their own attitude to others to a greater extent than low scorers (Scodel and Mussen, 1953).

Another concurrent validity study by Milton (1952) found a rank-order correlation of .73 between the average scale scores of students (sample $N = 390$) who preferred each of six Presidential candidates in

1952, and the researcher's ordering of those candidates on authoritarianism.

Christie and Jahoda (1954) cited the similarity between the F-Scale and a fascism index developed by Stagner as evidence of *face validity*.

As previously indicated, there is generally a close relationship between F-Scale scores and the Ethnocentrism scale developed by the same researchers; Christie and Jahoda (1954) report correlations ranging from .76 to .83 in various samples. This hardly suggests *construct validity*, however, since the items were explicitly chosen to discriminate on both scales during development.

Rokeach's (1960) investigations of dogmatism and opinionation led him to the conclusion that many of those scoring high on his dogmatism scale also tended to be right-wing authoritarians; he found that F-Scale scores correlated from .47 to .56 with his measure of "right opinionation," but from —.27 to .11 with "left opinionation." That is, the F-Scale tends not to be a general measure of dogmatism or opinionation, but locates persons whose belief system is opinionated *and* generally politically "right." Politically "left" persons, whether personally rigid or open, tend to score low on the F-Scale.

GENERAL COMMENT. Though the F-Scale appears to have some validity as a measure of "right" authoritarianism, the item content in 1971 has a somewhat dated feeling, carrying as it does some of the ideological overtones of the period immediately following World War II. Social class differences found in "authoritarianism" may be primarily a function of educational level, as examination of some of the interview summaries in Adorno et al. (1950) suggest. And, the spuriously high correlations with Ethnocentrism scales do not automatically lend weight to the idea that high F-Scale scorers must of needs be prejudiced.

For a time, in the 1950's, the F-Scale had wide, almost faddish use; researchers seemed to add the F-Scale almost automatically to any study, just because of its availability and its ideological attractiveness. That time is past, and it may well be that less ideological measures of personal authoritarianism (e.g., Harvey, Hunt, and Schroder's (1961) abstract/concrete cognitive style measure) or Rokeach's Dogmatism Scale (which see) are presently more useful.

Put another way: the variables (from anti-intraception to projectivity to conventionalism to superstitiousness) which made up the authoritarian syndrome in the late 1940's man (or may not) go together today.

For the present, the researcher using the F-Scale must do so with caution if he wishes a *personal* measure, and should consider developing new measures if he wishes a *political* measure of right (or left) authoritarianism.

REFERENCES

Adorno, T. W., Frenkel-Brunswik, E., Levinson, D. J., and Sanford, R. N. *The authoritarian personality.* New York: Harper, 1950.

Chapman, L. and Campbell, D. T. Response set in the F-Scale. *Journal of Abnormal and Social Psychology,* 1957, 54, 129–132.

Christie, R. Some determinants of the accuracy of social judgments among Army recruits. Unpublished paper read at Eastern Psychological Association meetings, 1952.

Christie, R. and Cook, P. A guide to published literature relating to *The authoritarian personality* through 1956, *Journal of Psychology,* 1958, 45, 171–199.

Christie, R., Havel, J. and Seidenberg, B. Is the F-Scale reversible? *Journal of Abnormal and Social Psychology,* 1958, 56, 143–159.

Christie, R. and Jahoda, M. *Studies in the scope and method of "The Authoritarian Personality."* Glencoe, Illinois: Free Press, 1954.

Eager, J. and Smith, M. B. A note on the validity of Sanford's authoritarian-equalitarian scale. *Journal of Abnormal and Social Psychology,* 1952, 47, 265–267.

Harvey, O. J., Hunt, D. E., and Schroder, H. M. *Conceptual systems and personality development.* New York: Wiley, 1961.

Leavitt, H. G., Hax, H., and Roche, J. H. "Authoritarianism" and agreement with things authoritative. *Journal of Psychology,* 1955, 40, 215–221.

Milton, O. Presidential choice and performance on a scale of authoritarianism. *American Psychologist,* 1952, 7, 597–598.

Rokeach M. *The open and closed mind.* New York: Basic Books, Inc., 1960.

Rosen, E. Differences between volunteers and non-volunteers for psychological studies. *Journal of Applied Psychology,* 1951, 35, 185–193.

Scodel, A. and Mussen, P. Social perceptions of authoritarians and non-authoritarians. *Journal of Abnormal and Social Psychology,* 1953, 48, 181–184.

UNITERMS.   Acquiescence; anti-Semitism; attitude; authoritarianism; authority; conservatism; conventionality; ethnocentrism; fascism; ideology; intolerance; personality; political.

—M. B. M.

23
Fundamental Interpersonal Relations Orientation–Behavior (FIRO–B)

AUTHOR.   William C. Schutz

AVAILABILITY.   Consulting Psychologists Press, Inc., 577 College Avenue, Palo Alto, California 94306

VARIABLES.   The FIRO-B measures two aspects of self-perceived interpersonal behavior, those *expressed* by self and *wanted* from others toward the self, along three dimensions: *Inclusion,* the need for association and interaction with others; *Control,* the need for dominance in relationships with others; and *Affection,* the need to establish relationships of love and intimacy towards others.

DESCRIPTION.   The FIRO–B consists of 6 Guttman scales of 9 items each, totaling 54 items. A simulated item is:

I like other people to decide what to do in a group.

1. usually   2. often   3. sometimes   4. occasionally   5. rarely   6. never

ADMINISTRATION AND SCORING.   The instrument is self-administering. The responses to items are dichotomized into accept/reject responses, according to scoring keys resulting from scalogram analysis of the responses of a population of 1500 college students in the Boston area (1000 Harvard freshmen and 230 Radcliffe freshmen made up the bulk of the sample). Scale scores are the raw totals of "accepting" responses across the 9 items in each scale, and can thus range from 0 to 9.

The six scale scores can be used directly as self-perceived measures of typical social behavior expressed by the self and wanted from others toward the self. The difference between the "expressed" and "wanted" scores (e-w) on each dimension is the tendency to originate behavior in a particular domain more than to receive it from others. Smith (1963) suggests the score can be seen as a measure of what the respondent finds rewarding.

The sum of expressed and wanted scores (e + w) is called the "interchange" score by Schutz; it is said to indicate the total amount of interpersonal behavior exchanged between the respondent and others (as viewed by him).

To compute a compatibility measure between any two persons, the difference between their "originator" scores, or their "interchange" scores is computed.

A children's form (ages twelve and up) is available; forms can be completed in about fifteen minutes. A hand key for scoring includes conversion scales for percentile scores. Norms for large populations are not available.

DEVELOPMENT.   The present FIRO–B has six direct predecessors. The first was a Q-Sort of 96 items, each of which expressed a feeling or action of someone in an interpersonal situation. Ss ranked the cards from "Most Like Me" to "Least Like Me." The need for an objective scoring method led to the scale analysis of three factors, then termed Dependence, Personalness, and Aggressiveness. New items were added, and the resulting form was administered to 500 naval enlisted men in a paper-and-pencil form; this led to a 13-scale form.

A set of four pairs of paragraphs, each pair representing an area of orientation and each paragraph describing diametric positions on the orientation, constituted the next form. Control was represented twice, once from a projected group leadership position, once from a group membership position. Respondents indicated the degree to which they were more nearly like one paragraph than the other (Likert scales). The present form represents a consolidation back down to two aspects ("wanted" and "expressed") of the three need orientations now labeled Control, Inclusion, and Affection.

CRITIQUE.   For Guttman scales the chief measure of reliability is *reproducibility*, which for five of the six FIRO–B scales is .94 and for the other is .93. For the expressed and wanted Inclusion scales one-month *test–retest reliability* coefficients are .82 and .75, respectively ($N = $ 126 Harvard students). Corresponding coefficients for the Control scales are .74 and .71 ($Ns = $ 183, 125). For the Affection scales the (one-week) test–retest coefficients were .73 and .80, expressed and wanted respectively ($N = 57$).

Data are not available on the reliability of the interchange or originator scores; the latter in particular is undoubtedly less stable as a difference score than its component parts.

Above-90% reproducibility lends weight to the *content validity* of the Guttman scales. Evidence of *concurrent validity* is not nearly so definitive. The manual merely alludes to six fields of research in which the FIRO–B has been utilized; it does not cite positive indications of validity. Schutz (1958, ch. 4) indicates that comparisons of FIRO–B profiles with political attitudes derived from other Guttman scales are generally in the expected direction, but these political attitude scale scores cannot be considered independent criterion measures for con-current validity. The manual indicates that scores for 12 occupational groups satisfy predictions made from stereotypes of these occupations. They clearly differentiate, for example, traveling salesmen, business school students, and medical school students from creative architects, physics majors, and members of Antarctic crews on both individual and total scale scores; a much higher level of interpersonal activity is self-reported by the salesmen and graduate students.

Efforts to predict group compatibility from FIRO–B scores have been uniformly successful with groups ranging from T-groups to string quartets. Since the compatibility measures are based on the originator and interchange measures, it may be that the reliability issues raised above are not serious.

It is not clear whether FIRO–B can be appropriately used as a criterion measure for programs (such as T-groups) aimed at changing interpersonal behavior. Smith (1963) did find that the "originator" (reward) scores for Control and Affection did tend to shift toward the median after T-group experience. This may be partially a regression effect, but Smith did find meaningful predictive correlates of such change in a later study (1967). Schutz and Allen (1966) predicted similar shifts and found them (but only via examining changes in correlations computed between before and after scores; no raw data are presented). In any case, the usefulness of the reward score (and the interchange score) rests on the assumption that two Guttman scales with the same range can (regardless of content) be meaningfully sub-tracted from or added to each other, which seems dubious.

The scores for the twelve occupational groups are the only ap-proximations to *norms*. Sample sizes are often small; seven of them are student groups in one major field of study or another.

Scale intercorrelations are a moderate problem. The two Inclusion scales intercorrelate at .49; the two Affection scales at .42. Also, ex-pressed Affection correlates with expressed Inclusion at .47 (all Ns = 1,430). The largest of the remaining 12 intercorrelations is .31; the median of all correlations is .22.

No consideration is given to the possibility of *response sets* (all items are worded positively), nor are the effects of *social desirability* considered. The user should also bear in mind the fact that Ss are re-porting self-perceived behavior.

GENERAL COMMENT.   The Guttman scales are well-constructed; admin-istration is easy, though subjects sometimes complain of item repetitive-ness. Inadequate norms are a drawback, as are the unknown effects of social desirability and acquiescence response sets. The predictive successes that the FIRO–B has scored, however, encourage its use as an aid to the composition of compatible groups, and perhaps as a change measure as well.

REFERENCES

Schutz, W. C. *FIRO: a three-dimensional theory of interpersonal behavior.* New York: Holt, Rinehart and Winston, 1958.

Schutz, W. C. *Manual: the FIRO scales.* Palo Alto: Consulting Psychologists Press, 1967.

Schutz, W. C. and Allen, V. L. The effects of a T-group laboratory on interpersonal behavior. *Journal of Applied Behavioral Science,* 1966, 2, 266–286.

Smith, P. B. Attitude changes associated with training in human relations. *British Journal of Social and Clinical Psychology,* 1963, 2, 104–112.

Smith, P. B. T-group climate, trainer style, and some tests of learning. Unpublished mimeographed paper, Sussex, England: University of Sussex, 1967.

UNITERMS.   Affection; behavior; compatibility; control; dominance; expression; inclusion; influence; interpersonal; intimacy; need; want; warmth.

—M. B. M.

24
Group Dimensions Description Questionnaire

AUTHOR.   John K. Hemphill

AVAILABILITY.   Educational Testing Service, Princeton, New Jersey 08540

VARIABLES.   The Group Dimensions Description Questionnaire measures 13 dimensions conceptualized by Hemphill as follows (verbatim): *Autonomy,* the degree to which a group functions independently of other groups and occupies an independent position in society; *Control,* the degree to which a group regulates the behavior of individuals while they are functioning as group members; *Flexibility,* the degree to which a group's activities are marked by informal procedures, rather than by adherence to established procedures; *Hedonic Tone,* the degree to which group membership is accompanied by a general feeling of pleasantness or agreeableness; *Homogeneity,* the degree to which members of a group are similar with respect to socially relevant characteristics; *Intimacy,* the degree to which members of a group are mutually acquainted with one another and are familiar with the most personal details of one another's lives; *Participation,* the degree to which members of a group apply time and effort to group activities; *Permeability,* the degree to which a group permits ready access to membership; *Polarization,* the degree to which a group is oriented and works toward a single goal which is clear and specific to all members; *Potency,* the degree to which a group has primary significance for its members; *Stability,* the degree to which a group persists over a period of time with essentially the same characteristics; *Stratification,* the degree to which a group orders its members into status hierarchies; and *Viscidity,* the degree to which members of the group function as a unit.

DESCRIPTION.   The Group Dimensions Description Questionnaire consists of 150 descriptive statements. Subjects indicate for each statement one of five Likert-type alternatives: (A) Definitely true; (B) Mostly true; (C) Neither true nor false; (D) Mostly false; (E) Definitely false. Statements are of the following form:

1. Members of the group lend each other money.
2. Certain members are hostile to other members.
3. The group has only one main purpose.

ADMINISTRATION AND SCORING.   The Group Dimensions Description
Questionnaire is self-administered without a time limit. Answers are
recorded on IBM Answer Sheet No. 1100 A 3870. A scoring key is provided; the alternatives (A) . . . (E) are scored either 1 . . . 5 or
5 . . . 1, depending upon whether the descriptive item is worded negatively or positively.

Scores on each of the 13 dimensions are obtained by summation of
the scores on the appropriate items for each dimension (which vary
in number from 5 to 15). A manual (Hemphill, 1956) contains normalized scores for a standard population. Normalized scores are expressed in terms of "stanines," an abbreviation for "standard nines."
Stanine 9 is assigned to the raw scores earned by the highest 4% of
the standard population. Stanines 8 through 1 (lowest) represent the
next 7, 12, 17, 20, 17, 12, 7, and 4% respectively, of the standard population. The manual contains a key for the transformation of raw scores
into stanines.

The population used for standardization contained 950 respondents,
made up of 5 subsamples. Data were collected in 1949. Sample A consisted of 100 college students and/or their close acquaintances who described 100 different groups, of which about one fourth were military
and another fourth were sorority or fraternity. Sample B consisted of
the faculty of a liberal arts college. Sample C, 185 women employees of
a large insurance company, provided descriptions of 19 office groups.
Sample D, 215 college students, described 9 member organizations of
the Religious Council of a large university. Sample E, 320 public school
teachers, described 45 school staffs (19 total-city, 19 high schools, 8
elementary schools).

DEVELOPMENT.   Eleven hundred items were assigned to 14 categories
(the final 13, plus "Size") by five judges. Of these 1100, 355 were retained; 200 descriptions of 35 groups were obtained with this item pool.
Internal consistency was checked by intercorrelating 54 items for each
of the 13 dimensions. The 54 items included all items keyed as belonging to the particular dimension, plus 5 items chosen at random from
items keyed to other dimensions, plus some items which judges had
rated as relating ambiguously to more than one dimension. For items
keyed to the dimension, the median correlation was .36, range .03 to
.78. For items randomly selected from other dimensions the median
correlation was .12, range .01 to .36. For items possibly related to the
dimension the median correlation was .15, range .00 to .50.

In order to test the mutual independence of the 13 dimensions,
tetrachoric correlation coefficients were computed between the "high"
and "low" categories of each pair of dimensions. Of the 91 pairs, 32

were significant at the .01 level of probability. Elaborated item comments made by the original five judges were searched for possible areas of dimension overlap; doubtful items were reworded or eliminated.

Next, 65 persons used the instrument on eight groups; no group had fewer than five respondents. An analysis of variance showed significant F values ($p < .01$) for all 13 dimensions.

For the final 150 items, intercorrelations were computed for Sample A, again to test for mutual independence of the 13 group dimensions. This time, 33 pair correlations were significant at the .01 level of probability. Hope for the independence of dimensions was then abandoned; instead, three factors were isolated and rotated; (I) Behavior Regulation Appearing as Social Structure; (II) Effective Synergy; (III) Primary Personal Interaction.

CRITIQUE. Estimates of *reliability* based upon the correlation of odd vs. even items (corrected for full length) for the 100 groups in Sample A had a median of .79 and a range of .28 (Hedonic Tone) to .92 (Autonomy). Estimates from 130 members of Sample B had a median of .72 and a range of .45 (Control) to .90 (Viscidity). Estimates from 83 members of Sample E had a median of .78 and a range of .49 (Hedonic Tone) to .88 (Autonomy).

Hemphill cautions that the *norms* provided "cover a wide but not universal sample of groups," and that "the normative data available to date (1956) are *not* to be construed to be representative of any hypothetical general population of groups, such as . . . the population of groups to which American people belong." At the same time, background data for the five samples (A through E) are sufficient to enable a prospective user to judge the relevance of any norm sample to his own projected population.

The manual's otherwise thorough discussion is weakened by the section on *validity*. Five sets of comparisons of evaluations are graphed; the numbers of evaluators are five, five, five, two, and two. The discussion is primarily limited to face validity. Though the evaluations within each set run roughly parallel, for the three sets containing five evaluators the mean differences across the 13 dimensions were 3.0, 3.6, and 3.4 stanines, respectively (three stanines can represent anywhere from 23% to 47% of the standard population; four stanines can represent from 40% to 59%).

The two sets of two evaluators represented a *predictive validity* experiment to differentiate two four-man laboratory groups, one of which contained two confederates who accepted the other group members and cooperated with them, the other of which contained (the same) two confederates who played rejecting and uncooperative roles. Expected differences materialized on the dimensions of Viscidity (4.5 stanines difference) and Hedonic Tone (4 stanines difference).

Response sets are guarded against by splitting the 150 items 69–81 between positively and negatively worded statements. Items pertaining to a particular dimension were placed contiguously, however, so that although an S would not know the name of the dimension being evaluated by any given item, he could detect the nature of the dimension common to a particular group of items. For example, the first twelve items are *transparent* in their concern with the degree to which members' actions are controlled by the group. An S not wishing to admit to iron-bound discipline or a brink-of-chaos state of affairs in his group could easily *fake* his responses.

GENERAL COMMENT.   The manual is clear and concise. The 13 dimensions are not nearly so mutually independent as is desirable. The normative populations are limited in nature, but thoroughly presented. The standard population is sufficiently large; it dates, however, from 1949. Some of the more reliable dimensions, such as Autonomy (mean reliability $= .88$), Intimacy (.83), Polarization (.83), and Viscidity (.88) can probably be used without undue concern. But unless further validity studies are completed, the entire Group Dimensions Description Questionnaire should be used with discrimination. Additional work with the three factor scores would seem useful.

REFERENCE

Hemphill, J. K. Group dimensions: a manual for their measurement. Research Monograph No. 87. Columbus: Bureau of Business Research, College of Commerce and Administration, Ohio State University, 1956.

UNITERMS.   Autonomy; control; flexibility; goal; group dimensions; hedonic tone; homogeneity; influence; intimacy; membership; participation; permeability; polarization; potency; satisfaction; stability; status; stratification; viscidity.

—R. B. E

25
Group Participation Scale

AUTHORS.   Harold B. Pepinsky, Lawrence Siegel, and Ellis L. Van Atta

AVAILABILITY.   Pepinsky, H. B., Siegel, L., and Van Atta, E. L. The criterion in counseling: a group participation scale. *Journal of Abnormal and Social Psychology*, 1952, *47*, 415–419.

VARIABLES.   The Group Participation Scale was designed to provide a measure of *effective individual participation* in a social group to serve as an intermediate criterion in studies of counseling outpatients.

DESCRIPTION.   The instrument consists of 24 Thurstone-scaled items in a "guess who" format. The respondent is asked to check (and rank order) the three items which give the most accurate description of his characteristic behavior in groups. Each member of a group is also asked to describe the other members of his group using the same technique. Sample items are:

Is a good follower.
Tries hard to do a good job.

ADMINISTRATION AND SCORING.   The scale is self-administering, as described above.

The self-score is the average of the item weight of the three items checked by self; the describer-score is an average of the weights of the three items attributed by each of his describers to the person being described.

No mention is made by the authors of subject reactions or difficulties in administration. Results obtained from students among four fraternity groups indicated high agreement between the ratings of students and expert judges.

DEVELOPMENT.   The scale was developed by operationally defining the "effectively participating group member" (criteria of effectiveness of participation included: 1) initiates, 2) defines, 3) sustains, and 4) directs), and by having three judges select 170 "guess who" items relevant to the definition. The items, randomly arranged, were presented to 38 social psychology students who rated the items on a nine-point scale, ranging from least effective, position 1, to most effective, position 9, in terms of the definition. Median and Q values were computed for the 38 ratings of each item (scale position 9 was eliminated because of the paucity of choices). Scale positions 1–8 yielded five items each with low Q values. These items were randomized and submitted to 20 "expert" social psychologists throughout the country. Their ratings were similar to those of the student raters. The final scale was submitted to four fraternity groups as a sociometric test; the operational definition of "effective participation" was not included.

CRITIQUE.   For a sample of six sections from a freshman orientation course in the College of Education at Ohio State University ($N = 147$), the split-half *reliability* coefficient ranged from .73 to .92, corrected by Spearman–Brown to .84 to .96.

An estimate of *validity* was obtained in two ways: 1) agreement of group's perception and teacher's perception of the individual's effective participation in the group; and 2) agreement of individual's self-perception and group's perception of his adequacy in the group. In a study by Buchheimer, teacher and student judgments correlated .50 for an N of 266 students. A factor analysis of data from several instruments showed that the Group Participation Scale loaded −.40 on a dimension defined as "social inadequacy." The variables loading positively on this dimension were areas on the Mooney Problem Check List: social psychological relations, .48; social recreational area, .40; and personal psychological relations, .32.

Miles (1965) found that self scores on the Group Participation Scale rose eight months after a two-week human relations training program (but did so for an untrained control group as well), suggesting that the instrument may be subject to social desirability effects (people feel they "should" become more effective over a period of time). However, Miles also found that his Open-End Perceived Change measure (which see) correlated .33 for an N of 34 school principals with the self score, and .37 with the score derived from averaging "other" scores given by five to seven work associates; thus some concurrent validity is suggested. The self and other scores correlated at only .06, however.

Norms have been obtained for 104 male undergraduates at the State College of Washington (the four fraternities) and the Ohio State population noted above.

GENERAL COMMENT.   This simple instrument has promise, but has seen no developmental work since its construction. It has little conceptualization and mostly face validity. The measures originally used to check validity were not independent of the actual measurement; nothing was said about behavioral checks. The normative sample is relatively restricted in range. The instrument seems to obtain a non-specific measure of "goodness of functioning" as seen by self and/or peers in a group. Peer nomination methods characteristically provide good data, and additional work aimed at restandardizing and validating this measure would be worthwhile.

REFERENCES

Martin, H. T. and Siegel, L. Background factors related to effective group participation. *Journal of Abnormal and Social Psychology,* 1953, *48,* 599–600.

Miles, M. B. Changes during and following laboratory training: a clinical-experimental study. *Journal of Applied Behavioral Science,* 1965, *1* (3), 215–242.

Pepinsky, H. B., Siegel, L., and Van Atta, E. L. The criterion in counseling: a group participation scale. *Journal of Abnormal and Social Psychology,* 1952, *47,* 415–419.

UNITERMS.   Behavior; competence; effectiveness; group; initiation; participation; socio-emotional; sociometric.

—E. H.
—M. B. M.

26
Human-Heartedness Questionnaire

AUTHORS.   Howard Schuman and John Harding

AVAILABILITY.   Robinson, J. P., Rusk, J. G., and Head, K. B. (eds.) *Measures of political attitudes*. Ann Arbor: Survey Research Center, Institute for Social Research, University of Michigan, 1968.

VARIABLES.   *Human-Heartedness*, qualitatively characterized as "sympathetic identification with the underdog," is the chief variable measured by the questionnaire; its absence is conceptualized as one component of *prejudice*. Prejudiced attitudes are seen by the authors (Harding and Schuman, 1961) as involving deviation from three ideal norms: *Rationality, Justice*, and *Human-Heartedness*. The Rationality instrument is reported elsewhere in this volume; for the Justice instrument see Robinson et al. (1968).

The instrument was designed for use with adults, though it appears usable with adolescents. Considerable effort was expended in developing an instrument which would suffer minimally from social desirability response set.

DESCRIPTION.   The instrument, entitled "Reactions Questionnaire," consists of 19 multiple-choice items, four of which are included as a control for response set. An item consists of a short description of a situation involving prejudice or discrimination toward members of a specific ethnic or racial minority. The following is a simulated example:

> A Negro girl attending the first day of classes in an elementary school never integrated until that day overhears a conversation by a group of her white classmates. One says, loudly enough to be heard by the Negro girl, "I'm glad we haven't any colored kids in gym, 'cause they always smell funny." How do you suppose the Negro girl reacts?
>
> *(1)* a. She probably feels sad, and maybe angry.
> *(4)* b. She wishes the school were segregated as before.
> *(2)* c. One needs more information to say definitely how she would react. It is hard for a non-Negro to know.
> *(3)* d. She probably has Negro friends, and so won't mind the statement after a little while.

The respondent is asked to rank each of the alternatives in order of their likelihood of occurrence, from 1 to 4. The authors' key (as shown in the example) gives a rank of 1 to the response which is most "human-hearted" (accepts fact of hurt being experienced by the minority group member), 2 to the next most, 3 to the next most, and 4 to the response

96

most denying that hurt has been experienced. The subject's ranks can be compared with these for each of the 15 items, and the sum of rank differences computed. This score can range from 0 to 120.

DEVELOPMENT. The original population for standardization of the instrument was a sample of 229 Boston adults; quotas were employed for sex, age, education, and religion to draw a sample typical of metropolitan Boston. Fifty-nine per cent of the respondents were Catholic. Members of minorities metioned in the instrument were intentionally excluded from the sample, as were those with inadequate English reading ability, usually those with less than six grades of school. Participants were paid nominally to complete several measures anonymously on the spot, of which the Human-Heartedness Questionnaire was only one.

On an 11-item version of the scale (scored by giving 1 for the most sympathetic response, 2 for blank or multiple checks, and 3 for all other responses), the median score was 25, with a skewing toward the unsympathetic end of the scale (20% chose nonsympathetic responses on 10 or 11 items; only 7% chose as many sympathetic responses). Corrected split-half reliability on this version was .76.

Since the 11 scored items were sympathetically answered by at least one third of the sample, while the two control items received less than 2% sympathetic responses, the authors inferred that response set was unlikely. The 2% was equally distributed among high and low sympathetic persons.

Validity of the early form was studied using three college samples. The following comparisons of scores were made using data obtained in a Southern state college, Northern Catholic colleges, and a Harvard race relations elective class (Schuman and Harding, 1963).

PERCENTAGES OF SYMPATHETIC RESPONSES [*]

Student Group	Male Sympathizers [**]		Female Sympathizers	
	%	N	%	N
Southern	21	33	32	19
Northern	53	71	48	112
Harvard race relations	72	39	88	8

[*] Percentages represent proportion of N scoring below a theoretical median of 22.
[**] Differences significant ($p < .01$).

For these three groups, small significant relations of sympathetic identification with age ($r = -.25$) and education ($r = .32$) were obtained.

Four additional items were added, plus two control items, and the instructions altered to their present form.

CRITIQUE.   Further *reliability* study has been completed by the authors (1963). The lowest internal consistency estimate obtained was .62; retest reliability (one month interval) for 30 students is .80.

Rubin (1967) reports 94% agreement on assignment of "ideal" rankings to the items of the revised form between himself and Schuman.

Concurrent validity has been further studied by Schuman and Harding (1963), who administered the early questionnaire with various measures of prejudice (questionnaires on cognitive beliefs, public discrimination, and social distance in personal relations) to the original and Catholic girls' college samples. Uncorrected *r*s with such measures were found to range from .14 to .44, means for the two samples being .36 and .30, respectively.

Fifteen respondents from the original standardization sample were interviewed, and two judges ranked the interview data for sympathetic identification, obtaining correlations of .69 and .31 between their rankings and the questionnaire responses. (The lower figure was obtained by the judge whose sample included four of the five subjects deliberately chosen for study because their interview data and questionnaire responses appeared incompatible.)

Rubin (1967) obtained some *construct validity* evidence using the revised form. He proposed that Human-Heartedness scores, since they involve acceptance of others, should be related to self-acceptance scores (Dorris et al.'s Sentence Completion Test, 1954). He found an *r* of .32 ($N = 50$, $p < .05$); he also showed a non-significant tendency for persons whose self-acceptance increased as a result of laboratory human relations training to show an increase in Human-Heartedness ($p = .16$).

GENERAL COMMENT.   Though this instrument, taken together with the Rationality and Justice measures developed by the authors, is probably the best available measure of attitudes underlying prejudice and discriminatory behavior (in the sense that it probably suffers little from social desirability response sets), insufficient current validity data are available. Explicit expression of attitudes toward race relations in particular have changed so much since 1961 that restandardization with a variety of norming groups would seem in order.

Inspection of the keyed responses suggests that low scorers may be *either* actively prejudiced against minority group members or generalized deniers/repressers. Further validity work should examine this possibility.

REFERENCES

Dorris, R. J., Levinson, D., and Hanfman, E. Authoritarian personality studied by a new variation of the sentence completion test. *Journal of Abnormal and Social Psychology*, 1954, *49*, 99–108.

Harding, J. and Schuman, H. An approach to the definition and measurement of prejudice. Unpublished manuscript, Department of Social Relations, Harvard University, 1961.

Robinson, J. P., Rusk, J. G., and Head, K. B. (eds.) *Measures of political attitudes.* Ann Arbor: Survey Research Center, Institute for Social Research, University of Michigan, 1968.

Rubin, I. The reduction of prejudice through laboratory training. *Journal of Applied Behavioral Science*, 1967, *3*, 29–50.

Schuman, H. and Harding, J. Sympathetic identification with the underdog. *Public Opinion Quarterly*, 1963, *27*, 230–241.

UNITERMS.   Acceptance; attitude; discrimination (race); empathy; ethnic; human-heartedness; identification; minority; norm; prejudice; race; sympathy.

—M. B. M.

27
Index of Adjustment and Values (IAV)

AUTHOR.   Robert E. Bills

AVAILABILITY.   Robert E. Bills, Department of Psychology, Alabama Polytechnic Institute, Auburn, Alabama 36830

VARIABLES.   The Index of Adjustment and Values is designed to measure the following variables: *self-concept; self-acceptance; concept of the ideal self; discrepancy between self-concept and the concept of the ideal self; perceptions of to what extent others accept themselves;* and *the importance of each of 49 personality traits.*

DESCRIPTION.   Currently the IAV comes in four forms, for use with school children in elementary (grades 3, 4, 5), junior high (grades 6, 7, 8), and high (grades 9, 10, 11) schools, and for adults and seniors in high school (12th grade).

The adult form of the IAV consists of a list of 49 adjectives, such as the following: charming; economical; logical; purposeful; successful; competitive. Ss respond a total of six times to each item, three with reference to how S perceives Self and three with reference to how others perceive themselves. The first response indicates how typical or characteristic the adjective is of the self (or of others in S's peer group): seldom; occasionally; about half of the time; a good deal of the time; most of the time. The second indicates how the S (or others) feels about his (or their) self-descriptions: 1) I (He) very much dislike (s) being as I am (he is) in this respect; 2) . . . dislike . . . ; 3) . . . neither dislike . . . nor like . . . ; 4) . . . like . . . ; 5) . . . like very much. . . . The third indicates how much of the time the S (or others) would like the trait to be characteristic of him (themselves); the response choices are identical to those of the first response.

The elementary school form contains 19 items such as:

Do you get scared?

Do you like the way you are?

Would you like to get scared?

Children answer either Yes, No, or Sometimes/Don't Care.

ADMINISTRATION AND SCORING.   The IAV booklet comes with an introduction and instructions on the cover; the administrator reads them aloud while Ss follow in their own booklets. The adult form of the IAV is self-administering without a time limit. The form designed for use in the elementary grades requires the administrator to read each item aloud as each child responds.

The possible responses are numbered so that the number of S's choice is the score for that item, with the exception of negative traits, whose score must be reversed (Seldom = 5, . . . , Most of the time = 1). The three columns of responses are then summed and become the scores for self-concept, acceptance-of-self, and concept of the ideal self, respectively. Scores range from 49 to 245. A discrepancy score is obtained from the absolute value of the difference between the self-concept and concept of the ideal self scores; the value of this score can range from 0 to ±196.

A four-fold typology is derived from the combinations of Self's acceptance-of-self scores and Others' acceptance-of-(their)self scores. If the Self's acceptance-of-self score is above the mean of 171.5, the sign is +; if below the mean, the sign is −. If the Others' acceptance-of-self score is equal to or greater than the Self's acceptance-of-self score, the second sign is +; otherwise it is −. The four types are, therefore, ++, +−, −+, −−. These four relationships can be expressed numerically by means of a conversion formula presented in the manual.

Norms are available for both Self and Others scores for all four forms of the test.

DEVELOPMENT.   From Allport's (1936) list of 17,953 personality traits, 124 were selected on two bases: frequency of occurrence in client-centered interviews, and clarity as an aspect of self-concept. Forty-four Ss were tested, and retested after three weeks with the same instructions contained in the present forms of the IAV. Average variations for each word and for the 44 Ss were calculated; items which showed a greater average variation than the average variation of the Ss on all of the items were eliminated, resulting in the present list of 49 items.

CRITIQUE.   Corrected split-half *reliabilities* (adult form) for Self scores are: .53 for self-concept; .91 and .82 (two samples) for acceptance-of-self; .77 for concept of ideal self; and .88 and .87 (two samples) for discrepancy scores. For Other scores the same Spearman–Brown indices are .92, .94, .73, and .92 for the four scores, respectively. For Self scores, sixteen-week test–retest reliabilities for a sample of 300 college students are: .86 for self-concept; .68 for acceptance-of-self; .58 for concept of ideal self; and .52 for discrepancy scores. For Other scores the corresponding figures are .84, .65, .69, and .40, respectively.

For the high school form, median split-half reliabilities for the three scores are .86, .90, and .84 on the Self form, .93, .96, and .97 on the Others form. For the junior high school form the split-half reliabilities are .90, .89, and .91 for Self scores ($N = 188$). Six-week test–retest reliabilities for Self scores are .70, .82, and .57 ($N = 173$). For the elementary school form split-half reliability scores (Self) are .48, .69, and .72 ($N = 80$).

To ascertain *concurrent validity*, Self scores for students at the University of Kentucky were compared with the Phillips Attitudes Toward Self and Others questionnaire, the California Test of Personality, and the Washburne S-A Inventory. Only the Phillips correlated significantly at the .01 level (.24 with acceptance-of-self and .56 with discrepancy scores). Omwake's comparisons (1954) of IAV acceptance-of-self and acceptance-of-others scores with the Phillips scale and the Berger scale (1953) showed correlations of .55 and .49, respectively, for acceptance-of-self scores, significant at the .01 level; acceptance-of-others scores were not comparable since the IAV asks for Ss perceptions of the degree to which others accept *themselves*. Comparisons of high and low discrepancy scores with six Rorschach factors chosen as indicators of depression showed significant differences on five factors for the two groups, with the high discrepancy scorers showing more Rorschach signs of depression (Bills, 1954).

Tests of *construct validity* have been confused by Bills' incorrectly using his Others' acceptance-of-self scores as equivalent measures of Self's acceptance-of-others—a distinction he was careful to draw in reply to Omwake's work. One study did show that Ss who are above the mean on self-acceptance report significantly ($p < .01$) fewer ailments than Ss who are below the mean on self-acceptance. Similarly, acceptance-of-self correlated significantly ($p < .01$) with rank in introducing oneself to members of an unfamiliar group. In a blame-for-unhappiness study, it was found that acceptance-of-self scores below the mean were correlated ($p < .001$) with perceived threat from self, and that scores above the mean were correlated similarly with threat from others. Studies of reaction time to trait words showed significantly longer times for words on which Ss indicated discrepancy between self-concept and concept of ideal self.

At least two studies have indicated that the Bills IAV measures *social desirability*. A judgment scale for the desirability of the ideal items was found to be nearly a perfect linear transformation of a similar judgment based on the Edwards Social Desirability Scaling Item Procedure (Cowen and Tongas, 1959; Spilka, 1961). And Crowne, Stephens, and Kelly (1957) found a correlation of .33 between Bills' self-acceptance score and Edwards' social desirability measure.

Bills does caution that the IAV has no *predictive validity*.

The *norming groups* are: for the adult form, 1728 students at the Universities of Florida, Louisville (Ky.), Minnesota, and Kentucky; for the high school form, 1599 seniors, 45% male, 54% female, from ten city schools, two rural schools, and four city and county consolidated schools in a total of eight states; for the junior high school form, two groups of $N = 826$ and $N = 398$; for the elementary school form, two groups of $N = 80$ and $N = 597$. No further description of the norming groups is given in the manuals. The norms are presented in raw frequency form, which puts the burden of computation of percentiles and standard scores on the user. Although the IAV is presumably not restricted in population, the absence in certain cases of adequate norms for the Others form should be noted.

The manuals report no comparisons of the Bills IAV and any of the standard student achievement measures.

GENERAL COMMENT. The validity of the Self form is more apparent than that of the Others form. Because it asks for S's perception of Others' perceptions of themselves, and not for S's perceptions of Others, the Others form should be used with caution. It is not clear that the Others form constitutes a wholly projective measure. Although Bills reports no respondent difficulties, the fact that Ss are asked to respond by filling in the number of the appropriate alternative could introduce error—since the same number indicates a different alternative on the acceptance-of-self column than it does on the self-concept and concept of ideal self columns. An answer sheet should be devised which would allow Ss to check preprinted alternatives. The extent of influence of social desirability remains unresolved. Users should take the precaution of measuring directly the social desirability of the 49 Bills traits.

REFERENCES

Allport, G. W. and Odbert, H. S. Trait-names: a psycho-lexical study. *Psychological Monographs*, No. 211, 1936.

Berger, E. M. The relation between expressed acceptance of self and expressed acceptance of others. *Journal of Abnormal and Social Psychology*, 1953, 47, 778–782.

Bills, R. E. Self concept and Rorschach signs of depression. *Journal of Consulting Psychology*, 1954, 18, 135–137.

Cowen, E. L. and Tongas, P. N. The social desirability of trait descriptive terms: applications to a self-concept inventory. *Journal of Consulting Psychology*, 1959, 23, 361–365.

Crowne, D. P., Stephens, M. W., and Kelly, R. The validity and equivalence of tests of self-acceptance. *Journal of Psychology*, 1961, 51, 101–112.

Omwake, K. T. The relation between acceptance of self and acceptance of others shown by three personality inventories. *Journal of Consulting Psychology*, 1954, *18*, 443–446.

Phillips, E. L. Attitudes toward self and others: a brief questionnaire report. *Journal of Consulting Psychology*, 1951, *15*, 79–81.

Spilka, B. Social desirability: a problem of operational definition. *Psychological Reports*, 1961, *8*, 149–150.

UNITERMS.   Acceptance; adjustment; approval; ideal; others; personality; projective; self; self-concept; values.

—R. B. E.

28
Hill Interaction Matrix

AUTHOR.   William Fawcett Hill

AVAILABILITY.   William Fawcett Hill, Youth Studies Center, University of Southern California, Los Angeles, California 90007

VARIABLES.   The Hill Interaction Matrix (HIM) was developed to serve as a systematic conceptual framework for understanding, describing, and doing research on group psychotherapy. As such, it is a scoring system for observation of *group behavior*, not an instrument. Verbal interaction is classified along two dimensions found useful in distinguishing various types of groups. One dimension focuses on the *Content* of group activity (what the group talks about). Four categories are used for this dimension: I) *Topic*, topics external to the actual group concerns; II) *Group*, conversation about the group itself; III) *Personal*, discussion in a historical manner, about the problem of a group member; and IV) *Relationship*, talking about the "here-and-now" relationships and reactions of members to each other.

Five categories comprise the second dimension of the matrix, *Work Style:* A) *Responsive*, little or no behavior takes place except in response to the leader's probes (typical behavior for severely regressed patients in mental hospitals or remotivation groups); B) *Conventional*, behavior similar to informal social group conversation (chit-chat, stylized transactions, social amenities, etc.); C) *Assertive*, behavior which asserts independence from group pressure and thereby does not accept or solicit help from group members; D) *Speculative*, behavior which maintains a problem orientation and in which someone does play the patient role, but the problem is delineated and controlled by the patient, with others only allowed to question or speculate on possible solutions; and E) *Confrontive*, the member playing the patient role is faced with his behavior or problem, and forced to work with it.

Both dimensions are ordered along an ordinal scale of therapeutic significance derived from theory. The Content dimension is divided into non-member-centered (I and II) and member-centered (III and IV) categories. The Work Style dimension is divided into pre-work (A, B, C) and work (D, E) categories. Groups which are member-centered and work-oriented are considered more effective.

DESCRIPTION.   The HIM is not an instrument, but a scoring system. Each verbal interaction is assigned to one of the 20 cells of the matrix, which is four-by-five, corresponding to the four Content categories and the five Work Style categories.

ADMINISTRATION AND SCORING.   The HIM is filled out by a judge, observer, group leader, or other scale user after listening to a tape, reading a session transcript, or viewing a group session. The rater indicates for each item how frequently the behavior in question appeared or how many members participated. For each cell above the A level of group activity there are four items, two describing member activity and two describing leader activity. In addition, there is one item for each of the A level cells and four non-specific items dealing with silence, resistance, and total volume of participation by the group leader. The ratings are entered on IBM cards and scored by computer. The computer print-out indicates the interaction occurring in each dimension and the total group pattern.

Instructions and norms are available to aid analysis and comparison of the groups. The HIM-G form can be completed by someone unfamiliar with the Matrix in about twenty minutes. The items are stated in behavior terms and are relatively easy to score. Interpretation is straightforward and easily comprehended.

DEVELOPMENT.   The first step in the development of the HIM was empirical. Several hundred psychotherapy group meetings were observed, recorded, transcribed, and studied intensively. Judgments of observers were compared with comments elicited from the group participants during stimulated recall sessions (during which a recording of a therapy session is played back to a participant; the recording is stopped at critical points, and comments on the feelings and intentions recollected are requested). From this study a two-dimensional matrix was progressively developed into the current 20-cell form.

The second step involved interviewing a large number of group psychotherapists, representing a wide range of psychological schools, to determine the essential theoretical ingredients in group psychotherapy. The empirical categories were then compared with psychodynamic and group dynamics theories, and placed on a hierarchy of therapeutic significance. As the scales were tested against further groups, revisions were made in the original matrix (HIM '54, HIM '56, HIM '62). These original observational studies were made on a statement-by-statement basis. Most of the reliability, validity, and normative material has been gathered using the early forms.

The latest revision, the HIM-G, has the judge score the group session as a whole in terms of percentages of types of activity observed. In addition, two forms of psychometric tests for individual behavioral style preference (HIM-A, HIM-B) have been designed, based on the typical behaviors found in each cell of the matrix.

CRITIQUE. Some *reliability* data have been collected on the statement-by-statement forms of HIM. Using three trained judges on three groups, interjudge agreement averaged 70% (the same data produced an *r* of .76 and a *rho* of .90). The main judge disagreements appear to lie in determining the explicit content or intent of the verbal inter-action. Using an unambiguous "typical statement" 64-item card sort, judges' reliability was 90%. Hill (1965) compares his reliability find-ings with those of ten other investigators with other observation schemes (Bales, Fouriezos et al., Heyns, and Thelen, among others), and finds his reliabilities at about the mean of those obtained in such studies.

The newer 72-item rating scale, HIM-G, has not been completely checked for reliability. Preliminary investigations found a rank-order correlation of .80 (nature of rank-ordering unspecified). It should be noted that since all the items run in one direction, *response bias* may inflate reliability findings; the authors do not discuss or indicate any attempt to control for this bias.

Validity, reliability, and normative data are based primarily on the earlier, statement-by-statement HIM form. *Validity* claims are based on HIM's demonstrated ability to distinguish between therapy groups representative of several schools of psychotherapy. Representative ses-sions from non-directive, group-analytic, psychoanalytic, guided group interaction, neo-psychoanalytic, and rational therapy groups were rated. Percentages of interaction appearing in the various cells were found to approximate the theoretical expectations of each method. Further, the groups were easily distinguishable. Two of the transcripts (Locke, 1961; McCarthy, 1950) are available in the literature to the reader who wishes to test HIM himself (or herself).

Homogeneous groups composed of members preferring the Relation-ship mode and the Personal mode were found, upon observation, to show patterns of high interaction in the Relationship and Personal categories respectively. No follow-up studies have been conducted to determine the validity of the therapeutic ordinal scaling of the matrix items.

To obtain *normative* data, over 1,200 members of the American Group Psychotherapy Association were solicited for typescripts or recordings of therapy sessions. Thirty-five usable protocols were ob-tained. These were supplemented by fifteen protocols from the author's files. The author's protocols were found not to differ significantly in diversification or proportion of styles from the thirty-five samples. Only complete sessions of therapy groups were used, and a therapist was represented by only one session of one group. Every statement in every session was rated. Ratings were organized for total volume in each cell and category. The cell volume was converted to percentage of total behavior. From these findings, "normed data" were developed to allow the researcher to compare the group with the sample population (supposedly representative of therapy groups in the United States). Each type of group therapy has a protocol associated with it; the HIM, therefore, provides systematic and discriminating quantitative values for therapy group interactions. Instructions are provided for graphing the group on a normative chart. Until further work is done with the HIM-G, the statement-by-statement HIM findings are used to provide normative comparisons for the HIM-G.

GENERAL COMMENT. The HIM-G (together with the HIM-A and the HIM-B individual measurements) has already been used in a number of studies on group composition and group behavior. The matrix categories seem to be well supported by empirical data, as well as by theoretical formulations. As the author suggests, work still needs to be done to determine the validity of the therapeutic value system. More normative data should be collected. Further study needs to be done on response bias in the HIM-B, HIM-A, and HIM-G. The reliability and validity of the HIM-G form, filled out post-session, are undoubtedly much lower than the figures obtained on a statement-by-statement basis. The instrument is recommended for research with groups.

REFERENCES

Hill, W. F. *Hill Interaction Matrix: a method of studying interaction in psychotherapy groups.* Los Angeles: Youth Studies Center, University of Southern California, 1965.

Hill, W. F. *Hill Interaction Matrix Scoring Manual.* Los Angeles: Youth Studies Center, University of Southern California, 1961.

Hill, W. F. *A supplement to HIM Monograph.* Los Angeles: Public Systems Research Institute, University of Southern California, undated.

Locke, N. *Group psychoanalysis.* New York: New York University Press, 1961.

McCarthy, R. G. Group therapy in alcoholism. *Quarterly Journal of Studies of Alcohol,* 1950, *11*, 309.

UNITERMS. Assertion; behavior; conformity; confrontation; content; group; interaction; interpersonal; observation; process; protocol analysis; relationship; therapy; work.

—D. G. L.

29
Interaction Process Analysis

AUTHOR. Robert F. Bales

AVAILABILITY. Bales, R. F. *Interaction process analysis*. Reading. Mass.:
Addison-Wesley, 1950. Scoring forms are available from Addison-
Wesley.

VARIABLES. Bales divides *interaction in a small group* into 12 mutually
exclusive and jointly exhaustive categories: 1) *Shows solidarity,* raises
other's status, gives help, reward; 2) *Shows tension release,* jokes,
laughs, shows satisfaction; 3) *Agrees,* shows passive acceptance, understands, concurs, complies; 4) *Gives suggestions,* direction, implying
autonomy for other; 5) *Gives opinion,* evaluation, analysis, expresses
feeling, wish; 6) *Gives orientation,* information, repeats, clarifies, con-
firms; 7) *Asks for orientation,* information, repetition, and confirmation;
8) *Asks for opinion,* evaluation, analysis, expression of feeling; 9) *Asks
for suggestion,* direction, possible ways of action; 10) *Disagrees,* shows
passive rejection, formality, withholds resources; 11) *Shows tension,*
asks for help, withdraws out of field; and, 12) *Shows antagonism,* de-
flates other's status, defends or asserts self. Categories 1–3 and 10–12
deal with positive and negative socio-emotional behaviors, respectively;
categories 4–6 and 7–9 deal with the initiation of or request for task behaviors.

A slightly revised version of the categories is presented in Bales
(1970); see below under Development.

DESCRIPTION. Interaction Process Analysis is not an instrument, but a
system for categorizing interaction of group members with each other
(although selves, the group as a unit or subunit within the larger group,
or the world outside the group may also be the focus of interaction).
Physically, it manifests itself in an Interaction Recorder (Bales and
Gerbrands, 1948), a moving wide paper tape upon which units of
interaction can be coded and recorded. (The scoring system can also
be used without the apparatus, and, with less validity, be applied to
verbal transcripts.)

Scoring forms are available. On these, the 12 categories are listed
down the left-hand edge of the form; an abscissa marked for every two
occurrences from 0 to 40 reaches to the right-hand margin.

ADMINISTRATION AND SCORING. Bales (1950) specifies a scoring procedure in which the group in question is observed through a one-way

window by two scorers and a third person who both records the meeting in anecdotal form and monitors a tape recording of the meeting. Bales emphasizes that both scorers must score all the interactions; no division of labor is permitted. Both speech (clauses in sentences) and gestures are scored.

The scoring itself is accomplished by numbering the 12 processes, assigning numbers to each actor, and designating the group as object of an interaction by 0. For example, the sequences "(1) 1-0" indicates that solidarity (1) has been shown by actor 1 (1-) with the group (0). "(8) 2-1" indicates that the interaction "Asks for opinion" occurred from actor 2 to actor 1. Provision is also made for coding interaction directed toward the self, or toward persons outside the group. Several indices are calculable from formulas in Bales (1950): Difficulty of Communication; Expressive–Malintegrative Behavior; Difficulty of Evaluation; Difficulty of Control over Situation; Directiveness of Control; Total Differentiation; Direct Access to Resources; Indirect Access to Resources; Degree of Control; Generalized Status; and, Interindividual Solidarity. Their psychometric properties are generally unspecified.

DEVELOPMENT.   In 1946, Bales attempted to formulate "some of the basic structural characteristics and dynamic processes one would expect to find in small groups, utilizing knowledge and impressions which are generally current in sociology, social anthropology, social psychology and psychology" (Bales, 1950). In an attempt to develop a context-free instrument, observers sat in on diagnostic sessions held at the Harvard Psychological Clinic by seven members of the Department of Social Relations, and made whatever notations they wished. These observations were collected, duplications were omitted, and the resulting list of categories was ordered according to theoretical preconceptions and used for further observation. Mechanical data collection difficulties were met by the development of the Interaction Recorder. After some work at the first National Training Laboratory in Group Development at Bethel, Maine, Bales began using the instrument in a laboratory seminar at Harvard. Continuing into the academic year 1948–49, Bales studied observer reliability, and reliability and validity of categories, and reduced them to their present 12.

A revised version of the categories has been presented in Bales (1970); Appendix 4 of that volume explains the changes, and connects them to a new interpersonal behavior rating system organized around the dimensions of "up/down," "forward/back," and "positive/negative." Category 1 is now labeled "Seems friendly" and category 12 "Seems unfriendly." Category 2 is now labeled "Dramatizes," and categories 6 and 7 are called "Gives information and asks for information." Content of other categories (except 3, 8, and 10) and the priority to be used in making choices between alternative categorizings in ambiguous circumstances, have also been changed. New norms are not available, although Bales gives estimates of how the changes may influence percentage distributions. Observer agreement rates are presumably no lower than those obtained with the original version.

CRITIQUE.   Bales (1950) recommends using *chi* square tests of goodness-of-fit for number of interactions scored in each category to determine when observers have reached a predetermined level of *reliability*. He suggests a probability level of .50 (not .05). Newell, Lewis, and Withall (1961), using a slight modification of Bales' 12 categories, reported inter-observer rank-order correlations of .99, .97, and .98, after six or seven hour-long training sessions.

Borgatta (1964) studied a variation of test–retest reliability, namely, the correlations between scores of persons in a five-person group with their scores later as members of three-person groups. Borgatta expanded Bales' 12 categories to 18 to obtain finer discriminations. Only 9 of the 18 categories correlated significantly in the two situations; the median significant r was .48. Borgatta got a significant r of .41 for the total number of interactions between the five- and three-person situations.

Newell, Lewis, and Withall (1961) found evidence of *construct validity* when they studied three styles of teaching an education course at the University of Wisconsin. They found significant differences between concept-oriented and case-study-oriented instructors in the proportion of use of the category *Asks for and Gives information* (higher for concept-oriented) and the category *Asks for opinion* (higher for case-study oriented) ($p < .01$); between concept-oriented instructors and learner-centered instructors in the proportion of use of the categories *Asks for and Gives information* and *Gives analysis* (higher for concept-oriented) and the categories *Gives suggestion or opinion* and *Asks for opinion* (higher for learner-centered) ($p < .01$); and, between case-study-oriented instructors and learner-centered instructors in the proportion of use of the categories *Asks for and Gives information* ($p < .05$) and *Gives analysis* ($p < .01$) (both higher for case-study-oriented) and the category *Gives suggestion or opinion* (higher for learner-centered) ($p < .01$).

Hamblin and Miller (1960) have shown Bales' 12 categories to be highly *intercorrelated* and their frequency to be correlated with group size (for *N*s from 2 to 12, $rs = .02$ to .52, median $r = .24$).

The only *norms* in Bales (1950) are profile charts of individuals or groups which are generally not representative of groups in the general population (including chess players, a non-directed group, a pre-school gang, thesis discussion group, five married couples). Bales (1970) supplies median rates for percentages of acts in each of the 12 original categories in 21 studies.

GENERAL COMMENT.   Bales' Interaction Process Analysis is the "grand-daddy" of operationalized group observation schemes and did much to aid early development in the small-group analysis field. The systematic nature of the underlying notions has been particularly useful in some classic studies of small groups (see, for example, Bales and Strodtbeck, 1951; Bales and Slater, 1955).

The training of observers is not a trivial task, but Newell, Lewis, and Withall (1961) suggest that it is not a trying one. While the Bales scheme is not widely used today in its original form, it remains the archetype in its field. The new form seems somewhat simpler in conceptualization and perhaps easier to use. Norms for it are needed.

REFERENCES

Bales, R. F. *Interaction process analysis.* Reading, Mass.: Addison-Wesley, 1950. (Out of print. Xerox copies may be obtained from University Microfilms, Ann Arbor, Michigan.)

Bales, R. F. *Personality and interpersonal behavior.* New York: Holt, Rinehart and Winston, 1970.

Bales, R. F. and Gerbrands, H. The "interaction recorder": an apparatus and check list for sequential content analysis of social interaction. *Human Relations,* 1948, *1,* 456–463.

Bales, R. F. and Strodtbeck, F. L. Phases in group problem solving. *Journal of Abnormal and Social Psychology,* 1951, *46,* 485–495.

Bales, R. F. and Slater, P. Role differentiation in small decision-making groups. In T. Parsons et al., (Eds.) *Family, socialization and interaction process.* New York: Free Press, 1955, pp. 259–306.

Borgatta, E. F. A note on the consistency of subject behavior in interaction process analysis. *Sociometry,* 1964, *27,* 222–229.

Hamblin, R. L. and Miller, K. Variations in interaction profiles and group size. St. Louis: Technical Report No. 3, Contract No. 816 (11), Small Groups Research Center, Social Science Institute, Washington University, 1960.

Newell, J. M., Lewis, W. W., and Withall, J. Use of a communication model to study classroom interactions. Paper read at the annual meeting of the American Educational Research Association, 1961.

UNITERMS.   Advice; agreement; antagonism; behavior; disagreement; dyad; group; information; interaction; observation; opinion; orientation; process; protocol analysis; socio-emotional; solidarity; suggestion; task; tension.

—R. B. E.
—M. B. M.

30
Interpersonal Check List (ICL)

AUTHORS.   Rolfe La Forge and Robert F. Suczek

AVAILABILITY.   Psychological Consultation Service, 1230 Queens Road, Berkeley, California 94708

VARIABLES.   The Interpersonal Personality System (Leary, 1957), attempts to classify varieties of interpersonal behavior according to eight pairs of basic interpersonal variables. These are: *Blunt/Aggressive; Competitive/Exploitive; Managerial/Autocratic; Responsive/Overgenerous; Cooperative/Over-Conventional; Docile/Dependent; Modest/ Self-Effacing;* and *Skeptical/Distrustful.* The variables are arranged in a circular continuum (circumplex) defining the theoretical relationship between them (the further separated on the perimeter of the circle, the smaller their theoretical similarity). The traits nearer the center (e.g., "cooperative") within each "octant" of the circumplex are considered to be of normal intensity, while those at the circumference (e.g., "over-conventional") are considered to indicate an abnormal degree of intensity of the same trait. These eight pairs of variables may be divided into five levels, in accordance with the operations that produced them:

Level I   Public Communication: overt behavior of the individual as rated by others.

Level II   Conscious Description: perceptions of himself and others.

Level III   Private Symbolizations: abstracts from the fantasy productions of an interpersonal symbolic self-image and symbolic world of others.

Level IV   Unexpressed Unconscious: interpersonal themes compulsively and systematically avoided.

Level V   Values: moral value judgments and ego ideals.

Form IV of the Check List actually measures only Levels I, II, and V.

The data may also be summarized in terms of two major axes: dominance–submission and love–hate. Using this model, all 16 interpersonal scores from one level can be summarized in a single point located with reference to the two axes.

The test is an interpersonal measurement, selecting for analysis those aspects of personality which concern a subject's relationship to others, and as such can be used in almost any setting, though the test was originally designed for clinical situations.

DESCRIPTION.   The Interpersonal Check List is made up of 134 items presented in a true–false form. An item on the test might be:

Able to be joyful.

The S is asked to think of this first as applied to himself, and either fill in the appropriate space on an IBM form (if the statement is true) or to leave it blank (if false). The subject is asked to do this for all 134 items. He is then asked to substitute in place of himself a series of others (e.g., his father, mother, spouse), and his own ideal (a quality or characteristic S would like to possess). Each reference figure is checked separately to allow for greatest concentration.

ADMINISTRATION AND SCORING.   Ten to fifteen minutes should be allowed for an S to complete the description of each person. 150-category IBM answer sheets are available which allow up to five figures to be described at one test administration. A scoring template is easily made for the answer sheet, and programs for IBM scoring are available (Schlotfeldt, undated). Scores are given for the 16 variables and four summary scores of dominance (Dom), love (Lov), average intensity (Ain), and number of items checked (Nic). Results can be plotted on a circumplex chart.

The authors consider the average intensity of the items the subject endorsed as True to be a good estimate of social desirability response set. "Intensity," as defined above, is measured by weighting an a priori ordering of the four items measuring one variable, such as "managerial" or "dictatorial."

DEVELOPMENT.   Four major forms of the ICL have been developed. The original source of items was a 334-adjective check list thought to be representative of trait lists extant in the psychological literature up to 1950. Form I was a selection of 106 of these words selected on an a priori basis by five psychologists. A posteriori analysis of the way in which these words were actually used by subjects led to subsequent changes. Corrections were made for misunderstanding the meanings of words, general tendencies to respond to positively or negatively valued words, and general tendencies to respond with fewer or more words. Form II had an explicit, two-level intensity dimension attached to each stimulus word, and Form III and Form IV each have a four-level intensity scale. An item analysis was done on Form IIIb with good items characterized as having high correlation with neighboring items and low correlations with distant items on the circle of variables. The list of satisfactory words from IIIb was used as the core for the subsequent check list. The various forms of the checklist have been administered to several thousand S's, including incoming patients in a psychiatric clinic, college students, dermatitis patients, obese women, and Air Force enlisted men.

CRITIQUE.   Initial test–retest *reliabilities* ranged from .64 to .77 (La Forge and Suczek, 1955). Average test–retest reliability over a two-week period on a female obesity sample was .73 for the 16 variables, and .78 for octants (form IIIa, $N = 77$). Given that such figures are based on 4-item or 8-item scales, they are surprisingly high. Schopler (1959) obtained a five-month test–retest reliability of .95 for the dominance summary score and .62 for love (self-descriptions). Descriptions of others had reliabilities of .74 and .72, respectively.

In a *construct validity* study, Luckey (1960a) studied the relationship between the congruence of self and ideal-self profiles and marital satisfaction. She sampled 42 couples from the top quartile and 33 couples from the bottom quartile of marital satisfaction measured by self-reports. For wives, the difference between their actual self and ideal-self ICL profiles significantly ($p < .01$) differentiated the "happy" marriages from the "unhappy" ones on scale 3 (Blunt/Aggressive versus Cooperative/Over-Conventional) and scale 4 (Skeptical/Distrustful versus Responsible/Over-Generous). For husbands, the actual-ideal discrepancies were significantly ($p < .01$) greater for the unhappy marriages on scale 1 (Managerial/Autocratic versus Modest/Self-Effacing), scale 2 (Competitive/Exploitative versus Docile/Dependent), and scale 4. When Luckey compared differences between ideal-self and spouse profiles the results were more striking. For wives, the differences between the profiles were much greater ($p < .01$) for the bottom "happiness" quartile than for the top on all four scales. The husbands showed almost the same degree of seeking ideal fulfillment in their mates; for them the differences were significant on scales 1 and 3 ($p < .05$) and scale 4 ($p < .01$).

Pursuing this study, Luckey (1960b) reported that in comparisons of self and same-sex parent profiles, wives in unhappy marriages perceived greater differences on scale 1 ($p < .05$) between themselves and their mothers than did the happily married wives. Husbands in unhappy marriages showed greater differences between themselves and their fathers on scales 1 and 4 ($p < .01$) and on scale 2 ($p < .05$). When she compared spouse profiles with other-sex parent profiles, Luckey found that among unhappy wives differences between their husband's and their father's ICL profiles were significantly greater than the same measures calculated for the happy wives on all four scales (for scales 3 and 4, $p < .01$). The unhappy husbands showed correspondingly larger differences between their ratings of their wives and their ratings of their mothers than did happy husbands on scales 3 ($p < .05$) and 4 ($p < .01$).

Romano's (1960) study compared ICL Level II responses with TAT cards 1, 2, 3BM or 3GF, 4, 6GF, 7BM or 7GF, 12M, 13MF, and 18BM or 18GF, but his evaluation of three married couples, while indicative of the diagnostic use to which the ICL can be put, does not constitute evidence of the ICL's validity.

Norms are presented for four groups in the Oregon Research Institute report (La Forge, 1963): psychiatric clinic out-patients, San Francisco State College students, United States Air Force survival instructors, and University of Illinois psychology students.

GENERAL COMMENT. The systematic conceptualization of underlying dimensions makes the ICL more useful than many check lists as a research tool. The instrument is easy to use and its directions are clear. Items are easily understood by subjects, and diverse enough to allow the subject to present himself and the others he describes in any fashion he wishes. This is a strength for such an instrument, especially if used in conjunction with other diagnostic tools; the data clearly reflect how the subject wishes to present himself in interpersonal situations. It should naturally be used with caution as the sole diagnostic tool for personality assessment. This tool is diverse in its possible applications; one interesting adaptation might be sociometric use in a classroom or other group situation. Adaptations of the scheme underlying the ICL have been made for the analysis of interpersonal behavior in therapy groups by Whitaker and Lieberman (1964) and in children's residential treatment settings by Raush, Dittman, and Taylor (1959).

REFERENCES

La Forge, R. Research use of the Interpersonal Check List. Eugene: Oregon Research Institute, 1963.

La Forge, R. and Suczek, R. F. The interpersonal dimension of personality: an interpersonal check list. *Journal of Personality*, 1955, *24*, 94–112.

Leary, T. *Interpersonal diagnosis of personality.* New York: The Ronald Press, 1957.

Luckey, E. B. Implications for marriage counseling of self perceptions and spouse perceptions. *Journal of Counseling Psychology*, 1960a, *7*, 3–10.

Luckey, E. B. Marital satisfaction and parent concepts. *Journal of Counseling Psychology*, 1960b, *24*, 195–204.

Raush, H. L., Dittman, A. T., and Taylor, D. J. The interpersonal behavior of children in residential treatment. *Journal of Abnormal and Social Psychology*, 1959, *58*, 9–26.

Romano, R. L. The use of the interpersonal system of diagnosis in marital counseling. *Journal of Counseling Psychology*, 1960, 7, 10–20.

Schlotfeldt, R. Scoring the Interpersonal Check List on the Burroughs 205 computer. Unpublished mimeographed paper, Portland, Ore.: University of Portland, undated.

Schopler, J. The relation between success as a therapist and differentiation of self from others. Paper read at American Psychological Association meetings, 1959.

Whitaker, D. S. and Lieberman, M. A. Assessing interpersonal behavior in group therapy. *Perceptual and Motor Skills*, 1964, 18, 763–764.

UNITERMS.   Acquiescence; aggressive; autocratic; blunt; competitive; conventional; cooperative; dependent; distrustful; docile; dominance; ego-ideal; exploitative; generous; love; managerial; marriage; modest; responsive; self; self-effacing; skeptical.

—M. E.
—R. B. E.

31
Interpersonal Competence Scoring System

AUTHOR.   Chris Argyris

AVAILABILITY.   Argyris, C. *Organization and innovation*. Homewood, Ill.: The Dorsey Press, 1965.

VARIABLES.   In his study of *interpersonal competence* in innovative organizations, Argyris first conceptualized all behavior as being at either the ideational (intellectual) level or the feeling (emotional) level. He then distinguished individual behavior from group norms.

Three pairs of behaviors describe the individual. *Owning up to* (ideas or feelings) is being aware of and accepting responsibility for ideas or feelings (versus *Not owning up to* ideas or feelings); *Openness* (to ideas or feelings) is enlarging boundaries of awareness and responsibility for ideas or feelings (versus *Not open* to ideas or feelings); *Experimenting* (with ideas or feelings) is taking a risk to self-acceptance in order to generate new information about ideas or feelings (versus *Rejecting experimenting* with ideas or feelings).

Three more pairs of behaviors relate the individual to others: *Helping others to own up* (versus *Not helping* others to own up); *Helping others to be open* (versus *Not helping* others to be open); *Helping others to experiment* (versus *Not helping* others to experiment).

The six norms (also paired) are: *Individuality*, the protection of and development of uniqueness; *Conformity*, the inhibition of or suppression of uniqueness; *Concern*, the support for the protection of and development of uniqueness; *Antagonism*, the opposition of support for the protection and development of uniqueness (Antagonism includes indifference); *Trust*, the inducement of risk-taking; and *Mistrust*, the inhibition of risk-taking. The scoring system was developed in innovative organizations, but is presumably intended for use in any group or organization.

DESCRIPTION.   Since it is a scoring system, no explicit form is required. The user merely records (from tape recording or transcript) instances of the behaviors categorized above. The basic units of scoring are verbal statements in group settings, such as

Why do you spend time raising these issues?

(which would be scored as *Not helping others to be open* about *feelings*), or

My distinct feeling is fear. You guys better stop talking or you'll get your-
selves into further trouble.

(which would be scored both as *Owning feelings* and *Conformity*).

ADMINISTRATION AND SCORING.   From tape recordings or transcripts of
the group's meetings, frequencies of each category are tabulated. Each
expression of a category is considered one unit; 200 units per hour is a
rough median figure for most groups. Some statements, however, contain contradictory behaviors, such as *Owning ideas* with *Conform ideas*.
These are termed "imbalanced behaviors" and each pair of imbalance
behaviors is recorded as such. Frequencies are multiplied by "potency"
weightings which Argyris has arbitrarily assigned to reflect the presumed relative difficulty of the various behaviors. For example, *Openness to ideas* has a potency of $+2$; *Not helping others to experiment
with feelings* has a potency of -7. The weighted scores are summed
under four headings: Individual Interpersonal Positive; Individual
Interpersonal Negative; Norms Positive; and Norms Negative. These
four scores are normalized to within a range of ± 1 by division by the
highest (or lowest) possible score in each category to produce an
index of competence. Scores are correctable for low numbers of interactions.

The final steps are to produce group competence scores (by summing
all the scores in each behavioral category over individuals), and imbalance scores (by summing raw frequencies). In addition, the rank
order of the categories (by raw frequency) and the changes over time
of rank order are often informative. A worked-out example is included
in Argyris (1965b); scoring sheets may be copied and run off by the
user.

DEVELOPMENT.   Argyris first defined three outputs of interpersonal
competence: awareness of relevant problems; ability to solve problems
so that they remain solved; and maintenance or strengthening of the
problem-solving process itself. Reasoning backwards, he derived categories of behavior he thought would directly facilitate or inhibit the
achievement of the three outputs. Argyris studied three groups: a
physical science industrial laboratory of 150 employees, 100 of them
professional or semi-professional; the ten-man executive committee of
"one of the largest research and engineering laboratories in the United
States," having nearly 3,000 employees; and the four-man board of
directors and their 18 executives of a firm which develops innovations
in management practices.

CRITIQUE.   Three studies of interobserver *reliability* without observer
discussion produced category agreements which ranged from .84 to .93,

with a median of .87. A single, and accidental, instance of score–rescore (by Argyris) reliability was .94.

Other reliability data (Argyris, 1965a) show an 86% figure for inter-observer agreement over 11 different meetings, and a total of 4,958 behavior units. In another study where no interobserver discussion occurred, there was 70% agreement on categorization, and 18% disagreement; in 12% of cases there was disagreement on unitizing. In still another study, Argyris and another observer examined 218 behavior units and obtained 80% agreement, 14% disagreement, and 6% unitizing errors.

Mention should be made, however, of the fact that the frequencies of categories observed in the reliability studies varied widely, from a high of 1,177 for *Owning ideas* to a low of 2 for *Not owning feelings*. Not all categories, therefore, have been checked for observer agreement to the same degree of accuracy.

Argyris' initial explorations of validity were primarily clinical and informal, and involved moderately successful predictions from knowledge of the three groups studied as to the rank order of frequencies in various categories of the scheme. He also undertook one change program (with the management innovation firm), which provided a more structured study of his theory's *predictive validity*. The board of directors met seven times "before;" held five weekly "change" sessions of about four hours each at which their interpersonal competence was openly explored; and met eight times "after." (Argyris was not present during any of the "after" sessions.) During the change sessions, comparison of the last two with the first three revealed an increase in *Concern ideas* and *Individuality ideas* norm scores (*chi*-square test significant at the .004 level), a decrease in *Conform ideas* and *Antagonism ideas* ($p < .001$), and a decrease in *Not helping others to own ideas* ($p < .0001$). The imbalance scores also decreased significantly ($p = .014$). And a comparison of the last two sessions before the change program with the last session (some fourteen months) after it showed that all individual and interpersonal scores had moved in the positive direction ($p < .001$), all norm scores had moved in the positive direction ($p < .001$), and the imbalance scores had decreased ($p < .01$).

As to *concurrent validity*, one study involved interviewing the board members fourteen months after the change sessions ended. The four-man sample is too small for statistical inference, but the flavor of the comments suggests that for at least three persons the change sessions produced a decidedly positive and lasting impact.

Since higher scores are defined as involving greater interpersonal competence, another form of concurrent validity study could legitimately involve examination of T-groups, whose objective is to increase the individual's interpersonal competence. Argyris (1965a) studied four T-groups in executive training programs ($N = 51$). Significant relationships ($p < .05$ or better) were found between high-middle-low competence rankings and the judgments of two trainers and an observer (though one of the trainers was Argyris). In two groups, also, participant satisfaction with the experience (as coded from open-end comments) agreed with competence scores for 17 of 21 cases.

In another study of the members of a T-group, Argyris (1965a) found a correlation of .83 between observers' competence scores for members, and the members' own evaluation of the group. Staff's evaluation correlated with competence at .77.

Argyris (1969) gives a summary of data recorded from 163 different meetings of 28 small groups in organizations. Though these cannot be termed *norms* for the instrument, the results give general guidelines as to what can be expected. In brief, about 75% of scores are accounted for by the categories *Owning ideas, Concern ideas,* and *Conformity ideas,* and another 20% are accounted for by *Openness to ideas, Individuality ideas,* and *Antagonism ideas.* Very little behavior occurs with respect to feelings (in contrast to findings when the instrument has been used in T-groups).

GENERAL COMMENT.   The user can rely on Argyris' scoring system to provide a parsimonious framework (with reasonable reliability and validity) for the analysis of interpersonal competence. Validity studies by other investigators with other instruments (e.g., Pepinsky et al.'s Group Participation Scale and Finney's Palo Alto Group Psychotherapy Scale, both of which see) would be welcome.

REFERENCES

Argyris, C. Explorations in interpersonal competence—I. *Journal of Applied Behavioral Science,* 1965(a), *1* (1), 58–83.

Argyris, C. The incompleteness of social psychological theory: examples from small group, cognitive consistency, and attribution research. *American Psychologist,* 1969, *24,* 893–908.

Argyris, C. *Organization and innovation.* Homewood, Ill.: Dorsey Press, 1965(b).

UNITERMS.   Antagonism; behavior; competence; concern; conformity; experimentation; feelings; idea; human relations training; individuality; innovation; interaction; interpersonal; management; norms; protocol analysis; T-group; trust.

—R. B. E.
—M. B. M.

32

The Interpersonal Perception Method

AUTHORS.   Ronald D. Laing, Herbert Phillipson, and A. Russell Lee

AVAILABILITY.   Laing, R. D., Phillipson, H., and Lee, A. R. *Interpersonal perception: a theory and method of research.* New York: Springer Publishing Co., 1966.

VARIABLES.   Even though the authors' work should be thought of as being more a method than a test, it is an ambitious quantitative undertaking. The authors identify variables which they understand to be central in *dyadic relationships.* They are: *Interdependence and Autonomy, Warm Concern and Support, Disparagement and Disappointment, Contentions* (fight/flight), *Contradiction and Confusion, and Extreme Denial of Autonomy.* Each category has a set of issues related to it. Sixty such issues are identified.

DESCRIPTION.   The instrument and method were built for analyzing dyads. The data come primarily from a study of married couples. However, the authors hope that the method will prove useful for studying two groups, two organizations, and two nations.

The sixty relationship issues are presented from three perspectives as follows. Given a dyad composed of Peter and Paul, each is asked three questions on each issue. For instance, Peter is asked 1) if he "is disappointed with Paul"; 2) how Paul would answer whether Peter is disappointed with Paul; and 3) whether he thinks Paul is disappointed with him. Paul is asked the same three questions about Peter.

ADMINISTRATION AND SCORING.   The full set of items creates the potential for the following types of analyses. First, Peter's view and Paul's on the same issue yields an agree–disagreement score. Second, if Peter is aware of Paul's view, regardless of whether there is agreement or disagreement, he is said to understand Paul. If he fails to recognize Paul's point of view, he is seen as misunderstanding him. In agreement and disagreement, direct *perspectives* are compared. In understanding, a direct perspective on one person is compared with the perspective of that direct perspective, or the *metaperspective,* of another. Even a third stage of analysis is possible by comparing two metaperspectives. Thus, if Paul realizes that Peter understands him, that is said to be Paul's *meta-metaperspective.* So three levels possible are: 1) agreement–disagreement; 2) understanding–misunderstanding; and 3) realization or failure of realization.

At least seventy minutes are required to complete the entire set of 60 issues. The respondent marks each item using one of four scale points, i.e., very true, slightly true, slightly untrue, and very untrue. The respondent must do this for each of 60 items, each of which has twelve subparts. This makes the task long and possibly boring.

Placing the responses in the scoring matrix proceeds easily enough, but moving from raw responses to interpretable scores is not a mechanical process. One needs considerable study of the book to begin seeing what patterns of responses mean.

DEVELOPMENT.   Out of theories which have given special attention to the dyad as a basic unit in understanding behavior, such as those of Mead, Cooley, Parsons, and Heider, the present authors have created a way of examining relationships between two persons.

From a list of 2,000 short phrases expressing issues such as honesty, respect, responsibility, and understanding, the authors eliminated synonyms and antonyms, and, through experience of using the issues with dyads, settled on 84 items which were then reduced to 60 following test–retest studies and item analyses. No data are given to describe the development. Original populations were married couples seeking help and married couples judged to have healthy relationships.

CRITIQUE.   No clear psychometric precedents exist for this type of instrument, which makes it difficult to know whether such concepts as transparency, fakeability, or response set apply. The "good" and "bad" directions of the issues are evident, and it is possible that one partner might take a generalized view of the other and answer with a stereotype. However, both members of the dyad answer all the issues, and it is difficult to imagine two persons' stereotypes as being perfectly comparable. There is a tendency for healthy couples to hold the view that everything is as it should be, even when they disagree. That is, some of the well adjusted couples consistently expected their partner to agree with their position, when on the actual agreement score they were in fact quite different.

Data are given on only two groups. One group consists of 12 married couples seeking help, referred to as disturbed marriages, and the other group of 10 couples supposedly satisfied with their marriages. Reliabilities were determined by retesting after four to six week periods. No coefficients of reliability are given, but percentages of agreement are computed for each issue and for each level of analysis described above. Percentages of agreement for each of the three levels of analysis range from 56% to 100%. However, for both the disturbed marriage group and the non-disturbed group, only eight items fall below 70%

agreement. The authors also compared percentage of agreement between synonyms such as "is good to" and "is kind to." The range of agreement is from 77% to 100% for the disturbed couples and 93% to 100% for the non-disturbed couples.

Even though the samples are small and very restricted, scores do differentiate the two groups significantly on such things as the number of agreements (higher for the non-disturbed couples at the .001 level), number of understandings (.001) and how often the agreements are in fact understood by each partner. Much more work needs to be done on other types of dyads, with larger samples.

GENERAL COMMENT.   Study of the dyad as an important social unit is long overdue in the history of psychology. The study and instrument developed by these authors has considerable potential for advancing our knowledge of relationships. At this point, the sample is far too restricted to draw generalizations, but promise is shown both in the theoretical development and the thoroughness of the authors' undertaking. The user of the Interpersonal Perception Method still needs considerable skill in converting raw data to meaningful interpretations. Hopefully, the authors' own research and the research stimulated by increased availability will help alleviate this problem. Caution should be used with this instrument until more research results are available.

REFERENCE

Laing, R. D., Phillipson, H., and Lee, A. R. *Interpersonal perception.* New York: Springer Publishing Co., 1966.

UNITERMS.   Agreement; autonomy; communication; dyad; empathy; interpersonal; marriage; perception; perspective; relationship; support; understanding.

—D. G. L.

33
Interpersonal Value Scales

AUTHOR.   William A. Scott

AVAILABILITY.   Scott, W. A. *Values and organizations.* Chicago: Rand-McNally, 1965.

VARIABLES.   This instrument is composed of twelve subtests of values: *Intellectualism, Kindness, Social Skills, Loyalty, Academic Achievement, Physical Development, Status, Honesty, Religiousness, Self-Control, Creativity,* and *Independence.* Items in the test are reproduced, grouped by subtest, in Scott (1965).

DESCRIPTION.   The instrument is composed of 240 items, each of the 12 scales being represented by 20 items. The S reads an item and indicates whether the statement expresses a quality or attitude that 1) he "always admires" in other people, 2) he "always dislikes" in other people, or 3) cannot say, since it "depends on the situation." Three simulated items are given below, similar to some appearing on the Intellectualism, Kindness, and Social skills scales, respectively.

always admire	*depends on situation*	*always dislike*	
_____	_____	_____	Continually trying to improve his information about the world.
_____	_____	_____	Helping others to fulfill their needs, even if they conflict with his own.
_____	_____	_____	Being competent at organizing smooth-running social functions.

ADMINISTRATION AND SCORING.   No data are given for testing time, but one should estimate approximately one hour. There are no special materials or instructions, nor are special skills required of examiners. Scott recommends a scoring procedure of crediting one point for each response in the direction of the variable being measured (e.g., *always admire* in each of the examples given above); other responses are scored zero. In each scale, half of the items are negatively worded (i.e., "Always dislike" scores one point). Separate scores are obtained for each of the 12 variables.

DEVELOPMENT.   A "representative sample of the student body at the University of Colorado" ($N = 218$) was used for analysis of the original instrument, composed of 60 items divided unequally among the 12 scales used. Results showed that the length of the original instrument was insufficient to permit an acceptable level of reliability. A new experimental version having 325 items was piloted with a group of 254 "general psychology students" at the University of Colorado. From the results of this application, the 240 items (20 for each of the 12 scales) of the present version were retained. Each item in the trial scales was correlated with the other items in its own scale and with the items of any other scale which correlated highly (.50 or more) with its scale. Any item in the trial scale with a mean intrascale correlation of less than .10, or with a mean intrascale correlation smaller than its mean correlation with the items of some other scale, was eliminated. This procedure was designed to enhance intrascale homogeneity and minimize interscale correlations.

CRITIQUE.   Using apparently the same sample of 254 students in a General Psychology course at the University of Colorado, the author computed homogeneity ratios and *reliability* coefficient estimates (Cronbach's alpha) for each of the scales. The latter ranged from .80 to .89. With this same sample, correlations with the scales of the original form of the test (60 items) ranged from .62 to .81.

As part of course work in test validation, 259 students in some of the General Psychology laboratories of the University of Colorado took a pilot version of the revised scales, containing 162 of the 240 items appearing in the final version of the scales. Scale scores on the *pilot* version were correlated with ratings assigned to the subject by two personal friends. Those *concurrent validity* correlations significant at the .001 level were: Religiousness (.52), Social Skills (.33), Kindness (.32), Independence (.27), Loyalty (.27), and Honesty (.23). Significant at the .01 level was Creativity (.17); and at the .05 level, Physical Development (.14), Self-Control (.12), and Academic Achievement (.11). These data are the sole validity data available in the author's text.

No *normative* data are available.

GENERAL COMMENT.   The author has supplied a purely experimental instrument, or rather, several sets of items which he hopes may be of use to other investigators. Clearly, the researcher who intends to use any of these scales must establish the validity of the instrument for the research application he has in mind, as well as supply his own norms.

The items themselves are generally *transparent;* when they are not, one is often inclined to feel that the variables being measured are contaminated by unrelated elements. For example, in the Intellectualism scale, several items deal with interest in current events, apparently under the supposition that this is an index of breadth of intellectual interests. Also, as is not uncommon in opinion and attitude scales, especially those expanded to enhance reliability, one frequently encounters items in the same scale which appear indistinguishable from one another in content. For example, two of the negatively-scored items in the Religiousness scale are: "Being an atheist" and "Denying the existence of God."

The scoring system suggested by the author (scoring each item one point if it is marked in the required direction, and scoring zero for any other response, including blank) has the practical virtue of irreducible simplicity. The author observes that this scoring system is rational in terms of the concept of value as absolute "good" or "bad," and states that the system furthermore yields intra-scale homogeneities as large as those of a three-point system (e.g., scoring each item 1, 2, or 3, with 2 the "Depends" condition), while yielding interscale correlations that are somewhat lower. Other researchers might wish to verify this result in their own groups. Guttman scaling might profitably be undertaken with the items.

Research workers interested in the variables these scales are designed to measure may find in them material valuable in assessing professed personal values. However, the lack of generally satisfactory standardization data means that the researcher must be prepared to support the validity of the instrument as part of his study.

REFERENCE

Scott, W. A. *Values and organizations.* Chicago: Rand-McNally, 1965.

UNITERMS.   Achievement; creativity; honesty; independence; intellectualism; interpersonal; kindness; loyalty; physical development; religiousness; self-control; social skills; status; values.

—L. J.

34
Leader Behavior Description Questionnaire (LBDQ)

AUTHORS.   John K. Hemphill and Alvin E. Coons

AVAILABILITY.   Bureau of Business Research, Ohio State University, Columbus, Ohio 43210

VARIABLES.   The Leader Behavior Description Questionnaire measures two components of *leadership behavior*: *Initiating Structure*, behavior which delineates the relationship between the leader and the members of his group, and which establishes well-defined patterns of organization, channels of communication, and means of goal attainment; and, *Consideration*, behavior indicative of friendship, mutual trust, respect, and warmth between the leader and the members of his group. The variables are thus essentially *task* and *socio-emotional* leader behavior.

DESCRIPTION.   The LBDQ is a 40-item Likert-scaled self-administering inventory. Fifteen items are addressed to Initiating Structure and fifteen to Consideration. Ten buffer items are not scored. Each item is a descriptive statement of the following type:

> He rules with an iron hand.
> He works without a plan.
> He is easy to understand.
> He is slow to accept new ideas.

Each item calls for a choice from among the following adverbs: always, often, occasionally, seldom, never.

ADMINISTRATION AND SCORING.   The LBDQ may be administered to either leaders (as a self-perception) or to their subordinates, individually or in small groups, and in two forms. Ss may be asked to describe actual behavior or ideal behavior. The purpose should be explained; the leader to be described by subordinates should be absent.

Leadership scores are averages of subordinates' scores; the authors recommend a minimum of four respondents per leader and note that additional respondents beyond the number of ten do not significantly increase the stability of the scores. The five responses are scored 4, 3, 2, 1, 0 for positive statements, and reversely for negative ones. A scoring key indicates the items relevant to each of the two dimensions; an IBM answer sheet is available. Means, standard deviations, and quartile scores are available on both dimensions for three samples: 1) 251 B-29 and B-50 USAF aircraft commanders; 2) 144 RB-47 USAF aircraft commanders; 3) 64 educational administrators.

DEVELOPMENT.   Hemphill and Coons developed the original 130-item form of the questionnaire; Halpin and Winer (1952) factor-analyzed the responses of 353 B-29 crew members who described 52 aircraft commanders. The factors identified as Initiating Structure and Consideration accounted for approximately 34% and 50%, respectively, of the common variance. Intercorrelation between the two dimensions was found to be .45 ($p < .01$). In a subsequent study based on a sample of 249 aircraft commanders, this correlation was found to be .38.

CRITIQUE.   Halpin (1956) indicates that the estimated *split-half reliability* is .83 for Initiating Structure and .92 for Consideration (both figures corrected for attenuation). Using a modified form of the questionnaire, Campbell's (1956) study of submarine crews reports split-half reliabilities ranging from .23 to .55 for self-descriptions by 69 commanding and executive officers and reliabilities ranging from .33 to .81 for descriptions by their subordinates.

There is some evidence of *construct validity*. Hemphill found that college department heads ($N = 22$) who were high on both Initiating Structure and Consideration led departments with a reputation among faculty (across departments) for being "well administered." However, Campbell (1956) found almost no correlation between the officers' self-descriptions and their crews' descriptions. It may be that subordinates' descriptions are more "valid"—they are on the receiving end of the superior's leadership behavior—but no third-party corroborating data are available, as in the Hemphill study.

In studies of *concurrent validity*, Andrews (1965) found that the Consideration scales of the LBDQ and the Organizational Climate Description Questionnaire correlated at only .03. Halpin (1954) found that with interaction effects partialled out Consideration scores correlated with a Crew Satisfaction Index, based on crew members' choices of an ideal crew from among members of their squadron, at .63 ($p < .01$). Initiating Structure correlated at $-.48$ ($p < .05$).

Halpin's study (1956) of 50 Ohio public school superintendents found that school staffs and boards were generally in agreement among themselves, but only in chance agreement with each other in rating superintendents. Only school staff scores versus self-description showed a significant correlation, (.37, $p < .01$) for Initiating Structure.

Miles (1965) found that LBDQ scores did not change after a human relations training experience undergone by 34 elementary school principals, though other data showed that Consideration-like behavior, at least, was seen on an open-end form completed by the same subordinates as having changed. It may be that averaging subordinates' scores contributes to score stability, or that the items measure stereotypes of leader behavior which change more slowly than actual performance.

No standard has been set for how much variance constitutes within-group agreement in evaluation and how much variance indicates disagreement.

The discrepancy in many studies between self and group descriptions suggests that the LBDQ is probably easily *faked*. Most items are positively worded; no compensation has been made for *response sets*.

The two groups of aircraft commanders and the group of educational administrators can by no means be considered *norming groups*. Furthermore, each of the RB-47 commanders was described only by his two fellow crewmen.

GENERAL COMMENT. The LBDQ is plausible, deals with factors central to leader behavior, and is easy to use. However, it appears to be insensitive as a measure of change. Halo effects have been noticed, as well as score sensitivity to raters' idiosyncracies (Charters, 1964). Scale intercorrelations indicate that the two dimensions are not independent. The LBDQ is probably best used in parallel with other measures of leader–group interactions. The two scores obtained for Initiating Structure and Consideration should properly be regarded as specific to the relationship of the leader to the group inventoried, rather than as having a firm value relative to scores of norming groups.

REFERENCES

Andrews, J. H. M. School organization climate: some validity studies. *Canadian Education and Research Digest*, 1965, 5, 317–334.

Campbell, D. T. *Leadership and its effects upon the group.* Columbus: Ohio State University, 1965.

Charters, W. W., Jr. *Teacher perceptions of administrator behavior.* U.S. Department of Health, Education and Welfare, Office of Education, Cooperative Research Project. No. 989. St. Louis: Washington University, 1964.

Halpin, A. W. The leadership behavior and combat performance of airplane commanders. *Journal of Abnormal and Social Psychology*, 1954, 1, 19–22.

Halpin, A. W. *The leadership behavior of school superintendents.* Columbus: Ohio State University, 1956.

Halpin, A. W. and Winer, B. J. *The leadership behavior of the airplane commander.* Washington, D.C.: Human Resources Research Laboratories, Department of the Air Force, 1952.

Hemphill, J. Leadership behavior associated with the administrative reputation of college departments. *Journal of Educational Psychology*, 1955, *46*, 385–401.

Miles, M. B. Changes during and following laboratory training: a clinical—experimental study. *Journal of Applied Behavioral Science*, 1965, *1*, 215–252.

UNITERMS.   Behavior;   consideration;   initiating structure; leadership; management;   organization;   socio-emotional;   subordinates;   superior; task.

—M. B. M.

35
Least Preferred Co-Worker Scales (LPC)

AUTHOR.   Fred E. Fiedler

AVAILABILITY.   Fiedler, F. E. *A theory of leadership effectiveness*. New York: McGraw-Hill, 1967.

VARIABLES.   The author's intent was to develop a theory explaining *group effectiveness* on the basis of *interpersonal perception*. Group effectiveness was seen as the efficacy of a team of individuals in performing a given task in a government, business, or industrial organization. Interpersonal perception was conceptualized as *assumed similarity*, the degree to which an individual sees a co-worker as similar to himself. Fiedler defines assumed similarity as involving emotional warmth and closeness versus distance and rejection in relation to others, thus liked persons are perceived as more similar to self than disliked ones. In particular, Fiedler was interested in the respondent's perceived similarity between himself and both his most and least preferred co-workers (LPC). Additionally, he was studying the effect on group performance of perceived similarity between one's most and least preferred co-workers.

"We have interpreted high LPC scores as indicating relationship and self-oriented needs, and low LPC as indicating task-oriented needs. The high LPC person is thus seen as obtaining need gratification from achieving a prominent position and success as a person. The low LPC person obtains need gratification from performing relevant tasks" (Fiedler, 1967, p. 181).

The scales are for use with persons who are leaders (or members) of groups charged with carrying out a task (e.g., basketball teams, boards of sales cooperatives, open-hearth furnace crews).

DESCRIPTION.   The instrument (several versions have been used) consists of 16, 24, or 30 paired adjectives describing opposite traits of persons. Each pair is an 8-point semantic differential scale allowing seven degrees between points on the scale. An example of an item (simulated) might be:

anxious   __:__:__:__|__:__:__:__ not anxious
            1   2   3   4 |5   6   7   8

ADMINISTRATION AND SCORING.   The semantic differential scale items require about ten minutes to answer. They are typically completed by respondents (leaders, and/or group members) who describe their most and least preferred co-workers: "the person with whom you can work best . . . not necessarily the person you like best," and "the person with whom you can work least well . . . [he] does not have to be the person you like least well . . . [but] had the most difficulty in getting a job done [with]." The respondent may be asked to think of persons in the immediate work group, or consider the array of persons known in the past (when the measure is used as a measure of personal predisposition toward others).

Two measures are obtained, the Assumed Similarity between opposites score (ASo) and the LPC score, a component of the former presumably measuring esteem for the least preferred co-worker. The ASo score is the square root of the sum of squared scale score differences (D-score) between the descriptions of the most and least preferred co-workers. Greater distances between a subject's perceptions of his most and least preferred co-workers are defined as constituting *low* ASo scores. The LPC score is simply the sum of the scale scores used to describe the least preferred co-worker, the complimentary one of each pair of bipolar adjectives being the high score. Each item is weighted with one to eight points and the LPC score is obtained by summing points for all items.

Fiedler (1967, pp. 39–44 and Appendix A) gives a copy of the instrument, explains clearly how to compute LPC and ASo scores, and gives means and standard deviations based on 320 persons.

Machine scoring, using the 602A IBM calculating punch, has been developed by Cleven and Meador (1957).

Norms are available for high school basketball teams, surveying teams, bomber crews, army tank crews, furnace crews in open-hearth steel shops, and farm supply cooperatives (Fiedler, 1958), and data from 53 studies of groups ranging from anti-aircraft artillery crews to therapists and their patients are reported in Fiedler (1967).

DEVELOPMENT.   Stephenson's Q-technique was originally used by the author to assess interpersonal similarity, and several types of scores evolved. Assumed Similarity (AS) deals with the degree of similarity perceived by the subject between himself and another. Assumed Similarity between others, ASo, as indicated above, refers to the difference between descriptions of the subject's most and least preferred co-workers. As a general mathematical model for studying perceived similarity evolved, a distance measure, D, was developed. Fiedler (1958) recommends its use rather than Q scores because of Warrington's (1953) and Cronbach, Gleser, and Rajaratnam's (1963) conclusions that Q-correlations discard information on individual differences in performance level, variability, and scatter.

Fiedler interpreted the Assumed Similarity between opposites score as a measure of psychological distance. Hence, one with a high ASo score is reportedly more concerned about interpersonal relations and about his associates' supporting and approving of him than is a person with a low ASo score. The latter is presumably more independent, less concerned with others' feelings, and more rejecting of those with whom he cannot complete an assigned job. Some early data (Golb and Fiedler, 1955) suggested that the low ASo person is more analytical and discriminating in seeing his co-workers than the presumably more accepting high ASo person.

The original population was a group of fraternity men (*N* unspecified) who gave answers yielding Assumed Similarity scores between most- and least-liked others. The study used a 76-statement Q-sort; correlations among self sort and the sorts for most- and least-liked others were the basic measure. A later version used in a study of basketball teams (*N* unspecified) asked subjects to choose the most and least applicable statements from among the 5 given in each of 20 Q-blocks. However, both this and the earlier sort were complex and time-consuming for subjects.

Warrington (1953) compared the Q-sort, Q-block, and a Likert-scaled set of 200 items (later item-analyzed to 60) with a sample of airmen (*N* unspecified in Fiedler, 1958). Higher reliabilities were found for the Likert-scaled items.

The decision to move to the final semantic differential format was based on the need for an instrument less demanding of subject time. Fiedler (1958) quotes an unpublished study by Rudin and Manis indicating that the shorter form correlated .66 and .78 for two samples of ROTC cadets with the 60-item scale.

See Fiedler (1958) for more detail on development.

CRITIQUE.   Split-half *reliabilities* of ASo scores for the Likert-scaled version (*N* = 132) and the semantic differential form (*N* = 200) were .91 and .93, respectively. Test–retest reliability (*N* = 562) for a two-month interval was .68 for two 40-item semantic differential versions.

Fiedler (1967, p. 44) gives a figure of "about .90" for a 20-item semantic differential form, with test–retest figures of .35 to .70. He also indicates that LPC and ASo correlate at between .80 and .90, "which is about as high as the reliability of the two scores will permit," and thus interprets the two scores interchangeably.

Construct validity has been the primary focus of attention. In his study of high school basketball teams, Fiedler found a correlation of —.69 between the informal team leader's ASo score and the proportion of games his team had won. He concluded that "the better teams chose relatively distant, reserved persons as informal leaders," a finding opposite to his expectations.

In a study of surveying parties, the correlation between informal leader's ASo score and team effectiveness was —.51. The instructor's ratings of accuracy correlated —.34 with student ratings of "best team;" Fiedler suggested this meant that effective teams sacrificed closeness and congeniality in interpersonal relations to attain greater efficiency.

In two *criterion validity* studies of ROTC cadets ($N = 30$), however, Fiedler found no consistent significant differences in ASo scores between men rated good and poor as leaders (leadership criteria unspecified).

Because they obtained correlations ranging from .45 to —.72 between ASo and radar bomb score in a study of B-29 crews, the authors "rejected the hypothesis that ASo by itself predicts good teamwork" (Fiedler, 1958). In basketball and surveyor teams, only the ASo score of the team's informal leader (most preferred co-worker) was related to group effectiveness. But in the bomber crew study, "accepted leaders with low ASo scores did not have crews which were effective in all performance criteria" (unspecified). This finding led to the examination of ASo scores in conjunction with 1) the degree to which the leader was accepted by the group members; and 2) the leader's relation to his "keyman" (the crew member, such as bombardier or radar operator, whose performance was crucial to crew success). The finding, replicated in a study of eleven tank crews, was that, for accepted leaders who endorsed (liked) their keymen, ASo correlated negatively (as predicted) with crew effectiveness. If the keyman was disliked, ASo correlated positively with effectiveness. Fiedler believed that the finding meant that "the accepted leader who maintains a moderate psychological distance from his keyman is able to get better performance than a leader who is either too distant . . . or too close."

In a study of 32 farm supply cooperatives comprised of comparable decision-making groups, the author was able to predict the ASo— effectiveness relationship accurately only if the general manager received the full allegiance of the most influential board member. The ASo scores of general managers who were thus legitimated correlated —.39 with net income of the cooperative. If the manager was also generally accepted by board members, the correlation rose to —.70. Keyman endorsement (see above) by the general manager raised the figure to —.74.

In general, then, as Fiedler (1958) indicates, "low ASo is *not* a leadership trait . . . [but] predicts team performance only in inter-action with other variables: the group's sociometric structure, the leader—keyman relationship, and the demands of the task." The exten-sive range of studies reported in Fiedler (1967) attempts to specify such relationships more precisely, with some success (see summary table of studies, pp. 134–141). The results are complex. E.g., leader LPC correlates negatively (about .5) with group effectiveness *if* leader–member relations are good, and if the task is structured, re-gardless of the leader's position power. But, if the leader's power is low and the task is unstructured, the correlation becomes positive (.47). The reader interested in these measures is well advised to read Fiedler's review and theoretical framework with care.

Appendix C to Fiedler (1967) also reviews correlations of LPC and ASo scores with biographical, response set, personality, interpersonal perception, and intelligence measures. Subject sampling and *N*s are unspecified. Only 9 of 154 such correlations were greater than .20.

A significant *response set* finding was that LPC and ASo correlated —.25 and —.40 with tendency to use extreme responses on a rating of similarity between most and least preferred co-workers. Pettigrew's category width scale (which see) correlated .15 and .16 with the two measures.

GENERAL COMMENT.   Fiedler's sustained interest in these measures, the thoroughgoing effort to develop a situational theory of leadership em-ploying them, and the careful retrieval of studies using them are to be lauded. The reader cannot assume a simple relationship between the measures and group effectiveness, but the measures do appear to be meaningful and useful. Careful study of Fiedler (1967) is essential for sensible interpretation of findings; the interested researcher will also need to collect data on variables such as leader acceptance by his group, position power, endorsement of keyman, etc. Thus LPC and ASo mea-sures, simple as they are, are not at all useful in isolation from other measures of group functioning.

REFERENCES

Cleven, W. A. and Meador, B. J. Punched-card calculation of the D-statistic. *Educational and Psychological Measurement*, 1957, *17*, 142–148.

Cronbach, L. J., Gleser, G., and Rajaratnam, N. Theory of generalize-ability: a liberalization of reliability theory. *The British Journal of Statistical Psy-chology*, 1963, *16*, 2.

Cronbach, L. J., Hartmann, W., and Ehart, M. E. An investigation of the character and properties of assumed similarity measures. Unpublished mimeograph paper, Urbana: Group Effectiveness Research Laboratory, University of Illinois, 1953.

Fiedler, F. E. *Leader attitudes and group effectiveness.* Final Report, ONR Project NR 170-106, N6-ori-07135, Urbana: University of Illinois Press, 1958.

Fiedler, F. E. *A theory of leadership effectiveness.* New York: McGraw-Hill, 1967.

Golb, E. F. and Fiedler, F. E. A note on psychological attributes related to the score Assumed Similarity between opposites (ASo). Technical Report No. 12. Urbana: Group Effectiveness Research Laboratory, University of Illinois, 1955.

Stephenson, W. *The study of behavior: Q-technique and its methodology.* Chicago: University of Chicago Press, 1953.

Warrington, W. G. The comparative efficiency of three test designs for measuring similarity between persons. Urbana: Group Effectiveness Research Laboratory, University of Illinois, mimeographed, 1953.

UNITERMS.   Acceptance; dissimilarity; distance; effectiveness; group; interpersonal; leader; organization; perception; rejection; semantic differential; similarity; sociometric.

—M. B. M.

36
Machiavellianism Scales (Mach Scales)

AUTHOR.   Richard Christie

AVAILABILITY.   Christie, R. and Geis, F. L. *Studies in Machiavellianism.* New York: Academic Press, 1970. Also in Robinson, J. P. and Shaver, P. R. *Measures of social psychological attitudes.* Ann Arbor: Survey Research Center, Institute for Social Research, University of Michigan, 1969.

VARIABLES.   A Machiavellian is defined by Christie and Geis (1970) as "one who views and evaluates others impersonally and amorally in terms of their usefulness for his own purposes." *Machiavellianism* is, therefore, "a perceptual and attitudinal personality disposition." The instruments as designed by Christie are used largely with adult populations; a modified version is available for children.

DESCRIPTION.   There are two Mach Scales in use at the present time. The Mach IV scale is a 20-item Likert-type scale composed of items and reversed items from an earlier scale (Mach II). Half of the items in the Mach IV scale are worded in such a way that agreement with the items is scored high in Machiavellianism while for the other half of the items disagreement is scored high. Simulated items of the Mach IV scale are:

> All people are good and kind most of the time.
> People are more concerned with their personal property than with the well-being of family members.

The Mach V scale was designed to control for the effects of social desirability. Mach V presents 20 triads of items within a forced-choice format; from each of the 20 triads the respondent must select one of the three statements as most characteristic of themselves and another of the three statements as least characteristic of themselves. Each triad consists of an item selected from the Mach IV scale, an item of equal social desirability but unrelated to Machiavellianism, and a third (buffer) statement of a more social desirable nature than either of the other two items, also unrelated to Machiavellianism. The response is scored as high Mach if the statement taken from the Mach IV scale is rated above the equally socially desirable but unrelated items. An item similar to those in the Mach V scale appears below:

A. To be a successful criminal often requires as much imagination as being a successful executive.
B. "A stitch in time saves nine" makes a lot of sense.
C. People are more concerned with their personal property than the well-being of family members.

ADMINISTRATION AND SCORING.   As all of the Mach scales are paper-and-pencil measures which take relatively little time to complete, a great deal of versatility is possible in the administration of the scales.

On the Mach IV scale, scoring for positively worded items gives a weight of $+7$ for "Agree strongly," $+6$ for "Agree somewhat," $+5$ for "Agree slightly," $+4$ for "Neutral responses," $+3$ for "Disagree slightly," $+2$ for "Disagree somewhat," and $+1$ for "Disagree strongly"; the scoring is reversed for negatively worded items. Scores for each item are summed, and 20 added to make the neutral scale score (4) correspond to a total score of 100. The range of scores is from 40 to 160.

The original scoring for the Mach V scale involved giving one point for an item in which the Mach IV statement is rated "most like me" and the matched, equally socially desirable item is considered "least like me;" or in which the Mach item was "most like me" and the matched item was omitted; or in which the buffer item (high social desirability) was "most like me" and the matched item was "least like me." When a Mach reversal item was involved, a point was given if the matched item was "most like me" and the Mach item was either "least like me" or omitted, or if the Mach item was "least like me" and the matched item was omitted.

A revised scoring system (Christie and Geis, 1970) was developed to "take full advantage of the fact that it is probably more Machiavellian to say the Mach item is most like and the matched item least like one-self—a two-step difference—than to say the Mach item is most like and omit the matched item or omit the Mach item and say the matched item is least like oneself—a one-step difference."

Mach item	Matched Item	Score
Most like	Least like	7
Most like	Omitted	5
Omitted	Least Like	
Omitted	Most Like	3
Least Like	Omitted	
Least Like	Most Like	1

(Reverse scoring applies for reverse-worded Mach items.) Scores are summed for 20 items and a constant of 20 added, providing a minimum score of 40 and maximum of 160, with neutral point at 100, rendering

Mach V scores numerically comparable (addable) to those of Mach IV. It would seem the Mach IV and Mach V scales could be readily adapted to machine scoring, though no appropriate forms have appeared to date.

DEVELOPMENT.   While at the Center for Advanced Studies in the Behavioral Sciences, Christie and others began focusing their attention on issues relevant to political and religious movements, and on the leaders of deviant radical and reactionary groups in particular. Of interest were psychological characteristics of leaders of such groups which made them "adept in handling others." First the researchers developed, by inquiry and logical analysis, "a behavioral description of the manipulator." This speculative description was reviewed by others at the Center, and a search of relevant literature, including Machiavelli's *The Prince* and *The Discourses*, was made. Seventy-one statements were taken from Machiavelli, made more relevant to modern social situations, and rephrased in terms of an attitude scale. After the first scale (Mach I) was presented to a group of readily available subjects, item analysis yielded three areas in which high and low scorers seemed to differ: a moral philosophy of life; a cynical view of human nature; and tactics in handling others.

Modification, deletion, or replacement was made of items which had not been shown to discriminate between high- and low-scoring persons. The revised 71 items (Mach II) were presented in Likert-type response format to three samples of college undergraduates majoring in psychology, sociology, and political science at Iowa, North Carolina, and Hofstra, total $N = 1,196$. Forty of the original 71 items were found to discriminate at an acceptable level ($p < .05$) between high- and low-scoring subjects. Twenty of these items were selected (10 original and 10 reversed items) on the basis of wording and variations in content. This 20-item scale was found to have a mean split-half reliability in nine samples of .79.

The Mach V scale was constructed using a forced-choice format to control for the effects of social desirability, to which the Mach IV seemed vulnerable. Its corrected split-half reliability for two college undergraduate samples ($N = 143$ and 173) was .56 and .54. The Mach IV reliabilities for the same samples were .72 and .75.

CRITIQUE.   *Reliability* is reported above.

Concurrent validity estimates derived from correlations between Mach IV and Mach V scores range from .60 to .67 in Caucasian and non-white male and female college student samples (total $N = 1,744$). However, the presence of much common item content undoubtedly raises these figures; other concurrent validity tests should be conducted.

Many *predictive validity* studies have been conducted. Christie and Budner (1962) found that first-year students attending an "elite medical school" had significantly higher scores on the Mach IV scale than did first-year students in "non-elite" medical schools.

Singer (1963) found that in two samples of 62 and 544 male undergraduates, there was significant positive correlation between Mach V scale scores and grade-point average, with students' academic ability held constant (partial r's of .39 and .24). There were presumably skills, not relevant to academic ability but probably more relevant to areas of interpersonal handling of others in which the higher Mach students were found superior.

Exline et al. (1961) reported a study of inducing students to cheat in which those who did cheat were accused by the experimenter. Persons scoring high on the Mach scales looked their accuser in the eye significantly longer while denying their own cheating than did low-scoring persons. Geis, Christie, and Nelson (1968) created a situation in which subjects were permitted and even encouraged to actively manipulate the performance on the Witkin Embedded Figures Test of another, supposedly naive, subject (actually an experimental confederate). Persons scoring above the mean of both the Mach IV and Mach V told significantly more lies and larger lies, in terms of feedback given to the experimental confederate about his performance on the experimental task. Also, high Machs engaged in approximately twice as much behavior coded as manipulative ($p < .005$). High Machs were found to engage in a wider variety of manipulative behaviors other than lying, and almost three times as much manipulative behavior of their own devising (i.e., not pre-coded by the experimenter as possible manipulations).

Lake (1970) in an impression-formation and interpersonal bargaining experiment, found that high Machs, in comparison with lows, were more likely to categorize others along Osgood's potency and activity dimensions (rather than the evaluative dimension); anticipated more aggression from competitive others; responded more rapidly to aggression from another with aggression (rather than defense); and were slower to react cooperatively to expected cooperation from others.

No *norms* as such have been reported, but Christie and Geis (1970) usually report means, standard deviations, and medians for the samples involved in the various studies included in their book.

GENERAL COMMENT.   In over fifty studies conducted by Christie, the Mach scales have generally showed themselves to be useful for research purposes, being able to differentiate between groups of high and low scorers in behavioral as well as perceptual terms. These encouraging validity results should not obscure the fact that both the Mach IV and V scales are quite unreliable, and should *not* be used to predict or interpret the behavior of individuals.

In choosing whether to use the Mach IV or Mach V scales, one should consider the possible effects of social desirability response on his research results.

REFERENCES

Christie, R. and Budner, S. Medical school value climates and "Machiavellian" orientations of students. In Merton, R. K. and Kendall, P. L. (eds.) *The student physician.* Vol. II. Cambridge, Mass.: Harvard University Press, 1962.

Christie, R. and Geis, F. L. *Studies in Machiavellianism.* New York: Academic Press, 1970.

Exline, R., Thibaut, J., Brannon, C., and Gumpert, P. Visual interaction in relation to Machiavellianism and an unethical act. *American Psychology,* 1961, *63,* 395–401.

Lake, D. G. *Perceiving and behaving.* New York: Teachers College Press, 1970.

Singer, J. E. Brains, beauty, birth order, and bunco artists. University Park, Penna.: Pennsylvania State University, unpublished mimeographed paper, 1963.

UNITERMS.   Amorality; cynicism; deception; exploitation; impersonality; Machiavellianism; manipulation; opportunism.

—D. G. L.
—M. B. M.

37

Measurement of Social Intelligence

AUTHORS.   Maureen O'Sullivan, J. Paul Guilford, and R. de Mille

AVAILABILITY.   Sheridan Supply Company, P.O. Box 837, Beverly Hills, California 90213

VARIABLES.   Using Guilford's "structure of intellect" model, this study attempts to demonstrate the existence of six factors which make up *behavioral cognition*. Behavioral cognition, in this study, means the ability to understand the thoughts, feelings, and intentions (psychological dispositions) of other people. The authors indicate that behavioral cognition is similar to what other psychologists have referred to as the "ability to judge people" (Taft, 1955); "empathy" or "accurate social perception" are other applicable labels.

Behavioral cognition is divided into six factor categories: 1) *Units,* elements of expressions, whether facial, vocal, gesture, or posture; 2) *Classes,* a set whose members possess a common attribute; 3) *Relations,* social relationships; 4) *Systems,* sequences of social behavior; 5) *Transformations,* alterations of the above (implying flexibility or creativity); and 6) *Implications,* extrapolations from given information to either its antecedents or its consequences.

DESCRIPTION.   The test items constructed for this instrument (which is comprised of 23 experimental tests) employ words, photographs, drawings, cartoons, silhouettes, stick figures, and tape-recorded sentences, sounds, and inflections. The various subtests are essentially multiple-choice.

It is not possible to include here all item types, but some examples follow. In the *cognition of behavioral units* test the respondent is asked to indicate comprehension of the behavioral meaning of an expression by choosing an alternative expression that conveys the same feeling. In the *cognition of behavioral relations* test, a pair of faces, one hostile-aggressive and the other withdrawing-protective, is displayed and the respondent is then shown a pair of hands which are hostile-aggressive and asked to find the other pair of hands out of three alternatives which demonstrates a withdrawal-protective position. In the *cognition of behavioral classes* test, a respondent is asked to choose the one of three cartoon strips in which a particular cartoon character responds differently than he does in the other two.

ADMINISTRATION AND SCORING.   The tests are presumably self-administering (except for the tape-recorded ones) but the skills required of the respondent are sometimes considerable (e.g., would S understand what he is to do in the following sample item?).

> Which alternative expression is related to the third given expression in the same way the second given expression is to the first?

Scoring procedures vary with the type of total score distribution obtained for each test. The authors state that where other than normal distributions were identified "appropriate scaling techniques" were applied, but these are not described.

Fourteen of the 23 tests require analysis of written responses. The authors claim that clerks can be taught to score these written responses.

DEVELOPMENT.   Beginning with the assumption that facial expressions, vocal inflections, postures, and gestures can act as cues equivalent to the emotional state underlying them, the tests utilized photographs, cartoons, and tape-recorded words and sounds.

The generation of items used one or more of three basic strategies. One was to construct a behavioral-cognition test by analogy to an existing structure-of-intellect test in another content area. A second strategy was to take a factor from the structure of intellect, describe it, and build a test for it. The third construction strategy relied heavily upon analogy or definition.

Initially, a pool of about 40 items for each of 23 tests was prepared and administered to about 30 examinees. For the multiple choice tests the response to each item was inspected for agreement with a rational key. If an item-response distribution was bimodal or platykurtic, the item was eliminated in the initial scoring of the test. For each test, dichotomization of the initial test scores at the median identified high and low scorers, who served as the criterion groups used in item analysis. Many of the tests used various correction-for-guessing formulae; the rationale for using one formula rather than another is not always clear.

The final standardization sample consisted of students of superior socio-economic standing. Initially, 306 eleventh grade students from a middle-class, chiefly Caucasian community were given the tests in periods of one hundred eleven minutes each for four days. Of the 306, 240 were retained in the final sample (110 boys and 130 girls) whose mean age was 16.7 and whose mean Henmon–Nelson IQ was 117.7 with a standard deviation of 16.9 and a range from 83 to 155.

CRITIQUE.   Both Kuder–Richardson and Spearman–Brown *reliabilities* were calculated for the scales; the two median coefficients were .53 (K–R) and .48 (S–B). Five of the tests have poor internal reliability: Social Relations (.29, .20); Picture Exclusion (.34, .35); Faces (.37, .39); Silhouette Relations (.45, .35); and Picture Exchange (.43, .38). Interscorer reliability correlations have ranged from .83 to .97 for four of the more difficult-to-score tests.

At the time of this report only *construct validity* had been reported. Given an initial battery of tests, some of which had been used in other studies of the structure of intellect and some of which were designed as behavioral cognition tests for this study, the validation of the six behavioral cognition constructs would depend on the ability of the new tests to yield factors which were statistically independent of the reference tests used to measure the original factors in the structure of intellect model.

In order to do this, all the tests ($N = 47$, including the 23 "social intelligence" measures) were submitted to the BMD 17 factor analytic program, which yielded 33 factors, of which the first 22 accounted for 95.7% of the variance. The 22 principal factors were then submitted to an orthogonal rotation program designed to maximize the similarity of the empirical factor matrix to a target matrix of loadings. Under rotation, the largest number of factors capable of maintaining communalities was 19. This number of factors was retained because better simple structure was achieved with it than with a smaller number. These 19 principal factors account for 92.5% of the variance.

The display of factor loadings demonstrates that the authors were, in fact, able to discover ways of measuring the hypothesized behavioral cognition factors independent of the standard structure-of-intellect measures. Only one of the 23 behavioral cognition tests loads significantly on a structure-of-intellect reference factor. Separation of behavioral cognition tests from reference tests suggests the following interpretations. The behavioral tests are not a function of general intelligence. General reasoning is not essential for superior performance on the social intelligence tests. Sensitivity to problems, semantic fluency, and originality are not involved in answering the items of the behavioral cognition tests. The behavioral cognition tests of implications are not related to the reference test of semantic implications. And spatial factors are not appreciable components of what is measured by the behavioral cognition tests. (It should be pointed out that *absence* of relation to the structure-of-intellect measures does not provide positive validity evidence that accurate social perception abilities are in fact being measured by the tests at hand.)

GENERAL COMMENT.　　While this attempt to measure social intelligence is impressive, some reservations must be noted. The authors point out that the normative sample is highly restricted and that whether more diverse samples would support the present factor structure is not known.

Instrument scoring procedures are not described thoroughly enough to allow this reviewer to be confident that scoring is indeed objective and in no way contributes to the results.

The authors also point out the need for both concurrent and predictive validity studies before practical usefulness is assumed. This need is present, not only for this battery, as we have indicated above, but for the past twenty years' worth of research on the ability to judge people. Research in this domain is conspicuously devoid of studies which demonstrate that the paper-and-pencil ability to judge people is in *any* way related to the way they *behave* toward others. Increased experimental use of this set of instruments may help to fill this gap.

REFERENCES

O'Sullivan, M. Guilford, J. P., and de Mille, R. *The measurement of social intelligence.* Los Angeles: Report No. 34, Psychological Laboratory, University of Southern California, 1965.

Taft, R. The ability to judge people. *Psychological Bulletin*, 1955, 52, 1–23.

UNITERMS.　　Creativity; cognition; empathy; flexibility; graphic; interpersonal; perception; social intelligence; social skill.

—D. G. L.

38
Meetings

AUTHOR. Matthew B. Miles

AVAILABILITY. Educational Resources Information Center (ERIC) Vol. I, Microfiche No. ED 042266 (Dale G. Lake, Final Report, Appendix, Cooperative Project for Educational Development, 1970). U.S. Office of Education, 400 Maryland Avenue, S.W., Washington, D.C. 20202

VARIABLES. This instrument is designed to measure *group problem-solving adequacy*. The 37 items were written to cover all stages of problem-solving, plus several continuing functions (summarizing, process analyzing, participation), plus items dealing with positive and negative climate. The stages of problem-solving supposedly sampled by items are: *agenda clarity and control; problem definition; diagnosis; solution generation; solution discussion; decision-making; implementation; follow-up. Solution adequacy* is also measured.

DESCRIPTION. Each item describes a function usually involved in problem-solving in a particular work group of which the respondent is a member. The respondent is asked to indicate the frequency of its occurrence on a seven-point scale. A typical item is:

People ask why the problem exists, what the causes are.

The respondent indicates how frequently this happens, from very frequently to very infrequently. An earlier version uses "very typical" to "not typical at all."

ADMINISTRATION AND SCORING. Scoring instructions indicate that 15 of the items are worded in a positive direction; the sum of responses on these can be seen as a score implying the presence of behavior indicating problem-solving adequacy such as, "When a decision is made, it is clear who would carry it out and when."

The remaining items are worded in a negative direction, but reverse-scored. This sum thus implies the relative absence of behaviors usually thought to represent adequate problem-solving. The sum of these two scores is used as an over-all score representing problem-solving adequacy. Scores provided by members of a given group can be averaged to produce an over-all adequacy score; presumably the instrument can also be used by observers or judges.

DEVELOPMENT.   This instrument is one of twenty created for the Co-operative Project for Educational Development (COPED). As such, it was initially field-tested on a small number of teachers and principals ($N = 150$) and then inserted in a package of twenty instruments and administered to more than 3,000 adults in twenty-one school systems ranging from rural to metropolitan. The entire package was administered at two points in time during one school year. Each instrument was then lifted and further developed by interested authors. Details of development are given in the COPED Final Report (Lake, 1970).

CRITIQUE.   *Test–retest* studies to date have yielded average item *reliabilities* of .60. An initial cluster analysis suggested four major clusters dealing with diagnosis, problem-solving process, decision quality, and use of group resources. The average item-intercorrelation was about .30. The positive sum correlates .89 with total score, and the negative sum .90 with total score.

Construct validity of the instrument was explored through the use of four separate factor analyses yielding three factors which have been named Decision-Making Effectiveness, Problem-Solving Adequacy, and Commitment (involvement in the meeting). The criterion for including an item in a factor was that it must have a .50 or better loading in at least three out of four analyses. The four studies included sample sizes as follows: 625, 48, 491, and 122 (all adults employed in school systems in the COPED study).

The items are *face valid* and as such are also open to faking in the "good" direction.

GENERAL COMMENT.   A body of experimental research literature exists to substantiate the importance of orderly problem-solving processes in groups. However, almost no research exists which attempts to measure such processes in natural work groups such as school faculties, work teams, and organizational task forces. This instrument is a step toward developing an adequate tool for measuring changes in problem-solving adequacy at the group level and understanding whether problem-solving by natural groups leads to greater productivity and satisfaction. It is still a relatively undeveloped instrument, and needs to be used with caution. In particular, concurrent validity studies comparing scores with other measures of group problem-solving (observation, ratings of protocols, etc.) are needed if confidence is to be placed in the instrument.

REFERENCE

Lake, D. G. Cooperative Project for Educational Development: Vol. I, Research Outcomes. (ERIC Microfiche No. ED 042268.) Appendix, Microfiche No. ED 042266. Contract OEG 3-8-080069-43(010), Project No. 8-0069, Washington, National Training Laboratories, 1970.

UNITERMS.   Agenda; behavior; commitment; decision-making; diagnosis; group; involvement; participation; problem-solving; process; summarizing.

—D. G. L.

39
Member-to-Leader Scoring System

AUTHORS.   Richard D. Mann, in collaboration with Graham S. Gibbard and John J. Hartman

AVAILABILITY.   Mann, R. D., *Interpersonal styles and group development*. New York: John Wiley & Sons, 1967.

VARIABLES.   Mann is interested in *actions taken by members of a self-analytic group which refer to the group's leader,* especially as these actions relate to the members' capacity for change and the group's ability to organize itself for work. The scoring system is designed for what might be termed the clinical diagnosis of the group. He distinguishes 20 variables: 16 indicate the *content* of the interaction; 4 are *levels* of interaction. The 16 content variables are in turn grouped under four headings: *Hostility* includes Moving Against, Resisting, Withdrawing, and Guilt-Inducing; *Affection* includes Making Reparation, Identifying, Accepting, and Moving Toward; *Authority Relations* include Showing Dependency, Showing Independence, and Showing Counter-Dependency; *Ego State* includes Expressing Anxiety, Denying Anxiety, Expressing Self-Esteem, Expressing Depression, and Denying Depression. The four levels are: *One,* both member and leader referred to directly; *Two,* the member referred to directly, but the leader symbolized by an equivalent figure from within the group; *Three,* the member referred to directly but the leader symbolized by an equivalent figure from outside the group; and *Four,* the member symbolized by an equivalent from either inside or outside the group and the leader referred to either directly or symbolically. Mann developed his scoring system with groups (such as T-groups) which were explicitly charged with becoming aware of their own group processes and individual members' feelings, and had deliberately non-directive but presumably authoritative leaders. Consequently, although the scoring system's applicability may extend to groups whose characteristics are less self-conscious, Mann's specific setting should be borne in mind.

DESCRIPTION.   No particular forms are involved; the scoring system is essentially a classificatory scheme for individual member-to-leader references in the verbal protocols of the group. The raw frequencies of the 20 variables for each member over the group's life constitute the basic output of the scoring system.

Mann, however, went on to find that these 20 variables loaded on six factors, which he termed Enactment/Dependent Complaining, Loyalty/Rebellion, Counter-Dependent Flight/Resistant Complaining, Colleague/Distress, and Involvement/Neutrality. While in future research the specific configuration of loadings of the 20 variables could be expected to deviate from Mann's findings, much of the richness of his research stems from this factor analysis. Thus, as Mann represents its full powers, the scoring system is a two-step process: the categorizing of acts and the factor analysis of the results. The acts themselves can vary from simple, overt declarations, such as

> (To leader:) "You're no help at all. You refuse to get off your high horse and be a real person!"

through multi-affect or ambivalent comments voiced seemingly to no one in particular, such as

> "There's too much hostility here. No one is willing to open up. Personally, it doesn't bother me, but if we're going to accomplish anything you better face up to it."

ADMINISTRATION AND SCORING.   From tape recordings of the group's meetings, the instances of member-to-leader references are recorded. For Mann, the system produced, on the average, 200 scorable acts per hour. For a new act to be scored for a member, the member must yield the floor and regain it. Reliable scoring is an art which requires two to three weeks to develop.

The frequencies are summed over the meetings (Mann's groups met 32 times for fifty minutes), percentaged, and factor analyzed.

After these capabilities of scoring and factoring are acquired, further analysis can proceed. For example, Mann has distinguished six *stages of enactment* through which each of his groups progressed: initial complaining, premature enactment, confrontation, internalization, separation, and terminal review. In addition, Mann also distinguished four styles of *interpersonal relation* (nurturance, control, sexuality, and competence); five aspects of *work* (enactment, expression, independence, involvement, and sensitivity); and six individual *roles* which are key to the group's progress toward genuine enactment (hero, moralistic resister, paranoid resister, male enactor, female enactor, and sexual scapegoat. (To the reader of this critique, this glut of next-level variables is no doubt bewildering. It is included here to suggest the extent of the full power of Mann's initially "innocent" 20-fold typology.)

Norms and standard scores in the usual sense are largely inappropriate in this context. What Mann has done is to provide a relativistic content through which each group moves with its own dynamics. The raw scores in each of the 20 original variables are expressed in percentage form, not to enable comparison with other groups (although different instances of the same type of group can be compared, as Mann does), but rather to establish base-line characteristics of the group, in reference to which individuals and subgroups move.

If fully applied as described above, this scoring system clearly devours much time and money.

DEVELOPMENT.   Bales' Interaction Process Analysis (1950) was the inspiration for Mann's approach to the self-analytic group. The Member-to-Leader Scoring System was developed from 1961 to 1963 in four sections of "Soc Rel 120," a Harvard Summer School course entitled "Social Relations: Interpretation of Interpersonal Behavior." In addition to case studies, the course analyzed processes taking place in the group itself.

Mann is not clear about the source of his sixteen content variables; they appear to be the result of some pre-data-analysis anticipation, crystallized by an a posteriori examination of the transcripts. The development of the analytical categories (enactment stages, interpersonal relations, aspect of work, and facilitative roles) proceeded sequentially and quasi-clinically via Mann's factor analysis, analyses of distributions of member-leader acts, examination of rank-order correlations between member and leader distributions of the 16 interaction content variables, analysis of concordance among leaders in over-attending or under-attending to the 16 variables, and session-by-session analysis of one variable seen as crucial to group movement (Enactment/Dependent Complaining). All this led to the second-level variables: four dimensions of group behavior; six styles of individuals confronting the group; four styles of individuals confronting the leader; five determinants of the group's capacity for work; and six roles which focused the group's movement toward its work goals.

CRITIQUE.   Two types of *reliability* are relevant here: interscorer agreement and score–rescore. For three pairs of scorers, the agreement on whether an act was of the same member-to-leader type ranged from .93 to .98. For four pairs of scorers, the agreement on which of the four levels of inference the act took place was greater than .90. Agreement on all of the 16 content categories ranged from .67 to .81, with a mean of .73. Half of all disagreements were on whether to double-score an act; this left a substantive disagreement ranging from 9% to 13%. Three pairs of scorers ranked five pairs of members as to which was higher in each of the 16 content variables. The interscorer agreement ranged from .87 to .92. Mann indicates that a three-year score–rescore study was made, but he omits findings.

Mann and his collaborators' analysis is post-dictive, after the fact; questions about *validity* are a bit elusive. One can envision a test of concurrent validity which compares some measures of group output with the relative length of time spent in internalization, for example, or with the relative mix of competence versus nurturance/control/ sexuality themes. Thus far, Mann has not attempted this. Rather, he has in his scoring system proposed an approach to investigating the dynamics of self-analytic groups that allows and encourages develop- ment of more nearly objective tests of the relationship of output to internal workings. He has proposed several sets of independent vari- ables whose correlations with output remain to be determined.

One possibly obvious caveat needs to be observed, and, in fact, Mann notes it himself, although his reference is not to his own work, when he writes, ". . . but the outcome of their work cannot help but reflect the particular observational systems which they employed and the different types of groups which they have observed." Not all self- analytic groups have to turn in papers to and write exams for their leaders (as these did). Whether Mann's dimensions are as applicable to self-analytic groups whose goal is not initially seen by the members as the individual acquisition of some subset of knowledge and the ability to impress the leader with one's mastery is not clear.

GENERAL COMMENT.   Mann's approach to the clinical diagnosis of group life is no easy do-it-yourself course. The scoring requires a subtle ear and a not-so-subtle computer for factor analysis. Moreover, Mann's account has him returning constantly to the tapescript of the sessions to check his findings and start new investigations. One aspect of his work, however, is valuable even to those who will never participate in or study a self-analytic group, and that is the professionalism with which he has conducted his research. Read simply as a social science whodunit, Mann's work is an absorbing model of the investigative process. The categories he ends with, or those he began with, may be arguable, but they are certainly fruitful—and his carefully-explicated, non-psychometric methodology is distinctly worthy of praise.

REFERENCES

Bales, R. F. *Interaction process analysis: a method for the study of small groups.* Reading, Mass.: Addison-Wesley, 1950.

Mann, R. D. *Interpersonal styles and group development: an analysis of the member-leader relationship.* New York: John Wiley & Sons, 1967.

UNITERMS. Affection; anxiety; authority; behavior; competence; control; counter-dependence; dependence; depression; ego state; hostility; human relations training; interaction; involvement; interpersonal; leader; member; nurturance; protocol analysis; relationship; role; self-esteem; sexuality; T-group; work.

—R. B. E.
—M. B. M.

40
Michigan Group Projection Sketches

AUTHORS.   William E. Henry and Harold Guetzkow

AVAILABILITY.   William E. Henry, Committee on Human Development, University of Chicago, 5730 Woodlawn, Chicago, Illinois 60637. Also: Henry, W. E. and Guetzkow, H. Group projection sketches for the study of small groups. *Journal of Social Psychology*, 1951, 33, 77–107.

VARIABLES.   The instrument focuses on the *structure, dynamics,* and *outcomes* of small face-to-face adult *groups* "meeting for purposes such as decision-making, training, formulating advisory opinions, and exchanging information." (The variables are specified in more detail below.)

DESCRIPTION.   The instrument consists of five 18″ × 21″ sketches (similar to TAT pictures). Data are collected by asking the members of a small group to discuss each sketch and make up a jointly-agreed-upon story. The five sketches, and the thematic material often elicited, according to the authors, are:

1. Conference Group (seven men around table): formal structure, goals, productivity, interpersonal relations in work settings, roles, division of labor.

2. Man in Doorway: individual-group relations, extrinsic–intrinsic motivation, attitudes toward contemplation of problems.

3. Two Men (older and younger man): dyad relationships, ascendance–submission, authority relations.

4. Woman and Man (older woman, younger man): assertion, dependence, breaking of established relationships.

5. Informal Group (four men): formality/informality, sincerity, emotional involvement.

As with all projectives, the assumption is made that the themes produced reflect characteristics of the producing unit (in this case, a small group). These themes may be directly content-analyzed, or quantified via a series of 21 six-point rating scales, in three general categories:

1. *Sociodynamics:* communication clarity, content–procedure ratio; information-provision; goal concentration; source of problems (group vs. superimposed); value-orientation; tension level; tension direction (support vs. opposition); pacing level (tempo); interdependence; personal affect.

2. *Group Structure:* participation spread; role differentiation; in-group feeling; individuality.

3. *Process Outcome:* reality orientation; adequacy of organization; creativity; satisfaction; motivation to carry out.

ADMINISTRATION AND SCORING.   Administrators present the pictures consecutively. They allow ten minutes (more if needed) between each viewing of the separate cards for the group to 1) compose a story about the one just seen, and 2) transcribe a copy of it in any manner they desire for the examiner. Initially, the group is told to answer the standard questions used in the Thematic Apperception Test, although these are not printed but verbally reiterated until the group, usually by the third viewing, is familiar with the task. Instructions stress composition of one story per picture, importance of group consensus about story produced, preference for a complete story (having a beginning and end), and the provision of a copy for the examiner. Groups are encouraged to proceed with their task in their accustomed manner without administrators' intervention (other than observing sketch-viewing, and imposing composition time limits).

Stories can be scored via content analysis of themes or through the rating scales (judges consider the five stories *in toto*).

DEVELOPMENT.   The measure grew out of an earlier one developed by Horwitz and Cartwright (1953) which involved scoring both the group's actual interaction and its verbal product.

The instrument was originally tried with four intact working groups (e.g., an editorial staff, a seminar); content analysis suggested correspondence between themes produced and actual group characteristics.

CRITIQUE.   No *reliability* coefficients have been computed, by the original investigators or by others. Both group reliability (test–retest) and interjudge reliability data are needed; in their absence, one must assume error variance in scores or themes.

Torrance (1955) studied the criterion *validity* of pictures numbered 1 and 5 with 71 Air Force B-29 bomber crews. On the basis of ratings by their superior officers, crews were categorized as "more effective," "less effective," or "drop-out." Torrance, utilizing a revised scoring method to assess group and individual perception, found consistent differences (usually approaching significance) between the three categories of crew, and he interpreted these as evidence of the better crews' relatively greater attractiveness to their members.

No *normative* data have been gathered, apparently.

GENERAL COMMENT.   The Group Projection Sketches instrument is not a test, but an interesting and (possibly) useful method of assessing group characteristics. Its operating properties are almost completely unknown, but Torrance's study suggests some plausibility for the claim that a projective method can yield data on group characteristics. Further empirical development is essential; links in the chain between actual group properties, the ebb and flow of interaction during the story production, the product, and the judgments of scorers are very tenuous indeed.

REFERENCES

Henry, W. E. and Guetzkow, H. Group projection sketches for the study of small groups. *Journal of Social Psychology*, 1951, *33*, 77–107.

Horwitz, M. and Cartwright, D. A. A projective method for the diagnosis of groups. *Human Relations*, 1953, *6*, 397–410.

Torrance, E. P. Perception of group functioning as a predictor of group performance. *Journal of Social Psychology*, 1955, *42*, 271–282.

UNITERMS.   Achievement; affect; ascendancy; communication; content analysis; creativity; decision-making; dependence; dominance; feelings; goal; graphic; group; individuality; informal; in-group; interaction; interdependence; interpersonal; motivation; participation; problem-solving; process; productivity; projective; relationship; role; satisfaction; structure; submission; task; tempo; tension.

—L. J. R.
—M. B. M.

41
Michigan Total Personality Inventory

AUTHORS.   Robert P. Quinn and Edward Lichtenstein

AVAILABILITY.   Robert P. Quinn, Research Center for Group Dynamics, University of Michigan, Ann Arbor, Michigan 48104

VARIABLES.   General *acquiescence* was conceptualized as the tendency toward agreement or disagreement "with personality or attitude questionnaire items regardless of content" (Quinn and Lichtenstein, undated), and was postulated as a specific personality variable as well as a source of bias on such tests. As a separate variable, the authors studied *social desirability*. Subvariables were content- and format-related forms of acquiescence, as elicited by 10 different measures.

DESCRIPTION.   An acquiescence and social desirability scale, comprised of items from subtests presumed to measure each variable, was constructed. Ten measures of the former and two of the latter were incorporated into the Michigan Total Personality Inventory. Some items are true–false, some are Likert scales, some involve an agree–undecided–disagree response, and some involve no question, but present empty Likert or true–false response modes (respondents are asked to compose questions and answer them in the spaces provided). Still other measures involve reaction to visual stimuli.

No target population has been specified; the battery is presumably aimed at "normal" adult populations.

Subscales are as follows: 1) Difference score, computed from 16 pairs of contradictory self-descriptive statements (Likert scale); 2) Social Acquiescence, calculated from 56 statements of attitude (Bass, 1956), presented in Agree–Undecided–Disagree form; 3) B-Scale (Fricke, 1957), 57 non-K MMPI items judged true 40% to 60% of the time by the original normative sample for MMPI; 4) Contradictory Maxims, using 21 Likert-scaled contradictory maxims (Leavitt, Hax, and Roche, 1955); 5) Plus Scale (Cohn, 1953), 29 MMPI items presumably discriminating between criterion groups of predominantly true and false respondents on MMPI; 6) Agreement Response Scale–Short Form, 15 Likert items, mainly self-descriptive (Couch and Keniston, 1960) and considered by the latter authors as constituting their best short scale for measuring the tendency to agree; 7); Information True Scale (Third Edition), 88 difficult items interspersed with 54 easy true–false items (Gage et al., 1957); 8) No Questions, 7 Likert, 7 agree–uncertain–

disagree, and 7 true–false types of responses being given, for which subject filled in item and checked his response; 9) Positive Response Scale (Kuethe, 1959), using the 10 Rorschach cards sequentially on a projector with verbal cues consisting of 25 presumably good form and 25 poor form responses with which respondents had to show either agreement (true) or disagreement (false); 10) Leading Questions, 27 substantive questions about a projected picture shown for one minute, about half of which queries referred to objects or persons *not* in the picture; and 11 and 12) Edwards' Social Desirability Scale and an Acquiescence-Free Social Desirability Scale of 32 true–false items (true response presumably socially desirable for 16 items, false for the 16 others).

ADMINISTRATION AND SCORING.   Because of the inclusion of Leading Questions and Positive Response Scales, both of which require timed projection of images onto a screen, the inventory is not self-administering. Administrators must manage and time the viewing of a street scene and the Rorschach cards (about ten minutes). No time limit is specified for the entire battery. Projections demand about ten minutes of the administration time.

Each subscale is scored separately for acquiescence, the method being used depending upon the format. The Difference Score is obtained by subtracting the score on positively keyed items from that on oppositely keyed ones for all 32 relevant items. The Social Acquiescence Scale is scored by summing the total number of "agree" responses on the 56 appropriate statements. The B-Scale score is determined by summing the true responses to items of that scale. Contradictory Maxims and Agreement Responses Scales are scored as Likert scales. The Information True Scale acquiescence score is derived by summing the true responses for the 88 "difficult" items. The "no question" responses were scored in the manners typical for each format used (Likert, AUD, true–false). For the Positive Response Scale, the total of true responses is the acquiescence score, and for Leading Questions, the total number of substantive statements which involved "succumbing" to the experimenters' questions about non-existent content constitutes that score. While Edwards' Social Desirability Scale response set score is obtained by summing true answers to socially desirable responses and false ones to undesirable ones, the scoring method for the Acquiescence-Free Social Desirability Scale was unspecified.

Norms were presented by Quinn and Lichtenstein (undated) for 100 college students in the form of means and standard deviations for each subscale in the entire battery.

DEVELOPMENT.   Prior to initial testing, preliminary item analysis revealed certain common MMPI items in the B, Plus, and Edwards' Social Desirability Scales. Thus, several items from these scales were removed "to eliminate spuriously high correlations among these three measures" (Quinn and Lichtenstein, undated). Additionally, in the Acquiescence-Free Social Desirability measure, the range of item favorability scores for socially desirable items was from 2.0 to 2.5, that of socially undesirable ones, from 3.4 to 4.0 (based on Heinemann's favorability ratings for MMPI items, as reported in Dahlstrom and Walsh, 1960, pp. 430–33).

One hundred paid female introductory psychology students at the University of Michigan were the original population (sampling techniques unspecified) to whom the battery was presented, along with the F-Scale (form 40–45) and the American Council on Education Psychological Examination (as a measure of scholastic aptitude).

Intercorrelations ($N = 100$) among all the acquiescence and social desirability subscales were computed, and several low negative intercorrelations were obtained. Additionally, the Difference Score measure correlated significantly and positively with Edwards' Social Desirability Scale, which casts some doubt on the validities of both these measures and on the constructs they presumably assess. Out of the 66 intercorrelations among 12 measures of acquiescence, 35 were reported as significantly positively correlated. Social Acquiescence appears to be the subscale most highly intercorrelated with other presumed measures of acquiescence; Positive Response Scale, the least.

Reliabilities of the various subscales were calculated by the authors. These are presented, with previous reliabilities generally reported by the original authors of each measure, in Table I, adapted from Quinn and Lichtenstein (undated).

Thus, coefficients of reliability were at an acceptable minimum level for only 3 of the 14 measures studied (Social Acquiescence, Information True, and Leading Questions).

On the basis of their factor analysis of the above-mentioned intercorrelations, the authors concluded that a general acquiescence factor exists and accounts for 31% of the variance among subscales. A second factor was obtained for acquiescence elicited by self-descriptive personality statements, while a third was called social desirability. Factors IV and V, respectively, were apparently No Question/true–false and Likert response factors.

The F-Scale loaded more heavily on the "general acquiescence" factor than eight of the presumed acquiescence measures.

The authors concluded that "isolation of a general acquiescence

TABLE I: Reliabilities of Subscales

Scale	Present Reliability (split-half)	Previous Reliability
Difference Score	.30	.61
Social Acquiescence	.90	.92
B	.29	.63[a]
Plus	.76	.76[b]
Contradictory Maxims	.68	
Agreement Response	.71	
Information True	.83	.86
No Questions (Likert)	.22	.68
No Questions (Agree—Uncertain—Disagree)	.10	
No Questions (True—False)	−.37	
Positive Response	.78	.70
Leading Questions	.80	
Edwards' Social Desirability	.78	.83
Acquiescence-Free Social Desirability	.47	

[a] Reported by Hanley (1961).
[b] Reported by Gage, Leavitt, and Stone (1957).

factor supported the implicit assumption of various investigators that acquiescence is not always limited in its generality to specific item contents or response formats." They also felt that appearance of the general acquiescence factor "established the convergent validity of those measures which loaded highly on it." Finally, they thought that of the scales purporting to measure acquiescence, only the Plus Scale had been demonstrated to be contaminated by social desirability. Bass' Social Acquiescence Scale and Leavitt, Hax, and Roches's Contradictory Maxims were considered "the most efficient measures of general acquiescence," loading .83 and .77, respectively, on the "general acquiescence" factor.

CRITIQUE.   *Reliability* of the subscales appears to be very low in most cases. Only Social Acquiescence, Information True, and Leading Questions met the commonly-cited minimum acceptable standard of $r = .80$ or better.

While *concurrent validity* seems fairly well established for some of the scales, it is not at all clear what variable(s) even these are measuring. That they in fact do measure general acquiescence (as contrasted with paper-and-pencil response sets) has not been conclusively demonstrated. One cannot be certain that the measures loading heavily on Factor I, called "general acquiescence" by the authors, are actually measuring a tendency toward agreement or disagreement regardless of situation or stimulus content.

Norms are insufficient for college populations, since the group tested was not large, was exclusively female, and homogeneous (college psychology students).

The Inventory's name is presumably aimed at concealing its purpose from respondents; whether subjects find any subscales, or the experience of the Inventory as a whole *transparent* is unknown.

GENERAL COMMENT. Quinn and Lichtenstein have performed a service too rarely provided: the assembly and intercorrelation of a variety of measures of the same variable. Their work is useful for the researcher who wants to know more about test-taking measures of acquiescent response set. Behavioral acquiescence needs more work; many more measures like Leading Questions and the Positive Response Scale need to be developed. The entire Michigan Total Personality Inventory should be subjected to further norming and validation efforts.

REFERENCES

Bass, B. M. Development and evaluation of a scale for measuring social acquiescence. *Journal of Abnormal and Social Psychology*, 1956, 53, 296–299.

Cohn, T. S. Factors related to scores on the F (Predisposition to Fascism) scale. Unpublished doctoral dissertation, University of Michigan, 1953.

Couch, A. and Keniston, K. Yeasayers and Naysayers: agreeing response set as a personality variable. *Journal of Abnormal and Social Psychology*, 1960, 60, 151–174.

Dahlstrom, W. G. and Walsh, G. S. *An MMPI handbook.* Minneapolis: University of Minnesota Press, 1960.

Fricke, B. G. A response bias (B) scale for the MMPI. *Journal of Counseling Psychology*, 1959, 4, 149–153.

Gage, N. L., Leavitt, G. S., and Stone, G. C. The psychological meaning of acquiescence set for authoritarianism. *Journal of Abnormal and Social Psychology*, 1957, 55, 98–103.

Hanley, C. Social desirability and response bias in the MMPI. *Journal of Consulting Psychology*, 1961, 25, 13–20.

Kuethe, J. L. The positive response set as related to task performance. *Journal of Personality*, 1959, 27, 87–94.

Leavitt, H. G., Hax, H., and Roche, J. H. "Authoritarianism" and agreement with things authoritative. *Journal of Psychology*, 1955, 40, 215–221.

Quinn, R. P. and Lichtenstein, E. The validity of acquiescence measures. Unpublished mimeographed paper, Los Angeles: University of California Medical Center, undated.

UNITERMS.   Acquiescence; approval; authoritarianism; disapproval; graphic; social desirability; response set.

—L. J. R.
—M. B. M.

42
Minnesota Importance Questionnaire (MIQ)

AUTHORS.   David J. Weiss, Rene V. Davis, George W. England, and Lloyd H. Lofguist, assisted by Richard S. Elster, Robert E. Carlson, and Lois L. Anderson

AVAILABILITY.   Weiss, D., Davis, R., England, G., Lofguist, L., and Elster, R. *Construct validation studies of the Minnesota Importance Questionnaire.* Washington, D.C.: Minnesota Studies in Vocational Rehabilitation: XVIII, Bulletin 41, Vocational Rehabilitation Administration, U.S. Department of Health, Education, and Welfare, 1964.

VARIABLES.   The Minnesota Importance Questionnaire was developed to measure *vocational needs,* need being viewed as a "need for specified reinforcing conditions in the environment" (Weiss et al., 1964). Dimensions included are presumably common to most working persons in American culture, and are conceptualized as *need sets.* The authors hypothesize that individuals' need sets depend on their having had "experiences . . . with the reinforcers appropriate to the needs represented in the set." Needs are also viewed as subject to change depending upon amount of work experience. Scales measuring the hypothesized subvariables are: *Ability Utilization; Achievement; Activity; Advancement; Authority; Company Policies and Practices; Compensation; Coworkers; Creativity; Independence; Moral Values; Recognition; Responsibility; Security; Social Service; Social Status; Supervision (Human Relations); Supervision (Technical); Variety;* and *Working Conditions.*

DESCRIPTION.   The MIQ is a 100-item self-report questionnaire, with content considered relevant to all job holders. The respondent is asked to state the degree to which he considers each item an important attribute for his "ideal job." Five response alternatives range from "Very Important" to "Very Unimportant." The items for the 20 ipsative scales, each comprised of 5 items, are spaced 20 items apart. Readability shows a "Flesch count" (see Farr, Jenkins, and Patterson, 1951) of 81, indicating that items are worded for a fifth-grade reading level. Some sample items are:

> I could be active much of the time.
> I could have a definite place in the community.

ADMINISTRATION AND SCORING.   Directions are clear and there is no time limit. The Minnesota Importance Questionnaire is essentially self-administering, with an average respondent time of fifteen to twenty minutes. The scales can be hand-scored by the administrator, who fills out a combination scoring-profile sheet and sums the result in each of the 20 subscales to obtain raw scores. In scales in which one item is unanswered, the administrator divides the total for that scale by 4, multiplies the result by 5, and rounds the new result to the nearest integer to obtain that subscale score. If more than one item per subscale is unanswered, the results are considered invalid. Scores are converted to T-scores by simply folding the scoring-profile sheet where indicated; the T-scores are then plotted on a profile chart.

Computer scoring for groups of 100 or more questionnaires can be arranged through the Regional Vocational Rehabilitation Research Institute, Industrial Relations Center, University of Minnesota, Minneapolis, Minnesota 55455.

Normative tables are provided, giving T-scores drawn from seven subsamples of the original populations (sampling methods and criteria for inclusion not fully explicated): general working population (excluding persons with physical disabilities), $N = 1,771$; employed workers with disabilities, $N = 507$; nonskilled blue collar workers, $N = 716$; nonskilled white collar workers, $N = 416$; skilled white collar workers, $N = 456$; managerial personnel, $N = 183$; and college students, $N = 503$. Additional normative data for the complete set of original populations ($N = 2,308$) are given as means and standard deviations for each of the 20 subscales of the Importance Questionnaire.

DEVELOPMENT. The original populations were a Work Adjustment Project sample ($N = 960$) and a sample of workers from two large firms in the Twin Cities area ($N = 1,348$). Neither group was representative of the general population, since all were volunteers and employed. Additionally, the former sample was heavily biased, due to inclusion of 507 workers with disabilities of various sorts (who also reported more years of formal education than the 453 non-disabled workers). The Twin Cities group somewhat over-represented young people (409 persons below age 45). Scale score distributions were found to be negatively skewed, most items having been considered "Important" or "Very Important" by the majority of these groups' members. The authors viewed these results as probably due to the effects of response set.

Test–retest reliabilities for the 20 subscales (rationale unspecified) were obtained by Weiss et al. for groups of 168, 92, and 189 college sophomores for ten-day, three-week, and six-week intervals respectively. These rs ranged from .64 to .88, the median r being .82 (our calculation) for the three groups. Variance among the groups for each scale was in some cases extensive, a fact Weiss et al. attributed to the relatively slight work experience of college sophomores.

Hoyt internal consistency reliability coefficients ranged from .77 (Compensation) to .91 (Social Service) with a median of .87 for the 20 subscales.

Intercorrelations among the subscales for the total original sample were all positive, Achievement and Ability Utilization having highest correlation ($r = .81$), and Working Conditions and Authority, along with Social Status and Moral Values having the lowest ($r = .08$). The mean r (our calculation) for all scale intercorrelations is .47, indicating that these subscales are certainly not measuring twenty separate dimensions.

Factor analysis yielded two clusters for subscales, accounting for 69% of common variance. The first included Company Policies and Practices, Achievement, both Supervision subscales, Ability Utilization, Security, Working Conditions—all loading at .40 or better. Security, Authority, Independence, Social Status, Responsibility, Creativity, and Variety constituted the other factor. These factor-analytic results lend further weight to the probability that the scales may not be measuring discrete variables.

An attempt at evaluating concurrent validity was made by assessing disability status as a presumed cause of differences between the subsamples of 507 workers with disabilities and the 453 with none from the Work Adjustment sample. On nine of the ten subscales (Achievement, Advancement, Company Policies and Practices, Co-Workers, Moral Values, Security, Social Service, and both Supervision scales) means of the non-disabled group were significantly higher (five at $p < .05$, two at $p < .01$). Those with disabilities had a significantly higher mean on the Independence subscale. Two other means were non-significantly higher (Authority and Social Status). The authors concluded that "status" needs are greater for the disabled than the non-disabled.

A study of occupational status differences constituted the authors' second attempt at assessing construct validity. They hypothesized that higher-status persons would show relatively greater satisfaction of needs for expressing creativity, giving social service, effecting achievement, and for compensation, and good working conditions. Four groups from the Twin Cities segment of the original population were studied: nonskilled blue collar ($N = 524$), nonskilled white collar ($N = 322$), skilled white collar ($N = 345$), and managerial ($N = 157$). These differed significantly in mean scores on every scale, and in scale variance, on all but four (Authority, Independence, Social Status, and Social Service). The authors concluded that "Ability Utilization, Achievement,

Advancement, Compensation, Creativity, Recognition, Responsibility, and Variety are 'reinforcer dimensions' relatively more characteristic of the managerial occupation than of the other three," based on the criterion of high mean and low variability as identifying reinforcement for a given occupation.

Employment status differences were evaluated by the authors as further evidence of construct validity. Such differences were predicted between an employed group (N unspecified) and a group of college students presumed to have had relatively little or no employment experience ($N = 503$, criteria for inclusion unspecified). Lower mean scores and greater variability on the Minnesota Importance Subscales were predicted for the latter group, and differences in the two groups' rankings of presumed needs were expected. Significant mean differences between the groups on 17 of the 20 scales of the questionnaire were obtained as predicted, the largest ones being reported for the Supervision and Company Policies and Practices scales. Those not differentiating the groups significantly were Ability Utilization, Social Service, and Social Status, although differences for these were in the direction predicted. Nineteen of the 20 subscale variances (not Authority) significantly differentiated the two samples. Subsequently Weiss et al. concluded that their scale measures "vocational needs in accordance with predictions" and that its validity was supported by the study.

CRITIQUE.   *Reliability* data have been reviewed above, and appear adequate, although *response sets* may be inflating the obtained figures.

The *validity* data reviewed above are plausible, but just why scores defined as "needs" should be higher for groups with more success experiences (employment, non-disablement, higher status) remains conceptually unclear. In some respects, the given definition of "need" seems to imply an orientation toward particular environmental "presses," to use Murray's term, rather than indicating needs as such.

The 20 subscales are clearly not measuring separate entities.

Norms do not seem adequate for normal adult populations. The managerial norm group N seems too small to use as a reference.

GENERAL COMMENT.   In its present form, the Minnesota Importance Questionnaire should not be used for individual counseling or prediction. Given more cross-validating studies, including replication by other investigators, the instrument could be of value in studying person's views of work environments.

REFERENCES

Farr, J. N., Jenkins, J. J., and Patterson, D. G. Simplification of Flesch reading ease formula. *Journal of Applied Psychology,* 1951, 35, 333–337.

Weiss, D., Davis, R., England, G., Lofguist, L., and Elster, R. *Construct validation studies of the Minnesota Importance Questionnaire.* Washington, D.C.: Minnesota Studies in Vocational Rehabilitation: XVIII, Bulletin 41, Vocational Rehabilitation Administration, U.S. Department of Health, Education and Welfare, 1964.

UNITERMS.   Ability; achievement; activity; advancement; authority; company policies and practices; compensation; co-workers; creativity; independence; moral values; need; recognition; responsibility; security; social service; social status; supervision; vocational; variety; working conditions.

—L. J. R.

43
Minnesota Teacher Attitude Inventory (MTAI)

AUTHORS.   Walter W. Cook, Carroll H. Leeds, and Robert Callis

AVAILABILITY.   Psychological Corporation, 304 East 45th Street, New York, New York 10007

VARIABLES.   The Minnesota Teacher Attitude Inventory measures the strength of *attitudes* which the authors feel are indicative of a teacher's capacity for interpersonal relationships with his pupils. As the items are constructed and construed by the authors, a high MTAI score indicates a "progressive," *pupil-centered, non-authoritarian orientation.*

DESCRIPTION.   The 150 items of the MTAI are statements of the following kind:

> Children should be seen and not heard.
> Most children are obedient.
> A teacher should not be expected to do more work than he is paid for.

The five responses run from "strongly agree" through "uncertain" to "strongly disagree."

ADMINISTRATION AND SCORING.   The inventory is self-administering, and takes less than an hour. The responses are not Likert-scaled; rather, each response is scored +1, 0, or −1, presumably depending upon prior item analysis. For example, in scoring the responses to "A teacher should not be expected to do more work than he is paid for," a response of "agree" is scored 0, the responses "disagree," "uncertain," and "strongly agree" are all scored −1, and "strongly disagree" is scored +1. Scores therefore can range from −150 to +150. Norms are available for high school and college students, for teacher trainees, and for experienced elementary and secondary school teachers. Student norms are subdivided by age; teacher norms, by amount of education.

DEVELOPMENT.   Starting from the teacher–pupil interaction literature, Leeds devised 378 normative statements of the type now found in the inventory, and rewrote them in both positively- and negatively-worded forms. Following a "known groups" strategy, these items were tested on two groups of 100 teachers who had been classified as "superior" or "inferior" according to three criteria: ability to win the affection of pupils; fondness for and understanding of children; and ability to maintain a desirable form of discipline. One hundred sixty-four items differentiated these two groups. These 164 items had a split-half reliability of .91 (Spearman–Brown correction). Scores on this form were then correlated with ratings of a third sample of 100 teachers of grades 4 through 6 with ratings by their principals, with ratings by Leeds himself based on a modified form of Baxter's Rating Scale of Teacher's Personal Effectiveness, and with ratings by pupils on a 50-item questionnaire. The correlations were .43, .49, and .45, respectively, all significant at the $p < .01$ level. The present form of the inventory contains 129 items from this work of Leeds; the remaining 21 items were devised by Callis.

CRITIQUE.   The corrected split-half *reliability* of the present form is .93.
      To test the *validity* of the final form of the Inventory, Leeds and Callis separately replicated the correlations among ratings outlined above. The correlations with principals', observers', and pupils' ratings were .46, .59, and .31 for Leeds' study and .19, .40, and .49 for Callis'. (Callis' sample came from grades 4 through 10 instead of grades 4 through 6 and he used two observers' ratings.) Sandgren and Schmidt (1956), however, found no relation between MTAI scores and critic teachers' ratings of effectiveness when they divided a sample of 393 student teachers into upper, middle, and lower categories according to MTAI scores. Male/female, elementary/secondary, and curriculum-based dichotomies were similarly unrelated to effectiveness. This lack of a relationship has been replicated by Oelke (1956) and Fuller (1951). An insight into the appropriateness of pupils' ratings as a criterion of predictive validity is provided by Della Piana and Gage (1955). Reasoning that a teacher's performance is a reflection of the values held by his pupils, they correlated MTAI scores with Leeds' "My Teacher" ratings from two samples of twenty classes. One sample contained classes whose pupils were most desirous of cognitive support (intellectual achievement)—as opposed to affective support (social–emotional need-satisfaction)—from their teacher; the other sample contained the classes least desirous of cognitive support. Samples were differentiated on the basis of forced-choice value inventories completed by the pupils. MTAI scores correlated with pupils' ratings in the most cognitively-oriented classes at .05, with the ratings in the least cognitively-oriented classes at .57 ($p < .05$).
      Several effects of *response sets* have been uncovered. Mitzel, Rabinowitz, and Ostreicher (1955) identified three sets: positive intensity, the ratio of "strongly agree" to all positive responses; negative intensity, the ratio of "strongly disagree" to all negative responses; and evasiveness, the number of "undecided" responses. The negative intensity set in-

creased the validity of the test scores; the positive intensity set had little effect; the evasiveness set diminished the test's validity. Budd and Blakely (1958) found that respondents who checked the "strongly" extremes had scores significantly higher ($p < .01$) than those who were more moderate in their responses. And Gage, Leavitt, and Stone (1957) found that scores based only upon the 112 negatively-worded items correlated with pupils' ratings at a higher level than did the entire 150-item inventory.

The evidence of *fakeability* is substantial. Stein and Hardy (1957) retested three samples of 24 education students. A control group given the standard instructions both times increased their mean score significantly, by 9.92 points. A group told the second time to fill out the inventory as they might if applying to a school system known for its "permissive atmosphere and pupil-centered point of view" registered an increase in mean score of 68.84 points. The third group was told to complete the inventory as if applying to a school system with an atmosphere opposite to that of the "progressive" one. This group of faked traditionalists registered a decrease in mean score of 141.68 points. Anonymity also affects scores, with signed inventories showing a mean increase of 7 points over unsigned inventories.

GENERAL COMMENT.   Although several studies have failed to establish a significant relationship between critic teachers' ratings of student-teacher effectiveness and scores on the Minnesota Teacher Attitude Inventory, it should be noted that such studies did not control for the attitudes of critic teachers themselves. The intervention of the values of the observers, pupils, principals is quite likely pronounced, as indicated in Della Piana and Gage's findings.

Fakeability is the MTAI's chief handicap, especially with regard to contemplated predictive use. It should be noted that if respondents are not advised about the intended use of their scores, and therefore do not know (and are not inferring) the direction in which to fake, the fakeability of the inventory becomes negligible.

If the potential user seeks to identify respondents along a "traditionalist/progressivist" continuum and can somehow assure "authentic" response, perhaps by building trust and/or keeping his purpose unspecified, the MTAI can serve him effectively and efficiently.

REFERENCES

Budd, W. C. and Blakely, L. S. Response bias on the Minnesota Teacher Attitude Inventory. *Journal of Educational Research*, 1958, 51, 707–709.

Cook, W. W., Leeds, C. H., and Callis, R. *The Minnesota Teacher Attitude Inventory.* New York: Psychological Corp., 1951.

Della Piana, G. M. and Gage, N. L. Pupils' values and the validity of the Minnesota Teacher Attitude Inventory. *Journal of Educational Psychology,* 1955, *46,* 167–178.

Fuller, E. M. The use of teacher–pupil attitudes, self-rating and general measures of general ability in the pre-service selection of nursery-school–kindergarten–primary teachers. *Journal of Educational Research,* 1951, *44,* 675–686.

Gage, N. L., Leavitt, G. S., and Stone, G. C. The psychological meaning of acquiescence set for authoritarianism. *Journal of Abnormal and Social Psychology,* 1957, *55,* 98–103.

Getzels, J. W. and Jackson, P. W. The teacher's personality and characteristics. In Gage, N. L. (ed.) *Handbook of research on teaching.* Chicago: Rand McNally, 1963, pp. 506–582.

Leeds, C. H. A scale for measuring teacher–pupil attitudes and teacher–pupil rapport. *Journal of Applied Psychology,* 1956, *40,* 333–337.

Mitzel, H. E., Rabinowitz, W., and Ostreicher, L. M. *Effects of certain response sets on valid test variance.* New York: City College, Division of Teacher Education, Office of Research and Evaluation (Res. Series No. 26) 1955.

Oelke, M. C. A study of student teachers' attitudes towards children. *Journal of Educational Psychology,* 1956, *47,* 193–196.

Sandgren, D. L. and Schmidt, L. G. Does practice teaching change attitudes toward teaching? *Journal of Educational Research,* 1956, *49,* 673–680.

Stein, H. L. and Hardy, J. A validation study of the MTAI in Manitoba. *Journal of Educational Research,* 1957, *50,* 321–338.

UNITERMS.   Attitude; authoritarianism; effectiveness; interpersonal; progressivist; teacher; teacher–pupil relationship; traditionalist.

—R. B. E.

44
Mood Adjective Check List (MACL)

AUTHOR.   Vincent Nowlis

AVAILABILITY.   Vincent Nowlis, Department of Psychology, University
of Rochester, Rochester, New York 14627

VARIABLES.   Nowlis defines *mood* as "the effect on a person of his own
configurations of activity." Configurations of activity are "fundamental
patterns of general functioning and orientation, such as level of activation, level of control, level of concentration, direction of social
orientation, and positive (pleasant) or negative (unpleasant) general
appraisal."

DESCRIPTION.   The MACL is a list of 140 adjectives. S indicates, by
checking one of four alternatives, the extent to which each adjective
describes his feelings at the moment of encountering the adjective. The
four alternatives are: definitely, slightly, undecided, definitely not.
Some of the adjectives used to assess mood are: nonchalant, irritated,
insecure, efficient, shocked, lonely, and mischievous. Of the total 140
items, 120 are distributed among four hypothesized dimensions: 1)
activation and deactivation; 2) pleasantness and unpleasantness; 3)
positive and negative social orientation; 4) control and lack of control.
Four adjectives (careful, earnest, meticulous, serious) were included
to monitor S's disposition to cooperate with the test administrators.
Six additional adjectives (hungry, in pain, intoxicated, lustful, sexy,
thirsty) were included to monitor recurring states which could influence S's responses. Ten adjectives were repeated among the last 28
to obtain reliability estimates.

A short form of the MACL exists which contains only 24 items, three
for each of eight factors the author isolated in the development of
the 140-item form.

ADMINISTRATION AND SCORING.   The MACL is self-administering. Nowlis
suggests that silence be required during administration so as not to
disturb S's moods. Scoring may be done by hand, using a 3-2-1-0
schedule for the four possible responses, or by a machine-scorable IBM
form (IBM Form I.T.S. 1000 A 158). For the short form, all 24 items
can be placed on a single IBM mark-sense card, which permits auto-
matic punching.

Profiles available are for a group of Navy enlisted men ($N = 140$) who were given a shortened, 40-word form of the MACL (Nowlis and Green, 1965). The same report includes response distributions to the 40-item form for a group of males and 124 females administered after a college final examination. Difference scores along 12 factors for mood changes in six experimental sessions with college males are presented in Nowlis (1965).

DEVELOPMENT. The 140-word form was administered to a group of approximately 450 college males at the beginning and end of six weekly one-hour sessions in a large auditorium. Various moods were induced through showing movies of Iowa corn-farming, Lincoln as President, the Nuremberg Trials, and a major surgical operation; and the silent-film comedy *The Freshman;* through an aggressive hoax; and through a contest for cash prizes. The results were combined into five separate data sets. Of the 130 items (excluding the 10 repeated ones), 34 were eliminated on the bases of skewed response distributions, low reliabilities, susceptibility to order effects, and patterns of correlation with other items. Using the 96 remaining items, 10 factors were extracted by the Thurstone centroid method from each of the intercorrelation matrices of each of the five data sets. The first 9 factors in each set were rotated to an oblique solution by the Pinzka–Saunders method.

In all five sets each of the following four factors emerged: Aggression, Anxiety, Surgency, Concentration. (The adjectives comprising the factor Surgency are: carefree, playful, witty, lively, talkative.) In four of the sets each of the following four factors was found: Fatigue, Social Affection, Sadness, Skepticism. One factor, Egotism, was found in three sets; two factors, Elation and Nonchalance, were found in two sets. A twelfth factor, Vigor, emerged from one data set.

All 96 variables were correlated with both their own axes and the other axes. The median correlation for axes within a factor was .45; the median value of all other correlations was approximately 0, with 87% of the values falling between +.29 and −.29.

It should be noted that the bipolarity of axes implied by the four originally-hypothesized dimensions did not emerge.

CRITIQUE. The ten repeated adjectives were subjected to six pairs of two tests of *reliability*: contingency coefficients, and Pearson *r*. Of the 60 coefficients (six tests of 10 adjectives), the lowest was .57, the highest .80. The mean of the range, however, for a single adjective was only .10. The 10-adjective *r*s ranged from .45 to .89; the mean of the range for a single adjective was .14. Rank-order correlations convinced

Nowlis and Green that the effect of S's merely remembering his response to the first of the repeated pair was unlikely to be a very important factor in these reliabilities.

Reimanis (1965) used an 8-factor, 30-word form of the MACL with 76 residents of a Veterans Administration home whose median age was 67. Test–retest *reliability* coefficients after periods ranging from two to five years for seven factors ranged from .50 to .66. The coefficient for the eighth factor, Aggression, was .38. Borgatta (1961) found test–retest *r*s ranged for college men from .40 (Fatigue) to .71 (Social Affection) and for college women from .07 (Fatigue) to .78 (Social Affection). Green (1964) tested 51 college men daily for 25 to 60 days. For eleven factors, scores on the second MACL correlated with the penultimate MACL ranged from .50 (Aggression) to .75 (Depression). Green also found, however, that intercorrelations for days 2, 3, 5, 7, 9, 16, 29, and 30 tended to increase, indicating either stereotyping of responses or increased accuracy with practice in responding.

Yagi and Berkum (1961), using a population of 147 enlisted personnel, concluded that 62% of their reports were suspect because of inconsistencies in checking either antonyms, factors believed to be bipolar, or the 10 repeated adjectives. As has been noted, however, Nowlis and Green's (1965) factor analysis has negated the hypothesized bipolarity.

The *validity* of the MACL could be threatened by the social desirability of the responses. However, Green (1964) had 51 college men and 87 college women rank 10 factors of a 39-word MACL for social desirability. When Ss were instructed to complete the 39-word MACL according to their present mood, only six of the 39 adjectives for the men and eight for the women correlated significantly with the social desirability ratings, with a maximum *r* of .50. Apparently indications of momentary feelings are less subject to social pressures than self-descriptions of more permanent traits or dispositions.

Certain *respondent difficulties* are possible. Subject-to-subject consistency of meaning for all the items is not assured. The conjunction of words (in one case, *careless* followed by *sexy*) can provoke a response which changes mood. An S's response may provoke vivid self-discovery or insight, again changing mood and perhaps cooperativeness.

GENERAL COMMENT.   On balance, this seems a good measure of transient subjective states. The factor analysis (Nowlis and Green, 1965) is very thorough. The MACL is easy to complete and understand, and requires a minimum of labored introspection. The absence of norms is a deficiency, but existing research utilizing the MACL is well-reported, and any set of norms would have to range across many populations and types of "normal" situations, such as the daily reports collected by Green (1964). The author's own appraisal seems appropriate: "The MACL is . . . useful for exploratory studies of various kinds. I cannot, however, recommend that it be used as the primary or sole index of the dependent variable or variables in a study."

REFERENCES

Borgatta, E. F. Mood, personality, and interaction. *Journal of General Psychology,* 1961, *64,* 105–137.

Green, R. F. The measurement of mood. Technical Report #16, Office of Naval Research: Contract Nonr-668 (12), 1965.

Nowlis, V. Research with the Mood Adjective Check List. In Tomkins, S. and Izard, C. (eds.) *Affect, cognition and personality.* New York: Springer, 1965.

Nowlis, V. and Green, R. F. Factor analytic studies of the Mood Adjective Check List. Technical Report #11, Office of Naval Research: Contract Nonr-668 (12), 1965.

Reimanis, G. Mood Adjective Check List in a VA domiciliary population. *Newsletter for Research in Psychology,* 1965.

Yagi, K. and Berkum, M. Some problems in the reliability of the Mood Adjective Check List. Paper read at Western Psychological Association meetings, Seattle, Washington, June, 1961.

UNITERMS. Affection; activity; aggression; anxiety; concentration; egotism; elation; fatigue; feeling; mood; nonchalance; sadness; skepticism; surgency; vigor.

—R. B. E.

45
Mother–Child Relationship Evaluation (M–CRE)

AUTHOR.   Robert M. Roth

AVAILABILITY.   Western Psychological Services, 1231 Wilshire Boulevard, Los Angeles, California 90025

VARIABLES.   The Mother–Child Relationship Evaluation measures four *maternal attitudes* which are hypothesized to intervene between a mother's past experiences and her present behavior towards her child. The variables are divided by the dichotomy of *acceptance* and *nonacceptance*.

After Symonds' (1949) work, *Acceptance* is represented by one variable, of the same name, and is an expression of adequacy in terms of sincerity of affect expression, interest in the child's pleasure, activities, and development, and the perception of the child as good. Nonacceptance is represented by three variables: 1) *Overprotection,* an expression of parental anxiety in terms of prolonged infantile care, prevention of development of independent behavior, and an excess of control; 2) *Overindulgence,* an excessive gratification of the child, along with a lack of parental control expressed in terms of oversolicitousness and excessive contact; and 3) *Rejection,* a denial of love and expression of hate towards the child in terms of neglect, harshness, severity, brutality, and strictness. Roth also postulates a confusion-dominance spectrum which indicates the degree to which one of the four attitudes dominates the relationship between mother and child. The manual (Roth, 1960b) states that the test is "primarily an exploratory and experimental one, rather than a refined clinical measurement"; the offering of clinical interpretations of cases in the manual, however, runs counter to this disclaimer.

DESCRIPTION.   The instrument contains 48 Likert-type statements, 12 for each variable. The five responses range from "strongly agree" through "undecided" to "strongly disagree." Some simulated items are:

> Children are people, just like adults.
> Children can never take care of themselves.
> A mother should take her child's side in a dispute.

ADMINISTRATION AND SCORING.   The booklet is self-administering without a time limit. Each item is keyed in the booklet to one of the four variables; the scoring of the responses (1–5) is indicated there as well.

Scores for each variable are the sums of the 12-item scores; the confusion-dominance score is the number of variable scores which exceed the 75th percentile and therefore ranges from 1 (dominance) to 4 (confusion). Roth suggests that administration, scoring, and interpretation can be completed in thirty minutes. Norms and standard scores are included in the manual; percentiles are printed on the back of the test booklet.

DEVELOPMENT.   Roth originally devised 100 items and tested them on a sample of eighty mothers, ages 25–35, from middle-class backgrounds in Austin, Texas. He calculated *phi*-coefficients to compare the top and bottom 26%, and selected the twelve most discriminating items for each variable. The mean *phi*-coefficients for the selected items were .49 (acceptance), .49 (overprotection), .44 (overindulgence), and .45 (rejection).

CRITIQUE.   The split-half *reliabilities* (corrected by the Spearman–Brown formula) of the four variables are .72 (A), .68 (OP), .58 (OI), and .62 (R).

Evidence of *concurrent validity* seems limited to correlations of the four variables with four scales of the USC Parental Attitude Research Instruments. For a sample of 45 mothers of high school students in a middle-class suburb of Chicago, correlations ($p < .05$) were found between Acceptance and the PARI scale of "breaking the will" ($-.34$), between Overprotection and PARI's "avoidance of communication" (.42) and between Rejection and "strictness" (.34) and "avoidance of communication" (.33). At the .01 level, the significant correlations were between Acceptance and "avoidance of communication" ($-.47$), between Overprotection and PARI's "fostering dependency" (.61), and between Rejection and "breaking the will" (.40). (Roth's Overindulgence scale was not correlated with the PARI scales in this study.) For *construct validity* Roth offers a mean correlation among the three non-acceptance variables of .45.

The *norms* are debilitated by the socio-economic narrowness of the validating sample; further, no information is given on sampling procedure, or on marital history, ages and number of children, or race of sample members.

Self-conscious mothers cannot but be aided in attempts to *fake good* by the placement of the items according to variable, discussion of the specific meaning of the variables, the percentile norms, and the scoring key to the responses—all of which are plainly printed on the test booklet itself.

In addition, many of the items are clichés of child-rearing practices

("Children should be seen and not heard") or are vague and subject to varying interpretations depending upon the inferred context or emotional set of the mother. Very few are couched in the first person; the entire test has an aura of having been sanitized.

GENERAL COMMENT.   The validity of this test, both concurrent and construct, remains to be demonstrated. Because it attempts to be relevant to an extremely sensitive and complex arena of human interrelationships it must be scrutinized with care. Unwarranted diagnostic inferences can too easily be read into scores for variables which are neither rigorously defined nor operationalized, and whose implications are not adequately investigated. The Mother–Child Relationship Evaluation is not recommended for general use. Much more work is needed in this area; the instrument is included for the researcher who may want to build more adequate theory and work at refining it.

REFERENCES

Roth, R. M. *The Mother–Child Relationship Evaluation,* Beverly Hills: Western Psychological Services, 1960a.

Roth, R. M. *Manual for the Mother–Child Relationship Evaluation.* Beverly Hills; Western Psychological Services, 1960b.

Symonds, P. M. *The dynamics of parent–child relationships.* New York: Bureau of Publications, Teachers College, Columbia University, 1949.

UNITERMS.   Acceptance; child; mother; overindulgence; overprotection; rejection; relationship.

—R. B. E.

46
Multiple Affect Adjective Check List (MAACL)

AUTHORS. Marvin Zuckerman and Bernard Lubin

AVAILABILITY. Educational and Industrial Testing Service, Box 7234, San Diego, California 92107

VARIABLES. The test was designed to measure *Anxiety* ("verbalizable"), *Depression,* and *Hostility* in persons with at least an eighth-grade reading comprehension level.

DESCRIPTION. Both 48-item and 132-item versions of the measure have been constructed, the former containing those items with the highest correlations to items in the longer format. For both long and short forms, a "Today" and a "General" test have been designed. The "Today" test is presumably relevant to describing present moods and feelings of the respondent, the "General" form being intended to describe longer-range tendencies in affect.

Currently, the scale consists of 132 adjectives, such as "jolly," "mollified," "purposeful," and "sad," descriptive of moods or feelings. The respondent checks the adjectives which he feels are applicable to his feelings.

ADMINISTRATION AND SCORING. The Multiple Affect Adjective Check List is easy to administer, and requires approximately five to ten minutes for completion. However, administrators must be present during testing for answering questions.

All items are keyed either plus ($+$) if checked or minus ($-$) if not. Separate hand scoring keys for the Anxiety, Depression, and Hostility scales are available from the publisher for both long and brief versions of the test. Total scores for each scale are computed separately by summing the number of plus items and the number of certain keyed items *not* checked.

Norms have been provided for groups of job applicants ($N = 200$), college students ($N = 75$), and five hospitalized psychiatric samples ($Ns = 69, 64, 43, 50,$ and 33). These are presented as group means and standard deviations for each of the three scales of the instrument separately. Six out of eight subgroups of the hospitalized patients differed significantly ($p < .05$) from both job applicant and college student groups.

DEVELOPMENT.   The first part of the measure was originally developed as a separate scale for the measurement of anxiety. It was called the Affect Adjective Check List (AACL), and was subsequently incorporated into the multiple affect instrument. Adjectives were collected from Gough's (1955) and Nowlis' (1953) check lists and from a thesaurus, to form a 61-item list intended to measure anxiety. Two successive item analysis studies were completed. The first (Persky, Maroc, Conrad, and den Breeijen, 1959) compared psychiatric patients rated as high-anxious with normals rated low on anxiety level on the basis of a psychiatric interview. On a 30-word form, 24 words yielded significant differences between the groups ($p < .05$). Of those, 12 were "anxiety plus" words (checked more often by the high anxiety group) and the remainder were "anxiety minus" ones (checked more often by the low anxiety group). In the second study (Levitt, Persky, and Brady, 1964), an attempt was made to measure the effects of a hypnotically-induced anxiety state in normal subjects. The Affect Adjective Check List scores, based on the first item analysis, increased significantly. Additional item analysis showed 38 words with "significant changes in checking frequency during the anxiety condition" (Zuckerman, 1960). Of the 38, 21 were "anxiety plus" and the rest were "anxiety minus." The resultant scoring key included 21 words which had shown significant effects in both of these studies.

To develop the Depression scale, Lubin had pairs of psychiatrists rate neuropsychiatric patients as "severely," "moderately," "slightly," or "not observably" depressed. Interjudge agreement correlations were .77 and .70 ($Ns = 60$ and 32). Forty-eight females and 47 males labeled "severely" or "moderately" depressed and 174 normal females and 100 normal males constituted the item-selection population. The criteria for item selection were: 1) ability to differentiate depressed from normal males and depressed from normal females; 2) a Lorge–Thorndike word-count frequency not above the eighth-grade level; 3) not already used in the Anxiety scales; 4) equal balance of plus and minus items.

For the Hostility scale, 20 freshman female college students were put in a hypnotic trance; 10 heard a taped hostility suggestion, the other 10 were controls. Of 132 adjectives, including the 21 Anxiety items and the 40 Depression items, 42 were checked significantly more often by the induced-hostile group. The 14 adjectives which overlapped the pre-existing scales were eliminated.

Intercorrelations among the three scales in the long version are high, with mean rs being .85 for Anxiety and Depression, .72 for Anxiety and Hostility, and .72 for Depression and Hostility in studies of 46 college males and females, 26 male psychiatric patients, and 47 female psychiatric patients. For the brief scales, the intercorrelations for 40 subjects were .82 (Anxiety and Depression), .31 (Anxiety and Hostility), and .47 (Depression and Hostility).

CRITIQUE.   Zuckerman et al. (1964) have found split-half *reliabilities* for 46 normal subjects of .79, .92, and .90 for the "Today" Anxiety, Depression, and Hostility subscales, respectively (long form). Using 52 college students, Sanders, Roehl, and Hillson (undated) obtained split-half coefficients of .74, .91, and .86 for the same indices. Datel et al. (1966) found *r*s for 48 army men of .81, .92, and .80, respectively. Lubin and Zuckerman (1965) found an *r* of .72 for the (AACL) Anxiety scale alone. In general, the internal consistency of the Anxiety subscale seems insufficient.

Retest reliabilities are lower than the split-half ones. Hayes (in press) reports .70, .65, and .54 for the three scales using the "General" format. These *r*s are naturally lower still when the "Today" format is used; Lubin and Zuckerman (1965) report .21, .21, and .15 over a seven-day period. The (AACL) Anxiety scale drops from a retest *r* of .68 to .31 when the format shifts from "General" to "Today." All in all, the reliabilities are modest, especially considering that they are reported for the long form only.

In *concurrent validity* studies, the General form of the Anxiety scale (unrevised) was found to correlate with a wider range of MMPI scales than the "Today" form in another validity study (Zuckerman and Lubin, 1965). Seven out of ten possible significant correlations were obtained between MMPI subscales and the "General" Anxiety subscale. The Anxiety subscales also correlated significantly with other measures of the variable, including the Welsh Anxiety, MMPI Psychasthenia, Maslow Security, Cattell IPAT, and Rosen Anxiety Reaction scales. The Hostility subscale was found to be correlated with the Psychasthenia and Schizophrenic MMPI subscales. The Depression subscale correlated significantly with the MMPI Depression and Schizophrenic subscales.

In a *predictive validity* study of 32 students given the "Today" form (Zuckerman, 1960), anxiety scores increased significantly on days immediately preceding examinations. Additionally, the rise was significantly greater for those obtaining low grades on these examinations than for those earning higher ones. In another study (Zuckerman and Biase, 1962), the above effects were replicated; it was also discovered that students who rated themselves as more worried about the exams before taking them scored significantly higher than those rating themselves as less worried.

Lubin and Zuckerman (1967) administered the MAACL to 43 persons attending four sensitivity training groups. During-group scores were higher (more positive) than pre-scores, suggesting that the instrument does measure emotional arousal. All three scores began low (—.7 standard score, implying much negative affect), and peaked at session 6 (.2 standard score), a point at which various evaluative ratings ("openness," "worthwhileness," "relevance") were highest. The three variables of the MAACL were highly intercorrelated in this study: Anxiety versus Depression, .92; Anxiety versus Hostility, .86; and Depression versus Hostility, .81, so it is likely that a generalized negative affect—perhaps anxiety—is all that is being measured. Thus, validity of the separate dimensions has not been demonstrated.

In a *fakeability* study (methods unspecified) none of the Multiple Affect Adjective Check List scales was found significantly correlated with the set in question. However, the version(s) (Today or General) used were not specifically named in the test manual. Checking *response set* was uncorrelated with scores on the unrevised 132-item original scale, but its effect has apparently not been ascertained for the short format.

GENERAL COMMENT.   The original scale development by the method of known groups and by hypnotic induction makes this instrument potentially useful. However, the original norm groups studied are, most of them, under 100, and sampling methods are often unspecified. On balance, the borderline reliability of the Anxiety subscale and the lack of validity studies distinguishing the three scales indicate that the instrument in its present form may be quite useful for studying generalized negative affect in aggregates (as in the Lubin and Zuckerman 1967 study of affect changes in T-groups) but is *not* appropriate for individual prediction or outcome purposes.

REFERENCES

Datel, W. E., Gieseking, C. F., Engle, E. O., and Dougher, M. J. Affect levels in a platoon of basic trainees. *Psychological Reports*, 1966, *18*, 271–285.

Gough, H. G. *Reference handbook for the Gough Adjective Check List.* Berkeley: Institute for Personality Assessment Research, University of California, 1955.

Hayes, C. V. The measurement of anxiety in sophomore nursing students using Zuckerman's AACL. *Nursing Research* (in press).

Levitt, E. E., Persky, H., and Brady, J. P. *Hypnotic induction of anxiety: a psycho-endocrine investigation.* Springfield, Ill.: Charles C Thomas, 1964.

Lubin, B. and Zuckerman, M. Affective and perceptual-cognitive patterns in sensitivity training groups. *Psychological Reports*, 1967, *21*, 365–376.

Nowlis, V. The development and modification of motivational systems in personality. In *Nebraska Symposium on motivation*. Lincoln: University of Nebraska Press, 1953, pp. 114–138.

Persky, H., Maroc, J., Conrad, E., and den Breeijen, A. Blood corticotropin and adrenal weight-maintenance factor levels of anxious patients and normal subjects. *Psychosomatic Medicine*, 1959, *21*, 379–386.

Sanders, R. A., Roehl, C. A., and Hillson, J. S. The Multiple Affect Adjective Checklist: a cross-validational study. Unpublished mimeographed paper, undated.

Zuckerman, M. The development of an Affect Adjective Check List for the measurement of anxiety. *Journal of Consulting Psychology*, 1960, *24*, 457–462.

Zuckerman, M., and Biase, D. V. Replication and further data on the Affect Adjective Check List measure of anxiety. *Journal of Consulting Psychology*, 1962, *26*, 291.

Zuckerman, M., Lubin, B., Vogel, L., and Valerius, E. Measurement of experimentally induced affects. *Journal of Consulting Psychology*, 1964, *28*, 418–425.

Zuckerman, M. and Lubin, B. *Manual for the Multiple Affect Adjective Check List*. San Diego: Educational and Industrial Testing Service, 1965. (See also Addendum to the Manual, 1966.)

UNITERMS.   Affect; anger; anxiety; depression; emotion; hostility; mood; personality; test anxiety.

—L. J. R.
—M. B. M.

47

Myers–Briggs Type Indicator (MBTI)

AUTHORS.   Isabel Briggs Myers and Katharine C. Briggs

AVAILABILITY.   Educational Testing Service, Princeton, New Jersey 08540

VARIABLES.   The Myers–Briggs Type Indicator consists of four dichotomous indices of *Jungian personality types: Extraversion–Introversion* (EI), whether perception and judgment are directed toward the environment or the world of ideas; *Sensation–Intuition* (SN), indicating dominant perceptual style; *Thinking–Feeling* (TF), which of these two modes of judgment is relied upon; and *Judgment–Perception* (JP), indicating which of these uses of the mind is relied upon in dealing with the environment.

DESCRIPTION.   The MBTI (Form F) consists of 166 forced-choice (typically two) items. Fifty-two items are word pairs, for one of which respondents indicate a preference. Some of the pairs are: theory–certainty, build–invent, casual–correct, who–what, sign–symbol. The remaining items are similar to the following:

Do you:
   A. rather prefer to do things at the last minute
   B. find it hard on the nerves

or,

When you have to do business with strangers do you feel:
   A. confident and at ease
   B. a little fussed or afraid that they won't want to bother with you

ADMINISTRATION AND SCORING.   The MBTI is self-administering, with no time limit. Almost all Ss at or above the senior high school level complete the Indicator in fifty minutes. Form F of the Indicator comes with a Standard IBM answer sheet, scorable by hand or machine, and scoring keys for translating difference scores on the four indices into preference scores. Scoring services, including a complete set of punched cards, are available from the Educational Testing Service. Difference scores yield four-element preference types, such as ESFJ (Extraversion–Sensation–Feeling–Judgment) or ESFP (the most common unrestricted adult female type), or INFP (the least common male type).

Norms are available for four groups of high school students, (*N* totaling 827); a wide variety of college student samples (total *N* = 6,301) and graduate school students (*N* = 159); a group of recently-employed college graduates (*N* = 350); and a group of public school teachers (*N* = 334). The manual (Myers, 1962) also includes percentile norms for high school and college males and females.

DEVELOPMENT.   The original items were administered in 1944 to a group of 20 friends and relatives whose type preferences seemed clear to the authors. After internal-consistency analysis, items having less than a .60 probability of predicting type preference were dropped. Between 1956 and 1958, 130 out of 200 new items were appended after being tested on 120 men and women already familiar with the Indicator. The lower limit of predictability was raised to .63; items were reworded and tested on three high school samples.

This form (D2) was administered to similar samples of 2,500 Pennsylvania high school boys and girls in college preparatory curricula at the 11th and 12th grade levels. From each sex, 200 students of each type preference, with compensation for the rarer introvert types, were used for tetrachoric item–test correlations. Two forms resulted: Form F, for the 11th grade up; Form E, for 7th to 11th grades.

Zero points on the scales are asserted to have real meaning; scores one point above and one point below the zero point are claimed to describe two distinct personality types. The zero points for the SN and JP scales were determined by the bimodality in the distribution of scale scores for 704 Dartmouth students (Class of 1961) and 711 Cal. Tech. students (Classes of 1958–1962). The TF scale zero point was set from scores of 170 Lexington VA Hospital mental patients. The zero point on the EI scale was identified by the discontinuity in the regression of intelligence scores on the scale scores for the male and female college preparatory students in 27 Pennsylvania high schools. The empirical and theoretical zero points closely coincide for the SN and TF scales, but not for the EI or JP scale.

Form F of the Indicator contains separate TF scales for males and females.

CRITIQUE.   The *internal-consistency reliability* of the type categories was determined by Stricker and Ross (1962) from a lower-bound reliability estimate developed by Guttman (1964) for qualitative items. The populations were 397 male and 614 female Massachusetts high school students and 300 male and 184 female Long Island University freshmen. The reliabilities for the EI scale ranged from .42 to .60; for the JP scale, from .42 to .59. Myers, however, asserts that the Guttman

statistic is inappropriate, since her scores were not originally dichotomous. Using tetrachoric *rs* and the Spearman–Brown formula,
she obtained median correlations of .83.

The internal-consistency reliability of the continuous (difference)
scores was estimated by Cronbach's alpha-coefficient (1951) for the
same four populations. The comparable results were: EI, .76 to .83;
SN, .74 to .80; TF, .64 to .74; JP, .78 to .84.

Forty-one Amherst students were retested after fourteen months and
compared with the 217 other members of their entering class for test–
retest reliability. Neither *chi*-square analyses of type distributions, nor
t-tests of differences in mean scores, nor F-tests for differences in
variances yielded any significant differences at the .05 level. The
product-moment correlations for the difference scores on the two
administrations were .73 (EI), .69 (SN), .48 (TF), and .69 (JP), all
significant at the .01 level.

To establish *concurrent validity,* several comparisions of the Indicator
with similar scales have been made. These scales include the Strong
Vocational Interest Blank, the Allport–Vernon–Lindzey Study of
Values, the Edwards Personal Preference Schedule, the Personality
Research Inventory, and the Gray–Wheelwright Psychological Type
questionnaire. Because it is also based on Jungian typology and measures EI, SN, and TF directly and JP indirectly, the Gray–Wheelwright
inventory is the most relevant measure of concurrent validity. Both
were administered to 47 members of two undergraduate psychology
classes at Golden Gate College (the ages ranged from 19 to 55). The
phi-coefficients between the corresponding type categories are .64 (EI),
.34 (SN), and .54 (TF), all significant at the .05 level or better. The
product-moment correlations for the continuous scores were .79 (EI),
.58 (SN), .60 (TF), and .41 (JP), all significant at the .01 level. The EI
scale is also highly correlated (.63 to .75) with the Extraversion scale
of the Maudsley Personality Inventory.

To establish *predictive validity* for academic criteria, male freshmen
at Wesleyan University ($N = 225$) and Cal. Tech. ($N = 201$) were
tested for relationships between Indicator continuous scores and 1)
freshman-year grade-point average; 2) over/under achievement (actual
grade-point versus grade-point predicted from the CEEB verbal and
mathematics SATs); and 3) (for Cal. Tech.) dropout during the freshmen year. No correlations were significant for the Cal. Tech. freshmen.

For Wesleyan freshmen, EI correlated negatively with actual grade-
point average ($-.18$), and JP correlated positively with actual grade-
point (.24) and over/under achievement (.27) (all significant at the .01
level).

For 201 freshmen at Cal. Tech. the SN and JP scales correlated negatively with verbal SATs (only) at —.20 and —.17, respectively ($p <$ .05).

The one study which examined vocational criteria showed significantly more turnover among employees classed as intuitive rather than sensing, and as perceiving rather than judging. When the effects of intelligence are controlled for, the partial correlation for the SN scale remains significant at the .05 level, but that for the JP scale loses significance.

In an extensive examination of *construct validity*, Stricker and Ross (1962) question six aspects of the Indicator's relationship to the Jungian typology: 1) the assumption of scale bipolarity; 2) the assumption of the comparability of the alternatives' scale position (i.e., is choice "A" as much thinking as choice "B" is feeling?); 3) the assumption that social desirability response sets improve measurement; 4) the setting of the zero points (to which Myers has replied); 5) the original type classifications made by the authors in 1942–44 (would they not have to have been competent Jungian analysts?); and 6) the absence of item analyses relating current internal consistency with the original empirical type classifications (which were based on an accidental sample of 20 and a low criterion of predictability—60%).

Respondent difficulties have been reported. For 39 graduate students in psychology and education, the choices were unrealistic, *item transparency* was noticeable, and the correspondence between personality and preference was questionable. Myers admits that it is possible to "throw" the MBTI, but not in a desired direction, she asserts.

GENERAL COMMENT.   Myers' manual is unusually large and thorough. Stricker and Ross' evaluation is even larger and more thorough. Their exceptions are well-taken, especially with regard to the MBTI's inability to make practical predictions and the need for more normative data for adults, particularly adults with little or no college background. The Indicator is easy to administer and score, and the types do have the virtue of being mutually independent. The relationship of the Indicator to its theoretical Jungian underpinnings has not been established, but many of its empirical features are known, and it elicits a large amount of information fairly efficiently. One aspect of the MBTI is reasonably clear: Any researcher who has both the Myers manual and the Stricker and Ross critique will be able to judge the MBTI's utility for his work quite accurately.

REFERENCES

Cronbach, L. J. Coefficient alpha and the internal structure of tests. *Psychometrika*, 1951, *16*, 297–334.

Guttman, L. The test–retest reliability of qualitative data. *Psychometrika,* 1946, *11,* 81–95.

Myers, I. B. *Manual: The Myers–Briggs Type Indicator.* Princeton: Educational Testing Service, 1962.

Stricker, L. J. and Ross, J. A description and evaluation of the Myers–Briggs Type Indicator. Research Bulletin RB-62-6, Educational Testing Service, 1962.

UNITERMS.   Extraversion; feeling; introversion; intuition; judgment; Jung; perception; personality; sensation; thinking.

—R. B. E.

48
Need Achievement Thematic Apperception Test (n Ach TAT)

AUTHORS.   David C. McClelland, John W. Atkinson, Russell Clark, and Edgar L. Lowell

AVAILABILITY.   McClelland, D. C., Atkinson, J. W., Clark, R., and Lowell, E. L. *The achievement motive*. New York: Appleton-Century-Crofts, 1953.

VARIABLES.   The *need to achieve*, defined as "concern over competition with a standard of excellence," is the variable intended for measurement. Actual success or failure of the respondent in goal attainment was not conceived as a relevant indicator of the need or motive to seek that goal. The measure is considered valid for studying achievement motivation cross-culturally in males and females, the former "ranging from the ninth grade level through college and perhaps to age 60" (McClelland et al., 1953).

DESCRIPTION.   A pictorial projective method for measuring achievement motivation was constructed, using cards 7BM, 1, and 8BM from the Murray Thematic Apperception Test, plus five additional pictures. Respondents are shown the pictures and requested to answer a standard set of questions designed to help them create a "story" from each of the images they have viewed. The pictures on the cards represent people interacting with a variety of objects, and are presumably vague enough to permit interpretation consistent with the respondent's motives. Projective questions resemble the following simulated examples:

What activity is occurring here, and who is involved?
What are the feelings of the person(s) depicted?

ADMINISTRATION AND SCORING.   Pictures are projected on a screen for twenty seconds apiece; respondents are permitted four minutes between each viewing for writing each "story." Each story is first scored separately according to two categories: Achievement Imagery (AI) and Doubtful Achievement Imagery (TI). To be scored in the former category a story must meet one of the following criteria: Either explicit or implicit *concern* over competing with a standard of excellence, including "self-imposed requirements of good performance"; some instrumental activitiy; or, "affective concern over goal attainment" (McClelland et al., 1953). Otherwise, the authors stipulate that the story must indicate either "unique accomplishment" or "long-term involvement" (criteria not explicated) if a score of Achievement Imagery is to be given. UI (Unrelated Imagery) is given when there is no evidence that achievement imagery is present.

When a story is considered indicative of achievement need, it is further scored according to seven subcategories: Stated Need for Achievement (N); Instrumental Activity (I+, I?, or I—, depending on outcome); Anticipatory Goal States (Ga+, Ga—); Obstacles or Blocks (B when personal, Bw when environmental); Nurturant Press (Nup), personal focus aiding the character striving to achieve his goal; Affective States (G+, G—, scored only once per story) and Achievement Thema (Ach Th), scored "When Achievement is elaborated in such a manner that it becomes the central plot of the story." All categories except Unrelated Imagery and Doubtful Achievement Imagery are scored +1, these two being given —1 and 0, respectively. Total scores for each story are added to calculate total achievement score.

Norms have been obtained for various groups. Lowell (1950) tested male college students ($N = 21$) under presumably neutral and achievement-oriented conditions. Veroff (1950) tested high school males ($N = 18$) and females ($N = 22$) each with male and female sets of pictures. These frequency distributions of scoring categories, group means, and standard deviations are presented in McClelland et al. (1953). Lowell (1950) also used the measure in modified (verbal) form with 21 ninth-grade Navajo males under aroused and non-aroused conditions. In a study of college women, "aroused" ($N = 26$) and "non-aroused" ($N = 27$), groups' means and standard deviations were obtained for each of these conditions. Roe (1951) scored nine TAT cards according to the method developed by McClelland et al. for measuring achievement need. She computed the mean and standard deviation for the above card series for 61 eminent scientists, ages 31 to 60.

DEVELOPMENT.   The original (1949) reliability check by the authors yielded an r of .95 between achievement scores of 30 subjects as rated by two judges of varying experience, using scoring system A. An average index of agreement of .91 in the score–rescoring of the various scoring categories was found for scoring system B (McClelland et al., 1953). In 1950, Atkinson found a score–rescore reliability (six months) of .95 for 32 subjects' 256 stories. In another study of interscorer reliability, an inexperienced judge's ratings (using scoring system B) correlated .96 with those of one with extensive experience for 24 subjects. In all these cases, the coders performed "blind," without knowing to whom a particular response belonged. Apparently, judges agreed beforehand not to score a category when in doubt.

Atkinson (1950) assessed the internal consistency of the four original and four additional pictures, with respect to whether each placed the respondent above or below his mean need achievement score. Only the "boy with violin" TAT Card No. 1 was found not to discriminate in 65% or more of cases ($N = 32$), and it was thus excluded from the test.

Subsequently, two three-picture forms containing the most equivalent pictures of the seven discriminating ones were constructed. Reliability of the six was reported as .78 (corrected) for 32 subjects.

The authors (1953) have suggested that cards depicting persons older than the respondents are more valid for measuring the need to achieve than those portraying younger ones. As a rationale, they cited empirical evidence (Tompkins, 1947) that cards eliciting regressive identifications are more likely to tap recall of prior situations in individuals' lives.

Item analysis revealed that the two cards containing more achievement cues (machinery, tools, desks, etc.—for persons in American culture) elicited significantly higher need achievement scores than those three containing fewer such cues. No significant sequence differences were found.

CRITIQUE.   Birney (1960) has commented that although considerable effort has been expended in demonstrating high interscorer and adequate comparable-item *reliability*, no convincing demonstration of test–retest reliability has been reported. Information on reliability is in general meager.

In a *validity* study designed to examine effects of non-intellective variables upon academic achievement (Applezweig, Moeller, and Burdick, 1956), 70 college women's grade-point averages and verbal scores on the Scholastic Aptitude Test were used as indices of achievement and intellectual ability, respectively. Six cards of the Murray Thematic Apperception Test were scored for achievement and affiliation motives, for the former according to the method of McClelland et al. described above. Both variables were found to correlate significantly ($r = .45$), but after further investigation the need affiliation measure was deemed invalid.

Norm groups tested have been too small to permit generalization to the populations from which they were drawn. The authors' conclusion that *"even girls project achievement striving primarily into the activities of men"* (McClelland et al., 1953) for example, was apparently based upon results for only 22 high school students in one culture.

As conceptualized, need achievement *theory* does not take into account neurotic versus healthy connotations of variations in need strength. A first step has been taken along these lines by Atkinson and Feather (1966) in acknowledging the situational dependence of other variables (such as incentive values and subjective probabilities) related to achievement situations.

A further conceptual problem lies in the operational procedures for establishing "arousal" and "neutral" conditions. Very often these do not seem sufficiently capable of either eliciting or "normalizing" achievement motivational level. See Klinger's (1966) very thorough review of this and other n Ach measures.

Finally, the original theory underlying the test does not adequately deal with the linkage between n Ach motives and actual success in reaching one's goal. Presumably, those higher in n Ach will turn out to accomplish more, and McClelland's analysis (1961) of material from a range of cultures shows that periods of industrial development are preceded by increases in n Ach, as measured by content analysis of children's readers.

But in the short run, such linkage cannot be presumed, and as Klinger's (1966) review shows, achievement behavior is not particularly associated with high n Ach as measured by the McClelland method. McClelland (1965) has proposed a very thoroughgoing theory of the acquisition of motives, which contains a set of propositions dealing with motive–behavior linkage. He also presents data showing that a course using the theory and designed to cause increases in n Ach imagery in stories written by Indian businessmen appears to have increased the proportion of the group who showed unusual amounts of entrepreneurial activity in real life from 25–27% to 65–67%.

Marlowe's criticism (1967) that more work is needed before any of the need Achievement tests currently available can be assumed to possess good construct validity seems justified. Thus, although the method is widely used to measure achievement motivation, as if its validity were known to be high, such is not necessarily the case. McClelland (1965) assumes the plausibility of the instrument (and uses feedback of scores to individuals as a means of altering n Ach levels). But the available information on achievement imagery and its relation to behavior is still much thinner than it should be.

REFERENCES

Atkinson, J. W. Studies in projective measurement of achievement motivation. Unpublished doctoral dissertation, University of Michigan, 1950.

Atkinson, J. W., and Feather, N. T. A theory of achievement motivation. New York: John Wiley, 1966.

Applezweig, M. H., Moeller, G., and Burdick, H. Multi-motive prediction of academic success. *Psychological Reports,* 1956, *2,* 489–496.

Birney, R. The reliability of the achievement motive. *Journal of Abnormal and Social Psychology,* 1959, *58,* 266–267.

Klinger, E. Fantasy need Achievement as a motivational construct. *Psychological Bulletin,* 1966, *66,* 291–308.

Krumholtz, J., Measuring achievement motivation: a review. *Journal of Counseling Psychology,* 1967, *4,* 191–198.

Lowell, E. L. A methodological study of projectively measured achievement motivation. Unpublished master's thesis. Wesleyan University, 1950.

McClelland, D. C. *The achieving society.* Princeton: Van Nostrand, 1961.

McClelland, D. C. Toward a theory of motive acquisition. *American Psychologist,* 1965, *20,* 321–333.

McClelland, D. C., Atkinson, J. W., Clark, R., and Lowell, E. L. The projective expression of needs: IV. The effect of the need for Achievement on thematic apperception. *Journal of Experimental Psychology,* 1949, *39,* 242–255.

McClelland, D. C., Atkinson, J. W., Clark, R., and Lowell, E. L. *The achievement motive.* New York: Appleton-Century-Crofts, 1953.

Marlowe, D. *A theory of achievement motivation* by Atkinson and Feather: a review. *Contemporary Psychology,* 1967, *12,* 557–578.

Roe, Anne. A psychological study of physical scientists. *Genetic Psychological Monographs,* 1951, *43,* 121–325.

Saddaca, R., Clark, R., and Ricciuti, H. *Content analysis of achievement motivation protocols: a working manual.* Princeton: Educational Testing Service, 1957.

Tomkins, S. S. *The Thematic Apperception Test.* New York: Grune and Stratton, 1947.

Veroff, J. A projective measure of the achievement motivation of adolescent males and females. Unpublished honors thesis, Wesleyan University, 1950.

UNITERMS. Accomplishment; achievement; affiliation; aspiration; competition; content analysis; goal; graphic; incentive; motivation; need; projective; striving; success.

—L. J. R.
—M. B. M.

49
Omnibus Personality Inventory (OPI)

AUTHORS.   Paul Heist, Harold Webster, and George Yonge

AVAILABILITY.   OPI Research Program, Center for the Study of Higher
Education, University of California, Berkeley, California 94720

VARIABLES.   The Omnibus Personality Inventory is just that—a compilation of separate *personality* scales from many previously existing
inventories. The scales are: *Thinking Introversion* (TI), a liking for
reflective thought and academic activities; *Theoretical Orientation*
(TO), a preference for the scientific method and scientific activities;
Estheticism (Es), diverse interests in and appreciation of artistic
activities, including literature and dramatics; *Complexity* (Co), a
tolerance of ambiguity and uncertainty, as opposed to certainty and
structure; *Autonomy* (Au), non-authoritarian attitudes and a need for
independence; *Developmental Status* (DS, Form C only), rebelliousness toward authority, particularly institutionalized authority; *Impulse
Expression* (IE), a readiness to express impulses and to seek gratification either in conscious thought or overt action; *Schizoid Functioning*
(SF, Form C only), attitudes and behavior which characterize socially
alienated persons; *Social Introversion* (SI), little interest in social contacts and responsibilities; *Religious Liberalism* (RL), a skepticism and
rejection of religious beliefs and practices; *Social Maturity* (SM),
flexible, tolerant, realistic, non-authoritarian thinking; *Masculinity–
Femininity* (MF), (for masculine respondents) weak esthetic and
social inclinations, few reports of adjustment problems, anxiety, or
personal inadequacies; *Repression and Suppression* (RS), inhibition,
prudence, caution; *Altruism* (Am, Form F only), affiliative and trusting
behavior in relations with others; *Practical Outlook* (PO, Form F only),
an interest in practical, applied activities and a high regard for material
possessions and concrete accomplishments; *Non-Authoritarianism* (NA,
Form C only, not profiled), low score on items extracted from the
California Authoritarianism (F) Scale; *Lack of Anxiety* (LA), low
scores on items from the Taylor Manifest Anxiety Scale; and, *Response
Bias* (RB, also termed Couch–Keniston (CK) on Form C), an attempt
to make a socially desirable impression.

The present forms of the OPI have been developed with and are
limited to college students of better than national mean intelligence.

DESCRIPTION.   The OPI is a true–false inventory which comes in three forms (C, D, and F). The number of items varies from 385 to 585, and are of the following (simulated) type:

> I sometimes become very angry over little things.
> I am not comfortable around members of the opposite sex.
> I do not like to be around crowds of people.

ADMINISTRATION AND SCORING.   The OPI is self-administering; the 585-item form requires two hours for completion. A 600-item form is available for machine scoring (Form I.T.S. 1100 A 182, Revised). Raw scores can be converted to profile scores for each scale either by referring to tables in the manual or by plotting them on OPI Profile Sheets, which are available from the Center for the Study of Higher Education. The Center does not offer scoring services.

In addition to profile scores, the manual contains norms based upon samples of 2,390 entering freshmen at the University of California and San Francisco State College, with a sex ratio corresponding to the source population.

DEVELOPMENT.   The original OPI contained 13 personality scales, over half of which came from the Minnesota Multiphasic Personality Inventory. The Minnesota T-S-E Introversion–Extroversion Inventory, the Vassar College Attitude Inventory, and the California Psychological Inventory provided the bulk of the remaining items. In the process of developing the A, B, and C forms, items were edited for psychometric inadequacy and relevance of content, based upon large samples of incoming freshmen.

CRITIQUE.   The Kuder–Richardson Formula 21 *reliabilities* for the scales range from .67 (RB) to .89 (PI), with a median of .87 ($N =$ 7,283). Corrected split-half reliabilities for 400 freshmen at the University of California ranged from .65 (RB) to .91 (PI and RO), with a median of .84. Test–retest reliabilities for three groups of students ranged from .79 (LA, 67 females) to .95 (IE, 71 males and females), with a median of .87.

This review cannot examine *validity* data for all the scales. Such evidence is, however, no better or worse than that from the OPI's antecedent inventories from which items were taken. Occasionally, weak results of concurrent validity studies are off-handedly treated; the .54 correlation between the Thinking Introversion scale and the Introversion–Extroversion scale of the Myers–Briggs Type Indicator (which see) is dismissed as illustrating "the well-known fact that similar labels do not insure that any two scales are assessing the same trait or dimension." The fact that the Masculinity–Femininity scale correlates at only $-.16$ for men and at $-.31$ for women with the Femininity scale on the California Psychological Inventory is not discussed. On the other hand, one can observe moderately good correlations (for example, the Religious Liberalism scale correlates with the Religious scale on the Allport–Vernon–Lindzey Study of Values at .66, the Esthetic scales on the two inventories correlate at .61, and the Theoretical Orientation scales at .62 (all at $p < .01$).

As to *construct* validity, the chief problem lies in the naming of the scales. It is not clear, for example, that low sociability and low esthetic orientation are necessarily defining traits of Masculinity; similarly, to term rebellion against institutionalized authority a key element of Developmental Status is clearly a judgment which may be disputed. Several of the scales do seem able to discriminate according to valid criterion measures—for example, Complexity divides prize-winning female artists from non-prize-winning artists by a whole standard deviation; it also correlates with three-judge rankings of the complexity of those artists' work.

Of the 182 scale *intercorrelations* reported, 18% are equal to or above .50 in absolute magnitude.

The *norms* and *profile scores* in the manual are undifferentiated by sex, despite obvious sex-related differences in the scale scores. Later normative data based on 3,540 men and 3,743 women have been published, but sex-differentiated profile scores are not yet available. *Item overlap* has been reduced considerably; the maximum overlap is 10 of the 24 Esthetic items with 10 of the 57 Masculinity–Femininity items.

GENERAL COMMENT.   The primary thing to consider about the Omnibus Personality Inventory is the wide range of scales its name implies. Judgments as to their usefulness and applicability must vary from scale to scale. Over all, only the absence of sex-differentiated norms impedes the comparison of college groups on a gross level. The later data allow the user to create profile scores by sex, but only at some personal expenditure. The administration (not to mention scoring) of the complete set of scales is time-consuming, and probably fatiguing enough to subjects to depress the validity of the instrument considerably. In any case, the predictive power of most scales for individuals is *not* established.

On balance, the OPI must be seen as a more or less grotesque monument to the "dustbowl empiricist" school of test construction. Somehow, it seems hard to assume that item number 422 (or 501 or 585) still makes sense to a college student groggy from two hours' worth of checking true–false items, even though it may have correlated empirically with some other non-test-taking response once, in the context of another, shorter instrument.

The Omnibus Personality Inventory may be a handy battery to have on the shelf, but it can only be recommended as a research tool for the user who keeps in mind its general limitations, and the idiosyncracies of each of the scales.

REFERENCES

Allport, G. W., Vernon, P. E., and Lindzey, G. *A study of values* (Rev. ed.). Cambridge, Mass.: Ho··ghton Mifflin Co., 1951.

Gough, H. G. *Manual for the California Psychological Inventory.* Palo Alto: Consulting Psychologists Press, 1957.

Heist, P. and Williams, P. A. *Manual for the Omnibus Personality Inventory.* Berkeley: Center for the Study of Higher Education, University of California, 1962.

UNITERMS.   Altruism; anxiety; authoritarianism; autonomy; complexity; estheticism; femininity; impulse expression; introversion; masculinity; maturity; personality; practicality; rebelliousness; religion; response bias; repression; schizoid functioning; social desirability; suppression; theoretical; value.

—R. B. E.
—M. B. M.

50
Open-End Perceived Change Measure

AUTHORS.   Douglas R. Bunker, Eric S. Knowles, Matthew B. Miles

AVAILABILITY.   Douglas R. Bunker, Program in Policy Sciences, State University of New York at Buffalo, 4224 Ridge Lea Road, Amherst, New York 14226

VARIABLES.   The Open-End Perceived Change Measure was originally designed to assess *perceived changes in interpersonal and work-related behavior,* as these are affected by laboratory human relations training. The measure is intended for use with normal adults, but may also be used "for [the evaluation of] any treatment aiming at behavior change, including psychotherapy" (Miles, 1965).

Though the original form of the instrument, developed by Miles, measured only a general "impact" of training on interpersonal and work-related behavior, a content-analytic scheme developed by Bunker (1965) includes 17 categories as follows:

A. Overt operational changes
   1. Communication
      a. Sending (expresses feelings, etc.)
      b. Receiving (listens, etc.)
      c. Unspecified (communicates better, etc.)
   2. Relational facility (cooperative, tactful . . .)
   3. Risk-taking (willing to take stand, etc.)
   4. Increased interdependence (involves others, dominates less . . .)
   5. Functional flexibility (less rigid, takes group roles easily . . .)
   6. Self-control (more disciplined, checks temper . . .)

B. Inferred changes in insight and attitudes
   1. Awareness of human behavior (understands motivation, sees people clearly . . .)
   2. Sensitivity to group behavior (aware of subcurrents in groups . . .)
   3. Sensitivity to people (more understanding of why people act as they do . . .)
   4. Acceptance of other people (patient, tolerates shortcomings . . .)
   5. Tolerance of new information (considers new points of view . . .)
   6. Self-confidence
   7. Comfort (relaxed, at ease . . .)
   8. Insight into self and role (better adjusted to job, etc.)

C. Global Judgments (all other: includes gross characterological references, references to consequences of changes, etc.)

DESCRIPTION.   The following open-end question is reacted to in writing
by subjects:

> Over a period of time, people may change in the ways that they work
> with other people. Since _____ [month of workshop or training ex-
> perience being evaluated], do you feel you have changed your behavior
> in working with people in any specific ways, as compared with the
> previous _____ [year, academic year, or other meaningful period]?
>   Yes_____.   No_____.

If yes, please describe:

A parallel form of the instrument is reacted to by a total of five or six
"describers," persons who associate with the subject, ordinarily in job
settings. They are asked, ". . . has he changed his behavior. . . ."

ADMINISTRATION AND SCORING.   This query is sent by mail to persons
having participated in the training or treatment experience to be
evaluated, as well as to members of any control groups being used.

Each subject is also asked to nominate eight to ten persons with
whom he is in regular working contact on the job, and who are in a
position to comment on his behavior. The subject is informed that the
research team will randomly select five or six associates as describers
and solicit their participation. The subject thus does not know who precisely describes his behavior, nor does he have responsibility for inducing describers to agree to participate.

The instrument is self-administering, and probably takes less than
five minutes for most subjects to complete.

In the Miles scoring scheme,* each separate change reported is given
one point, and verified changes—those listed both by the subject and
one of his describers, or by at least two describers—receive an additional point. Non-socially desirable changes are similarly scored and
given a minus sign (ordinarily, negative changes form less than 5%
of the total). Total score is the sum of all points.

In the Bunker–Knowles scoring scheme, changes are coded into the
17 categories (and indicated as positive or negative). A total score is
computed for the "self" descriptions, and another for the total number
of discrete changes mentioned by describers. A more conservative
verified change score is the number of changes in which two or more
describers concur (concurrence means placement in the same cate-

---

* This scoring scheme can be obtained by ordering document NAPS
01881, from MICROFICHE PUBLICATIONS, Division of Microfiche Systems Corporation, 305 East 46th Street, New York, New York 10017, remitting $2.00 for a microfiche, or $5.00 for a photocopy.

gory). (An additional self-describer agreement score can be derived: the number of self-reported changes which are confirmed by at least one describer.)

DEVELOPMENT.   This method of retrospective change measure using job associates' reports was originally developed by Buchanan (1957a, 1957b), for evaluating supervisory training. Miles (1965) created the present measure in a study of 34 elementary school principals, plus two control groups of $N = 29$ and 148, and produced a preliminary scoring manual. Bunker (1965) and Bunker and Knowles (1967) inductively developed the content-analytic categories, on a sample of 346 persons attending six training laboratories. After coder reliability checks, the scheme was revised to its present form.

Moscow (1969) translated the Bunker scheme and coding manual into Dutch, and found in a study of 52 T-group participants and 31 controls that categories B1 and B3 should be collapsed because of coder unreliability.

CRITIQUE.   No *test–retest reliability* data are available on the responses themselves. *Coder reliability* (agreement) was achieved at or beyond the 90% level by Bunker (1965) on his revised scheme; Moscow (1969) obtained 88% agreement on the unitizing of changes, and 82% on the assignment of changes to categories. Coder stability over time (unspecified) was found by Moscow to be 86%; Bunker found 90% stability in coding after an eighteen-month interval.

Content validity seems well established. Miles (1965) in an eight-month follow-up found that 73% of those principals attending a training laboratory showed change over a "base rate" of 2, using his scheme; only 17% and 29% of control groups did so. Bunker in an eight-to-ten-month follow-up (1965) found that 11 of the 17 categories in his scheme differentiated experimental from control subjects in his study of 346 training laboratory participants. The categories of "Communication Sending," "Risk-Taking," "Functional Flexibility," and "Self-Confidence" failed to do so. Valiquet (1968), however, found experimental/control differences in only eight categories, and keys this to a different emphasis in the programs being studied. Bunker and Knowles (1967) found that those exposed to three-week training laboratories had change scores significantly higher ($p < .05$) than those attending two-week laboratories.

Moscow (1969) found significant experimental/control differences as well, both for total describer changes ($p < .04$), and for the verified-change measure ($p < .06$). Fifty per cent of experimentals showed at least one verified change; 33% and 37% of control groups did so. The corresponding figures in Bunker (1965) are 67% and 30%; in Valiquet (1968) 73% and 20%; in Bunker and Knowles (1967) 77%, 58%, and 31%.

It can be argued that describers of persons attending a training laboratory will be biased, and thereby inflate their estimates of change. For this reason, the verified-change score is probably preferable as a more conservative estimate. Miles presents some predictive validity evidence to offset this concern, however: ratings by trainers of members' over-all gain as a result of the laboratory correlated .55 ($p < .01$) with the total perceived-change score eight months after the laboratory. Bunker (1965) reports an *r* of .32 with a peer-rating measure made during the laboratory. Moscow (1969) controlled for describer bias by using as controls subjects who had attended a non-T-group course on human relations; he did find significant experimental/control differences.

In any case, it is clear that the instrument should never be used without accompanying control group data to establish reasonable base rates of perceived change in untreated populations. Some illustrative data showing mean amounts of change are:

	Experimental	*Controls*
Miles, 1965		
(total score)°	4.4	1.2, 1.7
Bunker and Knowles, 1967		
describer total	9.14, 7.38	4.01
verified change	1.58, 1.11	.40
Moscow, 1969		
describer total	6.52	4.0, 4.25
verified change	.81	.37, .33

° Only Miles gives standard deviations; these are 3.9, 1.4, and 2.10 respectively, so the distributions are rather skewed.

It is possible that scores are influenced by the number of describers returning data; Miles, however (1965) found that number of describers correlated only .17 with total score in an *N* of 34.

No *norms* as such are available; however, the means of obtained scores are reported by Miles (1965). Bunker and Knowles (1967) and Moscow (1969) also report distributions. These data are all for adult normals, mostly from professional occupations; no data are available for populations seeking therapeutic help.

The instrument is simple, easy to administer and score. Return rates of 61% to 100% for "self" responses and 76% to 88% for describers were obtained by Miles; Moscow (1969) reports rates of 62% to 75%

for selves and 71% to 84% for describers; Bunker and Knowles report 64% to 74% for selves and 84% for describers; Valiquet (1968) obtained 58% to 65% for selves and "over 50%" for describers.

GENERAL COMMENT. The instrument is clearly sensitive to the general impact of human relations training experiences, when aggregated data are examined. The range of scores is narrow enough, however, that using them as measures of an *individual's* gain (except perhaps in a trichotomy of no change, some change, marked change) is clearly inappropriate. In addition, experimentation with the instrument in therapeutic settings is clearly desirable.

REFERENCES

Buchanan, P. C. Evaluating the results of supervisory training. *Personnel,* 1957(a), 33, 362–370.

Buchanan, P. C. Testing the validity of an evaluation program. *Personnel,* 1957(b), 34, 78–81.

Bunker, D. Individual applications of laboratory training. *Journal of Applied Behavioral Science,* 1965, 1, 131–148.

Bunker, D. and Knowles, E. Comparison of behavioral changes resulting from human relations training laboratories of different lengths. *Journal of Applied Behavioral Science,* 1967, 3, 505–523.

Miles, M. B. Changes during and following laboratory training: a clinical-experimental study. *Journal of Applied Behavioral Science,* 1965, 1, 215–242.

Moscow, D. T-group training in the Netherlands: an evaluation and cross-cultural comparison. *Mens en Onderneming,* 1969, 23, 345–362. Also in *Journal of Applied Behavioral Science,* 1971, 7(4), 427–448.

Valiquet, M. I. Individual change in a management development program. *Journal of Applied Behavioral Science,* 1968, 4, 313–325.

UNITERMS. Acceptance; awareness; behavior; change; communication; comfort; content analysis; flexibility; group; human relations training; insight; interpersonal; interdependence; job; risk-taking; self-confidence; self-control; sensitivity; T-group; tolerance; work.

—M. B. M.

51
Organizational Behavior Describer Survey (OBDS)

AUTHORS.   Roger Harrison and Barry I. Oshry

AVAILABILITY.   Dr. Roger Harrison, 35 Abingdon Court, Abingdon Villas, London W.8, 6 BT, England

VARIABLES.   The Organizational Behavior Describer Survey taps four dimensions of *interpersonal and group behavior* of managers and administrators, both line and staff: *Rational-Technical Competence,* a command of the intellectual and technical "know-how" required by one's position in the organization; *Verbal Dominance,* the exercise of ability to express oneself effectively; *Emotional Expressiveness,* voluntary or involuntary manifestation of feelings and emotions; and *Consideration,* the conscious attempt to give support and encouragement to the efforts of others in the organization.

DESCRIPTION.   The OBDS is a 25-item Likert-scaled inventory. The Rational-Technical Competence and the Verbal Dominance scales contain six items each; Emotional Expressiveness, five; Consideration, eight. An example from each scale follows:

He thinks quickly. (R-T)

He talks in a way that others listen to. (VD)

You can tell quickly when he likes or dislikes what others do or say. (EE)

He is tolerant and accepting of other people's feelings. (C)

Except for Emotional Effectiveness, the response choices are: Always; Almost always; Usually; Sometimes; Seldom. For Emotional Effectiveness the choices are: Always; Usually; Sometimes; Seldom; Never. The difference is to compensate for "ceiling effect."

ADMINISTRATION AND SCORING.   The OBDS is self-administering in about fifteen minutes. Scale scores are simple item-score sums within each scale.

DEVELOPMENT.   The OBDS was originally built using Argyris' (1962) two-factor theory of interpersonal behavior in organizations, Rational-Technical Competence and Interpersonal Competence. The first form of the OBDS contained 20 items, 10 for each of Argyris' factors. A factor analysis of the responses of 321 middle-level managers in a technical manufacturing concern produced three, not two, factors. In addition to the sought Rational-Technical Competence (24% of the variance) and Interpersonal Competence (22%), a factor titled Emotional Expressiveness emerged to account for 11% of total variance. The authors interpreted this as indicating an important distinction between receptivity to others' ideas and feelings, and expression of one's own ideas and feelings. These three scales were correlated with Fleishman's Supervisory Behavior Questionnaire, which also delineates two factors, Initiating Structure and Consideration (cf. Hemphill and Coons' Leader Behavior Description Questionnaire, reviewed in this book). The OBDS Interpersonal Competence scale had a median *r* of .62 with Fleishman's Consideration scale; the Rational-Technical and Emotional Expressiveness scales had a median *r* of .47 with Fleishman's Initiating Structure. In addition, the OBDS Emotional Expressiveness scale did not correlate with Fleishman's Consideration, and its correlations with its sister Interpersonal Competence scale was lower than that with the Rational-Technical scale.

From these results, a 36-item form was constructed and tested on a sample of 189 subordinates of middle-level managers. The same factor structure resulted. The current, 25-item, form retains the three factors, plus the Verbal Dominance items.

CRITIQUE.   The corrected Spearman–Brown split-half *reliabilities* of the scales are: Rational-Technical Competence, .83; Verbal Dominance, .84; Consideration, .92; and Emotional Expressiveness, .89. These *r*s are based on four samples with a median *N* of 80. The authors have not done conventional test–retest studies, but they have tested 11 samples with a median *N* of 49 before and after T-group experience. The *r*s for the four scales are .73, .71, .70, and .70, respectively, but one cannot say whether, in fact, these numbers were lowered from the mid .80s by the T-group process.

The largest scale intercorrelations are Rational-Technical Competence with Verbal Dominance (.69) and with Consideration (.36), and Consideration with Emotional Expressiveness (−.29).

A study of *interdescriber reliability* was, in the authors' words, "not very encouraging." Median correlations of the same person by self, superior, and subordinate were .14, .20, .14, and .30 for the four scales. The conclusion of the authors seems sound: "The data suggest, rather, that there is in fact considerable inconsistency in personal style, depending on some combination of the perceptual idiosyncracies of the observer and the behavior-determining role relationships between the observer and the individual described." Same-role (subordinate) correlations were not much better, however. For two samples for each scale the *r*s ranged from .15 to .56, with a median of .40.

The chief *validity* study of the OBDS consisted of comparing OBDS scores by self, supervisors, subordinates, and peers before T-group experience with post T-group participant (peer) ratings on ten variables: *Control* ("He has worked hard to influence others towards his point of view"); *Dependence* ("He has usually been willing to go along with what others want to do"); *Fight* ("He has been willing to disagree with or criticize others' ideas of actions"); *Support* ("He has been warm and supportive toward other members"); *Effectiveness* ("His overall effectiveness as a member has contributed significantly to the group's progress"); *Involvement* ("He has seemed interested and involved in the group's activities"); *Experimentation* ("He has been willing to consider and try out new ideas and ways of doing things"); *Understanding* ("He has helped clarify and make more understandable to others the events and processes in the group"); *Receptivity to Feedback* ("He has seemed to understand and learn from the reactions of others to his ideas and actions in the group"); and *Increased Effectiveness* ("As time has gone on, his overall effectiveness as a group member has increased"). Subjects were drawn from a population including YMCA and research and development managers.

Depending on the scales involved, from 8 to 17 samples with N's from 64 to 170 were available. The distribution of *r*s (one for each sample) was tested for a significant difference from zero, and the mean of *r*s for the sample was computed. The results are not striking. Examining findings at the .05 level or better, Verbal Dominance shows mean correlations of .22 with ratings of Control, .22 with Fight, and .15 with Effectiveness. Consideration correlates .22 with Support ratings, −.11 with Fight, .15 with Dependence, .11 with Experimenting, .06 with Receptivity to Feedback, and .10 with Increased Effectiveness. Emotional Expressiveness correlates .19 with Dependence, .20 with Fight, .10 with Control, and −.06 with Receptivity to Feedback. Rational-Technical Competence correlates .09 with Control, .11 with Fight, and .10 with Effectiveness. These mean correlations, even though they are depressed by the low relationship between the views of different samples (peers, self, superiors, and subordinates) are not encouraging.

For *norms* Harrison and Oshry (undated) include means and standard deviations along each scale for ratings of self, subordinates, and supervisors by T-group participants ($Ns = 74$ to 127), managers in a research and development company ($Ns = 51$ to 89), and YMCA managers ($Ns = 64$ to 170).

The authors do not discuss either *social desirability* or *acquiescence* effects. Since they have noted ratings to be susceptible to role expectations, and since all the items in the OBDS are worded as positive traits, both these response sets seem distinctly likely.

GENERAL COMMENT.   Scale reliability is reasonably good, and the OBDS is easy to administer and score. Harrison and Oshry's findings of the independent and often counterposed nature of receptivity to others versus expression of self is an important one, as is their general finding that T-group experience is more likely, in their words, to *unfreeze* behavior, rather than permanently change it, particularly after only one period of training. One hopes that they will investigate further the differential ratings provided by self, superiors, subordinates, and peers as, perhaps, a function of organizational structure, and also ferret out any response-set effects. In the meanwhile, the Organizational Behavior Describer Survey is substantial enough to recommend itself for experimentation, provided the present validity weaknesses are kept in mind.

REFERENCES

Argyris, C. *Interpersonal competence and organizational effectiveness.* New York: Wiley, 1962.

Harrison, R. and Oshry, B. I. The impact of laboratory training on organizational behavior: methodology and results. Unpublished paper, undated.

UNITERMS.   Activity; competence; control; consideration; dependence; dominance; effectiveness; expressiveness; fight; human relations training; organization; peer; role; subordinate; superior; support; T-group.

—R. B. E.
—M. B. M.

52

Organizational Climate Description Questionnaire (OCDQ)

AUTHORS.   Andrew W. Halpin and Don B. Croft

AVAILABILITY.   Don B. Croft, Director, Claude C. Dove Learning Center, College of Education, New Mexico State University, Box 3 AC, Las Cruces, New Mexico 88001. Also in Halpin, A. W. and Croft, D. B. *The organizational climate of schools.* Chicago: Midwest Administration Center, University of Chicago, 1963.

VARIABLES.   This instrument was designed to measure the *organizational climate* of elementary schools, though some data (Andrews, 1965) suggest it may be usable in secondary schools as well. "Climate" is defined loosely as an organization property analogous to personality. Broadly speaking, the instrument focuses on perceived social interaction between the principal and teachers, and among teachers. It is based on the assumption that a "desirable organization climate is one in which it is possible for leadership acts to emerge easily, from whatever source." Eight subscales are included; the first four refer to teachers' behavior primarily, and the last four to the principal's. *Disengagement:* the teachers' tendency to be "not with it"; corresponds to Durkheim's notion of anomie; *Hindrance:* teachers' perception that principal is burdening them with bureaucratic detail; *Esprit:* morale, implying social need satisfaction and job accomplishment; *Intimacy:* positive socio-emotional relations among the teachers; *Aloofness:* formal, impersonal, universalistic, nomothetic behavior by principal; *Production Emphasis:* close, directive supervision, with minimal influence accepted from teachers; *Thrust:* active task-oriented behavior of principal in setting example for teachers; and *Consideration:* principal's tendency to treat teachers "humanly."

Scores on these eight variables can be plotted as a profile. Six "climate profiles," along an "authenticity" continuum from openness/ functional flexibility on one end to closedness/rigidity on the other, are proposed: a. Open; b. Autonomous; c. Controlled; d. Familiar; e. Paternal; and f. Closed.

DESCRIPTION.   The instrument contains 64 items, like these:

Teachers volunteer for extra tasks.
The principal keeps his door closed.

For each item, S chooses a response from these alternatives: rarely occurs; sometimes occurs; often occurs; very frequently occurs.

ADMINISTRATION AND SCORING.   Respondents (teachers) work on a question booklet. The instrument is self-administering, and takes about twenty minutes. Scoring services are provided by Croft (see Availability address). Scoring output includes raw subtest scores for each subject, double standardized subtest scores for each subject, mean subtest scores for the school building, and climate difference scores showing how far the obtained climate differs from each of the six climate types. Distributions of the perceived climate types in each building, and a general openness score are also reported.

DEVELOPMENT.   The monograph by Halpin and Croft (1963) is unusually thorough in its description of developmental procedures followed. A pool of about 1,000 items was developed from analysis of critical incidents, interviews, the Leader Behavior Description Questionnaire, and the Hemphill Group Descriptions Questionnaire. An effort was made to locate items bearing on 1) task and socio-emotional orientation; 2) social control and social need-satisfaction, by both leader and group; and 3) leader behavior, group behavior, procedural regulation, and personality orientation. These items were screened to 600, and administered in four 150-item forms to 284 teachers in 17 schools, and further reduced to 160 items.

The final 8 subtests emerged from cluster analysis of responses from 91 teachers to the 160-item form, which was thereby reduced to 80 items, thence to 64 by cluster and content analyses. The subtests proved moderately independent (median subtest intercorrelation is .17). A factor analysis of the subtest scores suggested that a 3-factor solution was optimal, covering 62% of the variance. The factors were labeled Social Needs, Esprit, and Social Control.

Profiles were constructed via double-standardized subtest scores and factor-analyzed. The three *profile* factors emerging were labeled "authenticity" (openness of leader and member behavior), satisfaction (of task and socio-emotional needs), and leadership initiation (by leader and members). It appears (Halpin and Croft, 1963; Andrews, 1965) that the Esprit subtest is most crucial in ordering the six profiles along the presumed "open–closed" continuum.

CRITIQUE.   No *test–retest reliability* data are presented. Subtest split-half *reliabilities* range from .26 to .84, with median at .64. Odd versus even respondent subtest correlations range from .49 to .76, median .63. Communality estimates from the 3-factor solution range from .44 to

.68, median .65. No reliability estimates are available for the profile similarity scores.

Andrews (1965) concludes that the subtests of the OCDQ have good *construct validity,* but criticizes the "climate" scores; Brown (1965) criticizes the notion of specific climates, though a climate "continuum" similar to the Halpin–Croft one was found in his study. McFadden (1966), in a study of 30 schools, did not find the prototypic profiles reported by Halpin and Croft. Furthermore, there was no significant agreement between non-participant observers who (reliably) rated schools using the OCDQ and teacher responses from these schools, suggesting more validity problems. However, Ford (1966) found that schools with principals defined as psychologically healthy (high scores on Shostrom's Personal Orientation Inventory (which see) tended to have higher scores on Thrust and Consideration, and lower scores on Hindrance. Open-climate schools had principals with more self-acceptance, more acceptance of own aggressiveness, and greater capacity for intimate contact than principals in closed-climate schools.

In addition, Hughes (1968) did find that a sample of 11 high-innovative schools in Ohio was more similar to the open climate than to the closed. Low-innovative schools ($N = 13$) were more like the closed climate. The subscales differentiating high-innovative from low-innovative schools were Disengagement, Esprit, and Thrust (the latter at .10 level only).

Thus the validity evidence for the climate scores is somewhat supportive, but a good deal of ambiguity about their interpretation does remain.

Halpin (personal communication) reports that urban schools repeatedly show climate scores more on the closed end than do non-urban schools; it is not clear whether this is a function of size, presence of low-SES groups, or increased bureaucratization. Tremko (1969), in a study of 36 schools, found that the Open and Autonomous climates were more frequent in schools in middle-class socio-economic settings; Paternal and Closed climates were more frequent in schools in lower-class SES settings.

Some *concurrent validity* evidence is provided by Thomas (1970), who discovered that a human relations laboratory training program for principals appeared to cause shifts in their teachers' OCDQ responses toward more open climates; in addition principals were seen as improving on the Gross–Herriot Executive Professional Leadership (EPL) measure, and on the Miles–Bunker–Knowles Open-End Perceived Change measure (which see).

Anderson (1964) and Plaxton (1965) related OCDQ scores to personality variables (Cattell 16 PF and Vernon–Allport–Lindzey Study of Values; Myers–Briggs Type Indicator) with some success. Nicholas, Virjo, and Wattenberg (1965) found that "closed" and "less closed" schools differed in the kind of problem parents brought to the principal. Andrews (1965) discovered that the Intimacy subtest was most closely related to school achievement ($r = .29$). Steinhoff (1965) found that the factor structure of the OCDQ was "essentially similar" to that of Stern's College Characteristics Index, and that the OCDQ "was able to make fine distinctions between levels of the organization and between individual schools, thereby attesting to the validity of the instrument." Schmidt (1965) found plausible relationships between the OCDQ subtests and the Leader Behavior Descriptions Questionnaire (except for Consideration). For other studies using the OCDQ, see the review by Brown and House (1967).

The standard scoring and the profile similarity scores were, as of late 1970, still based on a six-state sample of 1,151 teachers in 71 schools. Work is currently under way to provide new norms based on a respondent pool of about 200,000. These will be welcome. Brown (1965), in 81 schools, found a 4-factor solution to be a better fit to the data, and identified eight rather than six climate types. This emphasizes the need for additional *norm* data.

The directions are clear and easy to follow. The items are clearly stated, and probably interesting to respondents. However, no attempt has been made to examine the *response set* problems of the instrument or the *social desirability* and *fakeability* problems inherent in such straight-forward items as "teachers at this school show much school spirit" and "teachers ask nonsensical questions in faculty meetings."

GENERAL COMMENT.   The instrument is thoughtfully developed, and represents a good blend of underlying conceptualization and empirical winnowing of items. It should not be used to make predictions about individuals, but seems quite workable for examining the proposed dimensions of climate at the level of the school building. The climate profiles as such are of uncertain value; their labels are quite far removed from the original item responses.

REFERENCES

Anderson, D. P. *Organizational climate of elementary schools.* Minneapolis: Educational Research and Development Council of the Twin Cities Metropolitan Area, University of Minnesota, 1964.

Andrews, J. H. M. School organizational climate: some validity studies. *Canadian Education and Research Digest,* 1965, 5, 317–334.

Brown, R. J. Identifying and classifying organizational climates in Twin

Cities area elementary schools. Paper read at American Educational Research Association meetings, 1965.

Brown, A. F., and House, J. J. The organizational component in education. *Review of Educational Research,* 1967, 37, 4, 399–416.

Ford, R. W. The relationship of psychological health of elementary school principals to the organizational climate of schools. Ed.D. dissertation, Syracuse University, 1966.

Halpin, A. W., and Croft, D. B. The *organizational climate of schools.* Chicago: Midwest Administration Center, University of Chicago, 1963.

Hughes, L. W. "Organizational climate"—another dimension to the process of innovation? *Educational Administration Quarterly,* 1968, 4 (3), 16–28.

McFadden, E. C. The non-participant observer and organizational climate. Ed.D. dissertation, Stanford University, 1966.

Nicholas, L. E., Virjo, H. E., and Wattenberg, W. W. *Effect of socioeconomic setting and organizational climate on problems brought to elementary school offices.* Detroit: College of Education, Wayne State University, 1965.

Plaxton, R. P. Relationships between principals' personality and the organizational climate of their schools. Edmonton, Alberta: University of Alberta, Unpublished Master's thesis, 1965.

Schmidt, W. G. Relationships between certain aspects of teacher behavior and organizational climate. Edmonton, Alberta: University of Alberta, Unpublished Master's thesis, 1965.

Steinhoff, C. R. Organizational climate in a public school system. Syracuse: Project S-083, Office of Education, U.S. Department of Health, Education and Welfare, Syracuse University, 1965.

Thomas, T. A. *Changes in elementary school principals as a result of laboratory training.* Eugene, Oregon: Center for the Advanced Study of Educational Administration, 1970.

Tremko, M. S. A study of school climate, socio-economic setting and in-service programs. Ed.D. dissertation, University of Illinois, 1969.

UNITERMS.   Activity; administration; aloofness; anomie; authenticity; autonomy; behavior; climate; consideration; control; esprit; initiating structure; intimacy; leadership; management; morale; openness; organization; peer; principal; school; socio-emotional; structure; superior; supervision; task; teacher; work.

—D. G. L.
—M. B. M.

53
Organizational Control Questionnaire

AUTHOR.   Arnold S. Tannenbaum

AVAILABILITY.   Arnold S. Tannenbaum, Survey Research Center, University of Michigan, Ann Arbor, Michigan 48106

VARIABLES.   Tannenbaum's Organizational Control Questionnaire produces a "control graph" which depicts two aspects of *organizational control*: the *Hierarchical Distribution of Control*, represented by the shape or slope of the curve; and the *Total Amount of Control* exercised by all levels in the organization, represented by the average height of the curve. Four curve configurations are distinguished: autocratic, where the amount of control increases with hierarchical ascent; democratic, where the amount of control decreases with hierarchical ascent; laissez-faire, where the amount of control remains relatively constant and low throughout the hierarchy; and polyarchic, where the amount of control remains relatively constant and high throughout the hierarchy. Organizations can be graphed for actual or ideal control, as well as active or passive control.

DESCRIPTION.   The questionnaire consists of four sets of questions, each set addressing itself to actual, ideal, active, or passive control. Within each set a Likert-type item asked something like the following:

> In general, how much influence or say do you feel each of the following groups has on what goes on in your department (or at your level)?

The groups listed are the relevant ranks in the hierarchy, such as president, executive board, plant manager, shop steward, membership, etc.

Responses are scaled from 1 through 5, with 1 representing "little or no influence" and 5 indicating "a very great deal of influence." The simulated item given above measures actual passive control. Items are rephrased to elicit the other types of control.

The control graph orders the levels of hierarchy along the abscissa, with the highest level nearest the origin, and the degree of control along the positive ordinate. Thus, the "democratic" curve is characterized by a positive slope, the "autocratic" by a negative slope.

ADMINISTRATION AND SCORING.   The questionnaire is self-administering and should require no more than twenty minutes for all control types and all hierarchical levels. For all respondents at a given level, scores for each level are averaged. These means are plotted on the graph; the points are connected with straight lines.

DEVELOPMENT.   Apart from expanding to the areas of passive and ideal control, the control graph and its questionnaire have undergone little change since Tannenbaum first employed them in a study of four unions in the Michigan area in 1956.

CRITIQUE.   The *reliability* of the questionnaire items is varied. Tannenbaum's (1961) study of the League of Women Voters showed correlations between the judgments of rank-and-file members and of local board members regarding the control exercised by the local president of .50; regarding the control exercised by the board of .18; and regarding the control exercised by the membership of .25. Smith and Ari (1964) found split-half reliabilities of .67 for within-level passive control, and .84 for total control across three levels of "plants" in a nationwide delivery service organization. The influence of managers upon supervisory personnel had a split-half reliability of .54. For the influence of managers upon the rank-and-file itself the figure was .53. No test–retest data are available.

As to *construct validity*, Tannenbaum (1961) found that for actual control within Leagues of Women Voters the degree of positive slope of the control curve (its "democracy") correlated with members' judgments of League effectiveness at .31 and with board members' judgments at .19. Total amount of control correlated with these two estimates of effectiveness at .29 and .25, respectively (all four correlations significant beyond the .05 level). The multiple correlation with effectiveness, using both positive slope and total control, was .42. Positive slope and total control are also related to member loyalty at .26 and .23 respectively ($p < .05$) in the League study, and to employee morale at .55 and .72 ($p < .01$) in the national delivery service study.

Positive slope and total control are not independent measures; they intercorrelate at —.67.

In constructing his graphs, Tannenbaum notes that in placing the levels of hierarchy and the control scores on the coordinates he has assumed equal scale distances between points. In the case of the placement of the hierarchical levels, this assumption is wholly unjustifiable and a bit dangerous. Also, the intervals in the amount of control scale should have been tested for equality. In the face of uncertainty, such assumptions are parsimonious, but they debilitate the concept of the slope as a measure meaningful in itself.

One *caveat*, which Tannenbaum recognizes, is that he may be measuring perceived control, not actual control. It seems plausible to argue that it is precisely and *only* perceived control that he is measuring.

Two additional handicaps: some hierarchical levels the user may wish to examine contain too few subjects for their responses to be reliable or stable. No norms are available; Baum and Sorenson's (1966) work suggests that from level to level responses are widely varied in distribution across amount of control exercised.

GENERAL COMMENT.   The Organizational Control Questionnaire and its offspring control graph have the advantage of being quite easy to adapt, administer, and score. Tannenbaum's idea is so straightforward that a user can develop his own test without recourse to the author's work. The scaling assumptions are very shaky, but some validity appears to attend the result. Little work has been done to develop the autocratic, polyarchic, and laissez-faire models. In sum, it is a modest graphic technique easily used and containing possibilities for improved utility.

REFERENCES

Baum, B. H. and Sorenson, P. F., Jr. Influence relationships as administrative organizational data. *Journal of Risk Insurance,* 1966, *31,* 63–71.

Smith, C. G. and Ari, O. N. Organizational control structure and member consensus. *American Journal of Sociology,* 1964, *59,* 623–638.

Smith, C. G. and Tannenbaum, A. S. Organizational control structure: a comparative analysis. *Human Relations,* 1963, *16,* 299–316.

Tannenbaum, A. S. Control and effectiveness in a voluntary organization. *American Journal of Sociology,* 1961, *67,* 33–46.

UNITERMS.   Autocracy; control; democracy; graph; influence; laissez-faire; management; organization; participative; polyarchy; power.

—R. B. E.

54
Orientation Inventory (Ori)

AUTHOR.   Bernard M. Bass

AVAILABILITY.   Consulting Psychologists Press, Inc., 577 College Avenue, Palo Alto, California 94306

VARIABLES.   The Orientation Inventory was constructed to measure three *orientations toward social behavior: Self-Orientation,* characteristic of a person who is more concerned about his own needs than those of others, more interested in intrinsic reward than intrinsic satisfactions of work; *Interaction-Orientation,* characteristic of a person who is consistently concerned with the group as a means for forming friendships, sharing things with others, providing security of belonging, and helping foster strong interpersonal relationships; and *Task-Orientation,* characteristic of a person who will try hardest to obtain the group's goals, solve its problems, overcome barriers preventing the successful completion of the group's tasks, and persist on assignments.

DESCRIPTION.   The Ori contains 27 forced-choice items which make up three ipsative scales. The items are stated in alternative-completion form with three alternatives, one for each of the scales. A sample item is:

I like: (A) Personal praise. (B) Cooperative effort. (C) Wisdom.

ADMINISTRATION AND SCORING.   The Ori is self-administering within twenty minutes. The examiner, however, should make sure that all items are completed. The respondent indicates his most preferred and least preferred alternatives. A most preferred alternative is scored 2; an unmarked alternative, 1; a least preferred, 0. An omitted item, therefore, results in a score of 1 being added to each scale score, narrowing the respondent's score on each scale. The manual contains T scores and centile scores for 523 male and 385 female college students from the South, Midwest, and Far West.

DEVELOPMENT.   The original items were constructed to provide three alternative completions, one of the alternatives presumably being acceptable to each orientation. After three independent internal-consistency item analyses, the 27 final items showed odd–even reliability estimates of .50 for Self-Orientation, .70 for Interaction-Orientation, and .64 for Task-Orientation ($N = 100$ college students). Bass et al. (1963) "guessed that the scales were not factorially pure" and that, therefore, "internal consistency estimates would be underestimates of the true reliability." They argued that *test–retest* reliabilities are a better measure of reliability. These figures are reported immediately below.

CRITIQUE.   The instrument's *reliability* is marginal, as might be expected of such a short test. For 84 college students, one-week test–retest correlations are: Self-Orientation, .73; Interaction-Orientation, .76; and Task-Orientation, .75. Stritch (1964), however, found test–retests of .63, .35, and .40, for 100 students after one-to-five day intervals; for a one-year interval ($N = 30$) Stritch (1964) found *r*s of .60, .35, and .40.

Research completed with the Ori shows promising *concurrent validity*. Bass (1967) describes research which shows that "as experimental Ss, task-oriented Ss are most likely to volunteer. Self-oriented Ss require pay. Interaction-oriented Ss prefer to work in a group; self-oriented Ss prefer to work alone. . . . Automobile buying behavior depends on orientation. For instance, self-oriented persons are more likely to buy bigger, more expensive cars. . . . With a few interesting exceptions, in small groups and large organizations, the task-oriented person is up-graded by observers, peers, and superiors."

Construct validity, however, is modest at best. Bass (1962) reports that Self-Orientation correlates significantly with such Cattell 16 P.F. scales as Aggressive-Competitive (.28), Immature-Unstable (.24), and Insecure (.19). Interaction-Orientation correlates significantly with the 16 P.F. scales Social Group Dependence (.28) and Warm-Sociable (.19). Task-Orientation correlates significantly with the Cattell scales Self-Sufficient, Resourceful (.33), and Controlled Will Power (.31). Although significant, these correlations are small in magnitude. Clearly some relations exist, but they are not strong enough to establish construct validity for the Ori.

Although Bass (1967) reports research with the Ori covering widely disparate groups, from an American team assaulting Mt. Everest to managers of English football teams, the only *norms* are those in the manual reported above. Both the manual and the review article are filled with brief glimpses of group means on the three scales, but only three of these include standard deviations as well.

The Ori is susceptible to *faking* and *social desirability* response sets. Bass (1962) got 82 seniors and graduate students to raise their mean Task-Orientation score 2.5 points, raise their mean Interaction-Orientation score 3.4 points, and lower their mean Self-Orientation score by 5.7 points while "faking good." With five samples of college students, Braun and Dube (1965) got lowered Self-Orientation (four to eight points) from all samples, whether ordered to fake an ideally adjusted person or make the best possible impression. Depending on which instructions they adopted, the samples raised or lowered Interaction-Orientation scores by from one to eight points, and four of them raised Task-Orientation by from four to ten points. The fifth sample dropped it by three points.

GENERAL COMMENT.   Bass has taken a theoretically simple model which suggests that persons may orient themselves towards others in quite consistent ways. He has suggested three and translated them into instrument form. The shortness of the resulting instrument makes it useful for a quick assessment of large groups of individuals, but its lack of reliability makes it inadequate for individual diagnosis. The Orientation Inventory holds much promise for research on group composition.

REFERENCES

Bass, B. M. *The Orientation Inventory: manual (research edition)*. Palo Alto: Consulting Psychologists Press, Inc., 1962.

Bass, B. M. Social behavior and the Orientation Inventory: a review. *Psychological Bulletin*, 1967, 68, 260–292.

Bass, B. M., Dunteman, G. H., Frye, R., Vidulich, R., and Wambach, H. Self-, interaction-, and task-orientation inventory scores associated with overt behavior and personality factors. *Educational and Psychological Measurement*, 1963, 23, 101–116.

Braun, J. R., and Dube, C. S. Faking studies with the Orientation Inventory. *Journal of Psychology*, 1965, 59, 207–210.

Stritch, T. M. Influence of orientation upon attitudes and performance. Hattiesburg: Final report, Project No. 896, Office of Vocational Rehabilitation, University of Southern Mississippi, 1964.

UNITERMS.   Achievement; affiliation; competence; interaction; occupation; orientation; self; task.

                         —R. B. E.

55
Palo Alto Group Psychotherapy Scale

AUTHOR.   Ben C. Finney

AVAILABILITY.   Ben C. Finney, Veterans Administration Hospital, 190 Heather Lane, Palo Alto, California 94305

VARIABLES.   The Palo Alto Group Psychotherapy Scale provides a measure of the *adequacy of interpersonal relations,* defined by the author as "the capacity of the individual to form intimate and personal relationships without anxiety and tension, relationships which are satisfactory and rewarding both to the individual and to the other party." The instrument is intended for use with patients undergoing group therapy.

DESCRIPTION.   The scale is an 88-item true–false inventory, with a "Don't know" response permitted. The items are brief descriptions of behaviors likely to occur in group therapy, such as (simulated):

> Spoke directly to another person, using his name.
> Talked on a subject of interest only to himself.
> Never admitted an error on his part.
> Never spoke unless encouraged to do so.

ADMINISTRATION AND SCORING.   Observers check each item according to whether it is true of the patient. Positive responses are underlined on the scoring form; a patient's score is computed by subtracting the number of "Don't know" responses from 88 and dividing the total of underlined responses by the resulting number. Scores are thus percentages of the total possible (for that patient) positive responses. The form appears to require about fifteen minutes to complete and score.

DEVELOPMENT.   It was decided that items would be selected empirically (from therapy notes on about 100 patients by approximately 30 leaders), rather than be generated according to a pre-formulated theory of interpersonal relationships. These items were reviewed by 15 therapists in the group therapy program on the maximum security ward at Palo Alto VA Hospital. The items they selected were scored on each of 41 patients on a maximum security ward by two to four observers. The final score for each patient on a given item was what the majority of the observers recorded. Each of the 15 judges then divided the patients which he knew into those that had "good" interpersonal relationships and those that had "poor" relationships. Then the data for each item were entered in a 2 ×2 table ("good" and "poor" patients versus "true" or "false"); using *chi*-square, 99 items were found which discriminated at the .001 level.

These 99 items were tried out clinically on several groups, and 40 new items were written to meet the deficiencies which appeared with the practical use of the scale. A new form of the scale was scored on 128 patients by 15 leaders who conducted 18 groups in the hospital. Eighty-eight items were found which discriminated among the three groups (upper one third of patients in the hospital in group therapy, middle third, bottom third) at the .01 level, 62 of these being items which had discriminated in the first item selection procedure.

CRITIQUE.   Scoring *reliability* is high, with both leader versus student nurse and student nurse versus student nurse intercorrelations being $r = .90$.

One indication of the *validity* of the scale is the rank-order correlation ($rho = .84$) between scale scores and group leaders' rankings of the same 128 patients. Finney points out, however, that in the absence of a demonstrated normality in the distributions, the non-parametric statistic *tau* might be considered more appropriate. The average *tau* was .67. Another study of 20 patients, each ranked by a psychiatrist, a psychologist, two nurses, and six aides, produced an average *rho* of .80 and a *tau* of .73. A study of 82 out-patients at various mental hygiene clinics showed a *rho* of .50 for similar rank-order correlations. This relatively lower coefficient results, according to Finney, from the smaller range of severity of maladjustment displayed by out-patients, as compared with the range exhibited by hospitalized patients.

No *norms* are available.

GENERAL COMMENT.   The Palo Alto Group Psychotherapy Scale appears to be an excellent instrument. Its ease of administration and scoring coupled with its high reliability and generally good validity recommend it. The user must keep in mind that the scale was developed for use with clinicially ill populations. One should also bear in mind the simplicity of the scale: it only purports to consolidate many bits of behavior into an easily-comprehended summary.

REFERENCE

Finney, B. C. A scale to measure interpersonal relationships in group psy chotherapy. *Group Psychotherapy*, 1954, 7, 52–66.

UNITERMS.   Behavior; competence; group; interpersonal; intimacy; observation; psychotherapy.

—R. B. E.

56
Perception of Organization Chart

AUTHOR.   Ellis L. Scott

AVAILABILITY.   (Research Monograph No. 82, 1956.) Bureau of Business Research, Ohio State University, Columbus, Ohio 43210

VARIABLES.   The Perception of Organization chart reveals *organizational perceptual errors* (deviations from the formal organizational hierarchy) of three types: *echelon errors,* where the respondent designates persons as being on his level of organization who are actually on the formal chart at higher or lower levels; *unit errors,* where the respondent designates persons as being within his unit or chain of command who are on the formal chart outside the respondent's immediate unit or chain of command; and *omissions,* where the respondent omits persons who are on the formal chart within his unit or chain of command.

DESCRIPTION.   The chart as printed is a simple, blank organization chart which includes two levels of line superiors, the respondent and three peers, and an echelon of four subordinates. The comprehensiveness of the chart may be increased or decreased to adapt to any particular organizational configuration.

ADMINISTRATION AND SCORING.   The respondent fills in the boxes in the chart as best he is able. Scott has developed 41 subvariables which are primarily counts of persons included or excluded at various levels, and sums and differences of these counts. (The utility of these subvariables is assessed below.) The basic scoring procedure consists of noting the discrepancies between the respondent's chart and the formal chart, and categorizing them as echelon, unit, or omission errors.

DEVELOPMENT.   Scott's (1956) study of 10 submarine crews was apparently the first use of this technique by him; no alterations in the technique have been developed.

CRITIQUE.   No *reliability* data are presented.
   The only evidence of *validity* is comprised of the modest correlations among petty officers between a composite measure (of status confusion and nonrecognition errors) and rank-order nominations of officers as "best peacetime" ($r = -.28$) and "best wartime" ($r =$

—.31). These two, however, are the only significant ones ($p < .05$) among 25 such correlations. (The other superior officer effectiveness criteria were "best all-around," "worst," and "best minus worst.")

Although Scott massaged his data thoroughly, the *norms* he presents (percentage of total errors falling in each category at each level of superior, peer, and subordinate) are the results of sampling a rather limited population (696 submariners).

GENERAL COMMENT.   This technique is included here because of its relative novelty. In a hierarchically-organized situation it is clearly valuable to have a sense of how the organization's structure is seen by its members. The straightforward evocation of their perceptions is the central merit of this device.

It is simple to devise, administer, and score, but the implications of the scores it provides have yet to be examined adequately. The 41 sub-variables stretch the data thin, as shown by their refusal to correlate with much of anything.

The interested user should also keep in mind that so-called "errors" may not be that at all, but simply indications of a discrepancy between the formal organization chart and the perceptions of an organization's inhabitants—a familiar phenomenon which may reflect self-delusion on the part of organizational chart-makers. The usefulness of the instrument would probably be improved if Ss were asked to fill out the chart as "it's supposed to be," and "as it really is," analogously to instructions for the Bass–Vaughan Pittsburgh Administrative Review (which see).

REFERENCE

Scott, E. L. *Leadership and perceptions of organization.* Columbus: Bureau of Business Research, Research Monograph No. 82, Ohio State University, 1956.

UNITERMS.   Authority; chart; echelon; management; organization; peers; perception; structure; subordinates; superiors.

—R. B. E.
—M. B. M.

57

Performance Record for the Personal and
Social Development Program

AUTHOR.   John C. Flanagan

AVAILABILITY.   Science Research Associates, 57 West Grand Avenue, Chicago, Illinois 60610. The guides are entitled "Teachers' Guide for the Personal and Social Development Program," "Manual for School Administrators and Supervisors," and "The Performance Record for the Personal and Social Development Program: Incident Sheet."

VARIABLES.   "The critical incident technique" is used to obtain eight types (categories) of *pupil behavioral performance in the classroom: Personal Adjustment; Responsibility and Effort; Creativity and Initiative; Integrity; Social Adjustment; Sensitivity to Others; Group Orientation;* and *Adaptability to Rules and Conventions.* Each category is divided into "behaviors needing improvement" and "behaviors to be encouraged."

DESCRIPTION.   The instrument is essentially a recording form which a teacher (or group worker, parent, or observer) can use to classify critical incidents in children's behavior, as it occurs in classroom settings (kindergarten through eighth grade). A sample item is as follows:

Group Orientation

A. Refused to participate in group activity; B. Talked out of turn or excessively and answered for others; C. Continually insisted on being first; D. Disrupted and annoyed the group; E. Exhibited poor sportsmanship in game; F. influenced others to ill advantage.	A. Offered to contribute to group activity; B. Provided something for benefit of group; C. Exhibited good sportsmanship in game; D. Communicated suggestion to the class; E. Showed independent thinking in the face of opposition for group benefit.

Date	Item	What happened	Date	Item	What happened

ADMINISTRATION AND SCORING.   The guide is broken into eight categories. Each category contains both positive and negative behaviors. Under each category heading is a series of subcategories which are operationally defined. The teacher notes, at the time of the incident or soon after, the subcategory letter best describing the behavior, the date of the incident, and a brief descriptive note to remind herself of the behavior. The recording period is generally considered to be several months. At the end of the period, the teacher (or other record-keeper) totals the positive and negative entries and attempts to assess the child's weaknesses and strengths. Guidelines are provided for interpretation and application of findings.

DEVELOPMENT. An observation guide was needed which would enable teachers (or others) to meet five basic criteria for adequate classroom performance measurement: a "typical" performance is measured; objective and precise facts of performance are collected; a large sample of behavior is used; observations are precisely classified and structured; and incidents are immediately recorded. The findings derived from such observation were for use by teachers in aiding normal elementary school pupils in grades kindergarten through eight to develop healthy and socially acceptable behaviors.

The observation protocol was developed in five stages. In the first stage, classes of teachers and student teachers at the University of Pittsburgh reported critical incidents of observed child behaviors from their teaching experience. The incidents involved behaviors seen as desirable or undesirable for the child's future development. In the second stage, the reports were converted to general categories, and systematic observations were made over two-week intervals by several hundred teachers from the Washington, D.C., and Pittsburgh school systems. Approximately 5,000 critical behaviors having important implications for personality and character development were reported. In the third stage, collected data were grouped into categories, which were revised and subdivided until all incidents could be meaningfully categorized. In the fourth stage, students in two college classes at the University of Pittsburgh were each asked to classify a sample of 20 incidents into the appropriate behavioral category headings. Revisions were made to eliminate problems encountered. The fifth stage was the final tryout of the instrument. Ninety-three teachers in the Pittsburgh and Washington, D.C., schools used the instrument. In general, teachers reported that the categories were appropriate for children at all levels from kindergarten to the eighth grade.

CRITIQUE. No *reliability* measures are reported.

No controls are provided to prevent the teacher's observations from being influenced by her general opinion of the child prior to and during the use of the observation guide.

Content validity is claimed by reporting that the instrument serves to classify all relevant behaviors. However, since no reliability data are reported, and no information is given on the empirical distribution of behaviors into categories, doubt remains.

The directions are clear, but not very rigorous. The teacher is essentially left to her own preferences in using the program. The decision as to what constitutes a significant incident in the life of the child is (naturally) left to the discretion of the teacher. Reporting is subjective.

GENERAL COMMENT.   The Performance Record does appear to be a useful aid to memory for the teacher. Recording of behavior is easier and more systematic. Implications for action can be drawn directly from the record, and improvement easily noted. However, to be used as a research instrument, the guide would need norm development, reliability determination, and some analysis of validity (e.g., are incidents omitted, distorted, over-emphasized, etc.?).

REFERENCES

Flanagan, J. C. *Teachers' Guide for the Personal and Social Development Program*. Chicago: Science Research Associates, 1956.

Flanagan, J. C. *Manual for school administrators and supervisors: The Personal and Social Development Program*. Chicago: Science Research Associates, 1956.

UNITERMS.   Adjustment; behavior; child; classroom; creativity; critical incident; development; group; observation; responsibility; sensitivity; student; teacher.

—D. G. L.

58
Person Description Instrument (PDI)

AUTHOR. Roger Harrison

AVAILABILITY. Roger Harrison, 35 Abingdon Court, Abingdon Villas, London W8 6BT, England

VARIABLES. This instrument was devised to study *interpersonal perception,* conceptualized in terms of dimensions people commonly use in perceiving others. Two broad subvariables in the perception of people are hypothesized: *interpersonal* and *non-interpersonal* construct domains. The former refers to the emotional aspects of face-to-face behavior, including dominance, comfort with others, and styles of expression. Non-interpersonal processes are competence, ability, status, wealth, marital status, industrious versus lazy work habits, physical characteristics, interests, and political and religious attitudes. Presumably, interpersonal constructs "represent functioning at a higher level of development than non-interpersonal constructs" (Harrison, 1967). The author hypothesized that such developmental differences reflect variance in field dependence as posited by Witkin (1962).

Harrison's general plan was to devise a non-free-response instrument for "discovering the major dimensions people use in the perception of others" (Harrison, 1967).

DESCRIPTION. The Person Description Instrument is a semantic differential device containing, in its latest format (PDI X) 27 items relevant to three factors. A factor designated Interpersonal Warmth and Acceptance consists of items for defensiveness, tact, sympathy, threateningness, consideration, acceptance of others, flexibility, acceptance of suggestion, and accommodatingness. One termed Power and Effectiveness in Work has high loadings on items labeled ability, informedness, competence, status, influentiality, prestige, responsibility, thoroughness, and industriousness. Lastly, the factor termed Activity and Expressiveness includes items identified as revelation of feelings, reservedness, enthusiasm, emotional expressivity, loudness, demonstrativeness, activity (versus passivity), committedness, and participation.

The items are presented in semantic differential form, like the following:

Thoughtful ＿＿＿ ＿＿＿ ＿＿＿ ＿＿＿ ＿＿＿ ＿＿＿ Thoughtless

ADMINISTRATION AND SCORING.   Depending upon the form of presentation utilized, the Person Description Instrument is proposed for assessing interpersonal values, social distance, and interpersonal discrimination. These alternative usages entail giving a different set of instructions for each. When a measure of interpersonal values is desired, the subject is asked to describe himself, his closest male friend, and his closest female friend. He is then told to choose the nine scales which he thinks constitute the best description for each person rated. Two interpersonal value scores are then calculated (by the administrator) by summing the number of times scales pertaining to the Interpersonal Warmth and Acceptance factor and those pertaining to the Power and Effectiveness in Work factor were selected as "best description."

To assess social distance, the scale again calls for describing three persons. The subject rates 1) someone especially enjoyable to work with, 2) someone of whom better understanding is desired, and 3) someone whose actions cause discomfort. These are to be actual individuals known to the subject.

To measure interpersonal discrimination, the administrator instructs a subject to describe himself and six additional persons, chosen to be as different from each other as possible, on each scale. Scales are presented in boxed semantic differential form, and the subject is told to place the numbers assigned to those described (1 to 6, and S for self) in appropriate boxes. A discrimination score is obtained by summing the total number of boxes used by the subject across all the scales. Discrimination scores can also be calculated for each of the factors, but factor analysis revealed a very large general discrimination factor, according to the author.

A concept preference score can be calculated by asking respondents to indicate a given number of scales which they feel provide the most adequate descriptive measure of others.

For each of these differing purposes, items from the separate factors are generally alternated. No order has been specified. The amount of respondent time needed to complete a testing is unspecified, but it does not appear necessary that administrators be present as long as instructions are clearly stated. Normative data have not, to this writer's knowledge, been made available.

DEVELOPMENT.   Brunswick's (1944) principle of representative sampling of perceptual acts constituted the method used by the author with an original population of 112 male and 48 female middle and upper-middle class persons. Subjects were aged 25 to 55, mainly college-educated, and were human relations training laboratory participants.

From a language pool of 3,200 responses obtained, 1,000 were randomly selected. These were found to constitute 18 categories representing "the major kinds of common meaning which could be discriminated by the experimenters" (Harrison, 1967). The initial instrument was comprised of 20 bipolar characteristics (construction methods not specified) cast in the semantic differential format described above.

A revised form included 113 seven-point scales covering 18 categories (criteria for inclusion not explicated). It was administered to 64 men and 22 women, yielding 119 separate descriptions of individual items. These were subjected to factor analysis.

Further revision produced a third version of the instrument (PDI III), items having been chosen from the four substantially-loading factors obtained previously. Additionally, items from the first factor were selected theoretically to represent areas of Interpersonal Health and Comfort, Power and Control, Consideration, and Intimacy and Openness. Methods of item selection were not explicated. Another factor analysis of this revised form, with data from 49 men and 20 women, was interpreted as showing that "the separation between interpersonal and non-interpersonal characteristics was maintained" (Harrison, 1967). No shifting of items between the two domains occurred, although the definition of factors within each was not as clear as had been hoped for.

Consequently, a fourth version of the instrument (PDI IV) was devised utilizing 50 items "from previous analyses which showed promise of giving well-defined factor structures" (criteria unexplicated) (Harrison, 1967). The 5-to-8-item clusters included were representative of 6 interpersonal and 4 non-interpersonal factors. The former were Mental Health and Interpersonal Comfort, Honesty, Intimacy and Openness, Consideration, Permissiveness, and Acceptance of Influence. Active Involvement, Ability, Status, and Responsibility were the non-interpersonal areas represented. Sixty-six male and 28 female human relations laboratory participants provided 282 descriptions for further factorial investigation. At first, the same basic separation between interpersonal and non-interpersonal domains, with some items shifting among factors within the former, was discovered. Additional statistical manipulation allowed "a more meaningful clustering of the interpersonal items" (Harrison, 1967), revealing seven presumably separate factors in that area.

A fifth revision produced a 40-item instrument (PDI V) ostensibly tapping areas similar to those in the fourth version. The methods used for this and other revisions prior to the tenth and present version of the instrument (PDI X, described in Harrison, undated) have not been described in detail by the author, to this writer's knowledge.

CRITIQUE.   Harrison states (1967) that internal consistency is probably high, due to the factor analytic development of the instrument. However, no studies have so far reported the size of *reliability* coefficients, thus use of the instrument in non-research contexts aiming at individual assessment is not appropriate. Reliability of the factor scores is probably in the same general range as that of other semantic differential instruments.

Similarly, *validity* data for the present form of the Person Description Instrument are scanty as reported. Harrison and Lubin (1965) found highly significant differences between trainer ratings of human relations laboratory participants designated as person- versus task-oriented ($N = 10$ apiece) on the basis of subject choice of scales yielding the "best description." However, they found no differences between peers' perceptions of these persons in testing a hypothesis that they would be perceived as "more different" than those of the laboratory population in general. Two trends approached significance ($p < .10$) in addition. One of these indicated a tendency, contrary to expectations, for person-oriented group members to be perceived by peers as learning less during the laboratory than task-oriented ones. The reversal may have been conditioned by the fact that training tends to encourage changes in the direction of learning to employ more person-oriented perceptual constructs. Those already facile in that area have less room to make such changes in themselves than those farther from their goal.

Validity for the measure of interpersonal discrimination was indirectly suggested by an analysis of discrimination scores (number of boxes used) and peer sociometric choices (N unspecified). Harrison (personal communication) indicates that high discriminators tended to be seen as obsessive and less effective as group members.

GENERAL COMMENT.   The Person Description Instrument is simple to use, and has had a good deal of developmental energy put into it, but the absence of reliability data and the paucity of validity information mean that it is only suitable at present for research purposes. The personality and behavioral correlates of scores should be thoroughly explored.

REFERENCES

Brunswick, E. Distal focussing of perception: size-constancy in a representative sample of situations. *Psychological Monographs,* 1944, No. 56 (Whole No. 254).

Harrison, R. The Person Description Instrument X. Washington: National Training Laboratories, mimeographed, undated.

Harrison, R. The structure and measurement of person perception. Unpublished manuscript, Yale University, 1967.

Harrison, R. and Lubin, B. Personal style, group composition, and learning: interpersonal perception and interpersonal behavior. *Journal of Applied Behavioral Science*, 1965, *1*(3), 286–294.

UNITERMS.   Activity; cognition; consideration; discrimination (cognitive); effectiveness; expressiveness; human relations training; influence; interpersonal; openness; perception; permissiveness; person; self; semantic differential; social distance; T-group; task; values.

—L. J. R.

59
Personal Orientation Inventory (POI)

AUTHOR.   Everett L. Shostrom

AVAILABILITY.   Education and Industrial Testing Service, San Diego, California 92107

VARIABLES.   The inventory was designed to measure overall *personal maturity,* based on Shostrom's interpretation of Maslow's and Goldstein's theories of *self-actualization.* Maslow (1954, 1962) has postulated a continuum of personality development, in which "neurotics" represent a deficiency-based character organization, "normals" a relatively more need-fulfilled type, and "self-actualizers" a structure relatively free of deficiency needs (needs for love, self-esteem, etc. having been met).

The Personal Orientation Inventory was designed to specify areas of personality health and deficiency, and is intended for clinical use in both diagnosis and prognosis. While the main variable is the general level of psychic functioning, there are ten subvariables, each represented by one of ten subscales, some of which have overlapping items. The subscales are: *Self-Actualizing Values,* the degree to which one holds values presumably held by self-actualizing people; *Existentiality,* the ability to respond according to situational demands without rigid adherence to principle; *Feeling Reactivity,* the extent of responsiveness to one's own needs and feelings; *Spontaneity,* the degree to which one is able to be spontaneous; *Self-Acceptance,* the extent of acceptance of oneself with one's imperfections; *Nature of Man,* a qualitative view of man as intrinsically good; *Self-Regard,* level of self-esteem; *Synergy,* the extent of one's realization that conventional dichotomies (e.g., selfish versus selfless) can be resolved (that one can be both selfish and selfless); *Acceptance of Aggression,* extent of tolerance rather than denial of aggressive impulses; and *Capacity for Intimate Contact,* extent of ability to form and sustain intimate relationships.

Two additional subscales consist of items not contributing to scores in the ten categories. These two remaining subscales are *Time* and *Support,* each yielding a ratio score to assess general personality effectiveness. *Time competence* refers to the ability to have faith in the future and to live a relatively more full life in the present. The time-competent person is able to meaningfully relate his past through the present to his future, while the time-incompetent individual has trouble doing so, tending to live relatively more in the past and future with guilts, regrets, resentments, and "idealized goals, plans, expectations, predictions, and fears" (Shostrom, 1966). The Support Ratio is based on Shostrom's interpretation of Riesman's theory of inner versus other directedness. The inner-directed person is seen as having internalized various authority figures, including especially parental influences, and as being obedient to their inculcated "guidance" principles. Conversely, other-directed people are viewed as being conformists, primarily motivated by fears of "what others will think" and by peer group influence extending beyond familiar and external authority.

DESCRIPTION. The Personal Orientation Inventory is a 150-item forced-choice scale of paired, "antithetical," self-characterizing statements. An item might resemble the following pair of statements:

I have thoughts about how I can give to others frequently.

I really don't think about giving to others.

ADMINISTRATION AND SCORING. Respondents usually require a minimum of 20 minutes with no time limit. Hand scoring can be accomplished with a key. By converting raw scores to standard ones, the administrator plots a profile which can be compared with profiles drawn from norm groups.

Additionally the two ratios, Time and Support, are computed by using the scores from the Time Incompetence subscale as the numerator and those from the Time Competence subscale as the denominator. Self-Actualized persons are proposed a priori to have time ratio scores of 1:8, normals, 1:6, and non-self-actualizing persons, 1:3.

The Support Ratio is similarly derived, but the numerator and denominator are drawn respectively from the Other-Directed and Inner-Directed subscales. Illustrative Support Ratios for a validating study (N and sampling methods unspecified) were 1:3, 1:2.5, and 1:1.3 for self-actualizing, normal, and non-self-actualizing groups, respectively. The ratio thus assesses independence in relative terms.

Percentile ratings for raw scores are given for a sample of 2,607 beginning college freshmen (1,514 males and 1,093 females). Profiles, means, and standard deviations from the Personal Orientation Inventory scores of norm groups have also been stated in the test manual for male supervisors ($N = 66$), student nurses ($N = 64$), Peace Corps volunteers ($N = 62$), male college juniors and seniors ($N = 150$), entering college freshmen ($N = 2,046$), high school students ($N = 412$), hospitalized psychiatric patients ($N = 185$), delinquent males ($N = 84$), and alcoholic males ($N = 20$).

DEVELOPMENT.   Items on the inventory were constructed from value judgment problems considered significant by psychotherapists in private practice, based on "observed value judgments of clinically troubled patients" seen "by several therapists over a five-year period" (test manual). Items were also derived from research and theory of humanistic, existential, and Gestalt psychologists including Maslow, Riesman, May, and Perls. Ellis' (1962) and Buhler's (1962) views of values as reflecting man's general affectivity and life orientation were germane to Shostrom's having constructed the inventory to explore patients' values as an indicator of their overall level of psychic functioning. Each item is stated twice, making the reversal of the value(s) supposedly in question explicit.

Test–retest reliability coefficients of .91 and .93 were obtained based on a sample of college undergraduates ($N = 48$) given the POI twice, a week apart. The reliability coefficients for the 12 scales of the Inventory ranged from .55 (Acceptance of Aggression) to .85 (Existentiality), with a median of .74.

Several validity studies have been conducted. In one (Shostrom and Knapp, 1966), the Personal Orientation Inventory and MMPI were administered to two groups of Ss, one beginning therapy ($N = 37$) and one advanced in therapy ($N = 39$), the latter with a mean time in therapy of 2.2 years. With respect to age, education, and sex distribution both groups are representative of patients in therapy in local clinics. Four MMPI scales (D, Pd, Pt and Sc) and all 12 POI scales differentiated between the two groups significantly beyond the .01 level. Thus, Shostrom (1966) has concluded that the POI measures characteristics crucial to the development of "harmonious interpersonal relationships among 'normal' populations."

Additionally, 11 of 24 rs were significant ($r > -.40$) when POI scales were correlated with the Depression (D) scales of the MMPI; Self-Regard and Inner-Direction scales correlated ($r > -.40$) with the D scale. It was found that high POI scorers advanced in the therapy group scored high on the MMPI K scale ($r > .40$), suggesting that excessively high POI profiles may be inauthentic.

Of the two groups, those advanced in therapy were found to exceed therapy beginners significantly on all 12 POI scales.

Another validity study (Shostrom, 1964) compared relatively self-actualized ($N = 29$) with relatively non-self-actualized ($N = 34$) adults chosen by certified clinical psychologists. Eleven of the 12 scales of the POI discriminated between the groups significantly, ten at the .01 confidence level and one at .05. The "Nature of Man" scale discriminated at the .10 level. On a standard-score profile chart developed from a norm group of 158 "normal" subjects, the means for self-actualized and non-self-actualized (neurotic) groups fell respectively at about 52 and 44 (averaged across all scales).

CRITIQUE.   The *reliability* information provided is meager, and only four of the ten scales show test–retest *r*s over .80. No information is given on internal consistency of the subscales.

Several additional *validity* studies have been carried out. Fox (1965) gave the POI to hospitalized psychiatric patients ($N = 100$). All scales significantly differentiated the hospitalized sample from both a self-actualized and a normal adult sample at the .001 confidence level. However, there is no information in the report as to sampling techniques used for selecting either the hospitalized or normal groups.

Yet another attempt at concurrent validation was made by Knapp (1965), administering the Eysenck Personality Inventory and the Personal Orientation Inventory to 136 undergraduates. Knapp assumed the former to measure neuroticism–stability and introversion–extroversion. Scores of 94 subjects were used for a correlational analysis of each of the 12 Personal Orientation Inventory subscales with the two Eysenck subscales, 15 out of 24 *r*s being reported significant. POI profiles were separately reported for the two experimental subgroups ("high neurotic" and "low neurotic," approximating the upper and lower 27% of the total sample scores on Form A of the Eysenck inventory). Ten POI subscales differentiated the experimental groups at $p < .01$, the remaining two, at $p < .05$. No independent judgment of neuroticism (other than Eysenck scores) was made.

Predictive validity seems reasonably well established in the sense of the POI's gross ability to discriminate relatively healthy from less well-functioning groups. However, it is important to note that little or no evidence is available to indicate *construct* or *concurrent* validity of the separate subscales, which are moderately intercorrelated. This is an important fault in a scale offered for clinical purposes.

The profile *norms* supplied are not wholly adequate for assessing adult and college student populations, since the sampling procedures were not specified.

A study to ascertain whether *item transparency* presents problems for the Personal Orientation Inventory outside of clinical situations is described in the test manual. The inventory was given to 86 introductory psychology students, who were instructed to "make a good impression" as though they were job applicants. Controls were another sample ($N = 136$) of introductory psychology students from the same college. The "fake good" sample mean profile was below that of the validating group for self-actualizers and below the T score of 50 on all but the Self-Regard and Nature of Man subscales. However, the possibility exists of mistaking a genuine self-actualizer's profile for "pseudo" or vice versa, even with the use of the MMPI K scale, as proposed in the manual.

GENERAL COMMENT.   The POI is offered as a measure of variables related to self-actualization—a domain of increasing clinical and research interest. Given the consistent differentiation among known populations by all subscales, it seems very promising, but in the absence of additional clinical and experimental data, the POI should be used for research purposes and group prediction, *not* for differentiated individual clinical diagnosis or prognosis. Validity studies on the ten subscales seem essential.

Items have not been equated for *social desirability*. Such equation could ameliorate the problem of high inauthentic scores that is a present source of difficulty in POI measurement.

An intercorrelational matrix suggests possible failure of some subscales to directly correspond to the variables presumably assessed. The mean intercorrelation among the 12 subscales (our calculation) is + .35, partially accounted for by overlapping items, but still high for indices of supposedly differentiated traits. Persons wishing to study variables related to psychological health are likely to be interested in refining and validating the POI subscales.

REFERENCES

Buhler, C. *Values in psychotherapy*. New York: Free Press, 1962.

Ellis, A. *Reason and emotion in psychotherapy*. New York: Lyle Stuart, 1962.

Fox, J. On the clinical use of the Personal Orientation Inventory. Mimeographed report, 1965.

Knapp, R. Relationship of a measure of self-actualization to neuroticism and extraversion. *Journal of Consulting Psychology*, 1965, *29*, 168–172.

Maslow, A. *Motivation and personality*. New York: Harpers, 1954.

Maslow, A. *Toward a psychology of being*. New York: Van Nostrand, 1962.

Shostrom, E. L. An inventory for the measurement of self-actualization. *Educational and Psychological Measurement*, 1964, *24*, 207–218.

Shostrom, E. L. EITS manual for the Personal Orientation Inventory. San Diego: Educational and Industrial Testing Service, 1966, pp. 5–37.

Shostrom, E. L. and Knapp, R. The relationship of a measure of self-actualization (POI) to a measure of pathology (MMPI) and to therapeutic growth. *American Journal of Psychotherapy*, 1966, *20*, 193–201.

UNITERMS. Aggression; creativity; feelings; growth; health; inner-directedness; intimacy; motivation; personality; psychotherapy; self-acceptance; self-actualization; self-esteem; spontaneity; time perspective; value.

— L. J. R.

60
Personal Values Inventory (PVI)

AUTHORS.   George E. Schlesser and John H. Finger

AVAILABILITY.   George E. Schlesser,* Colgate University, Hamilton, New York 13346

VARIABLES.   The Personal Values Inventory (PVI), College Student Edition, has resulted from research designed to identify *non-intellective factors related to academic achievement,* and "to predict academic achievement with as much validity as does a scholastic aptitude test, and yet be supplemental to and uncorrelated with the latter."

The PVI measures several aspects of academic motivation, and has scales entitled: *High School Record; Need for Achievement; Independence in Planning; Direction of Aspirations; Pre-College Peer Group Influence; Home Influence; Persistence; Self-Control and Deliberateness; Self-Insight; Overstatement;* and *Socio-Economic Status.* (See further description of variables under Critique section.) The authors indicate that their objective (above) has been achieved with the *Persistence* and *Self-Control and Deliberateness* scales.

DESCRIPTION.   The PVI is a battery of tests in two sections, administered together in a single booklet. The item format varies somewhat from subtest to subtest. Two hundred of the 208 items are of the true–false, yes–no, or multiple-choice type. The last eight items are paragraph descriptions to which the student responds by indicating how similar the descriptions are to himself. Some sample true–false items are:

My parents always showed trust and confidence in me.

My plans for the future seemed to work out well.

ADMINISTRATION AND SCORING.   There are two separate forms, one for men and another for women. Both contain the same orientation and the same number of questions. When administering the test there is no time limit, only an admonition to work rapidly and accurately. Most students finish in thirty to fifty minutes. Machine-scorable answer

* As of 1971, the instrument was not publicly available in the usual sense, but was usable by those colleges wishing to participate in cooperative research study. Current inquiries should be directed as above.

sheets are used; the Colgate Computer Center provides scoring services (individual data cards and program decks for an IBM 1620).

DEVELOPMENT.   In the fall of 1959 the College Entrance Examination Board approved a proposal titled "Measuring Long-Range Motivation Through the Use and Further Development of the Personal Values Inventory." The major purpose was to accelerate research and development of items for the PVI and to develop a valid instrument. Secondary purposes were to study the nature of academic motivation and to identify factors related to it. During five years of research, involving item and cluster analysis, and correlation with scholastic performance (grade point average, with ACE Psychological Examination Scores held constant), four editions of the PVI have been printed.

In 1962, after revision of the preliminary instrument, 12 four-year colleges were invited to participate in field trials of the instrument to obtain an additional check on validity. For these cooperating colleges (total $N = 3,934$), the correlation of SAT (verbal) with GPA ranged from .15 to .56, with a median of 37 (Schlesser and Finger, 1963). The correlations of PVI values scores with GPA range from .22 to .52, with a median of .41. One could conclude that the PVI contributes as much to the prediction of GPA as does SAT; its correlation with SAT is .10.

CRITIQUE.   *Reliability* coefficients have been calculated for the tests of the 1964 edition, which is the one still in use (1971). For the autobiographical part (Tests 1 through 7) they ranged from .80 to .84 and for persistence (Test 8) and self-control (Test 9) they are .90 and .80, respectively (Ns and samples unspecified).

The research results (Schlesser, 1965; Schlesser, Finger, and Lynch, 1969) on the *validity* of each test follow:

High School Record Self-Report (Test 1). This section of the test is designed to provide a simplified method of gathering information on high school marks. Test 1 correlates at a median of .47 with college GPA for students in twenty four-year colleges ($N = 3,754$). Actual average high school marks correlate at .41; this means that students' self-reports yield as good correlational information as the actual report.

Need Achievement (Test 2). This test is designed to measure the strength of a student's need for achievement. It covers a broader range than Direction of Aspirations (academic versus other) (Test 3), with which it correlates .45. With GPA it correlates .25.

Direction of Aspiration (Test 3). This attribute may be defined as the degree to which a student says he is personally involved in struggling for successful academic performance as he sees his past experience. Test 3 correlates .40 (median) with GPA. Thus, it is one of the better predictors of academic success.

Socio-Economic Status (Test 4). The Socio-Economic Status test seeks to gather data on family status by a simple, self-report procedure. It attempts to measure the attribute through items on amount of parent education, income, occupational level, and social and professional prestige. It is included as a variable for research, and as useful information for advisors. Its average correlation with GPA is −.10.

Influence of Pre-College Peer Group (Test 5). This test attempts to measure the extent to which the student's peer group has a potential for constructive or deviant influence. Its average correlation with GPA is .13, and as might be expected, low test–retest stability (between entrance and end of freshman year) was found ($r = .33$ and .39 for male and female samples of 100 each).

Home Influence (Test 6). This test may be defined as the extent to which the home contributes to the students' academic adjustment and supports a positive self-image, as reported by the student. It is more stable over the first year of college than Test 5 (.54 and .81 for males and females respectively), and correlates approximately .30 with GPA. In one college (unspecified) the coefficient was as high as .45 ($N = 400$).

Independence in Planning (Test 7). This test measures belief in planning; it is correlated with need for achievement at .40 for men and .44 for women, and goes only .22 with GPA.

Long-Range Persistence (Test 8). Persistence is defined as the extent to which a student considers himself a hard worker and what he thinks his reputation to be with respect to "persistence." The split-half reliability coefficient for this test is .90. It correlates, on the average, at .42 with the GPA. Test 8 is the most influential non-intellective measure with regard to academic success; it compares "very favorably with a median SAT-V and SAT-M correlation with GPA of approximately .33" (Schlesser, Finger, and Lynch, 1969, p. 16).

Self-Control and Non-Rashness (Test 9). The validity coefficient here is .32, but susceptibility to faking seems likely. The test attempts to measure the amount of self-control a student has (with respect to drinking, gambling, and wild parties) as well as foolish risk-taking—two characteristics of "muckers," according to the authors.

Test 10 is the sum of the results on Tests 8 and 9.

Faking or Overstatement (Test 11). This test measures the tendency toward overstatement or trying to appear better than one is (social desirability set). There is a direct relationship between this score and the scores on Tests 8 and 9; it is, in effect, a validity cross-check. Its GPA correlation is −.08.

Self-Insight (Test 12). This test can be defined as the extent to which a student knows that he uses many of the common defenses (such as rationalization and protection) to protect his ego or to avoid anxiety. It is an attempt to provide an index of a student's unrealistic plans or aspirations. The test has seemed of little predictive value even after several revisions, and is primarily related to scale 11 (overstatement), at —.42.

Percentile *norms* for 11 women's and 14 men's four-year colleges (plus some two-year college samples) participating in the study were available for the 1964 version for men and women, as are scale intercorrelations and validity coefficients (multiple R's with SAT, GPA, etc.).

GENERAL COMMENT.   The PVI seems possibly useful as an empirically-developed measure of non-intellective factors related to college academic achievement. A much wider norming group, drawing on a range of colleges and universities, would seem essential. In addition, concurrent validity studies with other measures (e.g., McClelland's and French's measures of need achievement (which see) would be desirable. More effort to develop a theoretical base for the instrument would also be fruitful.

REFERENCES

Schlesser, G. E. Measuring long-range motivation through the use and further development of the Personal Values Inventory. Colgate University, Hamilton, N. Y.; Progress report to the College Entrance Examination Board, 1965.

Schlesser, G. E. Measuring academic motivation through the development and use of the Personal Values Inventory. Unpublished mimeographed paper, 1963.

Schlesser, G. E. and Finger, J. H. *Personal Values Inventory (student form)*. Colgate University, Hamilton, N. Y., 1964.

Schlesser, G. E. and Finger, J. H., with Lynch, T. Measurement of academic motivation: a handbook for the Personal Values Inventory, College Edition. Mimeographed, Colgate University, Hamilton, N. Y., 1969 (Revised).

UNITERMS.   Achievement; aspirations, grade point average; peer; planning; self-control; socio-economic status (SES); values.

—J. L. M.

61
The Personality and Social Network Adjustment Scale

AUTHOR.   A. W. Clark

AVAILABILITY.   Clark, A. W. The Personality and Social Network Adjustment Scale: its use in the evaluation of treatment in a therapeutic community. *Human Relations*, 1968, *21*, 85–95.

VARIABLES.   Built on the assumptions of the social-context theory of behavior, this scale is designed to measure *"role-taking efficiency and psychological comfort"* in a therapeutic community. The variable proposed is seen as unidimensional, and is conceptualized as involving *adjustment* in societal, work, associational, and family groups, and within the patient himself. It is further proposed that adjustment (over time) should be achieved first in societal and associational relations, then in family relations, and finally intra-psychically.

DESCRIPTION.   The test consists of 17 items, 9 of which form a Guttman scale. A simulated example follows:

Please check the statement which best describes you.

I am

very friendly	moderately friendly	neither friendly nor unfriendly	moderately unfriendly	unfriendly

ADMINISTRATION AND SCORING.   The test takes an estimated three to five minutes to administer, and requires no special skills. A scoring key is provided in the reference cited above. Scores are determined by assigning a 1 or a 0 to each item depending on the response. Total score is the sum of 1's obtained. A higher score indicates better adjustment.

DEVELOPMENT.   The test was developed from assumptions common in the therapeutic-community approach to treatment of mental illness. "It claims that personality and social network form inter-related systems. Behavior, including psychopathological symptoms, flows from the interplay of forces in the systems . . ." (Clark, 1968). The scale attempts to tap selected areas of adjustment in the personality and social network system.

Working on the assumptions that adjustment is achieved in an orderly fashion across the societal, associational, family and self areas, and that more peripheral areas have less chance of generating conflict than more central areas, the authors carried out a scalogram analysis of the test items. The unidimensionality of the scale was tested using 43 patients randomly selected from 200. The coefficient of reproducibility was .89. Another independent sample of 88 patients was used, yielding a coefficient of .90.

CRITIQUE.   Test–retest *reliability* of .70 was reported over a period of four to six weeks with 62 psychiatric in-patients. No other reliability data are available. The coefficient of reproducibility is just within the range usually considered acceptable.

The predictive *validity* of the 17-item form was tested in a study using patients and students matched for age, sex, and marital status. Distributions of scores on the unidimensional scale were significantly different for the two groups, in the predicted direction.

A concurrent validity study, using the sample described above, found a correlation of .56 ($p < .01$) with the Cornell Index. The scale also correlated significantly ($r = .47$, $p < .01$) with adjustment as judged by four nurses and four fellow patients.

The shortened form of the scale involving the nine scalable items correlated .86 with the long form for an N of 228 patients. It correlated .47 with the Cornell Index ($p < .01$) and .42 with staff and patient ratings.

No *norms* are available beyond the scores obtained with the reliability and validity samples.

Fakeability, item transparency, response set, and *social desirability* would seem to play an important role in responses to these items; however, no data relevant to these issues are presented.

GENERAL COMMENT.   The instrument represents a plausible and probably useful approach to the evaluation of the interaction of personality (including psychopathological aspects) and immediate social systems. It does not suffer from the "disease model" assumptions which have been so frequently criticized. However, much additional work on reliability, validity, norms, and item response characteristics with a variety of populations is needed before it can be used as a criterion measure. The Personality and Social Network Adjustment Scale deserves further development.

REFERENCE

Clark, A. W. The Personality and Social Network Adjustment Scale: its use in the evaluation of treatment in a therapeutic community. *Human Relations*, 1968, *21*, 85–95.

UNITERMS.   Adjustment; family; group; personality; psychotherapy; social; therapeutic community; work.

—M. E.
—M. B. M.

62

Pittsburgh Administrative Review(PAR)

AUTHORS.   Bernard M. Bass and James A. Vaughan, Jr.

AVAILABILITY.   Management Development Associates, P. O. Box 7501, Oakland Station, Pittsburgh, Pennsylvania 15213

VARIABLES.   Intended for use with middle-level managers in large industrial organizations, the PAR consists of 14 subscales, 6 of which measure the *degree of attention* paid by the individual S to the following problem areas: *Intra-Organizational Decisions; Participation in Organization's Activities; Conflict; Coordination and Maintenance of Departmental Programs; Planning and Innovation;* and *Distribution of Rewards.* The other 8 subscales measure the *frequency of S's interaction* with the following loci of concern: *Boss; Peers; Subordinates; Rulebook; Self; Persons above S in Organization other than Boss;* and *Persons below S in Organization in Other Departments.*

In addition, the PAR contains a section of 10 items which ask for objective data on the organization's size and general nature, and on S's position within the organization.

DESCRIPTION.   The PAR is a 58-item questionnaire. The 48 items which generate the 14 subscales are of the following form:

In a conflict situation, I ignore how others at my level would handle it.

My own feelings dictate whether I will participate in a given activity.

Responses are to be one of the following modifiers: always; often; occasionally; seldom; never.

ADMINISTRATION AND SCORING.   Self-administering with no time limit (but requiring about thirty minutes to complete), the PAR as used by Vaughan and Bass was scored by an IBM 7070 Item Analysis Program (Bendig, 1962a). The 48 subscale items were scored by assigning weights of either 5 . . . 1 for "Always" . . . "Never" (for positively-worded statements) or 1 . . . 5 for "Always" . . . "Never" (for negatively-worded statements). For each of the six problem areas, eight item scores are added to produce the subscale score. Similarly, for each of the eight loci of concern, six item scores are added to produce the subscale score. Scores, therefore, range from either 8 through 40 (problem area) or 6 through 30 (locus of concern).

For the remaining 10 items, because of the discontinuous nature of the alternatives, only frequencies are tabulated.

DEVELOPMENT.   Vaughan (1963) computed the intercorrelation matrix for the 48 items which produce the 14 subscales, and performed a principal axis factor analysis, varimax rotation (Bendig, 1961, 1962b). Five factors were named: Consideration for Subordinate; Concern for Authority; Regard for Self; Distribution of Reward; General Organization Concern.

Vaughan has reported the complete correlation matrix and the unrotated and rotated factor loadings, including each item's communality. He has also reported partial summaries of the means and F values for several analyses of variance of the responses to the two sets of eight items (objective organizational data and S's position in organization).

The referent population consisted of 109 supervisors and managers from a large industrial producer of liquid-fueled rockets located on the West Coast of the United States. Subjects came from the following departments: research and development; engineering; engineering services (fabrication, and quality control); administrative services (procurement, technical services, and contracts); and operations (manufacturing, and testing).

Three levels of position within the organization were distinguished: upper managers ($N = 14$); middle managers ($N = 46$); lower managers and supervisors ($N = 49$).

CRITIQUE.   The Kuder–Richardson Formula 20 *reliabilities* for the problem-area subscales were markedly lower than those for the locus-of-concern subscales. The former ranged from .24 (Intraorganizational Decisions) to .40 (Coordination and Maintenance of Departmental Programs). The latter, despite the fact that they were constructed of fewer items, ranged higher, from .28 (Self) to .61 (Persons below S in Organization in Other Departments). Group means were substituted for missing data, making these reliabilities conservative. Nevertheless, Vaughan notes, "these reliabilities are much too low to be used for anything but large sample research."

The PAR is a self-descriptive questionnaire and as such possesses *face validity*. The PAR attempts to counteract the *response sets* which face-valid items invite by posing items in both negative and positive forms. Another device used to lessen the impact of response sets is to administer the PAR three times simultaneously; Ss are to indicate for each item: 1) what they actually do; 2) what they ought to do; and 3) what they would prefer to do. Directives 2) and 3) should anticipate if not call forth the major response sets which Ss might bring to the

PAR if asked only to indicate "what they actually do."

Based upon an apparent similarity between his Consideration of Subordinates factor and the Consideration factor on the Ohio State Leader Behavior Description Questionnaire, Vaughan asserts the PAR to have considerable *construct validity*. Items which constitute each of the first five (rotated) factors Vaughan extracted do seem to lend weight to the claim.

Vaughan anticipates that "the probability that (PAR) will prove to have significant factorial validity is very high . . . ;" the test manual, however, does not include any evidence in this direction.

GENERAL COMMENT.   Vaughan has done a thorough job of analyzing the results of his particular application of the PAR. He recognizes that while the organization from which he sampled is perhaps typical of large aero-space engineering firms, this type of company, with its high level of technical expertise among middle-level managers, is not representative of organizations in longer established fields of manufacturing.

On a more specific level, single-item reliability is extremely poor; subscale reliability only somewhat better. The PAR should not be recommended for assessment of individuals. Its major value lies in its potential ability to differentiate groups in large-sample research.

REFERENCES

Bendig, A. W. IBM 7070 item analysis program. *Behavioral Science,* 1962(a), 7, 125.

Bendig, A. W. IBM 7070 program for principal axis factor analysis. *Behavioral Science,* 1962(b), 7, 126–7.

Bendig, A. W. Normalized varimax factor rotation for the IBM 7070. Pittsburgh: University of Pittsburgh. Unpublished paper, 1961.

Vaughan, J. A., Jr. Surveying the man-in-the-middle of an industrial organization. Pittsburgh: Graduate School of Business, University of Pittsburgh, Technical Report No. 2, Contract N ONR 642(14), 1963.

UNITERMS.   Administrator; authority; boss; conflict; consideration; coordination; decision-making; effectiveness; innovation; interdepartmental relations; intraorganizational decisions; maintenance; management; middle-management; organization; participation; peer; planning; rewards; rules; satisfaction; self-regard; size (organization); subordinate; superior.

—R. B. E.

63
Problem Analysis Questionnaire (PAQ)

AUTHORS.   Roger Harrison and Barry I. Oshry

AVAILABILITY.   Roger Harrison, 35 Abingdon Court, Abingdon Villas, London W 8 6BT England

VARIABLES.   The Problem Analysis Questionnaire locates the blame or *cause of an interpersonal problem in an organization* in four possible places: *Self, Other, Self and Other,* and *Organization.* Within each *location* two *processes* are separable: *Rational-Technical* causes, those referring to the competence, energy, and initiative of either the Self, Others, or the Organization; and *Closedness,* those referring to the resistance of the Self, Others, or the Organization to change and influence. The PAQ also elicits estimates of the *personal characteristics* of both Others involved and Self along three dimensions: *Interpersonal Orientation; Status and Influence;* and, *Integrity and Dependability.* The authors anticipate using this instrument to measure the results of human relations training experience. They predict that the T-group experience will facilitate locating the blame more in oneself or self and others, and less in others or in the organization.

DESCRIPTION.   The PAQ has three parts. The first is a participant-provided description of the problem, which the authors believe serves to arouse mild anxiety (and hence attention?) in the respondent, thus increasing the validity of the responses. The second part consists of a total of 66 "cause scales." These cause scales are statements of possible contributions to the problem. They are divided among nine categories: Self/Rational-Technical; Self/Closed; Organization/Rational-Technical; Organization/Closed; Others/Rational-Technical; Others/Closed; Self and Others/Rational-Technical; Self and Others/Closed; and Situational. This last category, Situational, differs from Organizational in that it refers expressly to the possibility that the Self and Other(s) involved may be part of subunits which have different, and possibly opposing, goals in the organization. Here are some examples of the items in the cause scales:

> I have not planned adequately to meet this situation. (S/R-T)
>
> The organization resists suggestions aimed at producing change. (Org/Cl)
>
> The other person(s) and I have not taken enough time to sit down and talk about this problem. (S&O/R-T)

Both the other person(s)' and my jobs are such that we must work towards opposing goals. (Sit)

Next to the cause scales is a column headed "Contribution to Problem" under which five possible responses are offered: none, little, moderate, important, major. The third part consists of 18 items divided equally among three sets of semantic differential scales corresponding to the dimensions Interpersonal Orientation, Status and Influence, and Integrity and Dependability. The scales are 7-point; the respondent fills them out twice, once for Self and once for Others. Some examples follow:

Wants warm relationships	3 2 1 N 1 2 3	Wants cool, distant relationships
Likes to have his own way	3 2 1 N 1 2 3	Likes to find a compromise
Interested	3 2 1 N 1 2 3	Uninterested

ADMINISTRATION AND SCORING.   The PAQ is self-administering without a time limit. The time for completion varies, depending upon the length of the description of the problem, but should not be more than one hour. The description is not scored; it is included to arouse anxiety in the subject (and presumably to provide a focus of attention for the ratings). The second part, the cause scales, is scored on a 5-point system, from None (1) to Major (5). Each scale score is a simple sum. The third part is scored similarly, with a change of sign for responses on the negative side of the description traits.

DEVELOPMENT.   The only information on the development of the PAQ available for this review was that the current form is the third revision and reflects the results of factor analyses of the responses made by middle-level managers from industry and YMCA's attending T-group laboratories. (For a fuller view of a companion study see Harrison and Oshry's Organizational Behavior Describer Survey, reviewed in this volume.)

CRITIQUE.   The authors calculated scale *reliabilities* from the average inter-item correlation for each scale; for the cause scales, reliabilities ranged from .75 to .91, with a median of .86. For description scales, the internal consistencies were: Interpersonal Orientation, .66; Status and Influence, .81; and Integrity and Dependability, .94. For all these figures, $N = 150$.

The major scale *intercorrelations* are: Self/R-T and Self/CI, .62;

Organization/R-T and Organization/Cl, .76; and Other/R-T and Other/Cl, .53. This suggests that the Rational-Technical and Closedness scales are not independent, and, in fact, Harrison and Oshry (undated) calculated rank-order statistics (method unspecified) for the Rational-Technical/Closedness interrelationship: for Self, .43; for Other, —.63; for Organization, .83, the last significant at $p < .05$, one-tailed.

Oshry and Harrison (1966) provided some *predictive validity* evidence: 46 middle managers attending T-groups did experience an increase in attribution of self and own interpersonal needs as problem causes ($p < .05$) and a decrease in attribution of problem cause to others and the environment ($p < .05$). Other changes, all at $p < .05$, were: increased sensitivity to own interpersonal needs, increased perceived availability of self and others as resources for problem-solving, increased perceived control over problems. Ss saw no clear connection between the new perceptions and their translation into action. The authors assert "the data suggest that diagnostic orientations learned about self in relation to the T-group do generalize to learnings about self in relation to work," but point out that no control groups were involved, that only perceptual data were involved, and that no actual job measures were taken.

The *norms* given are means and standard deviations for 68 industrial managers and 67 YMCA managers.

The authors do not discuss possible *response sets*. With all the cause-scale items being worded negatively, as befits locating blame, the possibility exists that *acquiescence* may influence scores, particularly in consistently (and inappropriately) blaming either the Self or Other(s).

GENERAL COMMENT.   The Problem Analysis Questionnaire is interesting and possibly useful, but thus far insufficiently developed. It is included in this review as a handmaiden to Harrison and Oshry's Organizational Behavior Describer Survey (which see).

REFERENCES

Harrison, R. and Oshry, B. I. The Problem Analysis Questionnaire: I. methodology and technical data. Unpublished paper, undated.

Oshry, B. I. and Harrison, R. Transfer from here-and-now to there-and-then: changes in organizational problem diagnosis stemming from T-group training. *Journal of Applied Behavioral Science*, 1966, 2, 185–198.

UNITERMS.   Blame; competence; content analysis; dependability; human relations training; influence; integrity; interpersonal; openness; organization; other; process; role; self; status; task; T-group.

—R. B. E.

64
Problem Expression Scale (PES)

AUTHORS. Ferdinand van der Veen and Tom M. Tomlinson

AVAILABILITY. Ferdinand van der Veen, Wisconsin Psychiatric Institute, University of Wisconsin, Madison, Wisconsin 53706

VARIABLES. The Problem Expression Scale is one strand of the seven strands of the Process Scale developed by Walker, Rablen, and Rogers (1960) to measure *process or movement in psychotherapy*. The PES describes the *mode in which a person talks about his problems*. Except for the end points, each stage of the PES contains one positive and one negative description of the S's behavior. The seven stages are:

Stage 1   The individual does not talk about problems; i.e., wrongs, difficulties, confusions, conflicts, complaints, etc.

Stage 2   The individual talks about problems or problem situations, but not about his direct involvement in a problem situation or event.

Stage 3   The individual talks about his direct involvement in a problem situation or event, but not about his own reaction in or to the problem situation.

Stage 4   The individual talks about his own reactions in or to the problem situation, but not about the contribution of his own reactions to the problem.

Stage 5   The individual talks about the contribution of his own reactions to the problem, but not about his own understanding of his feelings, experiences, or attitudes.

Stage 6   The individual talks about his own understanding of his feelings, experiences, or attitudes, but not about an actual resolution in terms of changes in his feelings, experiences, or attitudes.

Stage 7   The individual talks about an actual resolution of the problem situation in terms of changes in his feelings, experiences or attitudes.

Intermediate stages of 1.5, 2.5, etc. are in principle possible; in order to make the PES cumulative each stage assumes the satisfaction of the definitions of all lower stages.

DESCRIPTION. The PES is a description scale which simply produces a single score (rating) for any speech segment of any length.

ADMINISTRATION AND SCORING. The rater may score live speech processes. The more convenient method is to rate tape-recorded segments or transcriptions. No norms are available. Profile charts for small highly specific populations (3, 5, and 15 institutionalized schizophrenics; 10 members of a T-group) have been reported.

DEVELOPMENT. The PES grew out of Rogers' exploration of a process conception of psychotherapy (Rogers, 1958; Rogers and Rablen, 1958) and the resultant Process Scale (which see), of which the other six strands scale a therapy client's reaction to his feelings and personal meanings, his manner of experiencing, his degree of incongruence, his communication of self, his construing of experience, and his manner of relating to others.

CRITIQUE. Van der Veen has reported two inter-rater *reliability* studies (1965, 1966). For two raters of 90 interview segments from 30 clients, the intercorrelation was .46. The agreement between raters for the 30 interviews was .60. The reliability of the averaged rating, as estimated by the Spearman–Brown formula, was .63. For two raters of 75 interviews, the correlation was .44. The Spearman–Brown reliability for the average of these two ratings was .62. Clark and Culbert (1965) have reported a Pearson r of .80 for two raters of the PES.

The PES appears to have *face validity* for Ss not engaged in psychotherapy, but this issue has not been studied explicitly.

In a *concurrent validity* study, the PES was found to have a rank-order correlation of .79 with the Barrett-Lennard Relationship Inventory (1962), which measures four theoretical variables: the therapist's empathic understanding of the client; the degree to which the therapist's regard is unconditional or unqualified; and the extent to which the therapist is congruent in his relationship with the client. For 15 schizophrenics, the PES had an r of .65 with congruence and of .62 with a combined score on the Relationship Inventory ($p < .01$ in both cases).

GENERAL COMMENT. Though the PES is psychometrically unsatisfactory (sketchy, poor reliability; insufficient study of validity), it is probably worth further development and application as a relatively non-reactive measure of "involvement in own problems" which could be useful in groups devoted to member improvement (therapy, training, counseling, etc.). Until additional work is done on the instrument, however, it cannot be employed with confidence in the study of individuals.

REFERENCES

Barrett-Lennard, G. T. Dimensions of therapist response as causal factors in therapeutic change. *Psychological Monographs*, 1962, *76*, No. 43 (Whole No. 562).

Clark, J. V. and Culbert, S. A. Mutually therapeutic perception and self-awareness in a T-group. *Journal of Applied Behavioral Science*, 1965, *1*, 180–194.

Rogers, C. R. A process conception of psychotherapy. *American Psychologist*, 1958, *13*, 142–149.

Rogers, C. R. and Rablen, R. A. A study of process in psychotherapy. Madison: University of Wisconsin, unpublished manual, 1958.

Rogers, C. R., Gendlin, E. T., Kiesler, D., and Truax, C. *The therapeutic relationship and its impact: a study of psychotherapy with schizophrenics.* Madison: University of Wisconsin Press, 1966.

van der Veen, F. Effects of the therapist and the patient on each other's therapeutic behavior. *Journal of Consulting Psychology*, 1965, *29*, 19–26.

van der Veen, F. Therapist behavior, client behavior and case outcome. Manhattan, Kansas: University of Kansas, unpublished paper, 1966.

Walker, A. M., Rablen, R. A., and Rogers, C. R. Development of a scale to measure process in psychotherapy. *Journal of Clinical Psychology*, 1960, *16*, 79–85.

UNITERMS.   Affect; attitudes; behavior; experiences; feelings; involvement; observation; problems; process; protocol analysis; reactions; resolution; self-understanding.

—R. B. E.

65
Process Scale

AUTHOR.   A. Walker, R. A. Rablen, and C. R. Rogers

AVAILABILITY.   Walker, A., Rablen, R. A., and Rogers, C. R. Development of a scale to measure process change in psychotherapy. *Journal of Clinical Psychology*, 1960, *16*, 70–85.

VARIABLES.   Various aspects are measured of *process or movement in psychotherapy*, including *Feelings and Personal Meanings, Incongruence, Communication of Self, Construing of Experience, Relationship to Problems*, and *Manner of Relating*.

DESCRIPTION.   This is not a scale, strictly speaking, but a conceptual scheme which served to guide the development of several other specific instruments (see van der Veen and Tomlinson's Problem Expression Scale and Barrett-Lennard's Relationship Inventory).

Rogers (1957) developed a formulation concerning the process of personality change in psychotherapy. After listening to tapes of therapeutic sessions, he was struck by what he began to see as a basic condition of therapy, which he describes as "the client's experience of himself as being fully *received*." He proposed that clients who feel received in therapy tend to move away from a general static stance toward life with rigid concepts, unrecognized relationship problems, and unexpressed feelings toward a stance of living "in flow," and relating openly and freely on the basis of immediate experiencing. Next, he developed a scale which was organized into several stages along this general continuum.

The scale, after some initial revisions, was presented by Walker, Rablen, and Rogers (1960). It was characterized as follows:

Strands	*Process Stages*		
	Low (I–II)	*Medium (III–V)*	*High (VI–VII)*
Feelings and personal meanings	Unrecognized Unexpressed	Increasing ownership Increasing expression	Living in flow Fully experienced
Experiencing	Remote from experiencing Unaware	Decreasing remoteness Increasing awareness	Lives in process of experiencing Uses as major referent

Strands	Process Stages		
	Low (I–II)	Medium (III–V)	High (VI–VII)
Incongruence	Unrecognized	Increasing recognition Increasing direct experiencing	Temporary only
Communication of self	Lacking	Increasing self-communication	Rich self-awareness communicated when desired
Construing of experience	Rigid construction Construction seen as fact	Decreasing rigidity Increasing recognition of own contribution	Tentative constructions Meaning held loosely to be checked against experience
Relationship to problems	Unrecognized No desire to change	Increasing responsibility assumed Decreasing danger felt	Problem not seen as external object Living in some aspect of problem
Manner of relating	Close relationships avoided as dangerous	Decreasing danger felt	Relates openly and freely on basis of immediate experiencing

The actual scale is not reviewed here; it does provide the theoretical notions underlying the instruments cited above, as well as several others (Kiesler's Congruence scales; Truax's measures of Empathy and Unconditional Positive Regard; Gendlin's Experiencing Scale).

The entire development of these scales and their relation to the study of therapeutic process is discussed in detail by Rogers, Gendlin, Kiesler, and Truax (1966).

GENERAL COMMENT.   This scale is included here because it appears to be a useful conceptual contribution to empirical understanding of the therapeutic process, and appears to have generated some useful instruments.

REFERENCES

Rogers, C. R. A process conception of psychotherapy. *American Psychologist*, 1958, *13*, 142–149.

Rogers, C. R. and Rablen, R. A. A study of process in psychotherapy. Madison: University of Wisconsin, unpublished manual, 1958.

Rogers, C. R., Gendlin, E. T., Kiesler, D., and Truax, C. *The therapeutic relationship and its impact: a study of psychotherapy with schizophrenics.* Madison: University of Wisconsin Press, 1966.

Walker, A., Rablen, R. A., and Rogers, C. R. Development of a scale to measure process change in psychotherapy. *Journal of Clinical Psychology,* 1960, *16,* 79–85.

UNITERMS.   Communication; experience; feelings; incongruence; interpersonal; problem; process; protocol analysis; psychotherapy; relationship.

—M. B. M.

66
Professional and Bureaucratic Employee Role Orientation Scales

AUTHOR.   Ronald G. Corwin

AVAILABILITY.   Corwin, R. G. The development of an instrument for examining staff conflicts in the public schools. Cooperative Research Program of the U.S. Office of Education, U.S. Department of Health, Education and Welfare, Contract No. 1934, 1963.

VARIABLES.   These scales were developed to distinguish between *attitudes* of *militant professionalism* and *bureaucratic employee orientation* among teachers. It was hypothesized that teachers subscribing to a professional role show greater initiative and have a higher rate of overt conflict than do teachers adhering to an employee status. Conversely, the latter were expected to be rather more submissive and compliant in relations with their administrations than the former. Professionalization was conceived of as a militant process involving teachers' seeking professional status for their occupational role. Professional and employee orientations are conceptualized as relatively independent, uncorrelated variables.

The scales were designed to be used in the public school system by both teachers and principals. Since no time limit need be observed, they can be utilized without direct supervision.

DESCRIPTION.   Two Likert scales were developed to measure the extent to which teachers subscribe to professional and employee roles. The professional status orientation scale consists of 16 items, the employee status orientation scale of 29 items. In all cases items were chosen from lists of interpersonal situations judged relevant to each concept by a panel of sociologists. As an example, Bureaucratic-Employee scale items resemble the following simulated one:

> Teachers should try to teach every child the same thing, so that education is as standardized as possible.

ADMINISTRATION AND SCORING.   The five alternatives for each item range from "strongly agree" to "strongly disagree," weighted from 1 to 5. Magnitude of scores on the professional scale is directly correspondent with the degree of professional orientation, while the relation between scores on the employee scale and intensity of employee orientation is inverse.

DEVELOPMENT.   For the original population, Corwin chose the 426 faculty members staffing seven Ohio and Michigan high schools, ranging in size from 9 to 120 teachers. The sample was reported as biased toward large schools and older teachers. Having recognized the bias, Corwin limited himself to preliminary hypothesis testing. Sampling techniques used in choosing the 284 teachers given the Employee and Professional scales are unspecified.

For validation of the scales, Corwin chose two methods. Indices of the rate of overt conflict of teachers with administrators were developed from taped interviews of a random sample of 146 teachers from the original population. These involved asking the teacher to describe any "incidents" involving himself or other faculty members, and to state how much tension existed between him and the rest of the faculty. The proportion mentioning severe conflict at least once correlates with that revealing the occurrence of major incidents in the interview, $r = .86$. A *rho* of .89 between the latter index and conflicts between teachers and administrators was reported.

As a second validational measure, a 12-item Initiative-Compliance scale was developed. Each item describes a conflict between teacher and administrator, and for every statement the respondent is asked to indicate the degree to which he would comply with the administrator's wishes, and what the consequences of refusing to do so in his school would be.

Forms used for determining discriminative power of the professionalism and employee orientation items were based on Compliance-Initiative scores of 222 teachers from the original sample. The 29 "most professional" teachers were chosen, since they ranked high on specified criteria (e.g., read professional journals at least five hours a week). "Generally opposite characteristics" to the above-listed high professional criteria were attributed to the 30 teachers judged "least professional." Criteria for judging 44 teachers as "most bureaucratic" were clearly stated (e.g., considered by principal as an excellent employee, at least one standard deviation below the mean on a check list of criticisms against the administration, etc.); the 19 "least bureaucratic" teachers were characterized as "generally opposite" to the "most bureaucratic" group (no definite criteria reported).

The final professional and employee role orientation scales discriminate on critical ratio tests and scale value difference ratios between persons having the highest and lowest total scores. Only items with a scale value difference ratio of .32 and above were used, and "most of the items have a discriminative power above .50" (Corwin, 1965).

CRITIQUE.   The split-half *reliability* of the employee scale is $r = .74$, or .84 after Spearman–Brown correction. The internal reliability of the professional scale is $r = .48$, or .65 after correction.

That the scales distinguish between groups most closely approximating high and low professional and employee norms was cited (Corwin, 1965) as evidence of their discriminatory power and *validity*. Also, a group (N unspecified) of university high school teachers reputed to be highly professionally oriented scored near the expected extremes on both scales. No information was given, however, regarding the precise extent of the discriminatory power of the scales in either of the last two instances.

The author claims that total scores of the employee and professional scales are uncorrelated, but no specific data are supplied. A significant difference was reported (confidence level not mentioned) between schools "in the proportion of faculty simultaneously highly committed to both orientations or simultaneously low on both, or simultaneously high on one and low on the other" (Corwin, 1965).

In examining *construct validity*, Corwin (1965) found that " 'initiative-taking' teachers . . . subscribe to significantly more professional and to fewer bureaucratic roles than 'compliant' ones . . . ," as he had hypothesized. "Support-seeking" teachers were intermediate on both Professional and Employee scales, but no significant differences were found between "support-seekers' " orientations and others' role conceptions. Also, conflict rate was "several times greater" for "initiative-taking" teachers than for "compliant" ones (mean conflict rate for the former was 1.02 conflicts per person; for the latter, .34 conflicts per person, significant at $p < .01$).

Corwin concluded that those involved in conflict as opposed to those uninvolved (as measured by interview data) tended in most instances to be more professional and less bureaucratic. However, only two differences were statistically significant. Also, he found that those admitting to the highest number of conflicts were the most professional and least bureaucratic persons.

Corwin defined "service bureaucrat" as one simultaneously more professional and more bureaucratic, and "functional bureaucrat" as one simultaneously more professional and less bureaucratic. Similarly, "job bureaucrats" are supposedly both less professional and more bureaucratic, and "alienated," those presumably simultaneously less professional and less bureaucratic.

"Functional bureaucrats" reported having participated in twice as many conflicts as "job bureaucrats," presumably indicating that "a more professional orientation contributes to militancy primarily when it is accompanied by a less bureaucratic orientation" (Corwin, 1965).

Statistical analysis of the compliance and rate-of-conflict validating criteria showed only two instances of significant differences among seven groups of professionally oriented teachers ($p < .05$ and $p < .01$), and six out of seven such differences among those with employee-bureaucrat orientations (five at $p < .01$ and one at $p < .05$).

In general, one feels that Corwin's conclusion as to the role of militancy in professional orientation must be viewed cautiously, in the light of the usage of taped interviews (which could have suffered from S mistrust) as the indices of conflict rate.

Directions are clear and unequivocal, but *fakeability* is possible, due to item transparency.

Normative data were obtained for a sample of teachers chosen on the basis of availability. Because of non-randomized sampling procedures and unspecified criteria for membership in some of the normative groups, these data should be expanded.

GENERAL COMMENT. These scales seem useful for examining the variables named, but are not especially reliable. Construct validity has not been demonstrated well enough to enable one to judge what the role orientation scales do measure. The operationalization of the variables is somewhat problematic. The inference that descriptions of "ought" behavior can characterize one as "professional" or "bureaucratic" may mislead the user to attribute the qualities inherent in an organization (or subsystem) to individuals.

In general, these scales should only be used at present in studies specifically designed to clarify their validity and reliability.

REFERENCES

Corwin, R. G. Militant professionalism, initiative, and compliance in public education. *Sociology of Education*, 1965, *38*, 310–331.

UNITERMS. Administrator; bureaucracy; conflict; compliance; employee; initiative; militancy; organization; position; professional; role; status; teacher.

—L. J. R.

67
Profile of Organizational Characteristics

AUTHOR.   Rensis Likert

AVAILABILITY.   Likert, R. *The human organization: its management and value.* New York: McGraw-Hill, 1967.

VARIABLES.   The Profile of Organizational Characteristics covers eight organizational variables: the *leadership processes* used; the *character of motivational forces;* the *character of the communication process;* the *character of the interaction-influence process;* the *character of the decision-making process;* the *character of goal setting or ordering;* the *character of the control process;* and the *performance goals and training.* The Profile is intended for use in describing the nature of managerial systems used in industrial organizations where the management system is not laissez-faire in character. Likert arrays four ideal-typical systems along a continuum: exploitive authoritative; benevolent authoritative; consultative; and participive group.

DESCRIPTION.   The profile consists of 51 scales of 20 intervals each. The intervals are grouped in four sets of five, corresponding to the four managerial systems, whose labels are *not* indicated on the form. One of the items for the variable "leadership processes used" is:

Extent to which Superiors Display Supportive Behavior toward others:

Display no supportive behavior or virtually none	Display supportive behavior in condescending manner and in some situations only	Display supportive behavior quite generally	Display supportive behavior fully and in all situations

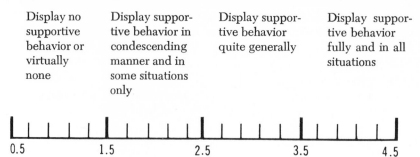

ADMINISTRATION AND SCORING.   For each item the respondent places an *N* at the point which describes his organization at the present time and a *P* at the point which describes his organization as it was one or more years ago, if he was in the organization at that time. Two other administrative procedures may be followed: the respondent may indicate what kind of organization he is trying to create by his management, or the kind of organization he would ideally like his to become.

Each form should require less than thirty minutes to complete. Scores are obtained by fixing the end points of the scales at .5 and 4.5, making each division represent an interval of .2, and computing the mean of the responses for a given organization. Scores, individual or mean, can also be plotted on a profile chart. Norms as such are not included; Likert's book (1967) does include several empirical profiles illustrative of the four systems and movements from one to another.

DEVELOPMENT.   Likert's initial 43-item form was found to have very high intercorrelations among the items; rarely were they below .50, and often they were above .80. The original form's Spearman–Brown reliability was .98. When the data were factor-analyzed, only one factor emerged. The total score correlated with that factor at 1.00. As a result, the system labels (exploitive authoritative, etc.) were removed from the form. In addition, in 24 of the 51 items the alternatives were reversed such that system 4 (participative group) was the left-most pole and system 1 (exploitive authoritative) was the right-most pole.

CRITIQUE.   The above-mentioned modifications reduced the range of the item intercorrelations, so that for managers who checked only the current status of their organization the split-half *reliability* (corrected) is .90. For two groups of managers who checked both current and past conditions, the intercorrelations were higher and the mean reliability, .98.

Likert summarizes several case studies of shifts in managerial systems in various organizations. Rather than establishing the *construct validity* of the profile, however, his evidence is more accurately interpreted as validating the superiority, in terms of increased productivity and morale, of system 4 (participative group management), which is the central argument of the book.

Despite the reversal of direction of 24 items, the problem of *response set* remains. The normative implications of the response alternatives remain quite clear; most alert managers would soon perceive that four distinct systems were being described. Given such awareness, one would expect a respondent tendency to decide in general terms which system is the best fit to his organization, and to make further consistent response within that subdivision. At least, Likert offers no evidence to the contrary.

GENERAL COMMENT.   The eight variables are not discussed individually to any satisfactory degree, nor are patterns of interaction among these variables considered. One might well want to know which of the eight, either singly or in combination, are most crucial to increased productivity, the most difficult to change, etc. Here the absence of norms is felt. Systems 1 through 3 are clearly labeled as inferior with respect to the criterion of increased productivity. Evidence for that general assertion is presented in Likert (1961), but is not sufficient in and of itself to recommend the instrument as a good measure of the variables at hand. The Profile of Organizational Characteristics is best used for diagnostic research, as in the study by Blumberg and Weiner (1970).

REFERENCES

Blumberg, A. and Wiener, W. One from two: facilitating an organizational merger. *Journal of Applied Behavioral Science*, 1971, 7 (1), 87–102.

Likert, R. *New patterns of management*. New York: McGraw-Hill, 1961.

Likert, R. *The human organization: its management and value*. New York: McGraw-Hill, 1967.

UNITERMS.   Authoritative; management; organization; participative; power; system; Theory Y.

—R. B. E.

68
Rationality Questionnaire

AUTHORS.   Howard Schuman and John Harding

AVAILABILITY.   Robinson, J. P., Rusk, J. G., and Head, K. B. (eds.) *Measures of political attitudes*. Ann Arbor: Institute for Social Research, University of Michigan, 1968. Also available from John Harding, Department of Child Development and Family Relationships, Cornell University, Ithaca, New York 14850.

VARIABLES.   The instrument measures the element of *rationality/ irrationality* in *prejudice*, including such phenomena as prejudgment, overgeneralization, and refusal to modify an opinion in the face of contradictory evidence. Rationality is one of three dimensions of prejudice conceptualized by the authors (Harding and Schuman, 1961). Prejudiced attitudes are seen as involving deviation from three ideal norms: *Rationality, Justice,* and *Human-Heartedness*. (The Human-Heartedness Questionnaire is reported elsewhere in this volume; for the Justice instrument see Robinson et al., 1968).) The instrument is designed to measure the "anti-pro" dimension of prejudice separately from whether the belief or attitude expressed is rationally supportable; thus, respondents can be classified as "rational," "irrational-anti," "irrational-pro," and "confused" (both "irrational-pro" and "-anti").

DESCRIPTION.   The questionnaire, entitled "A Survey on Groups," is composed of 48 items like the following:

A. Some American Indians are definitely much superior in intelligence to some white people.

B. Few if any American Indians are really superior in intelligence to any white people.

The subject is asked to circle the letter of the response which he believes is more nearly correct, then to indicate how sure he feels that his response is in fact the more nearly correct of the two ("not very sure," "moderately sure," or "very sure"). Of the 48 items, 24 are keyed as irrational-anti and 24 as irrational-pro. In the example above, a person scoring answer "B" would be given a score of 3, 4, or 5 depending on the certainty of his irrational-anti response; a person answering "A" would be given a score of 1 regardless of his certainty. Omissions are scored 2.

An irrational-pro item, such as:

A. The percentage of children born to unmarried mothers is higher among Negroes than white people.

B. The percentage of children born to unmarried mothers among Negroes is about the same as among white people.

would receive 3, 4, or 5 depending on how certain the respondent was of his "B" response; those choosing "A" get a score of 1. In each set of 24 items, one third deals with Negroes, one third with Jews, and the remainder with a variety of other ethnic groups (American Indians, Puerto Ricans, Japanese-, Chinese-, and Mexican-Americans). Respondents thus receive two scores, each with a possible range of 24 to 120. High scores signify irrational bias, whether it is pro or anti.

DEVELOPMENT.   The original standardization population was 229 Boston adults; quotas for sex, age, education and religion were employed to draw a sample typical of metropolitan Boston. Fifty-nine percent of the respondents were Catholic; members of minorities mentioned in the instrument were excluded. Groups of participants found in a variety of settings were paid a small amount to complete this and several other measures anonymously on the spot. Those with inadequate English reading ability (normally having completed less than six grades of school) were also excluded. The items do not appear to have been altered following this administration, but additional validity and norming data were collected from a sample of 112 freshmen women in a New England Catholic college, and a sample of 110 Radcliffe undergraduates.

Schuman reports some negative reactions from subjects, since the instrument "attempts to measure prejudice on the liberal side," which suggests item transparency.

CRITIQUE.   In the Boston adult sample, the irrational-anti scale has a corrected split-half *reliability* of .84, and the irrational-pro, .78. The Catholic college sample has reliabilities of .81 and .76, respectively.

The three ethnic anti subscales (Negro, Jewish, other) intercorrelate at an average of .51 for anti and .48 for pro in the Boston sample; thus, general tendencies to endorse (or refuse to endorse) irrational statemeans seem to be at work. The anti–pro correlations are —.47 in the Boston sample and —.61 in the Catholic college sample.

Concurrent validity is suggested by correlations with other measures of prejudice (social distance, discriminatory attitudes, California E scale, error choice technique, F-Scale, some miscellaneous prejudice indicators, and the Human-Heartedness Questionnaire). Correlations ranged from .28 to .71 for the anti scale, with a median of .62 for the Boston sample, and a median of .59 for the college sample. The pro scale correlations ranged from —.15 to —.52, with medians of —.43 and —.52, respectively. Thus, traditional measures of prejudice seem to load more on the irrational-anti side.

In the Boston sample, the proportion of respondents who were "rational" (below halfway point on both pro and anti scales) was 48% for those with a college education, and 9% or lower for all others. No college-educated respondent fell into the "confused" category (above halfway point on both pro and anti), and the proportion confused rose steadily as levels of education decreased (to 68% for those with grammar school only).

Finally a study of 73 selected Radcliffe undergraduates, all of whom scored as rational on the anti scale, but ranged from rational to irrational-pro on the irrational-pro scale, showed that "love prejudice" (irrational-pro attitude) tends to be associated with Social and Aesthetic (versus Theoretical and Economic) values on the Allport–Vernon–Lindzey Study of Values), with correlations obtained averaging about .30. Jewish students proved more rational than non-Jewish students on both the anti-Jewish ($p < .001$) and the pro-Jewish ($p < .10$) subscales.

Schuman and Harding also present interview-based descriptions of 15 persons classified into their fourfold typology (irrational pro, irrational anti, rational, confused).

No *norms* are provided beyond means and standard deviations for the Boston and Catholic college samples. Percentages of persons falling in the irrational-pro, irrational-anti, rational, and confused categories are given for the Boston and Radcliffe samples.

GENERAL COMMENT.   The instrument appears thoughtfully constructed, has adequate reliability for group studies, and plausible validity correlates. Norms for a much wider group of respondents should be obtained if the instrument is to be used further, including rural, non-student, and non-Catholic populations; further validity work by other investigators would be desirable.

REFERENCES

Robinson, J. P., Rusk, J. G., and Head, K. B. (eds.) *Measures of political attitudes.* Ann Arbor: Survey Research Center, Institute for Social Research, University of Michigan, 1968.

Schuman, H. and Harding, J. Prejudice and the norm of rationality. *Sociometery,* 1964, 27 (3), 353–371.

UNITERMS.   Attitude; ethnic; human-heartedness; irrationality; justice; minority; norm; prejudice; race; rationality.

—M. B. M.

69
Reactions to Group Situations Test (RGST)

AUTHORS.   Herbert A. Thelen and Dorothy Stock Whitaker

AVAILABILITY.   Herbert A. Thelen, Department of Education, University of Chicago, Chicago, Illinois 60637. Also in Thelen and Stock (1954, pp. 179–181).

VARIABLES.   The Reactions to Group Situations Test measures five modes of individual behavior in group situations drawn from Bion (1948–1951): *Pairing* (P), an individual or group expression of friendship, support, or partiality for another member or his ideas; *Fight* (F), a need to resent any of the other modalities, another member, or the total group, expressed directly by hostile attack or subtly by resistance to an idea or manipulation of the group; *Dependency* (D), a need to achieve security through reliance on external factors, expressed by statements before the group of inability to cope with problems or by demands for external structure or control by rigid procedures; *Flight* (Fl), a need to avoid the other modalities, expressed by mental or physical withdrawal or by diverting the group with irrelevant matters or humorous interjections; and *Work* (W), a need to engage in and master problem-solving activity, expressed by activity which is group-oriented and directed toward a group goal. In addition, 16 items either mix modalities or elicit attitudes toward self, leaders, other members, or the group.

DESCRIPTION.   The RGST is a 44-item sentence-completion projective. Items are constructed such that Ss respond with action or non-action verbs. Some simulated items are:

> When the group came to a standstill, John
> When the leader asked me what I thought, I said
> When Walter appeared to have lost interest, Fred

The RGST also exists (Thelen, 1967) in a 50-item, forced-choice form, with items similar to the following:

> When the group came to a standstill, John
> A. came up with a way to get back on the track.
> B. struck up a private conversation with one of the others.

> When Walter appeared to have lost interest, Fred
> A. asked him for his ideas.
> B. also started daydreaming.

ADMINISTRATION AND SCORING.   The 44-item form is self-administering within a time limit of twenty minutes. The 28 items which represent "pure" modalities are scored on three dimensions: *Accept–reject* refers to the overt response. Acceptance means that the S responds within the modality presented in the stimulus. *Overt–covert* distinguishes modalities expressly changed by Ss response (overt) from modalities indirectly expressed (covert). The scorer must assume the burden of deciding whether a response is covert, whether the S is not aware that he is communicating a shift in modality. *Manner of response*, the third scoring dimension, distinguishes among *feeling*, a non-overt expression of an emotion; *action-plus*, a voluntary overt response; *action-minus*, an inhibition or diminution of an ongoing action; and *ideation*, a non-overt cognitive response stressing wishes, wants, intellectualizations, and thoughts. The RGST allows for special scoring problems resulting from ambiguous responses. Scores on the RGST are frequencies of responses within these categories.

Sample cases are presented and scored in Stock and Thelen (1958, pp. 50–64), and in Thelen and Stock (1954).

DEVELOPMENT.   A prototypical form of the instrument was developed to predict behavior in training groups at Bethel, Maine, in 1949 by B. Rosenthal and W. Soskin, and extended by McPherson (1951), who found his version of a sentence completion test to be more effective than the TAT for predicting training group behavior. Gradolph and Stock report (Thelen and Stock, 1954) that a pool of 100 items was then used with 80 adult subjects. Those items showing stereotyped responses, or which did not differentiate among subjects for other reasons were eliminated. Validity and reliability studies (see below) were carried out with the 44-item form.

CRITIQUE.   No *reliability* data as such are available for subjects. Scorer reliability was assessed in a sample of 132 tests gathered at Bethel, Maine, before and after a training laboratory. The average agreement for the accept–non-accept category was 86.2%; for the feeling-action-ideation-ambiguous category, 78.8%; and for the overt and covert categories from 30 to 50% (where chance agreement would have been 16.6%).

In a *predictive validity* study, an unspecified number of clinicians threw Q-sorts (keyed to the RGST's variables) along a continuum to describe the group behavior of five subjects. The clinicians had only the Ss' RGST protocols on which to base their Q-sorts. Three staff members of the Human Dynamics Laboratory at the University of Chicago observed the five subjects for one hour of group interaction and then completed the same Q-sorts as did the clinicians. On the basis of Q-sort correlations, clinicians experienced with the RGST were able to predict the types of behavior Ss exhibited at least 80% of the time.

A series of studies using RGST are reported in Stock and Thelen (1958), which lend plausibility to the usefulness of the instrument in studying individual and group behavior. They include studies of group composition, group problem-solving effectiveness as a function of member scores, the relationship of scores to actual interpersonal and group behavior, and the prediction of differential gain ("trainability") as a result of T-group experience. See also Thelen (1967) for studies of classroom grouping using the forced-choice form.

A possible *respondent difficulty* for females lies in the fact that all the subjects to be identified within the RGST are males.

No *norms* as such are available, though Thelen and Stock (1954) report the percentages of 68 participants at Bethel who accepted each of the items.

GENERAL COMMENT.   The RGST has a coherent theoretical base, and appears to be a useful measure of aspects of individual behavior in a group situation which are not tapped by other instruments included in this volume. The reliability and validity data presented here are meager; users should assess these properties further, as well as referring to Stock and Thelen (1958). Other potential problems lie in the scoring of overt-covert responses and in the interpretation of the modality of dependency. Stereotypically, dependency is equated with passivity. Freudian theory asserts, however, that while on a deeper level this association is valid, at the overt level dependency may be expressed either passively or actively. For example, item 23 states:

> The leader got mad at the group, and Rob *reprimanded him.*

The response "reprimanded him" could be just such an active expression of dependency.

The Reactions to Group Situations Test is included here on the basis of its apparent fruitfulness and potentiality.

REFERENCES

Bion, W. R. Experiences in groups, I. *Human Relations,* 1948, *1* (3), 314–320. Subsequent installments were pubished in the same journal as follows:
II. 1948, *1* (4), 487–496.
III. 1949, *2* (1), 13–22.
IV. 1949, *2* (4), 295–304.

V. 1950, *3* (1), 3–14.

VI. 1950, *3* (4), 395–402.

VII. 1951, *4* (3), 221–228.

McPherson J. H. A method for describing the emotional life of a group and the emotional needs of group members. Unpublished doctoral dissertation, Department of Education, University of Chicago, 1951.

Stock, D. and Thelen, H. A. *Emotional dynamics and group culture.* New York: New York University Press (for National Training Laboratories), 1958.

Thelen, H. A. *Classroom grouping for teachability.* New York: John Wiley, 1967.

Thelen, H. A. and Stock, D. *Methods for studying work and emotionality in group operation.* Chicago: Human Dynamics Laboratory, University of Chicago, 1954.

UNITERMS.   Acceptance; avoidance; dependency; emotionality; fight; flight; group; human relations training; pairing; projective; T-group; work.

—R. B. E.

—M. B. M.

70

Relationship Inventory

AUTHOR. G. T. Barrett-Lennard

AVAILABILITY. Barrett-Lennard, G. T. Dimensions of therapist response as causal factors in therapeutic change. *Psychological Monographs*, 1967, 76, No. 43.

VARIABLES. The inventory includes measures of four variables in a dyad (two-person relationship): *Empathic Understanding*, the extent to which one person is conscious of the immediate awareness of another; *Level of Regard*, the affective aspect of one person's response to another (may include feelings of respect, liking, appreciation, affection, and any other positive affective response); *Unconditionality of Regard*, the amount of variability in one person's affective relation to another; and *Congruence*, the degree to which one person is functionally integrated in the context of his relationship with another, such that there is absence of conflict or inconsistency between his total experience, his awareness, and his overt communication.

DESCRIPTION. Each of the 64 items is a simple declarative sentence to which the respondent assigns a score from a 7-point scale running from "Yes, I strongly feel that it is true," (+3) to "No, I strongly feel that it is not true" (−3). Simulated items are:

He admires me as a person.

He knows what I mean.

Four forms exist in order to account for all combinations of female–male, client–therapist relationships.

ADMINISTRATION AND SCORING. The inventory is completed by both parties to the relationship (patient–therapist, husband–wife, etc.). The instructions for the instrument are simple and straightforward. Items are balanced between positive and negative scoring; scoring sheets are provided. Each of the four scales has a theoretical range of −48 to +48. Sample ranges are given in the monograph running from about −16 to +48. Scores for a group of "more changed" and "less changed" patients ranged from +5 to +48, and from −11 to +48 respectively.

DEVELOPMENT. The Relationship Inventory grew out of Rogers' explorations of a process conception of psychotherapy (Rogers 1957,

1958; Rogers and Rablen, 1958) and the resultant Process Scale (which see); its other six "strands" scale a therapy client's reaction to his feelings and personal meanings, his manner of experiencing, his degree of incongruence, his communication of self, his construing of experience, and his manner of relating to others.

Proceeding from this framework (see also Walker, Rablen and Rogers, 1960), Barrett-Lennard attempted to operationalize each of five aspects or dimensions of the therapist's attitudes and responses. In correspondence, the author says that revisions have been made based "(a) on item-analysis results from several samples of data obtained with earlier versions of the instrument, (b) on other considerations, such as achieving an exact balance of positively and negatively stated items in each scale, (c) on minor theoretical refinements, particularly in respect to the Unconditionality of Regard scale and (d) on the concern to alter or replace several items of a relatively abstract or verbally difficult kind." However, no item-analysis data were reported. The result of these development activities was a reduction of items from 74 to 64, and the decision (not explained) to drop one of the original scales, Willingness to be Known.

The original normative samples were patients at the Counseling Center, University of Chicago. The sample consisted of 42 clients with 21 different therapists; most of the clients were in their twenties or thirties, nearly all had some college education, and 60% were men.

CRITIQUE.   The correlations among the scales present a problem of interpretation. When each of the scales is correlated with the others for the client and the therapist separately, all but two of the intercorrelations are significant for the clients and *all* are significant for the therapists. Thus the scales are not measuring separate aspects of the therapeutic relationship. However, the author argues that the scales *should* be positively related. For example, he says, "A person's congruence is, theoretically, the primary factor determining his *potential* for empathically understanding the other."

An alternate interpretation is that the "good" direction of the items is fairly obvious. High intercorrelations among scales may be accounted for by social desirability, or by a general disposition toward the relationship, such as the degree of satisfaction.

Reliabilities, both test–retest and split-half, are satisfactory. Test–retest correlations reported are: Level of Regard, .84; Empathic Understanding, .89; Congruence, .86; Unconditionality of Regard, .90. Spearman–Brown split-half correlations range from .82 to .93 for clients, and .88 to .96 for therapists. Similarly, subsequent studies have reported satisfactory reliabilities of both types for all but the Willingness to be Known scale (dropped in the final version).

Several *construct validity* studies are now available. The author's initial study presents reasonably good evidence that high scores on the inventory by both therapists and clients were significantly related to change scores on the Taylor Manifest Anxiety scale, and a Q adjustment score.

No *norms* are available for the 67-item form.

Although the inventory started as a measure of variables in the therapeutic relationship, it has since been used to measure process in other significant relationships. Relationship Inventory scores of marriage partners were found to be correlated with the Burgess Marriage Adjustment Schedule (Thornton, 1960). In a study by Emmerling (1961) "good" teachers were found to be offering essentially the same *relationship* qualities to their pupils as therapists to their clients. Clark and Culbert (1965), using the PES Scale, found positive relationships between ratings of speech samples in a T-group and the scales of the Relationship Inventory. Other studies have been carried out on self-directed training groups (Berzon, 1964); student–parent relationships (Hollenbech, 1965); instructors and students (Kagan and Hungate, 1964); juvenile delinquents and parents (Rosen, 1961); and simulated counseling situations (Snelbecker, 1961).

GENERAL COMMENTS.   While the author suggests that the inventory can be used with any meaningful relationship, more data are needed to support this suggestion. Critical studies need to be carried out to help determine whether the four scales *are*, in fact, measuring four different aspects of relationships. More should be said concerning why the Willingness to be Known scale was dropped and what this means for the original underlying theory.

However, the inventory does seem to measure *something* of the adequacy of certain kinds of important relationships, and is linked to a general theoretical structure aimed at increasing understanding of the nature and effects of adequate relationships. Few measures (other than sociometrics) exist in this area; the researcher interested in relationship processes may use this instrument with caution—and can undoubtedly contribute to its further development.

REFERENCES

Barrett-Lennard, G. T. Prediction from counselor behavior of client perception and of case outcome. *Journal of Counseling Psychology*, 1961, *8*, 37–42.

Barrett-Lennard, G. T. Dimensions of therapist response as causal factors in therapeutic change. *Psychological Monographs,* 1967, *76,* No. 43.

Berzon, B. The self-directed therapeutic group: an evaluative study. *Western Behavioral Sciences Institute Reports,* 1964, No. 1.

Clark, J. V. and Culbert, S. A. Mutually therapeutic perception and self-awareness in a T-group. *Journal of Applied Behavioral Science,* 1965, *1,* 180–194.

Emmerling, F. C. A study of the relationships between personality characteristics of classroom teachers and pupil perceptions of these teachers. Unpublished doctoral dissertation, Auburn, Alabama: Auburn University, 1961.

Hollenbech, G. P. Conditions and outcomes in the student-parent relationship. *Journal of Consulting Psychology,* 1965, *29,* 237–241.

Kagan, M. and Hungate, J. I. The field instructor–student relationship in social work. Bound mimeographed report. Austin: Graduate School of Social Work, University of Texas, 1964.

Rogers, C. R. The necessary and sufficient conditions of therapeutic personality change. *Journal of Consulting Psychology,* 1957, *2,* 95–103.

Rogers, C. R. A process conception of psychotherapy. *American Psychologist,* 1958, *13,* 142–149.

Rogers, C. R. and Rablen, R. A. A study of process in psychotherapy. Unpublished manual, Madison: University of Wisconsin, 1958.

Rogers, C. R., Gendlin, E. T., Kiesler, D., and Truax, C. *The therapeutic relationship and its impact: a study of psychotherapy with schizophrenics.* Madison: University of Wisconsin Press, 1966.

Rosen, H. H. Dimensions of the perceived parent relationship as related to juvenile delinquency. Unpublished master's thesis, Auburn, Alabama: Auburn University, 1961.

Snelbecker, G. E. Factors influencing college students' person-perceptions of psychotherapists in a laboratory analog. Unpublished doctoral dissertation, Ithaca: Cornell University, 1961.

Thornton, B. M. Dimensions of perceived relationship as related to marital adjustment. Unpublished master's thesis, Auburn, Alabama: Auburn University, 1960.

van der Veen, F. The perception by clients and by judges of the conditions offered by the therapist in the therapy relationship. *Psychiatric Institute Bulletin,* 1961, *1* (10e).

van der Veen, F. Perceived therapist conditions and degree of disturbance: a comparison of conditions perceived by hospitalized schizophrenic clients and counseling center clients. Madison: Research Report No. 14, Psychotherapy Research Project, Wisconsin Psychiatric Institute, 1963.

van der Veen, F. Dimensions of client and therapist behavior in relation to outcome. American Psychological Association: *Proceedings of the 73rd annual convention of the American Psychological Association*, 279–280.

Walker, A. M., Rablen, R. A., and Rogers, C. R. Development of a scale to measure process in psychotherapy. *Journal of Clinical Psychology*, 1960, *16*, 79–85.

UNITERMS.   Acceptance; change; congruence; dyad; empathy; family; level of regard; liking; marriage; psychotherapy; relationship; unconditionality of regard.

—D. G. L.

71
Remote Associates Test (RAT)

AUTHORS.   Sarnoff A. Mednick and Martha T. Mednick

AVAILABILITY.   Mednick, S. A. and Mednick, M. T. *Research in personality*. New York: Holt, Rinehart and Winston, 1963.

VARIABLES.   The Remote Associates Test is a measure of the *associative process*, an ability considered to be fundamental to *creativity*. The authors envision the creative process as basically one of seeing relationships between seemingly "mutually remote" ideas, and forming them into combinations that are either useful or that meet specified criteria.

DESCRIPTION.   The definition above generates the structure of the test. An effective measure must provide elements from mutually remote associative clusters and have the subject find a criteria-meeting mediating link which combines them. The mediating link must be strictly associative rather than follow usual rules of logic, concept formation, or problem solving.

In the present form, the test items consist of sets of three words drawn from mutually remote associative clusters. One example might be:

> rat   blue   cottage

The subject is required to find a fourth word which could serve as a specific kind of associative connecting link between these disparate words. The answer to the example is "cheese." "Cheese" is a word which can form word pairs "rat cheese," "blue cheese," "cottage cheese," and thus can be an associative connective link. Another example might be:

> cookies   sixteen   heart

The answer to this example is the word "sweet," an association more remote than the first.

ADMINISTRATION AND SCORING.   Two forms of the Remote Associates Test (RAT) have been developed: one for the college level and another, still in an experimental stage, for the professional level. Most of the discussion that follows relates to the Form 1 of the RAT.

The Remote Associates Test can be administered to groups or individuals. Although it is not a speed test, there is a forty-minute time limit. Most examinees will have been able to complete the 30-item test during this time period. The test is easy to administer, with ample instructions and warm-up exercises on the front cover of the test booklet. If the test is being given to a group, the instructions are read aloud and the sample problems completed. If the test is being given to a single examinee he is told to read the instructions, fill in the examples, and then ask any questions he has about the procedures before continuing. The examinee's score is the number of items correctly answered. Where an examinee has written more than one answer to an item, credit is given if one of the answers is correct. Hand scoring is accomplished easily with aid of a strip key which lists the correct answers to the items.

DEVELOPMENT.   The problem of finding a relevant and reliable criterion is all-important to the conceptual foundation of the RAT. If no reliable criterion of the desired class of behavior is possible, then no validity is possible. Creativity research has typically employed criterion ratings of individuals by their superiors or other expert judges and/or ratings of an individual's productivity. Both these types of criteria have their drawbacks. In the case of judgment by superiors there is the constant danger of contamination by irrelevant characteristics of the rater, ratee, or setting; in the case of productivity, the factor of creativity is blurred again by the fact that one man may turn out many slightly creative products while another man may work for years on one highly creative thing.

Perhaps for these reasons, in the end the RAT researchers satisfied themselves with developing a list of items that could be validated by other word association tests, such as the Kent–Rosanoff Word Association Test or the Thorndike–Lorge Word Count. By choosing the three stimulus words from low-probability response lists, they assured remote association, yet they were able to find words that were familiar enough to be recognized by the majority of the population.

All the items in Forms 1 and 2 of RAT were selected on the basis of their empirical usefulness after one-year studies on college and professional people.

CRITIQUE.   Corrected odd–even *reliabilities* for the Remote Associates Test were .92 for 289 women at an Eastern college and .91 for 215 men at the University of Michigan.

In the first *criterion validity* study, which utilized a preliminary form of RAT, design-course instructors at a college of architecture rated 20 students on their creativity. The raters had been advising and evaluating these students in the creation of new designs and models for a minimum of one year. The correlation between students' RAT scores and the faculty rating of creativity was .70 ($p < .01$). These ratings showed a very low relationship to the Terman Concept Mastery Test scores as well as to grade-point averages.

In a study by M. Mednick (1963), RAT was administered to 43 psychology graduate students. Between one and two years later the RAT administrative research advisers, who were not aware of the RAT scores of their advisees, rated these graduate students on a research creativity checklist (a modification, along a Thurstone model scale, of a check list developed by D. W. Taylor). The internal reliability of the check list, or Creativity Rating Scale (CRS), was .93 (Spearman–Brown). Miller Analogies Test scores and grade point averages (GPA) were available for some of the students. The CRS scores were not significantly related to either the MAT scores or GPA. However, correlation between CRS and RAT scores was .55 ($p < .05$). Correlations between RAT scores and MAT scores and GPA were .11 and −.11, respectively.

Gordon (1966) investigated the relationship of RAT to the job grade classifications of scientists in a chemical firm. For 42 scientists there was a strong relationship between RAT score and job grade classification. Those scoring high on RAT tended to be rated high in terms of the job grade classification and, conversely, those scoring low on RAT tended to be classified low. Their relationship was stronger than might have been expected by chance (Kendall $Q = .84$; χ^2 $p < .05$).

Andrews (1962) found essentially zero correlations between RAT scores and supervisor's rating of the creativity of 214 research scientists and engineers working in several government laboratories. Zero correlations were also obtained when ratings of performance were used. However, Andrews found some evidence that certain social-psychological variables affected the manifestation of creative ability in some of the scientists. His findings suggested that an unfavorable environment or restrictive situation, i.e., one in which the scientists experienced low status, low influence, and poor communications channels, may have resulted in lowered creative performance.

In a study of scientists and engineers employed by an industrial research and development company engaged in research on defense systems, Gordon (1966) investigated the relationship between RAT scores and number of contract proposals written and number of research contracts won by these scientists. Of the 37 scientists studied, 17 obtained RAT scores of 18 or less, and 20 obtained scores of 19 or higher. The scientists in the high RAT group wrote 69% of all contract proposals written by the entire group. The high RAT scorers also won almost 81% of all contracts won by the group, and had higher mean contract value. Age, seniority, and number of times each was project engineer were controlled in this study; amount of education and level of intelligence were not.

GENERAL COMMENT. The problem with tests of creativity has always been the criteria against which they are to be measured. Creativity clearly requires some type of associational ability, but the Remote Associates Test criterion of verbal ability to concatenate words often heard or seen together effectively denies creativity in less literate persons. The increased number of successful contract proposals among high RAT scorers can be readily explained as due to their ability to turn out better written proposals. Creative persons with high verbal skills probably score high on the RAT, but some non-creative high-verbal persons may also do so. The user interested in a thoughtful discussion of these problems, and some very promising visual tests of creativity, along with some verbal tests which are uncorrelated with intelligence, should consult Wallach and Kogan (1965b); see Wallach and Kogan (1965a) for an overview of this work.

REFERENCES

Andrews, F. Creativity and the scientist. Unpublished doctoral dissertation, Ann Arbor: University of Michigan, 1962.

Gordon, G. The identification and use of creative abilities in scientific organizations. Paper presented at the Seventh National Research Conference on Creativity, Greensboro, 1966.

Mednick, M. T. Research creativity in psychology graduate students. *Journal of Consulting Psychology*, 1963, 27, 265–266.

Mednick, S. A. and Mednick, M. T. The associative basis of the creative process. Ann Arbor: HEW Cooperative Research Project No. 1073, University of Michigan, 1965. (A lengthy bibliography is included.)

Wallach, M. A. and Kogan, N. A new look at the creativity–intelligence distinction. *Journal of Personality*, 1965(a), 33 (3), 348–369.

Wallach, M. A. and Kogan, N. *Modes of thinking in young children: a study of the creativity–intelligence distinction.* New York: Holt, Rinehart and Winston, 1965(b).

UNITERMS. Association; creativity; verbal ability; vocabulary.

—R. B. E.

72
Repression–Sensitization Scale (R–S Scale)

AUTHORS.   John Altrocchi and Donn Byrne

AVAILABILITY.   Byrne, D., Barry, J., and Nelson, D. Relation of the revised Repression–Sensitization Scale to measures of self-description. *Psychological Reports*, 1963, *13*, 323–334.

VARIABLES.   The major variable is the behavior dimension *repression–sensitization,* which expresses two presumably alternative modes of *defensive adjustment.* Repressors "tend to use avoidance, denial, and repression of potential threat and conflict." Sensitizers tend to be alert to incipient threat and conflict and "to respond more readily with manifest anxiety [and] intellectual and obsessive defenses" (Altrocchi et al., 1964). The theoretical variable is thus the use of approach (sensitizing) defenses such as intellectualization, obsessive acts, and worrying as attempts to control threat, as contrasted with the use of avoidance (repressive) defenses such as denial, repression, and some (unspecified) kinds of rationalization.

Repression and sensitization have been conceptualized as antithetical endpoints on a continuum of defensive adaptations (Byrne, 1964). (Repressors have also been defined as having a relatively higher threshold for emotional matters than sensitizers.) In any case, the underlying variable purports to be descriptive of alternative systems of perceptual defense, and individuals are seen as tending to revert to either repression or sensitization as a general pattern. The assumption is that a given person does not tend to combine these defensive styles within his perceptual repertoire, but to use one to the relative exclusion of the other.

The scale was designed to test older adolescents and adults.

DESCRIPTION.   Altrocchi's original version of the 182-item scale was comprised of 6 partially independent true–false MMPI scales. The administrator subtracted the total of the T scores of the D plus Pt plus Welsh Anxiety subscales from the sum of T scores on the L, K, and Hy denial subscale. Of the total, 156 items were scorable; the remainder were buffers. High positive scores operationally defined sensitizers; high negative scores, repressors, with one point being given for every item scored in the sensitization direction. Simulated examples of true–false items resembling statements on the Repression–Sensitization Scale follow:

I am frequently troubled by passing headaches.

When their own gain is at stake, most people will not adhere strictly to moral precepts to obtain an advancement.

(In these instances "true" responses presumably signify sensitization.)

ADMINISTRATION AND SCORING.   Byrne observed areas of potential confusion in Altrocchi's scoring system because some items contributed to more than one score among the 6 MMPI scales used. In his scoring revision (Byrne, 1961), each item is scored only once; inconsistently scored items are eliminated. Again, high scores define sensitization; low scores, repression. Totals are obtained by simply summing points. Respondent time and time limits have not been stipulated.

Normative data for the first Byrne revision are available (Byrne, 1964) for 394 male and 230 female college students in an introductory psychology course and are presented as group frequency distributions, means, and sigmas. For Byrne's (1963) second revision the same statistics are presented for 733 male and 531 female college students.

Machine scoring is not available for the second revision; a hand scoring key (Form R for the MMPI) is available from the Psychological Corporation, 304 East 45th Street, New York, New York 10017.

DEVELOPMENT.   Altrocchi (1960) used senior student nurses at the Duke University School of Nursing as his original population. A sample of 88 of these (selection techniques unspecified) constituted the first experimental group. Methods involved testing these and a cross-validation group from the same population ($N = 64$) with the Repression–Sensitization Scale before and after a sixteen-week training period in psychiatric nursing. Subsequently, the 15 persons in each group having the highest positive scores were defined as repressors and the 15 with the highest negative scores were defined as sensitizers. A middle group was included for purposes of comparison Self–ideal discrepancy was evaluated by the Leary Interpersonal Check List (ICL), the only external criterion employed. As measured by their ICL responses, experimental and validational repressors were significantly more "aggressive–sadistic," "rebellious–distrustful," and "self-effacing–masochistic" than sensitizers. Altrocchi (1960) viewed these differences as distinguishing repressors' from sensitizers' self-concepts.

An internal consistency item-analysis was done for Byrne's revised 182-item scale. Responses to each question were correlated with total R–S score for samples of 130 undergraduates for each question. A revised scoring key of 127 cross-validated items was devised, each item correlating at $p = .001$ or better with total R–S score. With another sample ($N = 133$) the corrected split-half reliability coefficient and the coefficient of stability were each .88. A test–retest (six-week interval) reliability of .82 and a split-half reliability of .94 were obtained for another sample ($N = 75$).

In a construct validity study (Byrne, 1963), psychology clinic personnel and psychology interns had to decide on how repressors would respond to each item. Agreement of seven out of the nine judges was reached for 150 of the 182 test items. For 120 of the 156 items in the original scoring key and for 114 (90%) of the 127 items in Byrne's revised key, such agreement was also reached. In no instance did judges agree on a response in a direction opposite to the key.

In a concurrent validity study (Byrne et al., 1963) scores on the R–S Scale were compared with scores on a measure of "Hostility Incongruency." Correlations between original and revised R–S scores and each of three incongruency scores for 114 psychology students were equivocal: five significant differences out of nine comparisons for the revised scale; six out of nine, for the original. Altrocchi (1960) interpreted these data as implying that sensitizers, compared with repressors, have "more negative, i.e., hostile and submissive self-concepts . . . and therefore a greater discrepancy between self and ideal self."

In another validity study, Altrocchi (1961) used assumed dissimilarity scores to measure the degree to which Ss' perceptions of themselves differed from their percepts of others, and the degree to which they perceived differences between two others. The original operational definitions of sensitizers and repressors were retained, and Ss were drawn from the top and bottom quartiles of the psychiatric nursing population described above. Pre-training and post-training assumed dissimilarity scores were obtained for "repressors" and for "sensitizers" involved in one of two tasks: describing someone similar to themselves (e.g., a repressor describing another repressor) or someone different from themselves. In a second design, Altrocchi added a middle group whose task was to describe two people presumably different from one another (a "sensitizer" and a "repressor"). Results for the first design showed "assumed dissimilarity" scores for sensitizers were significantly higher than for repressors ($p < .01$), but they were not affected by the degree of similarity between the Ss and those they described. In the second design the only significant differences were determined by whether the two people described were similar or dissimilar; the tendency for sensitizers to assume more dissimilarity between others approached significance ($p < .10$). No strong evidence of consistent differences in interpersonal perception between sensitizers and repressors was obtained from analyzing ICL scores. Altrocchi (1961) further concluded that repressors have more positive self-concepts and are more homogeneous in self-description than sensitizers.

CRITIQUE.   *Reliability* does not seem a problem.

A study of the repression–sensitization dimension and leadership lends only mild support to claims to *construct validity*. Joy (1963) gave 300 male introductory psychology students the revised Repression–Sensitization Scale. Sensitizers were significantly less apt to be chosen as future co-workers, and were less interested in maintaining friendly relations. However, no differences among the "sensitizers," "neutrals," and "repressors" for threat-oriented and task-oriented conditions were found.

Some support for *criterion validity* claims stems from a study eliciting 35 psychology students' evaluations of themselves on Gough's Adjective Check List. "Repressors" saw themselves as "organized, persevering, rational, resourceful, and clear thinking"; "sensitizers" viewed themselves as "anxious, confused, disorderly, forgetful, and pessimistic" (Joy, 1963). However, the size of these differences was unspecified, and sampling techniques and criteria for inclusion in repression and sensitization groups were not stated.

Byrne (1964) concluded on the basis of reviewing several studies, including the following, that the *construct validity* of the Repression–Sensitization Scale has been moderately well established. Tempone (1962) examined perceptual defense in 244 undergraduates, classifying the lowest-scoring (on the R–S scale) 25% as repressors and the highest-scoring 25% as sensitizers. A significant interaction effect was obtained between repression–sensitization and success–failure on an anagrams task involving recognition of critical words. Byrne and Sheffield (1964) found that sensitizers rated themselves as significantly more anxious than repressors during an experimental situation designed to induce sexual and anxiety arousal. Lazarus and Alfert (1964) measured skin conductance and heart rate of 69 male students viewing a movie about subincision ritual. Using a median split of their R–S Scale score frequency distribution, they found fewer significant differences between repressors and sensitizers than had previous studies.

The repeated use of extreme groups by investigators mentioned here, and by others cited by Byrne, could have biased results in favor of obtaining artifactual differences. Thus, validity appears to be somewhat tenuous.

Joy (1963) has reported that R–S scores correlated $-.91$ with a measure of *social desirability* developed by Edwards ($N = 35$) and concluded that the R–S scale measures a continuum of relative acculturation. A considerably lower but still significant r of $-.37$ was obtained by Liberty et al. (1964) between a measure of social desirability designed by Crowne and Marlowe and R–S scores. The latter also loaded on a social desirability factor (Liberty et al., 1964, as reported by Byrne, 1964).

Normative data available are not appropriate for extra-college populations, and possibly, as Byrne (1961) cautioned, relevant only to the population at the University of Texas, from which the norm group was drawn. In none of the norm group studies were sampling procedures explicitly mentioned.

GENERAL COMMENT.   The repression–sensitization typology, while attractive, does not specify the plethora of defensive adaptations actually used by people. "Repressors" and "sensitizers" are persons who tend to rely on one of these defensive modes to the relative exclusion of the other; clearly other styles are possible. Studies on the R–S Scale that have also included groups of "expressors" are praiseworthy for this reason.

Until more information is available on its validity, the Repression–Sensitization Scale should be used only in validational studies employing a variety of external criteria. It is clearly not yet ready for use in making clinical diagnoses and prognoses. However, it appears promising, as Byrne (1964) has suggested, as a potential indicator of the relative presence of repressive versus sensitizing defenses in individuals' adjustment patterns. The social desirability aspect of the scale needs further developmental attention.

REFERENCES

Altrocchi, J. Interpersonal perceptions of repressors and sensitizers and component analysis of assumed dissimilarity scores. *Journal of Abnormal and Social Pychology,* 1961, 62 (3), 528–534.

Altrocchi, J., Parsons, O. A., and Dickoff, H. Changes in self–ideal discrepancy in repressors and sensitizers. *Journal of Abnormal and Social Psychology,* 1960, 61, 67–72.

Altrocchi, J. and Perlitsh, H. D. Ego-control patterns and attribution of hostility. *Psychological Reports,* 1960, 12, 811–818.

Byrne, D. The Repression–Sensitization Scale: rationale, reliability, and validity. *Journal of Personality,* 1961, 29, 334–349.

Byrne, D., Barry, J., and Nelson, D. Relation of the revised Repression–Sensitization Scale to measures of self-description. *Psychological Reports,* 1963, 13, 323–334.

Byrne, D. Repression–sensitization as a dimension of personality. In Maher, B. (ed.) *Progress in experimental personality research,* Vol. I. New York: Academic Press, 1964.

Byrne, D. and Sheffield, J. Response to sexually arousing stimuli as a function of repressing and sensitizing defenses. *Journal of Abnormal Psychology*, 1965, *70*, 114–118.

Crowne, D. P. and Marlowe, D. A new scale of social desirability independent of psychopathology. *Journal of Consulting Psychology*, 1960, *24*, 349–354.

Joy, V. L. Repression–sensitization. Address to the American Psychological Association, Philadelphia, August 1963.

Lazarus, R. S. and Alfert, E. The short-circuiting of threat. *Journal of Abnormal and Social Psychology*, 1964, *69*, 195–205.

Liberty, P. G., Jr., Fones, R. J., and McGuire, C. Age–mate perceptions of intelligence, creativity, and achievement. *Perceptual and Motor Skills*. 1963, *16*, 194.

Tempone, V. J. Differential thresholds of repressors and sensitizers as a function of a success and failure experience. Unpublished doctoral dissertation, Austin: University of Texas, 1962.

UNITERMS.   Anxiety; approach-avoidance; defense mechanism; dissimilarity; expression; hostility; inhibition; interaction; interpersonal; intellectualization; personality; repression; self-concept; sensitization; similarity; threat.

—L. J. R.

73

Responsibility, Authority, and Delegation of Authority Scales (RAD Scales)

AUTHORS.   Ralph M. Stogdill and Carroll L. Shartle

AVAILABILITY.   Stogdill, R. and Shartle, C. *Methods in the study of administrative leadership*. Columbus: Ohio State University, Bureau of Business Research, Research Monograph No. 80, 1955.

VARIABLES.   *Authority*, viewed as describing relationships among personnel in an organization and between one's responsibilities and his freedom to execute these, constitutes the first variable. *Responsibility*, the second variable considered, appears to be conceptualized as a concomitant subdivision of the first. *Delegation of Authority* has been conceptualized as determining which members of organizations shall have authority over given responsibilities (hence persons and activities).

The scales in question have been designed to measure these phenomena as *perceived level of obligation* (responsibility) and *perceived scope of action* in the organization (authority). The scores represent an individual's estimate of his own degree of responsibility, authority, and the extent to which he delegates authority to his assistants within the organization.

DESCRIPTION.   Three separate scales presumably measuring responsibility, authority, and delegation of authority have been constructed. These yield three sets of scores, which originally were used in a formula to derive a RAD Index:

$$\text{RAD Index} = \frac{\text{Authority Score}}{\text{Responsibility Score}} \times \text{Delegation Score}$$

According to Stogdill and Shartle (1948), the index is no longer in use, the separate scores having been found more useful. However, low index scores were associated with "high leadership status" (criteria unexplicated). Stogdill and Shartle considered the index as giving some indication of the relation between a person's estimate of his own status within an institution and willingness to let others manage their responsibilities.

The format involves 6 scales, each comprised of 8 items like the following simulated examples. Every item presumably represents a different orientation to one of the three variables:

I have the responsibility of supervising a number of others under me and of checking to see that their work is properly executed. (Responsibility)

I permit those I supervise to execute their duties with full freedom to exert their authority in whatever way they consider appropriate, but they must consult me on unforeseen matters. (Authority)

Instructions state that two scales describe degrees of authority, two others degrees of responsibility, and two more degrees of delegation and authority.

ADMINISTRATION AND SCORING.   These self-administering scales are designed for group or individual use. Subjects are required to indicate separately the most descriptive and second-most descriptive statement with respect to himself or another.

Items are assigned scale values, and the administrator sums those for the items in each scale checked by respondents to derive the score. The resulting three totals are each divided by four to ascertain final scores. High scores presumably indicate considerable perceived responsibility, etc.

No norms are currently available.

DEVELOPMENT.   The Responsibility, Authority, and Delegation of Authority Scales were designed to measure these phenomena as perceived by the person being evaluated, or as perceived by another who knows him well enough on an occupational basis to describe him. The original populations (sampling techniques unspecified) came from a naval district staff ($N = 34$), a naval air station ($N = 49$), a heavy cruiser ($N = 48$), a naval district staff ($N = 39$), ten submarines ($N = 66$), nine landing ships ($N = 51$), and a research command staff ($N = 187$). Each sample was divided into superiors and subordinates, according to status within their organization. The former were few in number in each organization, ranging from 8 to 15 for every sample but the research command staff ($N = 57$). Data for some individuals were used twice, in both superior and subordinate capacity. Correlations between scores of both these levels were obtained, using a self-description method of administering the three scales.

Significant relationships (.05 or better) between subordinates' and superiors' Responsibility scores were obtained only for air station ($r = .63$) and research command personnel ($r = .28$). Also significant were those between Authority scores for both roles in naval district staff ($r = -.72$) and research staff members ($r = .48$). For the latter, subordinates' Responsibility and Delegation scores correlated with those of superiors at .38 and $-.47$, respectively. Finally, Authority scores of subordinates in the research staff correlated at .33 with Delegation scores of superiors. Significant positive *and* negative correlations were thus found between subordinates' Authority scores, and superiors' Authority and Delegation scores, depending on the sample.

The authors' interpretation was that when superiors rate themselves high in Responsibility, their subordinates also evaluate themselves high on Authority and Responsibility. However, they thought that when superiors' self-ratings on Authority are high, subordinates are less able to clearly perceive their own Responsibility and Authority. Additionally, Responsibility and Authority scores of superiors were (nonsignificantly) negatively correlated to subordinates' Delegation ratings. Positive correlations of superiors' Delegation scores with all three scales for most subordinate groups were obtained. These were taken as evidence that when superiors delegate more, their subordinates rate themselves higher on all three variables with respect to *their* subordinates. However, the small size of the groups studied, and the substantial variation in relationships obtained from group to group, militate against an unambiguous interpretation.

CRITIQUE.   Stogdill and Shartle (1955) have reported *reliability* coefficients of "approximately .70 between equivalent forms of the R, A, and D scales. The test–retest reliabilities of the R and A scales are approximately .60 and that of the D scale is approximately .70" (Stogdill, 1957). Thus reliability as reported is not sufficiently high to permit accurate measurement of individual leadership behavior.

Criterion validity (comparing self-ratings with descriptions by others) was assessed by Stogdill (1957). Correlations between these methods were reported as .70 for Responsibility, .27 for Authority, and .33 for Delegation (*N* unspecified).

Stogdill also reports a study by Browne (Stogdill, 1957, p. 75) showing that executives' salaries in a manufacturing plant correlated at .48, .41, and .49 with the R, A, and D scales respectively, lending some weight to the *construct validity* of the measures; presumably upper, better-paid managers have more responsibility and authority, and also delegate more. In six military samples, the three measures also correlated positively with level in the organization at from .06 to .73, median .27.

The measures showed few if any correlations with sociometric scores in three military organizations.

The RAD scores showed little or no correlation with leader communicative behavior in six military organizations (*N* from 15 to 69), but leader "organizing" behavior tended to correlate negatively (nonsignificantly) with the Delegation score, while "representing" leader behavior tended to go positively with it (significant *rs* .28 to .35). Finally, Delegation scores correlated positively with nominations of submarine squadron leader ($N = 69$) as good peacetime, wartime, and all-around leaders—as well as with their rank and time in position. Authority scores tended to do likewise, but less strongly; Responsibility scores showed no relationship.

In general, the validity evidence tends to be inconsistent from organization to organization, and not powerful. Further, the relatively high intercorrelations obtained among the variables lead one to suspect the *theory* of being incomplete, since the author does not appear to have accounted for such relationships. Stogdill discusses the meaning of his findings in some detail (1957, pp. 81–84), and the interested user is referred to that treatment.

Norms are needed to further clarify the validity and applicability of the scales, as well as for purposes of comparison of scores.

GENERAL COMMENT.   At present, because of meager information on reliability and uncertain validity, the RAD Scales should only be used for group evaluations, and should not be used in clinical or other settings to assess individual performance. The authors' stipulation that the RAD Scales were intended for research only deserves note. Investigators interested in studying leadership and the use of power in organizations may want to use (and contribute to the future development of) these scales.

REFERENCES

Stogdill, R. M. and Scott, E. L. Responsibility and authority relationships. In Stogdill, R. M. (ed.) *Leadership and structures of personal interaction.* Columbus: Research Monograph No. 84, Bureau of Business Research, Ohio State University, 1955.

Stogdill, R. M. and Shartle, C. L. Methods in the study of administrative leadership. Columbus: Research Monograph No. 80, Bureau of Business Research, Ohio State University, 1957.

Stogdill, R. M. and Shartle, C. L. Methods for determining patters of leadership behavior in relation to organization structure and objectives. *Journal of Applied Psychology,* 1948, 32, 286–291.

UNITERMS.   Authority; control; delegation; employee; employer; leadership; management; organizational; planning; power; responsibility; supervisor.

—L. J. R.

74
Role Construct Repertory Test (Rep Test)

AUTHOR.   George A. Kelly

AVAILABILITY.   Kelly, G. A. *The psychology of personal constructs.* Vols.
I and II, New York: W. W. Norton, 1955.

VARIABLES.   The Role Construct Repertory Test does not attempt to
measure variables previously conceptualized by the author; it seeks,
rather, to elicit from the respondent the major templates he attempts
to lay over reality. A *personal construct,* as Kelly develops the term,
is a channel of psychological movement. "In its minimum context a construct is a way in which at least two elements are similar and contrast
with a third" (Kelly, 1955). Three elements are the minimum required
for a construct; the two which are similar are termed the "construct";
the third is called the "contrast." For example, two roles may be seen
as having in common the element "easygoing," and a third role may be
specifically contrasted by having the element "hypertensive." In Kelly's
theory, these three elements define a path along which psychological
movement does or can take place. The clinical diagnosis of these paths
and their qualities in a psychotherapy client (or in any person) is the
object of the Rep Test.

DESCRIPTION.   The Rep Test comes in nine forms which cover a range
of contexts, include or exclude the self, vary in administrative procedure slightly, or are intended for group use. The simplest form, the
Minimum Context Form, consists of a sort totalling 24 $3'' \times 5''$ cards,
each bearing a role title such as the following:

> Your mother.
> A girl you did not like when you were 16.
> The person whom you would most like to be of help to.

All the forms for individual administration contain 24 cards; the group
form asks for 15 role occupants. The most complex (and most easily
scorable) form, the Grid form, asks for 22 role occupants, and groups
them so: self (1); family (4); intimates (4); situationals (3—minister,
physician, neighbor); valencies (4—rejected, pitied, threatening, attractive persons); authorities (3—accepted and rejected teachers, boss);
and values (3—successful, happy, and ethical persons).

ADMINISTRATION AND SCORING.   The clinician hands the client each card
and asks him to write on the card the name of a person who fits the role

description printed at the top. No names are repeatable; if, for example, the person a client would most like to be of help to is his mother, he must make a second choice. When the cards have been filled out, the examiner chooses combinations of three cards according to one of several sequences suggested by Kelly. He then presents them to the client and asks, "In what *important way* are two of them alike but different from the third?" The examiner records the subject's response for sort number 1 both as to construct (the way in which the two are like) and contrast (the way in which the third is different). The number of sorts made depends upon the clinician's experience, both with the Rep Test and with patients generally. One study has suggested that 40 sorts do not elicit appreciably less information than do 80 to 100. An average number of sorts (30) can easily require an hour to obtain.

Scoring is more difficult; and the term "scoring" as such applies only to the Grid form, elaborated upon in a lengthy and mathematically sophisticated chapter in Kelly's first volume (1955) and further explicated in Bannister and Mair (1968). For the other forms, protocols are analyzed, rather than scored, and Kelly suggests 24 distinguishable types of constructs: for example, permeable; linking through contrasts; linking through figures; situational; preemptive; dependency; conventionalized; and perseverations. The mere typology of constructs, however, does not constitute an analysis of the protocol. The clinician must first be familiar with Kelly's theory of personality (a theory which specifically eschews established concepts such as *ego, emotion, motivation, reinforcement, drive, unconscious,* and *need*), of which the Rep Test is a practical embodiment. Only then do the constructs elicited reveal any import for diagnosis. The clinician knowledgeable in personal construct theory will be able either to guide the client along what have been revealed to be his channels of psychological orientation to a more healthy position, or to reorient those channels along a more helpful dimension—to change the client's constructs toward those embodying less anxiety, fear, or paralysis. The Rep Test (except for the Grid form) can be utilized efficiently only by a clinician both experienced in therapy and wholly familiar with the content of Kelly's treatise.

DEVELOPMENT.   To delineate the development of the Rep Test, it is necessary to trace the development of Kelly's theory of the psychology of personal constructs, from his first realization that the *whys* of clinical practice were often left assumed and unanswered, through his own view of the evolution of psychology from phenomenology through Gestalt theory, up to his 1955 expression of his own synthesis. Such is not within the scope of this volume.

292

CRITIQUE. Kelly rejects the concept of *reliability* as unsuitable to the Rep Test; he prefers to discuss its *consistency,* and refers to studies of hospital patients and of college students which showed that on two administrations of two different but equivalent forms of the test, the average agreements in constructs used were 69% and 70% in the two groups respectively. The standard deviations were 6% and 8%. Fjeld and Landfield (1961) found a two-week test–retest correlation of .79 between constructs elicited by the same elements and one of .80 between constructs elicited by new elements ($N = 80$ normals). They also found that when subjects chose their own elements with regard for role titles, they repeated 72% of the role title occupants. Pedersen (1958) found an average agreement of 77% between persons chosen to fill role titles in two separate administrations one week apart.

Bannister and Mair (1968, p. 180) quote reliabilities of the Grid form which "fall largely within the range .60 to .80." For ten persons who used the Grid to rank-order ten photographs of persons, the six week test–retest figure was .86. In another set of three studies of normals and schizophrenics, retest reliabilities (N and time unspecified) were found to be .60, .72, and .80 for normals, and .33, .35, and .18 for schizophrenics. Mair and Boyd (1967) compared fourteen-day test–retest reliabilities for 20 subjects, using both a split-half grid and a rank-order grid. The latter proved more stable, with correlations of .72, .57, and .57 for the constructs "like mother, like self, like father." The split-half grid produced figures of .43, .59, and .52.

No evidence of *validity* is presented in Kelly's (1955) work. Instead, a sample Rep Test protocol is analyzed, questions for the respondent's therapist are formulated as a result of that analysis, and the extensive comments of the therapist based on six sessions with the client are presented with an obvious, if not explicitly stated, view to the points of coincidence between the two analyses. The lengthy comparison is summarized by the statement, "The foregoing account should serve to illustrate what is meant by checking clinical hypotheses based on tests against psychotherapeutic experience. This is an *illustration* of the possible usefulness of the test, not an experimental proof of its validity." Bannister and Mair (1968) give evidence drawn from single case studies (arsonist, frigid woman, agoraphobic, opposite sex identifier) which emphasize the individual–specific focus of the Rep Test.

Bannister and Mair (1968, pp. 191–194) also report two *concurrent validity* studies. In one, voting behavior of 74 subjects was successfully predicted from the size of the correlation between the Grid score on "sincere" and the respective Grid scores for "Conservative," "Labor," and "Liberal." The other study (N unspecified) found that subjects whose

Grid showed a close relationship between the "like me" and "needs approval," and those whose Grid showed a close relationship between "like I'd like to be in character" and "like the experimenter" were more influenced by experimenter reinforcement in a verbal conditioning experiment.

The concept of *norms* is somewhat irrelevant to this test; *respondent difficulties*, however, are central. Kelly offers an adequate discussion of 6 types of constructs which are difficult to handle systematically, such as a subject's saying, "These two are alike; they're from the same town," and the followup procedures necessary to increase the level of specificity in responses.

GENERAL COMMENT.   The Role Construct Repertory Test is the practical application of an elaborate, original, and sophisticated theory of personal psychology. Kelly's theory challenges, this writer suspects, the most experienced clinical therapist. As indicated above, this is not an instrument to be used readily by any but the most advanced diagnostician, and then only after he has become thoroughly familiar with both the theory and practice of the test. Kelly's theory, however, is so comprehensive and his elaboration is so absorbing that his two volumes commend themselves to the professional clinician.

The Grid form of the test requires less clinical sophistication, and in fact stimulated the development of Harrison's Person Description Instrument (which see).

REFERENCES

Bannister, D. and Mair, J. M. M. *The evaluation of personal constructs.* New York: Academic Press, 1968.

Fjeld, S. P. and Landfield, A. W. Personal construct consistency. *Psychological Reports*, 1961, 8, 127.

Kelly, G. A. *The psychology of personal constructs.* Vols. I and II. New York: W. W. Norton, 1955.

Kelly, J. V. A program for processing George Kelly's Rep Grids on the IBM 1620 computer. Unpublished manuscript, Columbus: Ohio State University, 1963.

Mair, J. M. M. and Boyd, P. R. A comparison of two grid forms. *British Journal of Clinical and Social Psychology*, 1967, 6, 220.

Pedersen, F. A. A consistency study of the R.C.R.T. Unpublished master's thesis, Columbus: Ohio State University, 1958.

UNITERMS.   Categorizing; clinical; cognitive; construct; diagnostic; personality; protocol analysis; psychotherapy; psychological space; role.

—R. B. E.

75

Rosenzweig Picture-Frustration Study (P-F Study)

AUTHOR. Saul Rosenzweig

AVAILABILITY. Dr. Saul Rosenzweig, 8029 Washington Street, St. Louis, Missouri 63114

VARIABLES. The Rosenzweig Picture-Frustration Study produces 15 scores. Three measure the *direction of aggression: Outward; Inward;* and *Passive.* Three measure the *type of aggression: Need-Persistence,* conceptualized as constructive aggression; *Ego-Defense,* conceptualized as destructive aggression; and *Obstacle-Dominance,* conceptualized as a response which is blocked before it can assume the form of either of the other two types. Nine additional scales are formed from the combination of these two three-fold measures. For the outward reactions, the need-persistence type is termed *extrapersistive,* the ego-defense type is termed *extrapunitive,* and the obstacle-dominance type is termed *extrapeditive.* The corresponding three adjectives for the inward reactions are *intropersistive, intropunitive,* and *intropeditive.* For the passive reactions they are *impersistive, impunitive,* and *impeditive.* Forms for children (ages 4 through 13), adolescents (12 through 18), and adults are available.

DESCRIPTION. Each of the 24 pictures in a form features a frustration situation between two persons. One person has said something either to frustrate or to indicate frustration in the other. The subject identifies with this other person and indicates that person's response. The facial expressions depicted are purposely vague to ease projection.

ADMINISTRATION AND SCORING. The projective responses can be either oral or written. Oral responses are clearly richer in terms of nuance and intonation than written responses, but they are difficult to compare and expensive to preserve/transcribe on tape.

The set of 24 items can be completed orally in from fifteen to twenty minutes. Each response is scored for direction and for type of aggression; the raw scores are converted to percentages of the total (24) responses. By comparison with norms, composite Group Conformity Ratings can be determined. The responses to the first 12 items can be compared with those to the last 12 to assess trends. Scoring samples in the manual are thorough, although on occasion scoring is possible only after further and possibly leading inquiry. Norms are available in the manual for all three forms for American subjects, and elsewhere for

French, Italian, German, Japanese, and Indian children. (See Pareek, 1959.)

DEVELOPMENT. In 1928 Rosenzweig began investigating the interrelationships among personal frustrations, needs, and creativity. From laboratory investigations of repression, displacement, and projection he posited the concept of frustration as exemplifying a psychodynamic approach to these phenomena. The Picture-Frustration Study started as a projective in a four-part battery known as the F-Test. This battery contained, in addition, a behavioral test which tapped types of reaction to frustration, and two questionnaires, one asking for anticipated (real) responses to frustrating situations and one asking for ideal responses to the same situations. This projective part was first used in 1941, in a study of susceptibility to hypnosis as related to preferred mechanisms of ego defense and to modes of intermediate reactions to frustration. The original form contained 32 items which included depictions of needs for approval, freedom, nurturance, etc., and of privation, deprivation, and conflict. The sex of both the frustrating and frustrated characters was varied. In the final 24-item form 14 items are *ego*-blocking (obstacle); 8 of the remaining 10 are *superego*-blocking (accusation or incrimination).

CRITIQUE. In discussing *reliability*, Rosenzweig (1960) contends that traditional measures, such as split-half (first–second or odd–even) techniques, "violate the deliberately nonlinear plan of . . . the P-F in which the items, though they do aim to elicit certain general functions or traits, are also intentionally *diverse* so as to sample various aspects of experience." His major valid point seems to be that a subject may, over the course of the test, become aware of his mode of response (such as blaming others) and consciously change it, and that this shift naturally undermines standard measures of reliability, including test–retest. While the objection to reliance on test–retest is valid on the grounds that one may expect personality changes to occur independently of any conscious effort to effect change over time. Rosenzweig's a priori suspicion of split-half measures is not so defensible. What one wants, after all, is an index of the consistency with which the items tap the presumed personality traits. If a subject shifts his mode of response, then the projective is "unreliable" because it encourages him to adopt behavior which is less preferred or even atypical and which is indicative only of the responses he would make in the real world if subjected to a similar rapid sequence of frustrating situations in unrelated contexts (a highly improbable experience). In addition, Rosenzweig's trend scores are first-half versus second-half; odd–even reliabilities should not be affected by such trends. All this being said, the odd–even reliabilities are not good. For a group of 44 10- and 11-year-olds the rs for the direction of aggression were Outward $= .82$, Inward $= .57$, and Passive $= .62$ (all $p < .01$). For the type of aggression they were Need-Persistence $= .46$, Ego-Defense $= .28$, and Obstacle-Dominance $= -.04$. These latter results were significant only for the Need-Persistence score. For 45 12- and 13-year-olds the figures were Outward $= .68$ ($p < .01$), Inward $= .32$ ($p < .05$), Passive $= .60$ ($p < .01$), Need-Persistence $= .13$ (nonsignificant), Ego-Defense $= .23$ (nonsignificant), and Obstacle-Dominance $= .36$ ($p < .05$). Thus, only the *direction* of aggression scores can be said to have consistency. It should be added that although Rosenzweig recommends post-test interviewing to determine the level of response tapped (opinion, overt, or implicit), he does not indicate that subjects commonly report the kinds of shifts which, he argues, explain the low reliability scores. Interscorer reliability is good; two studies showed initial agreement scores between two judges of .80 for the child form and .85 for the adult form, and all differences were resolved in conference.

Validity data are inconclusive. One study of 60 private school children ages 4 through 7 years compared P-F scores with teacher ratings of social adjustment in five categories: socially adequate (unaggressive); socially adequate (aggressive); shy, timid, and insecure; destructively aggressive; and asocial or withdrawn. Rosenzweig (1960) reports each group's punitiveness scores, which measure the direction of ego-defensive aggression, but he confuses the results by such statements as, "The extrapunitiveness tended to be of the obstacle-dominant type. . . ." By his own terminology, however, obstacle-dominance aggressions are classified as peditive, not as punitive, responses. Later he writes, "The extrapunitiveness in this group, while chiefly of the ego-defensive type, was also commonly need-persistive." In the face of this inconsistency the results of this study are inconclusive.

Ferguson (1954) showed that the lower half of superego scores corresponded to those subjects in the higher half of home and parental instability, but this study is vitiated by Rosenzweig's contradictory statements that the 32 subjects had "serious behavior problems" and that they "were not . . . clearly different from the normal standardization group."

Mirmow (1952) used the method of successive clinical predictions to assess P-F validity. In this technique investigators attempt to predict P-F scores for subjects known to them through psychological histories and test data. After comparing the actual results to their hypothesized ones, they predict again for a new group of subjects. Presumably, the P-F reveals its own validity. The 24 subjects, ages 7 through 14, were patients at a child guidance clinic. The three judges attempted both to predict actual P-F scores and, for the last 19 subjects in the series, to select a particular subject's record book from a group of five unidentified such books. The blind identification improved significantly from the first ten to the last nine. The composite (three-judge) predictions of P-F scores correlated significantly with actual scores for the *direction* of aggression and for Group Conformity Ratings, but the composite scores did not correlate significantly for the *type* of aggression.

Construct validity poses problems, especially in the light of the fact that aggression and sex role are usually linked. Rosenzweig finds no sex differences in child and adult samples, but, of the 24 situations in the child form, girls have only 8 opportunities for same-sex identification, while boys enjoy the remaining 16. In 7 of these 16, the boy is responding to a female adult, while in only one is the girl responding to a male adult. The adult form contains 16 males and 6 females to be identified with (two are unclear); no female is pictured as responding to a male. (See Moore and Schwartz (1963) for data and comment.) The adolescent form is balanced for sex identification with frustrater and frustrated and with peer and adult frustraters. Significant sex differences result, with males being more aggressive, both inward and outward (Rosenzweig, 1970).

One problem of theory which has been noted is that of determining the level at which responses are taking place. It is not clear whether a subject's responses indicate everyday behavior, his own interpretation of his everyday behavior, wish-fulfillment behavior, or ideal, socially desirable behavior. In an interesting study (itself a minor classic on the validity of paper-and-pencil tests), Borgatta (1951) compared the frequency of hostile (extrapunitive) responses to the P-F Study, in a series of role-played episodes paralleling the test situations, and in deliberately frustrating situations occurring in the actual experimenter-subject interaction. The level of hostility was considerably higher in the P-F responses than in either of the more behavioral measures; the role-played responses were much closer to real behavior than to the paper-and-pencil responses. This suggests that P-F scores (at least for extra-punitiveness) are nearer something like wish-fulfillment (given the usual social inhibitions centering around the expression of aggression) than to actual, perceived, or socially desirable behavior. And in a similar study involving playlets which dramatized the first 12 items in the P-F, Wechsberg (1951) found that in 22 normal children, ages 7 through 12, P-F scores corresponded to scores on a self-concept questionnaire, while in 22 maladjusted children P-F scores corresponded more nearly to implicit levels tapped by the playlets. But for the two populations taken together there were no consistent differences between P-F scores and either the self-opinion questionnaires or the playlet responses.

In an early investigation of (relative) *predictive validity,* a 32-item form of the P-F was matched against an open-ended questionnaire (administered four months after the P-F) taken by 40 public school children, ages 9 through 13. Three teachers who had known each subject for at least one year were asked to choose between individual P-F and matching questionnaire responses for the item which more nearly described the subject's overt everyday behavior. The teachers significantly ($p < .01$ or $.05$) preferred 14 of the 32 P-F items. For the set of 32 the P-F was preferred to the questionnaire at the .01 level of significance. But Mehlman and Whiteman (1955) showed that P-F scores did *not* predict actual behavior in frustration situations.

GENERAL COMMENT.   The Rosenzweig Picture-Frustration Study has found its chief use in the testing of theoretical constructs of frustration mechanisms. Not all the nine categories occur with equal frequency or have equal construct validity. The reliability of scores for type of aggression is virtually nonexistent. The problems of response level, of sex-fairness, and of the effects of follow-up inquiry reinforce the recommendation that the Rosenzweig Picture-Frustration Study be used only as an adjunct on a theoretical or experimental level to other, more direct, measures of behavioral responses to frustration.

REFERENCES

Borgatta, E. F. An analysis of three levels of response: an approach to some relationships among dimensions of personality. *Sociometry,* 1951, *14,* 3–52.

Ferguson, R. G. Some developmental factors in childhood aggression. *Journal of Educational Research,* 1954, *48,* 15–27.

Mehlman, B. and Whiteman, S. L. The relationship between certain pictures of the Rosenzweig Picture-Frustration Study and corresponding behavioral situations. *Journal of Clinical Psychology,* 1955, *11,* 15–19.

Mirmow, E. L. The method of successive clinical predictions in the validation of projective techniques with special reference to the Rosenzweig Picture-Frustration Study. Unpublished doctoral dissertation, St. Louis: Washington University, 1952.

Moore, M. E. and Schwartz, M. M. The effect of the sex of the frustrated figure on responses to the Rosenzweig Picture-Frustration Study. *Journal of Projective Techniques and Personality Assessment,* 1963, *27,* 195–199.

Pareek, U. Rosenzweig Picture-Frustration Study—a review. *Psychology Newsletter,* 1959, *10,* 98–114.

Rosenzweig, S. The Rosenzweig Picture-Frustration Study, Children's Form. In Rabin, A. I. and Haworth, M. R. (eds.) *Projective techniques with children.* New York: Grune & Stratton, 1960.

Rosenzweig, S. Sex differences in reaction to frustration among adolescents. In Zubin, J. and Freedman, A. M. (eds.) *The psychopathology of adolescents.* New York: Grune & Stratton, 1970.

Wechsberg, F. O. An experimental investigation of levels of behavior with special reference to the Rosenzweig Picture-Frustration Study. Unpublished doctoral dissertation, St. Louis: Washington University, 1951.

UNITERMS.   Aggression; frustration; defense; ego; hostility; persistence; projective; punitiveness; superego.

—R. B. E.

76

Russell Sage Social Relations Test (RSSR)

AUTHORS.   Dora E. Damrin, William E. Coffman, and William A. Jenkins

AVAILABILITY.   Educational Testing Service, Princeton, New Jersey 08540 (publisher) and Hillcraft Industries, Route 3, Traverse City, Michigan 49684 (for purchase of building blocks used in test)

VARIABLES.   *Group problem-solving skill,* as related to discipline versus efficiency, is the variable presumably evaluated by the test. It was developed for use with children in grades 4 through 8 to measure an area of their growth designated "Social Relations." It was constructed to assess skills, knowledge, and behavior patterns relevant to *group planning* and *action.* Aspects of these phenomena are exemplified by such traits as the ability of the child to be both leader and group member at different times, as well as his capacities to make suggestions, listen to those of others, abide by group decisions when he has opposing views, etc. Subvariables are: *freedom; interest; discipline; discussion skill; knowledge of organizational skill; task-centeredness; procedural skill; quality of plan; operational skill;* and *problem success.* Subsequent to its origin, the Russell Sage Social Relations Test has also been considered appropriate for use with adults.

DESCRIPTION.   The test requires the group to build three structures, of graded levels of difficulty, from blocks distributed among the members. These are a house, a footbridge, and a dog, respectively in ascending order of complexity. An assembled model is visible for comparison. All children in a classroom are to be equally involved in the task of fitting together 36 notched, interlocking plastic blocks, which are initially distributed to all class members. They are instructed that their score is improved the faster they build the model, and that the test measures how well they work together. Twenty-six of the blocks are cubes, the remainder, triangles, and all are colored red, blue, or white.

The group's planning and action are recorded by an observer.

ADMINISTRATION AND SCORING.   Since a time limit is observed (fifteen minutes for the construction of each figure, *not* including the time spent by the group in planning how they will proceed), administrators must be present. Group work is timed from when the construction actually starts until fifteen minutes have elapsed, or a figure is completed, at which time the examiner tells members their score in terms of length of time taken.

The test is administered in two operationally defined stages, the first being a phase called "Planning" stage and the second a construction period. Observations of group behavior in each stage are recorded on different standardized sheets. When the rater must check off aspects of planning or execution patterns, a given category is scored plus or minus if the behavior describes a majority or minority of the group, respectively. In both phases various types of characterizations of the group interaction are denoted on the scorer's forms and these are checked off as they occur as overt behavior. Thus the scorer must be keenly and responsively perceptive to the activity of those being examined. Sensitivity to details of the group process is essential.

Examples of categories to be noted by the observer are Group Participation (subdivided into such components as Individual, Chorus, and Noise) in the Planning stage and Execution Pattern (subdivided as Plan in Effect, Plan not Followed, and No Plan) in the Operations stage. Every category and subcategory has been extensively defined.

Each of the vertical columns on the check lists of behaviors presumably represents about a minute of time. Ostensibly, the resulting pattern of checks provides a graphic picture of trends in group functioning over the time period required to complete each of the tests.

For description of the Planning stage, the observer is asked to denote the plan decided on, and to note type of examiner intervention needed, if any. Observation sheets for the Operations stage also make provision for completion time, examiner's remarks, and number of errors in final product.

A single scoring sheet is used for all three building tasks to summarize data from the observation records. Scoring is accomplished by coding planning behavior into eight content divisions, operations behavior into five. A "1" is placed in every category describing the class during planning; a "2" in every one describing operations behavior, and a "3" in every category describing interaction during the third task (phase unspecified). Scoring scales require examiners to abstract essential behavioral trends from the observation period; they include descriptive categories representing the variables, such as Freedom, Interest, and Discipline. Respondent total time is estimated at one hour, in the presence of a trained observer and a trained examiner.

DEVELOPMENT.   Results of studies using the authors' original populations (91 classes, grades 3 to 6, N's and sampling methods unspecified) yielded important information about the Russell Sage Social Relations Test. Apparently, it measures differently in accord with group size above and below a given range (20 to 30 children). The authors report ease in training persons with some education to administer the test according to standardized techniques. Children's behavior appeared to reflect the type of classroom experience provided by teachers (cf. Lippitt and White, 1943). Scores tended to vary more between schools than within schools, possibly in accord with local school climate. Retested groups rarely exhibited diminished eagerness and cooperation on the second as compared with the first administration when told examiners were interested in seeing how much better they could do than they had done. Finally, for adult and children's groups skilled and unskilled in cooperative group planning analogous scores were obtained, indicating the possible validity of the test for measuring such skills in adult groups as well.

No reliability study was completed by the authors, but observer reliability between Damrin and each scorer she trained for work with the original groups was estimated at .75 (part–part reliability) before such training was considered adequate. The rationale for not employing test–retest methods was that the test is designed to measure dynamic variables that are subject to change over time.

Construct and *predictive validity* were not considered relevant to the problems engaged by the test. From the original design of the RSSR, the variables under consideration were modified. For the Planning stage, these became Participation, Involvement (educed interest and concern with task), Communication, Autonomy (independence from examiner's help or restraint), Organizational Techniques, and Final Plan. For the Operations Stage, variables became Involvement, Atmosphere (psychological tone-quality of group), Activity (of those not actively building), and Success (amount of time utilized). Scoring was also revised, every group being scored 1 to 5 on each variable.

The theory was further refined to account for variables which limit performance. Limiting variables are conceptualized as reflective of self-discipline and technical knowledge (of group organizing). During planning, these are presumably Involvement and Autonomy, and during construction, Atmosphere and Activity.

Some additional revisions were also made in the observers' coding system. The following code for use with childrens' groups during the initial parts of the planning stage was adapted:

++	active interest of the majority of the group
+−	active interest of about half of the group
−+	active interest of a small minority of group members
−−	no one is actively interested

For Operations, Atmosphere is evaluated according to seven varieties of possible psychological tone. Involvement is similarly assessed according to two categories, Activity (of non-builders) using four designations, and Success by indicating time needed for completion (or the lack of ability to finish). These constitute a brief summary of the scoring revisions, which have been elaborated in detail by Damrin.

CRITIQUE.   Rippy (1960) reports an interproblem *reliability* of .90 found by Bowers and Soar (1960).

Scores showed no relation to OSCAR (Medley and Mitzel, 1958, 1959) in classroom observation scores, Rippy (1960) found. Apparently, *validity* has not been thoroughly investigated by the authors or other experimenters.

Norms are suggested by the authors' having specified nine types of groups. However, no normative data as such are offered.

A further problem seems to be that *scorer difficulty* has been encountered, possibly due to the complexity of the rating system, and its requirements for combining quick and keen observation with recording precision.

GENERAL COMMENT.   The basic idea of the test is sound: it gives promise of exploring classroom group processes directly through a standardized task, rather than by projective devices, ratings, or other indirect means. However, it appears that substantial sensitivity to group processes is necessary for both administering and scoring the Russell Sage Social Relations Test correctly. The need for a trained observer *and* a trained scorer may prevent the test's widespread classroom use.

Investigators interested in studying group processes, especially as these are affected by educational experiences such as group therapy and human relations training, should investigate further the reliability and validity of the Russell Sage Social Relations Test. Until validation is accomplished the test is *not* workable for evaluation of training or group interaction (or other variables presumably dependent on the latter).

REFERENCES

Bowers, N. D. and Soar, R. S. Characteristics of teachers who use group activities. Paper read at the annual meeting of the American Educational Research Association, 1960.

Damrin, D. E. Report on the development of the Russell Sage Social Relations Test. Unpublished mimeographed manuscript, Princeton: Educational Testing Service, undated.

Damrin, D. E., Coffman, W. E., and Jenkins, W. A. The Russell Sage Social Relations Test: a measure of group problem-solving skills in elementary school children. Unpublished mimeographed draft, Russell Sage Foundation, 1954.

Lippitt, R. and White, R. K. The social climate of children's groups. In Barker, R. G., Kounin, J. S., and Wright, B. A. (eds.) *Child behavior and development*. New York: McGraw-Hill, 1943.

Medley, D. M. and Mitzel, H. E. A technique for measuring classroom behavior. *Journal of Educational Psychology*, 1958, *49*, 86–92.

Medley, D. M. and Mitzel, H. E. Some behavioral correlates of teaching effectiveness. *Journal of Educational Psychology*, 1959, *50*, 239–246.

Rippy, L. Certain relationships between classroom behavior and attitude and personality characteristics of selected elementary teachers. In Bowers, N. D. and Soar, R. S. (eds.) *Studies of human relations in the teaching-learning process*. Nashville: Technical Report, Cooperative Research Program, U.S. Office of Education, 1960.

UNITERMS. Behavior; child; classroom; discipline; discussion skill; efficiency; freedom; group; interaction; interest; observation; performance test; planning; problem-solving; productivity; self-discipline; task.

—L. J. R.

77
Self Concept Scale

AUTHORS.   Mohindra P. Gill and Vincent R. D'Oyley

AVAILABILITY.   Mohindra P. Gill and Vincent R. D'Oyley, c/o Request
Instrument and Subscale Key, The Ontario Institute for Studies in
Education, Ontario, Canada

VARIABLES.   The Self Concept Scale is derived from Roger's (1951)
idea of self, which "implies that many single self-perceptions standing
in relation to each other exist for the same individual." Thus, every
statement a person makes in evaluating himself can be considered a
sample of his *concept of self*. This scale involves the individual arrange-
ment of a number of self percepts along a subjective continuum of
"like me" and "unlike me." This is done for both *self as perceived* and
ideal self. From factor analysis, 8 subscales were identified for the
perceived-self half of the scale, for both boys and girls. These are:
*Achievement-Related Characteristics; Acceptance by Peers and
Teacher; Self-Confidence; Self-Perceived Originality; Feeling of Adequacy; Reaction to School Program; Concentrating Ability;* and *Self-
Satisfaction*. Six ideal self factors were identified and formed into
subscales. These were: *Self-Confidence and Achievement-Related Characteristics; Originality (desired)* (similar to Self-Perceived Originality
above); *General Characteristics; Acceptance by Peers and Teachers*
(same as above); *Self-Satisfaction;* and *Reaction to School Program*.
The instrument has been constructed primarily for use by high-school-
age males and females in an academic setting.

DESCRIPTION.   The Self Concept Scale consists of two sets of 65 inventory statements rated on a Never/Sometimes/Usually/Always scale.
The first set represents the real self, the second set the ideal self. A
simulated item is as follows:

Most of my teachers like me.

ADMINISTRATION AND SCORING.   The test takes an estimated thirty
minutes to administer and can be completed by groups. It is possible
to use machine scoring, although this must be adapted by the individual
investigator. Identification of items relating to specific subscales can
be obtained from the authors of the scale. Means and standard deviations on the perceived self and ideal self subscales by sex of student
are given in Gill and D'Oyley (1968).

DEVELOPMENT. A number of self-concept theorists (Brookover, 1959; Lecky, 1961; Rogers, 1951) have discerned the student's self-concept as a potentially facilitating or limiting factor in academic achievement. According to the authors, however, empirical studies (Davidson and Lang, 1960; Payne and Farquhar, 1962; Roth, 1959; Shaw, Edson, and Bell, 1960) "have failed (a) to make their self-concept [measures] even plausibly relevant to the behavior under study and (b) to validate their instruments." The scale was designed to measure self-perceptions of high school students regarding both themselves and their school experiences by asking questions related to contemporary perception of self and ideal self. Items were gathered by reviewing the relevant literature. Comments on the face validity of the pooled items were obtained from psychologists, guidance counselors, and 9th grade students.

CRITIQUE. Test–retest *reliability* was obtained by readministration of the test to 67 students eight weeks after the first administration. For perceived self for boys $r = .69$; for ideal self, $r = .60$. For girls, perceived self was .60, while ideal self was .67. The subjects were 9th grade students from five academic high schools in Toronto. Hoyt internal consistency for perceived self for boys ($N = 227$) was .89; for girls ($N = 187$), .91. Ideal self internal consistencies (same Ns) were .92 for boys and .89 for girls.

Predictive validity was tested using the factorially defined dimensions as predictors with average final marks as the criterion. The validity coefficients for total scores for perceived self were .42 for boys and .38 for girls. Ideal self correlated with final marks at .25 for boys and .19 for girls. While no specific data are presented, the authors note that scores on the perceived self scale for both boys and girls, the Achievement Related Characteristics scale, were the highest, followed by Self Confidence and Acceptance of Peers and Teachers. The total score on perceived self correlated .11 (boys) and .11 (girls) with the CAAT 1 verbal reasoning test.

More recent or more extensive *reliability* data, especially for the separate, factorially defined subscales, are not reported, and seem needed. No further *validity* studies are reported, and the validities of the separate subscales are largely unknown beyond face validity.

No data are given concerning *response sets* or *item transparency*, either of which could account for appreciable variance in an inventory scale.

Norms beyond the 9th grade and including more disparate school systems should be obtained.

GENERAL COMMENT.   As a school-system-specific measure of self concept the measure is insufficiently validated. Further psychometric
work, especially cross validation and replication, as well as concurrent
validity studies with other self-concept measures should be undertaken.

REFERENCES

Brookover, W. B. A social psychological conception of classroom learning.
  School and Society, 1959, 8, 84–87.

Davidson, H. H. and Lang, G. Children's perceptions of their teachers' feelings toward them related to self-perception, school achievement, and behavior. *Journal of Experimental Education*, 1960, 29, 107–118.

Gill, M. P. and D'Oyley, V. R. The construction of an objective measure of
  self concept. Paper read at the annual meeting of the American Educational Research Association, Chicago, 1968.

Lecky, P. *Self-consistency: a theory of personality*. Edited and interpreted
  by Frederick C. Thorne. New York: Shoe String Press, 1961.

Payne, D. A. and Farquhar, W. W. The dimensions of an objective measure
  of academic self-concept. *Journal of Educational Psychology*, 1962, 53,
  187–192.

Shaw, M. E., Edson, E., and Bell, H. M. The self-concept of bright under-
  achieving high school students as revealed by an adjective check list.
  Personnel and Guidance Journal, 1960, 39, 193–196.

Rogers, C. R. *Client-centered therapy: its current practice, implications, and
  theory*. Boston: Houghton Mifflin, 1951.

Roth, R. M. Role of self-concept in achievement. *Journal of Experimental
  Education*, 1959, 27, 265–281.

UNITERMS.   Acceptance; achievement; adequacy; confidence; ideal;
originality; peer; satisfaction; school; self; self-concept; student;
teacher.

—M. E.

78
Self-Perceptual Q-Sort (SPQS)

AUTHORS.   Herbert A. Thelen and Dorothy Stock Whitaker

AVAILABILITY.   Herbert A. Thelen, Committee on Human Development, University of Chicago, Chicago, Illinois 60637

VARIABLES.   The Self-Perceptual Q-Sort, like the Thelen-Stock Reactions to Group Situations Test (which see) measures six modalities of self-perceived *individual action in a group setting: Dependence,* a need to rely for support and direction on the leader, the total group, or established structure; *Counter-Dependence,* an insistence on maintaining independence of leadership; *Pairing,* a need to establish close personal relationships with other members, and to conduct group interaction on an intimate, personal level; *Counter-Pairing,* a need to keep relationships with others formal and impersonal and to conduct group interaction on a formal, impersonal, intellectual level; *Fight,* a tendency to express negative, aggressive feelings; and *Flight,* a tendency to inhibit negative, aggressive feelings in the group, and to withdraw generally.

DESCRIPTION.   Each of the six modalities is represented by 10 statements, totaling 60 cards in the Q-Sort. Some simulated statements are:

> Uncomfortable when others made personal remarks about him. (Counter-pairing)
>
> Takes role of mediator in arguments. (Flight)

ADMINISTRATION AND SCORING.   Subjects rank the 60 cards from "most like me" to "least like me," while placing the cards in a specified frequency distribution, approximately normalized. The differentiation of subgroups based upon preferred modalities requires that the members' Q-Sorts be factor-analyzed, a resource-consuming process. Individual Q-Sorts can be scored on the basis of a Guttman weighting of the responses in each of the specified frequency groups for each modality.

DEVELOPMENT.   No background on the development of the Q-Sort was available for this review.

CRITIQUE.   The only *reliability* evidence available for this review is that for four judges' assignment of the 60 statements to each of the six modalities, the range of "misplaced" items was 0 to 8, with a mean of 4.7. No single item was consistently misplaced.

Available *validity* studies are limited. Based upon a factor analysis of Q-Sorts, three "pure" subgroups were distinguished within a single group: A, having high leadership aspirations; B, having high needs for expression; and C, having a high passive orientation. The combinations of AC and BC were also extracted. On the basis of 2,810 statements from 14 group meetings, the rank order of subgroups according to participation (number of contributions per subgroup) differentiated among the three subgroups at the $p < .01$ level. Similarly, the group having high leadership aspirations contributed over 45% of the leadership bids; no other subgroup contributed more than 17%. Third, all the subgroups except C chose within their own subgroup when daily asked "Which member was the best spokesman for your point of view?" The C group's passivity may explain its inability to choose a spokesman consistently. This within-group choosing was also significant at $p < .01$.

As far as it goes, the *theory* behind the Q-Sort appears reasonable. Briefly summarized, the working hypotheses are: 1) the structure of a group can be seen as built upon subgroups; 2) the basis of association within a subgroup is a communality of purpose among its members which can be discovered through factor analysis of self-perceptual data; 3) the members of a subgroup tend to act together to achieve their common purpose; and 4) the dynamics of the total group are revealed as cooperation and competition among the various subgroups. The discovery, however, of the dynamics of interaction in any group is left to the user.

No *norms* were available for this review.

GENERAL COMMENT.   The Self-Perceptual Q-Sort is included in this volume merely as a companion to the Thelen–Stock Reactions to Group Situations Test. The psychometric data presented here are not adequate for a considered judgment as to its usefulness. Potential users should, however, be aware of its existence and possible utility as an adjunct to the RGST.

REFERENCE

Thelen, H. A. and Stock, D. *Methods for studying work and emotionality in group operation*, Chicago: Human Dynamics Laboratory, University of Chicago, 1954.

UNITERMS.   Behavior; dependence; fight; flight; group; pairing; Q-Sort; subgroup; work.

—R. B. E.

79
Social Insight Test

AUTHOR.   F. Stuart Chapin

AVAILABILITY.   Consulting Psychologists Press, 577 College Avenue, Palo Alto, California 94306

VARIABLES.   The test was designed to measure *social insight*, conceived of as "the ability to recognize in principle in a given situation: 1) the existence and operation of specific substitute responses such as projection, rationalization, regression, sublimation . . . etc.; and 2) the need of some specific stimulus to adjust group conflicts or tensions . . ." (Chapin, 1942). No limitations were made for use of the test with particular populations. Apparently, it was intended to measure social insight of normal adults.

DESCRIPTION.   Chapin's Social Insight Test is a two-part multiple-choice questionnaire. Part I contains 16 questions; Part II, 9. Instructions for Part I are to select the most appropriate or logical response while those for Part II are to choose the response yielding most satisfaction and least embarrassment to the person described in the item. Each item has a paragraph describing an interpersonal situation followed by four alternative response choices. Presumably, the correct response is the one which supplies the most probable reason for the behavior described or the most likely consequences it will have. The following is a simulated item example:

Part I   Mrs. Jenkins was a guest at a party, where she did not know the hostess well. On leaving, she inadvertently called the latter by the name of someone else. She excused herself for the mistake, corrected her error, and left for her own home. Why did she make the mistake of calling an acquaintance by the wrong name?

a.   She had wanted to deny feeling uneasy about her dislike of her hostess, calling her by the name of someone distant she also did not care for.

b.   She had not known the hostess well enough to remember her name correctly.

c.   She was not the sort of person who is good at recalling names.

d.   The hostess must have had a particularly hard name to pronounce properly, and Mrs. Jenkins had not wished to embarrass her by mispronouncing it.

(Key: "Correct" answer is a.)

ADMINISTRATION AND SCORING.   Scores are weighted 1, 2, or 3, according to differentiating power as ascertained by item analysis. High total score (summed weights of correct answers) is interpreted as evidence of the individual's possessing social insight. Hand scoring keys are available. Respondent time has been estimated at less than thirty minutes, and no time limits have been stipulated by the author.

Norms for various groups have been made available by Gough (1964) as means and standard deviations of their scores. Ns were 1,012 males and 318 females (no information available on sampling methods). Data are shown separately for such subgroupings as graduate students, medical students, and military officers.

DEVELOPMENT.   An original volunteer population of 375 graduate students and social agency personnel in the Minneapolis–St. Paul area was studied. Initially, 65 of these were independently rated by others in their own agency who were asked to name persons they felt had greater than average "social insight." These 65 individuals were selected (by unspecified technique) from 110 persons judged on that quality. The biserial r between the ratings of co-workers and Social Insight Test scores for these groups was .21. Chapin (1942) assumed that the correlation reflected group differences and supported validity claims for the instrument.

Another validational check involved obtaining a correlation for 33 students between scores on social insight and those on the author's Social Participation Scale, a measure of participation in community organizations; the r found was .15, interpreted as consistent with the earlier findings reported above and as evidence of the validity of the Social Insight Test for measuring that variable. The correlation between these sets of scores for 156 social workers was reported as .18. Finally, for 185 students and social workers a non-significant r of .09 was obtained.

As a third validational test, mean social insight scores of groups of 68 social workers and 46 clerical workers were shown to differ significantly in the expected direction.

To ascertain the relative discriminating power of the 45 items originally included in the test, an item analysis was conducted. As an independent criterion, Social Participation Scale scores were again used. The 25 items with critical ratios ranging from .60 to 2.10 were retained in the final version of the test. Subsequently, the 14 items with critical ratios from .60 to 1.30 were assigned a weight of 1. Six items ranging from 1.40 to 1.90 in their critical ratios were given the weight of 2. Finally, 5 items with critical ratios of 2.00 were given weights of 3.

Chapin found that 110 subjects' revised Social Insight Scale scores correlated .36 with ratings by executives, a finding which he reported as "probably significant." Correlations between Social Participation Scale and Social Insight Scale scores increased (naturally) as a result of revision. (Chapin has hypothesized that those who score high on the former by being organization officers do so because of their greater than average social insight.) Significant *r*s between these sets of scores were also found for groups of 33, 156, and 185 subjects. Finally, 68 social workers differed in social insight from 46 secretaries (level of significance unspecified). However, Chapin felt that the coefficients were not large enough to permit prediction of individual scores.

An odd–even item correlation on the long form yielded an *r* of .60 ($N = 41$) and an *r* of .41 between scores on Part I and those on Part II of the Social Insight Test. Chapin (1942) did not consider these results to have demonstrated the reliability of the scale.

CRITIQUE.   Gough (1965) has reported obtaining odd–even *reliability* for 100 adult males of .64 (corrected for length, .78). Although these coefficients indicate a gain in dependability from Chapin's studies, the level of internal consistency does not warrant use of the scale for any clinical or individual assessment purposes. No test–retest data are presented.

Validity has been investigated by various experimental designs. Criterion validity of the Social Insight Test was studied by Gough and Heilbrun (1965), who found significant differences in the expected direction between groups of 38 high and 34 low scorers on the Chapin test. The criterion was a "drop-out score" on the need scales of the Adjective Check List. High-scoring persons tended to have Adjective Check List profiles resembling those of "students tending toward early termination of counseling" (Gough and Heilbrun, 1965). However, it should be noted that early termination of a therapeutic relationship can be indicative of neurosis as well as of health. Hence one must wonder whether social insight, presumably a concomitant of psychic well-being, is actually being measured.

McDermid (1965) correlated social insight scores for 58 members of an engineering staff with ratings of creativity by their co-workers and supervisors. Coefficients obtained were .14 and .21, respectively, the criteria being intercorrelated moderately ($r = .30$).

Gough (1965) further found the test to be related to measures of intellectual ability. Significant median *r*s for 1,012 males and 318 females were obtained (for subgroupings of these samples) between scores on seven intellectual and cognitive measures and those on the Social Insight Test. Correlations with age, education, height, and weight ranged from —.07 to .12. Subsequently, a correlation of .19 between social insight scores and a scale presumably measuring innovation as a personality variable was obtained. This *r* and one of .00 with a measure of socialization (median for 297 males) were interpreted as supporting the improbability of scoring high on insight due to oversocialization. Low to moderate correlations with all but the Achievement via Independence and Intellectual Efficiency subscales of the California Psychological Inventory were obtained. These subscales presumably measure various components of ego-strength, such as self-acceptance, dominance, and social presence. Thus, one should expect higher *r*s than those obtained between Social Insight Scale scores and these measures.

Gough and Heilbrun (1965) administered the Chapin Social Insight Test to 66 honor students in engineering and 45 research scientists. Subsequently these subjects were each described on the Gough Adjective Check List by ten raters. Adjectives with the highest mean correlations with scores on the Chapin test were reported as shrewd, alert, active, interests wide, courageous, pleasure-seeking, imaginative, outspoken, and aggressive. Some of the 15 with the lowest mean *r*s with Social Insight Test scores were listed as spineless, conventional, conservative, shallow, loyal, cautious, and self-denying. Thus Gough (1965) concluded that the high-scorer on the Chapin scale is "an insightful, perceptive, quick, imaginative, and resourceful person . . . relatively free in the expression of impulse. . . ." Conversely, he saw the low scorer on the Social Insight measure as "less able, more constricted, and less confident . . . too methodical and conventional to be a very attractive individual." These hypotheses regarding traits of high and low scorers on the Social Insight Scale were interpreted as further supported by the results of Q-Sort descriptions completed by interviewers of each of the above groups of students and scientists. Raters' and interviewers' training were not specified.

The possibility that the items simply measure the subject's learned ability to "psychologize" about interpersonal relations, apply conventional categories of explanation, and so on, should not be overlooked.

GENERAL COMMENT.   More evidence on both validity and reliability should be obtained before the Social Insight Test is used for individual measurement. Refinements in the test to increase correlations with variables such as those on the California Psychological Inventory would be valuable. Persons interested in studying positive (healthy) aspects of psychic activity may want to investigate the instrument further.

REFERENCES

Chapin, F. S. Preliminary standardization of a social insight scale. *American Sociological Review*, 1942, 7, 214–225.

Gough, H. G. A validational study of the Chapin Social Insight Test. *Psychological Reports*, 1965, 17, 355–368.

Gough, H. G. and Heilbrun, A. B. *Adjective Check List manual*. Palo Alto: Consulting Psychologists Press, 1965.

McDermid, C. D. Some correlates of creativity in engineering personnel. *Journal of Applied Psychology*, 1965, 49, 14–19.

UNITERMS.   Activity; ego-strength; empathy; insight; interaction; interpersonal; sensitivity; social.

—L. J. R.

80
Stages of Moral Development Scoring System

AUTHOR.   Lawrence Kohlberg

AVAILABILITY.   Kohlberg, L. *Stages in the development of moral thought and action.* New York: Holt, Rinehart and Winston, 1961.

VARIABLES.   This scoring system distinguishes six *stages in the development of moral judgment. Stage 1* is characterized by an orientation toward obedience and punishment, with either deference to superior power or prestige, or avoidance of "getting into trouble." *Stage 2* is a naively egoistic orientation which holds that the morally correct action is that which instrumentally satisfies the self's needs and occasionally others' needs; it equates instrumental usefulness with moral value. *Stage 3* is characterized by an orientation toward obtaining approval from and pleasing or helping others; it stresses "good boy" behavior, conformity to stereotypical role behavior. *Stage 4* equates morality with actions which maintain existing authority and social order; one "does one's duty" and supports the existing social order for its own sake (in colloquial terms, "law and order"). *Stage 5* is characterized by a contractual, legalistic orientation which sees morality in terms of the avoidance of the violation of the will or rights of others; it defines right action in terms of standards which have been critically examined and agreed upon by the whole society; it looks, for example, to the spirit of the Constitution rather than to the letter of the law. *Stage 6* bases moral judgment upon conscience or principles which encompass the broadest logical universality and consistency, such as the Golden Rule, or the categorical imperative. The six stages relate to 25 *aspects of intentionality* studied by Piaget (1948) grouped into 8 categories: value; choice; sanctions and motives; rules and authority; positive justice; and punitive justice. Some of the aspects are: considering motives in judging action, self-condemnation, and rights of possession or property.

Conceptually, Kohlberg's stages can be applied to any population, child or adult. Because they represent a developmental sequence, however, much of his work has been with children and adolescents.

DESCRIPTION.   Since it is a scoring system, Kohlberg's typology of stages can be applied to any situation relating to morality. Kohlberg himself (1963, 1964) has developed a set of 13 dilemmas designed to reveal a subject's stage of moral development. Several of them evolve from the following scenario:

In Europe, a woman was near death from cancer. One drug might save her, a form of radium that a druggist in the same town had recently discovered. The druggist was charging $2,000, ten times what the drug cost him to make. The sick woman's husband, Heinz, went to everyone he knew to borrow the money, but he could only get together about half of what it cost. He told the druggist that his wife was dying and asked him to sell it cheaper or let him pay later. But the druggist said, "No." The husband got desperate and broke into the man's store to steal the drug for his wife. Should the husband have done that? Why?

At each point in the development of the scenario the respondent is asked several questions, such as:

Did the druggist have a right to charge that much when there was no law actually setting a limit to the price? Why?

ADMINISTRATION AND SCORING.   Kohlberg's questionnaire is self-administering. Scoring involves isolating instances of the 25 aspects (for example, "I was only following orders") and assigning a stage to each (in this case, Stage 1). Scoring is not easily mastered, and requires a substantial amount of practice and refinement. The appendix to Kohlberg (1961) contains an explanation of scoring procedures.

The mode across all the responses is the subject's score; Kohlberg has found that for children approximately 50% of all responses fall under the same stage. Kohlberg (1961) reports profile charts for several types of populations—child and adult, Western and Oriental, and technological and primitive societies.

DEVELOPMENT.   Kohlberg's approach is cognitive-developmental, and traces its antecedents from J. M. Baldwin (1906), J. Dewey (1930), G. H. Mead (1934), Piaget (1948), and Loevinger (1966). He tested 12 moral dilemmas on a population of 75 Chicago youths ages 10 through 16, divided roughly equally between middle- and working-class backgrounds. A factor analysis of the scores revealed a common first moral factor; the 9 dilemmas showing the best intercorrelations of stage scores and interjudge reliability were retained.

CRITIQUE.   The interjudge *reliability* ranges from .83 to .93, depending upon the length of training of the raters. Test–retest reliability ranges from .65 to .80. (For children and adolescents, test–retest refers to relatively short intervals, since the scoring system was designed for longitudinal studies of moral development, and therefore changes in scores are to be expected.)

Kohlberg's questionnaire shows *construct validity*, in that correlations of stages across the different moral dilemmas ranged from .31 to .75 in early studies, with a median of .51. More recent studies have produced intersituation correlations in the .80s. Predictive validity studies have shown a correlation of .72 between scores at age 16 and in the mid-20s for $N = 24$. For eight middle-class youths $r = .92$ between scores at age 13 and at age 24, and $r = .88$ between scores at age 16 and at age 24. Concurrent validity studies have shown correlations with teachers' ratings of moral conscientiousness of .46 and with teachers' ratings of fair-mindedness with peers of .54. The correlation of moral development scores with peer ratings of moral character was .58 in one study. In Milgram's obedience study (1963), four out of six Stage 6 subjects disobeyed orders and ceased giving the increasingly severe electrical shocks to a stooge, while only three of 24 subjects at lower moral stages stopped. And at Berkeley, 80% of Stage 6 subjects and 50% of Stage 5 subjects participated in the original free-speech sit-in, while only 10% of Stages 3 and 4 subjects sat in. All in all, the validity evidence is appealing.

Kohlberg does not treat the problems of *response sets* or *fakeability;* it is up to the user of this scoring system to apply it to data which have been controlled for these effects.

GENERAL COMMENT.   Kohlberg freely admits that his Stages of Moral Development scoring system is vulnerable to attack because it presumes that Stage 6 is somehow superior to Stage 5, which in turn is "better" than Stage 4, and so forth. Whatever the debate about the merits of *action* taken at the various stages, the typology of stages is demonstrably a Guttman-scalable hierarchy of *comprehension.* In terms of cognitive development, therefore, the assignment of Stage 6 to the superior level is justifiable. The scoring system's full implications and utility have yet to be elaborated. For example, Kohlberg is just beginning studies of the conditions which promote the utilization of each of the 25 aspects of intentionality. The six stages, however, are well established, and their representation of development from dependence to individual moral autonomy is an appealing and easily related concept.

REFERENCES

Baldwin, J. M. *Social and ethical interpretations in mental development.* New York: Macmillan, 1906.

Dewey, J. Experience and conduct. In C. Murchison (ed.), *Psychologies of 1930.* Worcester: Clark University Press, 1930.

Kohlberg, L. The development of children's orientations toward a moral order. 1. Sequence in the development of moral thought. *Vita Humana,* 1963, *6,* 11–33.

Kohlberg, L. Development of moral character and ideology. In M. L. Hoffman (ed.), *Review of child development research*. Vol. 1. New York: Russell Sage Foundation, 1964.

Kohlberg, L. *Stages in the development of moral thought and action*. New York: Holt, Rinehart and Winston, 1961.

Loevinger, J. The meaning and measurement of ego development. *American Psychologist*, 1966, *21*, 195–217.

Mead, G. H. *Mind, self, and society*. Chicago: University of Chicago Press, 1934.

Milgram, S. Behavioral study of obedience. *Journal of Abnormal and Social Psychology*, 1963, *67*, 371–378.

Piaget, J. *The moral judgment of the child*. Glencoe: Free Press, 1948.

UNITERMS.   Adolescent; child; cognition; content analysis; development; intentionality; judgment; morality; projective; socialization.

—R. B. E.

81
Teaching Situation Reaction Test (TSRT)

AUTHORS. John B. Hough and James K. Duncan

AVAILABILITY. Duncan, James K. and Hough, John B. *Technical review of the Teaching Situation Reaction Test.* Available from Dr. Kenneth C. Murray, College of Education, West Virginia University, Morgantown, West Virginia 26506

VARIABLES. The instrument was designed to measure *attitudes toward teaching behavior.* Low scores on the instrument are purported to indicate a teacher who prefers "indirect" behavior (cf. Flanders, 1964), defined as behavior more accepting, empathizing, and facilitating student freedom. High scores are thought to indicate a teacher who prefers "direct" behaviors, seen as rejecting, punitive, and freedom-restricting.

DESCRIPTION. The present instrument (1966 edition) is composed of 48 items, each a specific situation and four possible options for handling it; they are to be ranked in terms of their importance. A shortened situation (adapted) and a sample set of options follow:

> You work in a school system which is carrying out a series of innovative experiments. One of these involves a project designed to improve children's general adjustment to the social and cultural environment. A heterogeneous (along physical, mental, and social lines) group of children has enrolled for the class; it totals twenty-five children aged thirteen through fourteen. The class is called "Teen Topics."
>
> It meets during the last scheduled period of the day on Mondays and Wednesdays of the second semester. Arrangements include the possibility of class trips, and informal discussion with the teacher after class.
>
> The principal has invited you to teach this class, and you have accepted. You have a free hand to develop it, a teacher-counselor to help you, and an adequate supply of instructional materials. The gains in adjustment made by your pupils will be studied.
>
> You will meet for the first time with the class tomorrow.
>
> It will be important that you have planned for:
>> (a) the pupils to get to know each other well.
>> (b) explanation of the grading system to be used.
>> (c) ways to develop student interest.
>> (d) explanation of your complete program for the semester.

Several such situational items with alternate choices are supplied for each of the 9 clusters of situations included in the TSRT. These always involve the same basic classroom group, and cover planning, the first day, after four sessions, the eighth session, midterm, after the twentieth session, the twenty-fourth session, the thirtieth session, and later.

From the respondent's point of view, the directions are largely concise and clear. They are ambiguous in that they do not indicate the basis for ranking. They say, "The most desirable choice should be labelled 1 and the least desirable, 4." The respondent might ask, "Desirable for whom, and to what end?" The actual description of the general setting suggests the answer: desirable for the child's adjustment.

ADMINISTRATION AND SCORING.   The test is scored (see Duncan and Hough, undated) by determining correspondence of rankings to the key. Development of the key is not described, but it appears to be based on the authors' a priori judgments. An item score of zero would show perfect correspondence; thus, lower scores indicate better performance.

The major skill required of the respondent is that of reading and remembering the specifics of a school situation through 48 complicated questions and 9 subsituations. This skill is perhaps familiar to teachers.

No specific indices, profiles, or other scoring procedures are reported. In the studies reported, means and standard deviations of each item are used.

DEVELOPMENT.   The report acknowledges that "the theoretical formulation was neither carefully developed nor fully elaborated. The test itself was the only formal expression of it." While the TSRT is still being developed, the authors do note that earlier studies led to an expansion of the number of items from 36 to 48. Four validity studies and three reliability studies have been included in the basic report.

CRITIQUE.   In one *reliability* study (Hough and Duncan, 1965) 84 preservice teachers took the TSRT twice in eight days: $r = .84$. No internal reliability studies are reported.

The intention of the authors is to demonstrate that the TSRT can be an effective predictor of good teaching. The first criterion used to test this assumption is that of grades in student teaching. A significant relationship (tetrachoric r of .51) was found between TSRT scores and such grades (Hough, 1965). Hough and Duncan (1965) also report a significant difference ($p < .05$) between TSRT scores of student teachers ranked by supervisors as "best" ($N = 10$) and "poorest" ($N = 11$) of a group of 48.

The authors note that student teaching grades and performance both reflect subject matter competence, which the TSRT is not designed to measure. This suggests an added source of uncontrolled variance in the relations reported.

The TSRT also discriminated experienced teachers nominated by administrators as "best" ($N = 19$) from "poorest" ($N = 19$) in a group of 72; in-service teachers ($N = 110$) also differed ($p < .05$) from pre-service teachers ($N = 419$).

Five *concurrent validity* studies have been completed by the authors to establish the relationship between the TSRT and the MTAI, the Barrett-Lennard Relationship Inventory, the Dogmatism Scale, a measure appraising the teacher's use of structure in the classroom, and the California Test of Mental Maturity. Significant but low (.28 and .31) correlations are reported with the CTMM and MTAI respectively (Hough and Duncan, 1965). The authors do not suggest *why* these correlations were studied (i.e., no theoretical reasons are given), nor do they suggest what the correlations might mean in terms of what it is that the TSRT is measuring.

In another study (Hough and Duncan, 1965) each of the items of the TSRT was examined by selecting from an experimental group those classified as high (top 27%) on human relations skills (as measured by the Barrett-Lennard Relationship Inventory) and those who were low (bottom 27%). This procedure yielded 14 items which discriminated the high and low scorers via *chi*-square analyses (.20 level or better).

Two item analysis studies, one with the Dogmatism Scale and a second with a ranking of student teachers on high and low use of structure, showed that twelve and ten items, respectively, yielded significant *chi*-squares at or beyond the .20 level.

These three *item analysis* studies leave much to be desired. The choice of correlates (dogmatism, human relations skills, etc.) does not seem to have any clear theoretical basis. Technically, since no actual distributions or means are reported, it is never clear in what direction a particular item discriminates. In addition, the use of extreme-scoring groups with *chi*-square, while helpful in locating items, overestimates the actual usefulness of the TSRT in discriminating known groups.

In a *construct validity* study, Murray and Duncan (1968) examined the items and decided that they measured factors of objectivity, sociability, control, confidence, reflectiveness, and empathy. They factored the TSRT total score for 238 pre-service students, plus scores on the objectivity and sociability scales of the Guilford–Zimmerman Temperament Survey, the F-Scale, the Confidence scale of the 16 P.F. Questionnaire, the Reflective scale of the Thurstone Temperament Schedule, and the Intraception (empathy) scale of the Edwards Personal Preference Schedule. Factored TSRT subscores were also correlated with these concurrent measures. The authors concluded that TSRT subscores tend to relate negatively to control, as measured by the F-Scale, and positively to empathy, as measured by the EPPS Intraception scale. However, the highest correlation obtained was .24, and the factor structure for males and females differed very substantially.

The authors report two studies of *fakeability* (Hough and Duncan, undated). In the first, one group was asked to take the test as "they honestly felt" ($N = 35$) while a second was asked to take the test to get a "good" score. The difference was not significant. A second study compared two groups of 27 student teachers using the same directions; no difference was found.

No *norms* as such are provided. Duncan and Hough (undated) give means, standard deviations and ranges for four samples (N from 42 to 106) who completed the second revision (1964 edition).

GENERAL COMMENT.   The authors have pointed out this is an exploratory instrument to be used for research purposes, and that caution must be exercised in its use. Continuing developmental studies are needed.

The instrument's major shortcoming is its lack of theoretical background. While the authors were admittedly empirical about its development, their efforts to specify construct validity (Duncan and Hough, undated) are still largely descriptive and non-theoretical. The twelve so-called subscales derived from factor analysis are not specified (which items, what loadings are involved?), and the evidence relating these scores to empathy and control is ambiguous. The primary need now is to gain clarity about what the TSRT is (or ought to be) measuring. The instrument is included in this collection because it deals with an important area of practice, which is itself undergoing rapid changes toward certification based on performance measurement.

REFERENCES

Amidon, E. Behavioral change in pre-service teacher preparation: an experimental study. Philadelphia: College of Education, Temple University, 1964.

Flanders, N. A. Some relationships among teacher influence, pupil attitudes and achievement. In B. J. Biddle and W. J. Ellena, *Contemporary research on teacher effectiveness.* New York: Holt, Rinehart and Winston, 1964, pp. 196–231.

Hough, J. B. and Duncan, J. K. Exploratory Studies of a Teaching Situation Reaction Test. Paper read at the annual meeting of the American Educational Research Association, 1965.

Duncan, J. K., with Hough, J. B. Technical review of the Teaching Situation Reaction Test. Mimeographed, undated. Morgantown, West Virginia: West Virginia University. (Available from Dr. Kenneth C. Murray.)

Murray, K. C. and Duncan, J. K. A study of the construct validity of the Teaching Situation Reaction Test. Paper read at the annual meeting of the American Educational Research Association, 1968.

UNITERMS.   Classroom; confidence; control; creativity; empathy; indirect-direct; influence; teacher.

—D. G. L.
—M. B. M.

82
Test of Diagnostic Skills

AUTHORS.   H. J. A. Rimoldi, John V. Haley, and Hermelinda Fogliatto

AVAILABILITY.   Rimoldi, H. J. A., Haley, J. V., and Fogliatto, H. The
Test of Diagnostic Skills. Loyola Psychometric Laboratory Publication
No. 25. Chicago: Loyola University, 1962.

VARIABLES.   The test was originally designed to measure *clinical diagnostic ability* of physicians and medical students. However, the underlying technique has subsequently been considered by Rimoldi et al.
(1962) as a potential indicator of the more general processes of
problem-solving and *thinking*. It has been used by the author (with
appropriate content variations) with children as well, in testing *mathematical reasoning* skill. More recently, Rimoldi et al. (1963) have suggested the possibility of using the test as "a training device for clinical
thinking." Thus, it is viewed as a useful evaluative measure for persons
at different levels of training, in varying content domains.

DESCRIPTION.   The Test of Diagnostic Skills is really a technique rather
than a test of specific content. As such, it is best described in terms of
directions to respondents. Readers should keep in mind the possibility
of transposing these directions, as well as the content of the examination, so that areas other than medical diagnostic ability may be explored.

The test consists of a series of cards, on the reverse side of which
appears information relevant to the knowledge being examined. For
example, if the knowledge that leads to sound medical diagnostic skill
is being tested, information normally obtained from a patient's medical
history, laboratory studies, and physical examination is given on the
cards. The front side of each card is visible to the S and contains a
question answered by the information on the reverse. When S selects
a question, the card is turned over so the information is visible. Initially,
S (in the medical version) is also given two cards supplying data on
admission to the hopsital and patient's complaints. His task is to select
from the larger series of cards only those questions he feels he needs
answered in order to arrive at a diagnosis. Presumably, the better his
diagnostic ability, the fewer extraneous cards he will choose to make an
expert-like final diagnosis, and the more similar his choices of information will be to those made by experts.

Thus, what is being tested in general, regardless of subject matter variations, is the ability to ask fruitful diagnostic questions.

ADMINISTRATION AND SCORING.   There is no time limit for the Test of Diagnostic Skills. Respondents are permitted as many or as few "questions" (numbered cards) as they may desire to "ask." However, Rimoldi et al. (1963) have noted that "a typical (medical) clinical case can be presented in a set of 50 to 75 cards." Group or individual administration is possible, and specific content or information can be excluded or added as required. A subject receives the answer to his question by reading the card's reverse side. Either experimenter or respondent records the number of each card, and thus the order in which cards are used.

Two types of scores have been utilized: 1) those based on the *amount* of information requested; and 2) those based upon the *order* in which information is requested. A third measure is the *utility* score, which is a weighted average of the "utility indices" of the cards selected. The utility index of a given card for a given group of subjects (such as 20 first-year medical students) is, roughly, the proportion of subjects choosing that card. (The actual formula subtracts 1 from the N of the group, and 1 from the N of those choosing the card, so that if a card is chosen by only one person in the group, the utility is defined as zero.) Cards not selected do not contribute to these three scores.

Normative performance curves can be plotted, using the cumulative utility index total (of experts) as the ordinate and number of cards as the abscissa. Theoretical maximum and minimum curves can be plotted (the former beginning with the highest-utility items and proceeding to the lowest, which should be the most economical diagnostic sequence), and the curve actually followed by any given subject examined. Rimoldi et al. (1962) show sample curves for 4 subjects; second administrations of the test clearly move toward the maximum curve.

Norms given include mean number of questions asked, and mean utility scores for 87 medical school juniors, 129 medical school seniors, and 41 physicians for Test 2 and Test 4 of the series.

DEVELOPMENT.   The original population of 64 subjects (sampling technique unspecified) consisted of 6 professors of surgery, 8 interns, 24 senior class medical students, and 16 junior class surgery students. All were tested with three sets of cards prepared as described above from three hospital case records by two physicians. Utility indices for cards were computed from the professors' choices. Students' performances were then compared with professors' in terms of utility scores. Significant agreement among professors' card sequences was obtained (coefficient of concordance, $W = .79$). The five experts whose scores were most highly intercorrelated were used as the source of the "experts' sequence" against which student performance was evaluated. Five or six estimates of student ability (e.g., course grade-point average, comprehensive exam mark) were also obtained. The student sample was biased in containing a preponderance of those with high marks and "a small dispersion of values." Although differences in the expected directions were obtained among juniors, seniors, and experts, the authors neglected to indicate statistical significance.

Validity has been studied for some of the test series constructed. The authors (Rimoldi et al., 1958) considered the Test of Diagnostic Skills (Form C) "sensitive enough to appraise levels of medical training and experience [and] diagnostic ability in relation to levels of training." According to Devane et al. (1960), means of utility scores for 87 juniors, 129 to 147 seniors, and 41 physicians showed significant differences as predicted for Tests 2 and 4 (F significant at .01 level). These findings applied to Part I (clinical interview and history), but *not* to Part II (physical examination) for Test 2, and *not* to Part III (laboratory tests).

The mean number of cards selected (in Part I only) was also significantly different, as predicted, in both Tests 2 and 4. In sum, better-trained people choose fewer cards, with higher utility indices.

More recently, the technique has been applied to the study of problem-solving (Rimoldi et al., 1963).

CRITIQUE.   Test 2 and Test 4, administered to the three samples described above, showed moderate part–part *reliability* as evidenced by significant correlations for number of cards chosen among the three parts of each test (averaging about .45 for Test 2 and Test 4). Utility score intercorrelations for the parts are also significant, averaging about .35 for Test 2, and .20 for Test 4.

Haley (1960) interpreted the change in utility score between administrations of each version to intervening learning. However, no test–retest reliabilities have been reported, and one does not know whether to attribute such score differences to a lack of reliability or to variability due to causes such as learning, or to practice effects on a fascinating task. Thus the *validity* of the Test of Diagnostic Skills cannot be said to have been fully demonstrated, despite the fact that known groups have been successfully differentiated.

The *norms* and performance curves given do not give sufficient information about sampling methods to provide a meaningful reference for individual comparisons. However, the normative data available do appear to have some utility for comparing and evaluating group performances.

GENERAL COMMENT.   The Test of Diagnostic Skills appears very promising as a technique for evaluating processes underlying thinking, learning, and problem-solving. The authors' conceptualization of these areas as ones deserving analytic exploration is commendable. Investigators interested in studying this domain are heartily encouraged to use the method, provided they ascertain the reliability and validity of their content-specific versions of the Test of Diagnostic Skills (e.g., therapeutic, educational or consulting diagnosis of individual, interpersonal, group, or organizational functioning). The instrument also appears to have considerable value in training for adequate diagnosis.

REFERENCES

Devane, J., Rimoldi, H. J. A., and Haley, J. V. A comparison of the performance of two student groups and physicians in the Test of Diagnostic Skills. Loyola Psychometric Laboratory Publication No. 10. Chicago: Loyola University, 1960.

Haley, J. V. The effect of learning on performance in the Test of Diagnostic Skills. Loyola Psychometric Laboratory Publication No. 11. Chicago: Loyola University, 1960.

Haley, J. V. Effects of training on the Test of Diagnostic Skills. Loyola Psychometric Laboratory Publication No. 30. Chicago: Loyola University, 1963.

Rimoldi, H. J. A., Devane, J., and Grib, T. Testing skills in medical diagnosis. Loyola Psychometic Laboratory Publication No. 2. Chicago: Loyola University, 1958.

Rimoldi, H. J. A., Haley, J. V., and Fogliatto, H. The Test of Diagnostic Skills. Loyola Psychometric Laboratory Publication No. 25. Chicago: Loyola University, 1962.

Rimoldi, H. J. A., Devane, J., Fogliatto, H., and Esdmann, J. A program for the study of thinking. National Science Foundation Publication No. 28. Project N. G-19844, Washington: National Science Foundation, 1963.

UNITERMS.   Clinical; cognition; diagnosis; information processing; insight; medical; performance test; problem-solving; reasoning; student; thinking.

—L. J. R.
—M. B. M.

83
Test of Insight

AUTHOR.   Elizabeth G. French

AVAILABILITY.   French, E. G. Development of a measure of complex motivation. In Atkinson, J. W. (ed.) *Motives in fantasy, action, and society.* Princeton: Van Nostrand, 1958, pp. 242–248.

VARIABLES.   The French Test of Insight presumably measures motives conceptualized as complex motives or acquired drives. *Achievement need,* the need for the attainment of a standard of excellence, and *Affiliation need,* the need for warm, supportive interpersonal relations, are the motives French selected to measure. Motivation is viewed as an intervening variable, not directly observable; according to French (1956), its presence can only be inferred from behavior. She assumed that individuals with "high needs" will tend to interpret the behavior of others in terms of those needs and, further, that interpretations of people who expect to be successful will be made in defensive terms.

DESCRIPTION.   Two forms having 10 items each have been developed by the author. Each item consists of a short descriptive statement of a personal characteristic. The examinee is told that this is a test of his understanding of why people behave as they do. The examinee is instructed to read each statement and write his opinion of what the person must be like, why the person behaves as he does, and what the results of this behavior are likely to be. If the examinee has more than one explanation of the person's conduct, he is instructed to write the one he feels to be the most important.

Three examples of items similar to those used in the Test of Insight are given below:

Charlie always gives in when an argument becomes heated.
Jack always tries to stand out in a group.
Mike said, "Just stand back and watch how I do it."

ADMINISTRATION AND SCORING.   Administration is straightforward, requiring no special skills. The author states that twenty to twenty-five minutes is usually sufficient.

French originally stipulated that in scoring for the two motivations, every separate idea within each item response was to be assessed against 13 categories of item content (such as Desire for goal (A+); Expectation of failure (Ga—); and failure to attain goal (G—). Since some responses are irrelevant to achievement motives as defined, items may have no score, one scored category, or several scored categories. An item may also have both plus (+) and minus (—) scores, depending on whether the response indicates a hope-of-success or fear-of-failure orientation, respectively. Total score involves calculating the sum, regardless of sign, of all unit scores, each having been assigned a unit weight. Total positive and negative scores, as well as total scores on any category, may be tabulated. Additionally, a simple count of items to which relevant response is made reportedly correlates in the .80s with the counts described above.

It should be noted that definite criteria for deciding whether a response indicates the presence of Achievement or Affiliation motives are not specified in detail by French. Thus, the skill of the administrator in evaluating test data is a primary factor in the content analysis of responses for expression of motivational level and style. Some training in content analysis appears to be necessary if interpretations are to be valid.

Subsequent revisions in scoring have been developed. Miles (1965)* devised a mode of scoring each item for Affiliation/Achievement, and Success/Failure. After determining interscorer reliabilities, he compared French's empirical judgments with empirical and a priori judgments of three scorers for weighted versus unweighted Achievement and Affiliation scores and subsequently inaugurated the use of weighted scores. In the revised system, one point is given for imagery consistent with item (Affiliation response to statement which is expected to elicit Affiliation response), two points for imagery following an ambiguous statement (presumably indicative of aroused Achievement or Affiliation motives), and three points for imagery in response to a statement expected to elicit opposite content (an Affiliation response to Achievement-oriented item). In the final revised scoring scheme for use when entire items are scored for content (Miles, 1965), three possible scores for assessing optimism/pessimism about the chances for need satisfaction in the Achievement and Affiliation domains were elaborated. Thus, for each of these need variables Goal, Threat, and Neutral orientations are possible. A Goal scoring indicates relevance to success or warmth (Achievement + or Affiliation +), a Threat scoring indicates failure or

---

* For a copy of this scoring scheme, order document NAPS 01881, from MICROFICHE PUBLICATIONS, Division of Microfiche Systems Corporation, 305 East 46th Street, New York, New York 10017, remitting $2.00 for each microfiche or $5.00 for each photocopy.

exclusion-rejection (Achievement — or Affiliation —) and a Neutral scoring indicates content unclassifiable as to Goal or Threat but clearly inferring Achievement or Affiliation motives (Achievement 0 or Affiliation 0). Responses which involve non-Achievement or non-Affiliation content are ignored in tabulating Total Affiliation and Total Achievement scores. These totals are the summed weightings of all Achievement and Affiliation scores (scores for each variable tabulated independently) for all categories—Goal, Threat, and Neutral. Additionally, he has stipulated rules for scoring (a) ambiguous responses, such as "aggressiveness," "cooperativeness," etc. and (b) specific content not elsewhere explicitly categorized, such as "fear of being wrong" (Achievement —) or "being insulted" (Affiliation —).

Norms are available in the form of means and standard deviations of scores for the following groups: 180 college men and 540 college women for Affiliation need only, using revised scoring of Miles (Exline, 1960); 137 airmen in basic training (French, 1956) for Achievement and Affiliation needs (original scoring); 144 male U.S. Air Force students in Officer Candidate School (French, 1956) for Affiliation motive only (original scoring).

DEVELOPMENT.   Sherrifs' (1948) and McClelland's use of projective techniques for evaluating motivation were combined by French, who adopted the former's use of a questionnaire format and the latter's method of scoring for "need Achievement." Using a military group for her original population, the author decided upon a verbal device and administered her Test of Insight to three groups of approximately 70 pre-flight cadets. Items were selected for inclusion in two 10-item forms, Forms I and II, based on the trial testing of 50 of these items on a sample of Air Force cadets ($N = 185$). The first four statements on each test reportedly elicited Achievement and Affiliation imagery almost equally frequently. Items number 5, 8, and 10 had been scored for Achievement imagery for over 50% of the respondents, equally for positive and negative categories. The sixth, seventh, and ninth items evoked more Affiliation imagery. The judgments used in arriving at these figures were those of two independent scorers of two samples' protocols ($Ns = 30$ and 37); interscorer reliabilities were 88% and 91% agreement, respectively. Items paralleled these for Affiliation motives. Motivation scores on the preliminary forms of the test were not found to correlate with observers' judgments of motivation and goal-attainment. The test scores, however, showed low but significant ($r = .19$) correlations with sentiment and questionnaire responses pertaining to Achievement and Affiliation. Scores for Achievement and Affiliation showed no significant intercorrelation.

CRITIQUE.   Himelstein and Kimbrough (1960) used psychology students
in a *reliability* study. Calculating test–retest coefficients for Achievement and Affiliation scores for males and females separately, they
found *r*s ranging from —.02 to .70; for alternate forms, no significant
correlations were found. They also found positive skewness in the
frequency distributions of scores. In general, reliability data for the
unrevised and revised French Test of Insight have been scant, the samples studied have been too small to permit valid generalization.
However, Willerman et al. (1957) analyzed the internal consistency
of their modified multiple-choice version of French's test (*N* = 90).
Having discarded a few items (criteria for retention of items not explicated), they developed a 25-statement projective form, from which
9 statements were presumed to reflect positive achievement orientation;
5, fear of failure. Data on the *internal consistency* analysis of the items
used were not presented, thus lending no further information on the
reliability. Test–retest reliability is low (French, 1955).

   The subsequent revision in scoring (Miles, 1965) included calculating interscorer reliabilities for two independent scorers, who scored unit
and item separately for Affiliation, Achievement, and Goal Orientation.
Twelve Test of Insight protocols completed by school principals were
rated. Correlations were respectively .34, .48, and —.19 for unit scoring and .43, .55, and .16 for item scoring. For a second group of 12
tests, these investigators evaluated the intercoder reliabilities of the
same three variables for item-scoring and obtained *r*s of .64, .44, and
.78, respectively. Additionally, weighted versus unweighted scoring
methods (as described in the "Administration and Scoring" section of
this review) correlated .96 and .94 for Achievement and Affiliation
scores respectively (*N* = 80).

   In a study of *construct validity* with a sample of 90 males in Officer
Candidate School, French (1955) obtained results consistent with the
following hypotheses: 1) increase in achievement motivation score is
a function of previous motivational level; 2) performance is more related to motivation scores than to relaxed, task-involved, and extrinsi-
cally-motivated experimental conditions; 3) performance scores relate
most closely to motivation scores when similarity of motivational cues
in each situation is minimized; and 4) when Affiliation cues pre-
dominate over Achievement cues, performance is related to Affiliation
motivation scores rather than to Achievement need scores.

   Criterion validity was supported by another study (French and
Chadwick, 1956) in which 144 Air Force males (sampling methods
unspecified) were given the Test of Insight and a sociometric questionnaire to measure popularity. French hypothesized an increase in
approach (positive) and avoidance (negative) responses on an affilia-

tion-rejection dimension, contingent on maximizing affiliation cues without stressing either component. Also, she predicted that total motivational level would not be related to popularity, but that "relative goal or threat orientation" would be, popular persons being "more goal- and less threat-oriented than unpopular ones." Finally, persons with high affiliation need were expected both to be more aware of the extent of their popularity and to estimate themselves as having greater popularity than those with low affiliation motives. These predictions were generally supported.

A *predictive validity* study (French, 1956) involved giving the Test of Insight to 256 airmen equated for intelligence and, subsequently, measuring results of task-relevant and feeling feedback on separate groups. The expected interaction between kind of motivation (Affiliation or Achievement) and kind of feedback was significant at .001 (i.e., persons with high nAch responded better to task-relevant than feeling-oriented feedback). However, the Achievement motivation group failed to perform better under conditions emphasizing the individual rather than group nature of a task. No independent criterion other than the Test of Insight was used to assess motivation of persons constituting the groups.

Klinger (1966) has questioned the *construct validity* of projective measures of motivation, including French's and McClelland's, citing the discrepant results and plethora of existing motivation theories. He observed that all nAch measures now in use are uncorrelated empirically, that experimental "arousal" conditions designed to arouse achievement motivation against which criterion validity can be assessed have not been fully explicated, and that "data from performance measures in all but two studies fail to confirm that the experimental instructions designed to arouse motives did so, even though most of them obtained effects on fantasy [Achievement need]." Klinger noted that on brief experimental tasks the French Test of Insight, unlike other projectives purporting to measure Achievement need, produced almost consistently significant measures. However, this uniformity cannot necessarily be generalized to include long-term performances signifying Achievement motivation, such as grade-point averages.

The *norms* thus far provided have not been adequate, because information is lacking as to whether raw scores or standard scores were presented, and, in the case of those provided by French, no statement is made as to sampling techniques employed.

GENERAL COMMENT.   The French Test of Insight appears to show considerable promise as a measure of achievement and affiliation motivation, as these were originally defined. However, more information on both validity and reliability using random samples and external criteria other than fantasy measures of motivation is needed before the test can be considered for individual diagnostic or prognostic work. The author designed the test for use in motivational research. If it is used together with such criteria of affiliation and achievement motives as judges' observation of affiliative behavior and task performance, with controls for the usual socioeconomic variables (age, sex, education, intelligence, income, etc.), the French Test of Insight may provide useful information.

REFERENCES

Exline, R. Effects of sex, norms, and affiliation upon accuracy of perception of interpersonal preferences. *Journal of Personality,* 1960, *28,* 397–412.

French, E. G. Some characteristics of achievement motivation. *Journal of Experimental Psychology,* 1955, *50,* 232–236.

French, E. G. Development of a measure of complex motivation. U.S. Air Force Personnel and Training Research Center Research Bulletin, AFPTRC-TN-56-48, 1956.

French, E. G. Development of a measure of complex motivation. In Atkinson, J. W. (ed.), *Motives in fantasy, action, and society.* Princeton: Van Nostrand, 1958, 242–248.

French, E. G. The interaction of achievement motivation and ability in problem-solving success. *Journal of Abnormal and Social Psychology,* 1958, *57,* 419–428.

French, E. G. and Chadwick, I. Some characteristics of affiliation motivation. *Journal of Abnormal and Social Psychology,* 1956, *52,* 296–300.

Himelstein, P. and Kimbrough, W. W., Jr. Reliability of French's Test of Insight. *Educational and Psychological Measurement,* 1960, *20,* 737–741.

Klinger, E. Fantasy need achievement as a motivational construct. *Psychological Bulletin,* 1966, *66,* 291–308.

Miles, M. B. Changes during and following laboratory training: a clinical-experimental study. *Journal of Applied Behavioral Science,* 1965, *1,* 215–242.

Sherrifs, A. C. The "Intuition Questionnaire": a new projective test. *Journal of Abnormal and Social Psychology,* 1948, *43,* 326–337.

Willerman, B. et al. *Preference for working individually or in groups.* Minneapolis, University of Minnesota, 1957. (Tech. Rep. No. 6, Contract N8 ONR-66216)

UNITERMS.   Achievement; affiliation; attainment; failure; friendship; goal; group; interpersonal; liking; motivation; need; performance; projective; rejection; success; threat; warmth.

—L. J. R.

84
Ways to Live Scale (WTL)

AUTHOR.   Charles Morris

AVAILABILITY.   Morris, C. *Varieties of human value*. Chicago: University of Chicago Press, 1956.

VARIABLES.   Morris' Ways to Live Scale (also called "Paths of Life") seeks to outline an individual's values, or *ethical and philosophical orientation towards life*. No variables as such are conceptualized; rather, 13 short summaries of approaches to life are presented to the subject for his consideration.

DESCRIPTION.   Each of the 13 paragraphs attempts to combine several descriptive statements into a coherent, unified world view. Rather than simulating a Way and risking distortion, this review simply repeats Morris' own (1956) short summaries of each Way: *Way 1:* Preserve the best that man has attained; *Way 2:* Cultivate independence of persons and things; *Way 3:* Show sympathetic concern for others; *Way 4:* Experience festivity and solitude in alternation; *Way 5:* Act and enjoy life through group participation; *Way 6:* Constantly master changing conditions; *Way 7:* Integrate action, enjoyment, and contemplation; *Way 8:* Live with wholesome, carefree enjoyment; *Way 9:* Wait in quiet receptivity; *Way 10:* Control the self stoically; *Way 11:* Meditate on the inner life; *Way 12:* Chance adventuresome deeds; *Way 13:* Obey the cosmic purposes.

ADMINISTRATION AND SCORING.   Subjects rate each Way on a 7-point Likert-type scale, from "I like it very much" (=7) to "I dislike it very much" (=1). In addition, subjects rank order the 13 Ways, both to check on the individual ratings and to resolve identical ratings. No scores are produced; the rank orderings merely reflect an individual's preference profile. Fairly extensive norms are available, both for college students in the United States and students in India, Japan, Norway, and mainland China (1948 sample).

DEVELOPMENT.   Morris originally constructed seven "paths of life" from combinations of three basic components of human personality, identified as "Dionysian," a tendency to release and indulge existing desires; "Promethean," a tendency to manipulate and remake the world; and "Buddhistic," a tendency to regulate the self by restraining its desires. Six paths resulted from combinations of relative strengths of these three components (high, medium, low); the seventh represented all three at roughly equal strength. Ways 8, 9, and 10 were added at the suggestions of several hundred college-age respondents who found none of the seven paths to their liking; Ways 11, 12, and 13 were the result of further suggestions from respondents and a desire to add more extreme alternatives. No attempt was made to include modes of life which could be considered abnormal, destructive, or malevolent.

CRITIQUE.   Test–retest *reliability* coefficients on two populations were .87 ($N = 20$, three-week interval), and .78 ($N = 30$, fourteen-week interval). "Rank-order correlations made on the ratings of the first six Ways averaged .93 for 56 college women" (three-week interval). The mean test–retest reliability of the 13 individual Ways is .67 for 21 students over a three-week interval.

Morris' only study of *validity* involves 90 students who completed the Allport-Vernon-Lindzey Study of Values as well as a 5-point scale version of the Ways to Live scale. The sample group scored significantly above the Allport-Vernon norms for Theoretical and Aesthetic scores and significantly below the norms for Economic, Social, and Political scores. Those who liked Way 1 (preserve) had significantly high Social scores and low Aesthetic scores; Way 2 (independence), high Aesthetic and low Social and Economic; Way 3 (concern), high Social and Religious, low Social and Economic; Way 4 (festivity), high Theoretical and Aesthetic, low Religious; Way 5 (group participation), high Economic, low Aesthetic and Theoretical; Way 6 (master), High Economic, low Aesthetic; Way 7 (integrate), high Theoretical, low Religious; Way 8 (carefree), high Economic, low Aesthetic and Religious; Way 9 (receptivity), high Religious, low Theoretical, Economic, and Political; Way 10 (self-control), high Religious, low Theoretical and Aesthetic; Way 11 (meditate), high Religious; Way 12 (adventure), high Economic; Way 13 (obey cosmos), high Religious and Social, low Theoretical, Aesthetic, and Political.

In a very interesting investigation of the 13 Ways, Dempsey and Dukes (1965) broke the paragraphs down into 110 constituent sentences which they had 230 college students Q-Sort. They then calculated inter-item *r*s within each Way and produced 13 intercorrelation matrices. All but two Ways contained negatively correlating statements; 42 statements out of the 110 correlated negatively with at least one other statement in its own Way. (Seven of these came from the same Way.) The mean part-part correlations for the 13 Ways ranged from .02 (Way 9) to .39 (Way 12); the mean of the 13 means was .17.

The mean part-whole correlations ranged from .10 (Way 9) to .44 (Way 12).

Dempsey and Dukes have developed short forms of each Way. For these short forms the part-part correlations range from —.01 (Way 9) to .67 (Way 4), with a mean of .36 (excluding Way 8, which is a single statement in the short form). The part-whole correlations for the short forms range from .14 (Way 6) to .52 (Way 13), with a mean of .39. Test–retest reliability of the short form is .80 ($N = 230$).

The original Morris items show a correlation of .68 ($N = 19$) between students' personal preference ratings and ratings of how one "ought" to live. This figure may serve as a rough measure of the impact of social desirability upon the responses. The *norms* for the United States at the college level include breakdowns by college, sex, religious affiliation of parents, color (a sample of Negro males and females at Howard University), economic status, and population of childhood locale.

GENERAL COMMENT. As it now stands, Morris' Ways to Live scale provides individual profiles useful chiefly in comparison with group norms. His norms, however, are roughly two decades old; it is clear that today's students do not retain the *Weltanschauungen* of their parents. Certainly, an inter-generational study would be a valuable use for the WTL. The problem of negative correlations among the constituent parts of Ways suggests, however, that future work should be done with Dempsey and Dukes' short forms. Lacking current normative data, the user might best employ the (modified) Ways to Live scale for inter-group comparisons. The reliability data are not complete enough to allow recommendation of the WTL for individual assessment.

REFERENCES

Dempsey, P. and Dukes, W. F. An examination and revision of Morris' *Paths of Life*. Unpublished mimeographed paper, Davis, California: Institute of Behavior Assessment, University of California, 1965.

Morris, C. *Varieties of human value*. Chicago: University of Chicago Press, 1956.

Osgood, C. E., Ware, E. E., and Morris, C. Analysis of the connotative meanings of a variety of human values as expressed by American college students. *Journal of Abnormal and Social Psychology*, 1961, 62, 62–75.

UNITERMS. Life-view; values; world-view.

—R. B. E.

SECTION II

Compendia Reviews

A
CSE Elementary School Test Evaluations

AUTHOR.   Ralph Hoepfner and the staff of the School Evaluation Project, Guy Strickland, Gretchen Stangel, Patrice Jansen, and Marianne Patalino

AVAILABALITY.   Center for the Study of Evaluation, Graduate School of Education, University of California at Los Angeles, Los Angeles, California 90024. Copyright 1970.

TESTING AREAS COVERED.   Activity; adjustment; arithmetic operations and concepts; arts and crafts; Boldness; Capitalization; citizenship; civics; creativity; Dance; dependence; Foreign language; friendliness; Geography; geometry; grammar; Health and safety; history; hostility; hypothesis formation; Interests; Language skills; listening; Mathematical skills; measurement; memory; muscle control; music; Need achievement; neuroticism; Penmanship; physical education; physical skills; problem solving; punctuation; Reading, attitude toward; reading comprehension; reading skills; reasoning; rebelliousness; reference skills; religious belief; School orientation; scientific processes; self-esteem; sex education; shyness; singing; social organization, knowledge of; socialization; sociology; speaking; spelling; sportsmanship; statistics; Temperament, personal; temperament, social; Word recognition; writing skills.

DESCRIPTION.   This volume includes 204 tests (or test batteries—the total number of scales is about 1,600) aimed at the measurement of objectives for elementary education (Grades 1 through 6). It is conceived as a preliminary portion, aiming at "needs assessment," of a larger Elementary School Evaluation Kit, which will also include instruments aimed at program planning, evaluation of program implementation, evaluation of progress, and evaluation of outcome.

The tests are keyed to a list of 145 goals of elementary education, and are indexed both by goal and test title. The instruments are presented in a tabular format, organized according to the list of goals, separately for grades 1, 3, 5, and 6. For each instrument, the variable measured, instrument title and availability, and a series of ratings covering measurement validity, appropriateness for examinees, administrative usability, and normed technical excellence, plus a total judgment of worth in these four areas, are provided. Sources of the ratings are described below. In essence, the CSE Elementary School Test Evaluations are just that: the systematic presentation of judgments about the worth of a wide range of instruments. The instruments themselves, their format, precise descriptions of variables, background information, and so forth are not presented.

CRITIQUE.   With such an approach, everything depends on the adequacy of the evaluation process. In this case, a psychometrician and three graduate assistants with competence in statistics, counseling and guidance, and classroom teaching served as evaluators, using a systematically worked-out rating scheme. Each instrument was classified according to the educational goal (or goals) it appeared to measure (commendably, sometimes not that claimed by the authors), and a series of ratings was made in each of the four major areas (validity, appropriateness to examinees, administrative usability, and technical excellence). Summary "grades" of Good, Fair, Poor were computed for each of these areas. The raters relied wholly on the instrument itself and supporting technical and administrative manuals, and did not consult the broader research literature.

In general, the specific criteria used, and the systematic and explicit method of proceeding, are to be commended. To have a common set of criteria applied across this gigantic pool of instruments is itself a contribution. However, it is of note that "normal technical excellence" was the criterion of least importance, which is a bit disturbing, especially in light of the fact that the most frequent grade given in this category was "Poor." (In passing, frequency distributions of the final grades given, perhaps within broad categories of educational goals, would be extremely illuminating.)

The fact that only publishers' manuals were relied on is a distinct weakness; it is well known that conflicting or non-supportive evidence does not usually find its way into such publications. Accordingly, the ratings appearing in this volume are probably generous.

The authors claim that *all* measures "that are prepared for or potentially useful for evaluations within the elementary school, and that are generally available to educators and researchers" were evaluated. This is a large claim, and is probably 80–99% true (depending on one's definition of "generally available").

GENERAL COMMENT.   This collection is undoubtedly useful, and generally meets the five criteria for judgment suggested by the authors: conciseness, currency (up-to-dateness), educational relevance, objectivity, and consistency. It can serve as a useful locater mechanism for particular instruments focused on particular educational objectives. The user will, of course, still have to purchase, examine, and judge the instrument—and (if the stakes are high) is advised to look at more detailed reviews in other compendia, including non-publisher/author research data. *Caveat emptor.* CSE Elementary School Test Evaluations is not quite a *Consumer Report* for the instruments it includes, but it is very helpful.

—M. B. M.

B
Family Measurement Techniques

AUTHOR. Murray A. Straus

AVAILABILITY. University of Minnesota Press, Minneapolis, Minnesota 55455. Copyright 1969.

TESTING AREAS COVERED. (partial listing) Acceptance; achievement; activity; adaptability; adjustment; adolescent; advice-giving; affect; affection; aggression; agreement; altruism; ambition; anger; anxiety; approval; authoritarian; autonomy; avoidance; Background; belonging; breast-feeding; Child; child-rearing; cohesiveness; communication; community; companionship; compatibility; competence; competitiveness; compliance; confidence; conflict; conformity; conscience; consensus; consistency; contraception; cooperation; creativity; criticism; Dating; decision-making; defense; delinquency; democracy; dependency; depression; deprivation; development; deviance; discipline; divorce; dominance; Economic; education; emotionality; empathy; employment; equalitarianism; eroticism; esprit; esteem; ethnicity; expectations; expressive; Familism; family; father; fear; feeding; flexibility; freedom; frustration; Goals; growth; guilt; Happiness; health; home; homemaking; hostility; Ideal; identification; ideology; impulses; indulgence; inferiority; initiative; insecurity; instrumental; intellectuality; intelligence; interaction; interest; intropunitiveness; intrusiveness; involvement; irritability; Jealous; judgment; Kin; Leadership; life style; loneliness; love; Machismo; marital role; marriage; maternal; mental health; mobility; model; modernism; mood; moral; mother; motive; motor development; Nagging; narcissism; needs; neglect; neurotic; norms; nurturance; Obedience; objectivity; obligation; observation; occupational choice; Oedipal; overprotection; Parent; passivity; peer group; performance; permissiveness; personality; philosophy; play; power; praise; prejudice; premarital; prestige; problem-solving; projective; punishment; punitiveness; Q-sort; Rapport; reciprocity; recognition; recreation; rejection; religion; responsibility; responsiveness; restrictiveness; reward; rigidity; role; Satisfaction; school; security; self; self-concept; self-confidence; self-realization; sex; sex role; sexuality; shame; siblings; sociability; socio-emotional; socioeconomic status; spouse; stability; standards; status; strain; strictness; submission; success; supervision; support; sympathy; Task; tension; threat; toilet training; tolerance; traditionalist; trust; Understanding; Value; verbalization; Warmth; weaning; work.

DESCRIPTION.   Family Measurement Techniques contains abstracts of 319 instruments, focusing on one or more of the following domains: adolescent, 20; child, 75; family, 63; parent, 129; premarital, 20; and spousal, 81. To be included, a measure had to be based on at least three indicators (ruling out most indices and simple counts); deal with action or disposition to act in a family (or "proto-family") setting (although a few more general instruments useful in the family setting, such as the Bell Adjustment Inventory, the Blacky Test, Bales' Interaction Process Analysis, the Minnesota Counseling Inventory, and the Rorschach appear); and be described in some publication or be available through the American Documentation Institute, or the National Auxiliary Publications Service. The search domain was the psychological and sociological literature from 1935 to 1965.

Measures are listed alphabetically by author. For each, there is an abstract, usually 400 to 600 words in length, covering: authors; test name; variables measured; description of test; sample item (usually the first one); validity evidence (often as inferred by the abstracter); sample size and characteristics; sampling methods; reliability; length of measure; norms (also generously interpreted by abstracter); availability; and references (all subsequent to original that could be located).

Indexes covering authors, instruments, variables, and family role (adolescent, parent, etc.) are provided.

CRITIQUE.   Straus has used well the skills he employed as associate editor of *Sociological Abstracts*: the abstracts here are models of what can be done in a limited space. As with the Johnson and Bommarito volume (which see), the decision to provide abstracts only, without critical comment, deprives the reader of useful comparative judgment. Fortunately, Straus has provided some general critique elsewhere.*

The author straightforwardly points out that 56% of the measures abstracted had no reliability data whatever provided by the authors, and comments knowledgeably on the problems presented by the roughly similar proportion of studies without validity data. He points out ruefully that while for psychological instruments, the reviewer's task is usually that of deflating validity claims to a reasonable level, for

* M. A. Straus, Measuring families. In H. T. Christensen (Ed.) *Handbook of marriage and the family.* Chicago: Rand McNally, 1964, pp. 335–400. He also cites L. W. Hoffman and R. Lippitt, The measurement of family life variables, in P. H. Mussen (Ed.) *Handbook of research methods in child development.* New York: Wiley, 1960, pp. 945–1014, as a useful critical source.

sociological instruments the task is more nearly that of ferreting out possible validity correlates in data, and locating meaning in the measures blithely provided by authors.

Norms in turn are almost never mentioned, and Straus in some cases simply had to resort to reporting marginals from frequency distributions, or means.

In the face of this, Straus urges quite reasonably that the compendium instruments be treated as a source of useful measurement ideas, to be expanded, altered, or adapted as the researcher sees fit. Not all researchers will be this intelligent or responsible, so some perpetration of useless measures will doubtless occur.

GENERAL COMMENT.   Family Measurement Techniques is a thoughtful, well-organized collection of measures varying widely in their adequacy. The author's approach to his task is articulate, self-aware, and reasonable; one could hardly do better with the task of collecting instruments from a field with less than adequate standards for instrumentation. This compendium should do much to improve things, and to make researchers interested in the family more aware of the state of inquiry in that field.

—M. B. M.

C

Handbook of Research Design and Social Measurement (2nd ed.)

AUTHOR.   Delbert C. Miller

AVAILABILITY.   David McKay Company, Inc., 750 Third Avenue, New York, New York 10017. Copyright 1970. (1st edition, copyright 1964.)

TESTING AREAS COVERED.   Achievement orientation; adjustment; alienation; anomia; attitude; authoritarianism; Cohesiveness; community attitude; conservatism; culture; Family; Group; group dimensions; group dynamics; Inferiority; interaction; Law; leadership; leisure participation; Marriage; morale; Neighborliness; norms; Participation; personality; political participation; powerlessness; satisfaction; social distance; social participation; socio-economic status; sociometric; solidarity; structure; supervision.

DESCRIPTION.   The *Handbook* includes 35 instruments in the domains above. For each one, brief comments are included on: the variables measured; a description; where published; reliability; validity; scores; and utility. Research references and availability are given. In most cases the instrument itself is included.

In addition, Miller mentions, and gives references for 78 indices and measures employed during 1965–68 in the *American Sociological Review* (a period beginning after the compendium by Bonjean et al. (1967) (which see). He also lists 175 attitude measures described in Shaw and Wright (1967) (which see), and gives a table from Bonjean et al. showing the 50 measures most frequently used and cited in four major sociological journals from 1954–1965.

This listing of measures does not do full justice to what the volume is: a true handbook for social researchers covering an astounding range of practical information in its 432 pages. It includes guidelines for every phase of research design and operation; a review of frequently-used methods; library documentary resources; help on questionnaires and interviews, and on all frequently-used scaling methods; a listing of social science data libraries in the United States; directories of research centers, world-wide; a bibliography of research methods guides; an extensive section on methods of statistical analysis; a listing of major funding agencies and other support programs; guidelines for research costing; criteria for rating research reports; and guides to journals, annual meetings, fellowships and grants! It is altogether an impressive collection, likely to be of considerable use to researchers concerned with social variables.

CRITIQUE.   The focus of these comments is solely on the instruments included.

The user should know that the label "sociometric" as used by Miller refers not only to sociometric measures in the usual peer-nomination sense, but to any measure dealing with "social structure and process" (as contrasted with demographic measures, or psychological and social-psychological scales). Some "psychological" measures, such as the MMPI and the F-Scale, are nevertheless included.

The author points out that "literally thousands" of measures of social variables exist. His choice of 35 was based on a determination of variables most frequently focused on, followed by a choice of those instruments with most validity, reliability, and ease of use. It must be said that the results are uneven; several instruments (and simple indexes) are included without evidence of more than face validity. However, the information provided, though rather skeletal, does give sufficient basis for a decision about whether to investigate the instrument further. The author also provides useful comparative commentary across the instruments in a particular section (e.g., leadership) to aid the user in choosing.

The material provided on each instrument generally occupies only one to two pages (exclusive of the instrument itself and references). This often results in extreme scantiness of coverage, particularly with widely-used (and debatable) instruments such as the F-Scale. The reader can form some idea of how much of a problem this presents by comparing Miller's presentations of Bales' Interaction Process Analysis, Hemphill's Group Dimensions Descriptions Questionnaire, and the F-Scale, with descriptions of the same instruments in the present volume. In general, detailed critical judgments on the strengths and limitations of the instruments are not offered, and the data available on properties of the instruments are summarized briefly, rather than given directly.

Having the scales themselves available for examination is a distinct advantage; the user can often form a more direct idea of what the instrument is like and its potential usefulness for his purpose. However, this method by definition meant that the pool of instruments drawn on tended to be limited to those already available in scholarly journals; test publishers are notoriously reluctant to allow such reproduction.

GENERAL COMMENT.   As a general research handbook for the social (primarily sociological) scientist, this volume is almost unparalleled;

it is nearly a do-it-yourself kit for researchers. Its comprehensiveness means, however, that the instruments presented are discussed with less care than is desirable if a researcher is to make an informed decision about whether to proceed with a particular instrument.

—M. B. M.

D

Improving Educational Assessment and An Inventory of Measures of Affective Behavior

AUTHORS.   Walcott H. Beatty (Ed.) Inventory prepared by Donald J. Dowd and Sarah C. West

AVAILABILITY.   Association for Supervision and Curriculum Development, National Education Association, 1201 Sixteenth St., N.W., Washington, D.C. 20036. Copyright 1969.

TESTING AREAS COVERED.   Achievement motivation; adjustment; alienation; anal character; anxiety; articulation; attention; Behavior, classroom; Child-rearing, attitudes toward; climate; classroom; congruence; creativity; counseling, evaluation of; Delinquency-proneness; deviance; dissatisfaction; Education, attitudes toward; emotional handicapping; emotional maturity; emotions; empathy; expectations; extroversion; Gratification, delay of; guidance, attitude toward; Handicapping conditions, attitude toward; human nature, beliefs about; Identity; impulsivity; inference; interaction, classroom; interest; interpersonal relations; incentives; intellectual maturity; involvement; Law, attitude toward; Morale; motivation; Needs; neuroticism; Peer status; personality; positive regard; professors, attitude toward; psychomotor functioning; punishment, attitudes toward; "Ragging," attitudes toward; reading, attitudes toward; reading readiness; Science, attitudes toward; self-acceptance; school, attitude toward; school bus, attitude toward riding; self-concept; self-esteem; self-expectations; self-ideal; self-regard; social competency; social distance; Teacher behavior; teacher performance; teaching, attitudes toward; teaching, problems of; tests, attitudes toward; Undisciplined students, identification of; Values.

DESCRIPTION.   The *Inventory* covers 133 instruments (of which 4 are techniques rather than tests as such; e.g., a response latency measure applicable to personality tests), organized into eight domains (attitudes, creativity, interaction, motivation, personality, readiness, self-concept, and miscellaneous). They are presumably seen as relevant to the assessment of affective variables in educational settings. Of the 133, 59 are education-specific, dealing with teachers or students; the remainder are usable in any setting.

The capsule descriptions for each instrument are very brief (usually less than 400 words), and include authors' identity and instrument availability; a brief description of the instrument and the variables measured; and allusion to or reporting of available reliability and validity data. Sample items are occasionally given. Few evaluative or critical comments are made. In essence, the *Inventory* points the reader toward a number of instruments, indicating that further information must be collected by the reader.

The instruments are indexed by author, by title, and by abbreviations associated with titles—but not, curiously, by variables measured.

The earlier section of the book, Improving Educational Assessment, contains articles on the purposes of assessment (R. Tyler); language, rationality and assessment (R. E. Stake); evaluation seen as data for decision-making (D. L. Stufflebeam); and a general discussion of emotion in education (Beatty).

CRITIQUE.   The domain searched by the authors, the time period covered, and the search methods employed, remain unknown. Similarly, criteria for instrument inclusion are unspecified. The reader should note that for 56 of the instruments, reliability and validity data are either not mentioned, or cited as unavailable. Though a number of the instruments are cited as usable for research purposes only, a phrase indicating that the instrument in question should not be used for individual diagnostic purposes appears only once in the entire *Inventory*.

In a few cases, it is not possible from the description to understand precisely what the instrument purports to measure. In perhaps a third of the instruments, it seems fair to say that the variables do not seem to have been developed in any systematic way (i.e., with reference to theoretically coherent constructs). Evidence of cross-validation (or even of use by other investigators) is rarely mentioned. For only 36 instruments (one quarter of the total) is a book or journal publication cited; the reader is ordinarily referred to the test author for more information.

These facts are consistent with the inference that the authors simply requested test nominations from some population (perhaps the Association for Supervision and Curriculum Development membership) and did not engage in any other search.

GENERAL COMMENT.   Though it is useful to have a listing of instruments specifically focused on the educational domain, this book is flawed by incompleteness of search, and the inclusion of many instruments which appear on the face of it to have little merit. The careful researcher can use the book for scanning purposes, but he will have to do a good bit more work to find out whether any particular instrument included is worth his use.

Finally, the label "affective" as used in the title seems only to refer vaguely to any measure which is not "intellective." A good book of instruments in this domain is much needed, but it should be organized around a coherent notion of what "affective" means in relation to educational processes and outcomes.

—M. B. M.

E

Inventory of Drug Abuse Research Instruments

AUTHOR. Ernest W. Ferneau, Jr.

AVAILABILITY. Boston City Hospital Psychiatry Service, Mattapan Chronic Disease Hospital, 249 River Street, Mattapan, Massachusetts 02126. Inventory is sent on request; instruments and bibliographies at 35¢ a page (U.S.A.), or 50¢ a page (foreign).

TESTING AREAS COVERED. Addiction; adjustment; alcohol; alienation; Drug abuse; drug effects; drug information; drug use; drug use, attitudes toward; Life history; life philosophy; L.S.D.; Marijuana; Personality; Tobacco.

DESCRIPTION. The Inventory of Drug Abuse Research Instruments is "an archival source for the collection, storage, duplication, and issuance of pertinent research instruments and related material (e.g., bibliographies) to aid in drug abuse research and in the development of more such instruments." As of Spring, 1971, it contained about 50 instruments, listed under the headings of attitudes, subjective effects of drugs, differentiation of abusers from others, drug access and extent, education and knowledge, and program-related and evaluation measures.

The Inventory is simply a listing (apparently, of any instrument forwarded), with no information on the instruments themselves. Instruments may be listed in a "restricted" category, requiring the author's approval before use is granted. Only instruments and bibliographies are supplied on request; reports are listed as "a courtesy and aid" but are not available.

CRITIQUE. A listing of this sort may be useful, but is essentially uneconomical; in the absence of information, the researcher must request a much larger pool of instruments than he needs. The fact that only institutional affiliations are given in most cases, without identification of principal investigators, is further limiting. At the very least, the supplying of keywords or Uniterms would be helpful, and involve minimum cost.

GENERAL COMMENT. A potentially useful service, but one which will require much more differentiated description and evaluation of instruments if it is to be helpful, even in this specialized field.

—M. B. M.

F

Measures of Occupational Attitudes and Occupational Characteristics

AUTHORS.   John P. Robinson, Robert Athanasiou, and Kendra B. Head

AVAILABILITY.   Publications Division, Institute for Social Research, University of Michigan, P.O. Box 1248, Ann Arbor, Michigan 48106. Copyright 1969.

TESTING AREAS COVERED.   Alienation from work; automation; attitude toward; Career orientation; class identification; Financial benefits; Government, attitudes toward working for; Identification with organization; inner–other directedness; Job activities; job satisfaction, general; job satisfaction, specific features; Labor, orientation pro-, and attitude toward; labor and management, attitudes toward; leadership; Meaning of work; mentally ill, opinions about work of; misanthropy; motivation; Occupational mobility; occupational ratings; occupational situs; occupational values; older persons, attitude toward employment of; organizational characteristics; organizational control; Respect; Sales, attitude toward; satisfaction; self-improvement; self-reliance (independence from supervision); socio-economic status; status inconsistency; supervision; Tension, job-related; Union and management, attitudes toward each other; Vocational interest; Working conditions.

DESCRIPTION.   Eleven of the eighteen chapters in *Measures of Occupational Attitudes and Occupational Characteristics* contain reviews of a total of 80 test instruments, grouped under the headings above. The authors' criteria for assessing these instruments are clearly set forth in a separate chapter, and are similar to those used in this volume: sample adequacy; norms; reliability (primarily test–retest); homogeneity (item intercorrelation, item–test reliability, split-half reliability, reproducibility); discrimination of known groups (construct validity); and, "other procedures," which include response sets, fakeability, respondent difficulties, and scale independence. Typical items, and ease of administration and scoring are indicated.

The consistency of the reviews varies, but not detrimentally so. One writer may be numerically specific in his reporting of reliability or validity studies, while another comments more generally ("Some evidence for stability over time is reported by Hulin. . ."). The reviews are short, usually about 300 words and rarely more than 500. Each of the eleven evaluative chapters is prefaced by a short summary of its findings.

Of the remaining seven chapters, the first is introductory and sets forth the selection and evaluative criteria. Chapter 2 is a short overview of the past seventy years of research on work and the worker in the United States. Robinson's and Athanasiou's "reviews of reviews" cover occupational norms and differences in job satisfaction, and job attitudes and occupational performance in two more chapters. The three remaining chapters discuss multi-dimensional analyses of job satisfaction, status inconsistency, and occupational similarity.

CRITIQUE.   Robinson, Athanasiou, and Head's approach to test-critiquing generally parallels ours; naturally, we approve. Perhaps one reservation should be noted: although they are concerned with the problems of response sets, their criticism of fakeability and acquiescence does not fall so heavily or so often as ours would, had we reported the same instruments. Particularly in the testing of individuals whose advancement possibilities are likely to depend appreciably on a supervisor's estimate of their job attitudes, the potentiality for these two response sets seems considerable.

The review chapters are well and thoroughly, though not exhaustively, done.

GENERAL COMMENT.   *Measures of Occupational Attitudes and Occupational Characteristics* consistently gives accurate assessments of the form and scope of the significant instruments within its charge. Its evaluations of psychometric qualifications are usually terse, but sufficent for the potential user to judge the instruments' utility accurately for his purposes.

—R. B. E.

G
Measures of Political Attitudes

AUTHORS. John P. Robinson, Jerrold G. Rusk, and Kendra B. Head

AVAILABILITY. Publications Division, Institute for Social Research, University of Michigan, P.O. Box 1248, Ann Arbor, Michigan 48106. Copyright 1968.

TESTING AREAS COVERED. Acquaintanceship; activity, political; Business, attitude toward big; Citizen duty; civic competence; civil liberties; Communists, attitude toward; competence, political; conservatism; cosmopolitanism; cynicism; Democratic attitudes; Efficacy, political; ethnocentrism; Foreign aid; foreign policy; Government (India), attitude toward; Information, political; integration, attitude toward; internationalism; isolationism; issue familiarity; issue involvement; issue orientation; involvement, political; Liberalism; localism; Medicine, attitude toward socialization of; militancy; Nationalism; Negroes, attitude toward; norms, political; Opinion leadership; Pacifism; participation, political; partisanship, issue; patriotism; party image; personage admiration; political system, attitudes toward; power, attitude toward sources of; prejudice; progress, concern with; Race, attitude toward; race, identification with race stereotypes; races, community relations among; radicalism; Social attitudes; social distance; social welfare; socialism; Soviet Union, attitude toward actions of; Tolerance; Underdog, identification with; Vietnam, attitude toward U.S. policy in; War, attitude toward.

DESCRIPTION. Ten of the 15 chapters in *Measures of Political Attitudes* contain reviews of a total of 95 instruments, grouped under the headings above. The authors' criteria for assessing these instruments are clearly set forth in a separate introductory chapter, and are similar to those used in this volume: sample adequacy; norms; reliability (primarily test–retest); homogeneity (item intercorrelation, item–test reliability, split-half reliability, and reproducibility); discrimination of known groups (construct validity); and, "other procedures," which include response sets, fakeability, respondent difficulties, and scale independence. In almost all cases, the instrument is reproduced in full. The ease of administration and scoring is also indicated.

  The consistency of the reviews varies somewhat, but not detrimentally so. The reviews are short, about 300 words, and rarely more than 500. Each of the ten evaluative chapters is prefaced by a short summary of its findings.

Of the remaining four chapters, Chapter 2 is a review by Alfred Hero of the major trends, both general and comparative, of public reaction to government policies in the United States over the past thirty years. Chapter 13 contains longitudinal studies taken from the Survey Research Center's election studies of the following traits: party identification; attitudes toward government principles; domestic policy; civil rights and racial attitudes; international attitudes; war-related attitudes; political activity; attitudes toward the political system; and personality variables. Chapter 14 contains the tables of contents of two Appendix volumes (which are separately bound), *Measures of Occupational Attitudes and Occupational Characteristics* and *Measures of Social Psychological Attitudes*. Chapter 15 contains the contents of the related volumes *Sociological Measurement,* by Bonjean, Hill, and Mc-Lemore (1967); *Scales for the Measurement of Attitudes,* by Shaw and Wright (1967); and *Handbook of Research Design and Social Measurement,* by Miller (1st edition, 1964).

CRITIQUE.   Robinson, Rusk, and Head's approach to test–critiquing generally parallels ours; thus we tend to approve. As with the other volumes from ISR, we note a reservation: although the authors are concerned with the problems of response sets, their criticism of fake-ability and acquiescence is less frequent than the instruments deserve. Particularly in the testing of political attitudes in a society with a tradition of singling out attitudes as being "un-American," the potentiality for both faking and acquiescing is considerable. To the extent that voting behavior, for example, is hypothesized to be relatively free of such influences by virtue of its being done in secret, to that extent are measures susceptible to faking or acquiescent response set impaired in their usefulness. In general, Robinson, Rusk, and Head's execution closely parallels that of this volume, though it is less intensive.

GENERAL COMMENT.   Like its companion volumes, *Measures of Political Attitudes* consistently gives accurate assessments of the form and scope of the significant instruments within its charge. Its evaluation of their psychometric qualifications is usually brief, but enables the potential user to form an accurate assessment of the instrument's utility for his purposes.

—R. B. E.

H
Measures of Social Psychological Attitudes

AUTHORS.   John P. Robinson and Philip R. Shaver

AVAILABILITY.   Publications Division, Institute for Social Research, University of Michigan, P.O. Box 1248, Ann Arbor, Michigan 48106. Copyright 1969.

TESTING AREAS COVERED.   Adjustment; alienation; ambiguity; anomie; anti-Semitism; Bible, attitude toward; Church, attitude toward; commitment, religious; competence, personal; conviction, intellectual; Dogmatism; Ego-strength; ethnocentrism; Faith in people; fascism; Helplessness; Machiavellianism; misanthropy; New Left, concurrence with attitudes of; Opinion leadership; Power, distribution of; powerlessness; purpose in life; Rejection; religion, attitude toward; religiosity; rigidity; Self-concept; self-consistency; self-esteem; social desirability; social responsibility; status concern; Toughmindedness; trust; Values.

DESCRIPTION.   Eight of the ten chapters in *Measures of Social Psychological Attitudes* contain reviews of a total of 106 test instruments, grouped under the headings above. The authors' criteria for assessing these instruments are similar to those used in this volume: sample adequacy; norms; reliability (primarily test–retest); homogeneity (item intercorrelation, item–test reliability, split-half reliability, and reproducibility); discrimination of known groups (construct validity); and "other procedures," which include response sets, fakeability, respondent difficulties, and scale independence. Almost all instruments are reproduced in full; ease of administration and scoring are indicated. The reviews are brief, about 300 through 500 words. Each of the eight evaluative chapters is prefaced by a short summary of its findings. The remaining chapters are a brief introduction and a review by Robinson of the major attempts to measure "life satisfaction" and "happiness" over the past 15 years. Robinson looks at five aspects of these investigations: descriptions of the studies in which global assessments of satisfaction have been obtained; the stability and reliability of these global assessments; variations in reported satisfaction by sex, marital status, age, social status, status incongruence, race, employment status, religious affiliation, and urban versus rural residency; relationships between reported satisfaction and other attitudes; and relationships between satisfaction and behavior.

CRITIQUE. *Measures of Social Psychological Attitudes* is Appendix B to Robinson, Rusk, and Head's *Measures of Political Attitudes* (Appendix A is Robinson, Athanasiou, and Head's *Measures of Occupational Attitudes and Occupational Characteristics*). In reviewing each of these three volumes, we have noted and favored the similarity between their approach to test–critiquing and ours. We have remarked about the other two volumes that their criticism of instrument vulnerability to fakeability and acquiescence has been milder and less frequent than ours would have been. In this volume, however, Shaver in particular has been careful to note these possibilities, especially in his reviews of 27 measures of authoritarianism, dogmatism, and related measures, an area notoriously beset by acquiescence problems. As with the other volumes, we would perhaps have reviewed the same instruments at somewhat greater length, but this is a minor distinction.

GENERAL COMMENT. As with its companion volumes, *Measures of Social Psychological Attitudes* consistently gives accurate assessments of the form and scope of the significant instruments within its domain. The evaluations of instruments' psychometric properties are usually terse, but perfectly sufficient for the potential user to form an accurate judgment of the instruments' utility for his purposes.

—R. B. E.

I

Mirrors for Behavior: An Anthology of Classroom Observation Instruments

EDITORS.   Anita Simon and E. Gil Boyer

AVAILABILITY.   Research for Better Schools, Inc., 1700 N. Market St., Philadelphia, Pennsylvania 19103. Copyright 1970.

TESTING AREAS COVERED.   Activity; affective; Classroom; cognitive; counseling; Dyad; Family; feedback; Group; Interaction; Non-verbal behavior; Observation; Physical environment; procedure; psychomotor; psychotherapy; pupil; Role; Structure; student; supervision; Teacher; T-group; Verbal behavior.

DESCRIPTION.   The 14 volumes in the *Mirrors for Behavior* series are special editions of the *Classroom Interaction Newsletter*. Simon and Boyer have collected 79 observation instruments. All of them are usable in the classroom, though 15 were originally developed for use in other settings (counseling or therapy, industrial work groups, training groups). Of the 79 instruments, 12 are only for use in observing individual behavior, 5 only for dyads, and the remainder are multipurpose or for use with groups of 3 or more persons. Fourteen instruments focus solely on teacher behavior, 7 on pupil behavior, and the remainder do both. Only 8 instruments are designed for use with a specific subject matter (e.g., mathematics).

For comparisons, the editors preface each instrument with a check list of its major features: system dimension (affective, cognitive, work process, behavior); type of communication recorded (verbal, nonverbal); subject of observation (teacher only, student only, teacher and student); data collection method; audiotape or videotape requirement; personnel required for observation; number of coders required; coding units; and uses of the instrument (research, training, supervision). A concise description of the dimensions of classroom activity upon which the instrument focuses, and the administration and coding procedures follow. The specific behaviors which the instrument records are listed in detail at the end of each instrument's summary. Also included are observer reliability procedures, any available reports of interjudge reliability, a list of supplementary materials available, and, of course, the availability of the instrument. The reader can profitably compare the Simon–Boyer treatment of Argyris' Interpersonal Competence Scoring System, Bales' Interaction Process Analysis, and the Hill Interaction Matrix, with the reviews in this volume.

The instrument summaries are preceded by a 24-page review of the rationale, approach, and lines of development of classroom observation instruments, with emphasis on the increasing importance of affective processes to learning in the classroom.

In the early pages of *Mirrors for Behavior*, the authors print not only abstracts of each of the 79 instruments, but also summary tables indicating the focus of each system, (affective, cognitive, psychomotor, role, activity, procedure, physical environment); the coding units used (category, speaker or topic change, time unit, etc.); whether audio, video, and/or multiple observers are needed; settings and populations in which the system has been used; the size of system observed (person, dyad, or group); and the purposes of observation (research, training, or evaluation).

CRITIQUE.   The 79 instruments constitute a comprehensive, probably nearly exhaustive, sample of the field. The specific listing of the variables which each instrument records allows the potential user to choose the observation scheme which coincides most nearly with the approach he wants to take toward viewing interaction, in or out of the classroom. The question of how the data produced by each instrument are to be reduced, interpreted, and applied tends to be overlooked here. In fairness to Simon and Boyer, this process lies outside their intended scope. It would, however, have been a valuable addition to this compendium had they included some of the interpretations and consequences which authors of the various instruments have lent to their results.

GENERAL COMMENT.   This extensive compendium performs a real service; it points the researcher toward all the significant work in classroom observation. Even without a discussion of the implementation of test results, *Mirrors for Behavior* is extremely useful. It must be considered the primary source for anyone wishing to observe interaction, especially in the classroom.

—R. B. E.

J
Objective Personality and Motivation Tests: A Theoretical Introduction and Practical Compendium

AUTHORS.   Raymond B. Cattell and Frank W. Warburton

AVAILABILITY.   University of Illinois Press, Urbana, Illinois 61803. Copyright 1967.

TESTING AREAS COVERED.   Cattell and Warburton have developed a set of what they term "primary objective personality test factors," 21 in number; the general testing area they are concerned with is, therefore, personality assessment. The tests they report, however, encompass the broadest definition of "personality," as measured by instruments focused on psychologalvanic response through music preferences to ability with tongue twisters.

Cattell and Warburton are concerned with the relationship of the varied tests to their 21 dimensions of personality. Each of these 21 dimensions is defined by two poles, which are listed separately below. The numbers in parentheses following each pole label are the Universal Index (U.I.) numbers which the authors have assigned to each dimension, so that although 42 poles are listed separately here the reader can establish each dimension by matching the pairs of U.I. numbers.

Adjustment (24); anxiety (24); apathy, skeptical (27); assurance, rough (28); Comention (cultural conformity) (20); cortertia (cortical alertness) (22); Dismay (33); dissofrustance (dissociation of frustrating recollections) (30); Ego, narcissistic (16); excitation (35); exuberance (21); exvia (extroversion) (32); Homespunness (26); Inconautia (impracticalness) (34); independence (19); inhibition (17); invia (introversion) (32); involvement (27); Lack of will (29); Manic smartness (18); mobilization of energy (23); Objectivity (20); Passiveness (18); pathemia (22); practicalness (34); Realism (25); regression (23); responsiveness, wholehearted (29); Sanguine poise (33); self-sentiment, narcissistic (26); self-sentiment, strong (36); self-sentiment, weak (36); stolidness (30); stolparsomonia (somnolence) (35); subduedness (19); super-ego asthenia (28); suppressibility (21); Tensinflexia (psychotic tendency) (25); trustingness (17); Unassertiveness, secure, disciplined (16); Variability, impulsive (31); Wariness (31).

DESCRIPTION.   The bulk of Cattell and Warburton's 687 pages is devoted to a compendium of 412 instruments, prefaced by an explication of their primary objective test factors, and by six extensive cross-indices.

Each test is outlined as follows: Two titles are given, one with which a psychologist would label the test, and the other presented to the subject. The age-range, length of test in minutes, number of forms, and formal structure of the test follow. Next the authors indicate which of 2,366 Master Index variables can be derived from the test. Where appropriate, a variable is followed by a two-letter code which signifies the general means by which the test attempts to prevent faking. (Some examples are: unexpected tasks; puzzling purpose; physiological responses.) Paragraphs on the theory, the rationale, and the design of the test follow. The summaries end with sample items and brief descriptions of the administration and scoring procedures. Other than the loadings, if they are known, of each variable on Cattell and Warburton's 21 personality factors, *no psychometric data whatsoever are presented. And, only half the tests have undergone two or more factor analyses to check the replicability of factor loadings.*

The remainder (beginning) of the volume contains ten chapters devoted to an appraisal at some length of the state-of-the-art of objective personality tests, the proper criteria for their construction, and the *raison d'etre* for Cattell and Warburton's scheme.

CRITIQUE.   With six cross-indexes, and some tolerance for neologisms, the reader is almost guaranteed of finding which of the 412 tests may be useful to him. And the tests do exhibit wide ranges of approach, areas of interest, and methods. The complete absence, however, of any psychometric data means that any judgment of utility to the potential user is severely limited. But an even more serious, and quite incomprehensible, debility of this work is the utter absence of attribution or availability of the tests themselves. *No authors are named for any test.* The introduction implies that half are the responsibility of Cattell and half of some twenty colleagues at the Institute for Personality and Ability Testing (IPAT) whose location is also nowhere indicated. (It is at 1602 Coronado Drive, Champaign, Illinois 61820.) Warburton's address *is* given, in a note expressing a readiness to receive specifications of further objective personality tests. Also, *nothing but an occasional clue is given as to the individual test's whereabouts.* Once intrigued by a test, a potential user must presumably write Cattell at IPAT, or Warburton in Manchester, England.

GENERAL COMMENT.   It is not quite fair, and would certainly be unprofessional to describe this compendium of tests as "useless." But it is fair to say that in the 687 pages of *Objective Personality and Motivation Tests* Drs. Cattell and Warburton give no explicit information whatsoever as to the validity, consistency, and transferability of their tests, despite their long chapter on the indispensability of those qualities; that they give no credit to the authors of any of the tests; and that they indicate no direct means of obtaining any of the tests. These baffling omissions make this book of severely limited value.

—R. B. E.

K

Published Standardized Tests: An Annotated List for Junior Colleges

AUTHOR.   Dean W. Seibel

AVAILABILITY.   Educational Testing Service, Princeton, New Jersey. Copyright 1967.

TESTING AREAS COVERED.   *Published Standardized Tests* is concerned with five areas of testing: ability; achievement; interest inventories; pupil skills; and vocational.

The *ability* tests cover: Mechanical; mental, general; Non-verbal; numerical; Spatial; Verbal.

The *achievement* tests cover: Algebra; arithmetic; art; arts, general; Biology; Calculus; chemistry; Economics; English, general, and listening comprehension; Foreign language, aptitude, and general; French; Geometry; German; government or civics; Greek; Health; Hebrew; history; Italian; Latin; literature (English); Mathematics, general; music; Phonics; physics; Reading, diagnostic, and general; Russian; Science, aptitude, and general; social sciences, general, and miscellaneous; Spanish; spelling; Trigonometry; Vocabulary; Writing.

The *pupil skills* tests cover: Library usage; Social; study.

The *vocational* tests cover: Bookkeeping; business; Clerical and secretarial; computer programming; Drawings, engineering and structural, ability to read; driving (motor vehicle); Electrical sophistication; Nursing; Photography; Selling; supervisory practices; Teaching.

DESCRIPTION.   Seibel searched the catalogs of 23 test publishers for those entries which were conceivably relevant to usage by teachers and administrators in junior colleges. All are pencil-and-paper instruments; none are personality inventories, nor are any designed for clinical situations. Also, instruments aimed at higher-level college and graduate students have been weeded out. In addition to the title and publisher for each of the 330 tests he selected, Seibel gives its length in minutes and the number of forms the test comes in. The comments on the tests' features are brief: the variables covered, a description of the test, and the number of scores produced are summarized in about forty words. Where appropriate, references to the volume and page of Buros' *Mental Measurements Yearbooks* on which the test also appears are noted. A list of the publishers' addresses completes the book.

CRITIQUE.   Comments on the tests are terse to the point of being barely informative. Seibel omits any and all psychometric data, on the curious assumption that this "kind of information is extremely difficult to interpret and can change as rapidly as results of new research studies or new standardization programs are made available." Also, Seibel assumes that the "fact that a publisher places enough emphasis on test publishing activities to warrant producing a catalog or descriptive booklet devoted to tests indicates, we believe, that the tests so identified will probably meet at least some minimum standards of quality and utility." Our experience in compiling this book has frequently been otherwise.

GENERAL COMMENT.   *Published Standardized Tests* is a book of pointers. The information it gives is sufficient only to identify the existence of tests. Any judgment of utility of a particular instrument must depend on the potential user's obtaining substantive information from the test's publisher, Buros or other compendia, and available research.

—R. B. E.

L

Scales for the Measurement of Attitudes

AUTHORS.   Marvin E. Shaw and Jack W. Wright

AVAILABILITY.   McGraw-Hill Book Company, 1221 Avenue of the Americas, New York, New York 10020. Copyright 1967.

TESTING AREAS COVERED.   This volume contains 176 attitude scales, organized into eight chapters, devoted to attitudes toward social practices; social issues; international issues; abstract concepts; political and religious systems; ethnic and national groups; significant others; and social institutions.

The following topic listing should be read as including "attitude toward" after each item; except for the first. Attitude; abstract concepts; Biological characteristics; Conflict; Economic practices; economic systems; education; educational institutions; educational workers; ethnic groups; Family; Health; heterosexual practices; Institutions; international conflict; international issues; Jews; Law; legal issues; Negroes; Philosophical issues; political issues; political systems; Religious practices; religious issues; religious systems; School; school courses; self; significant others; social institutions; social issues; social practices; social problems; social systems; status.

DESCRIPTION.   The information on each of the 176 attitude measures (not all are strictly scales, as the authors point out) is quite thorough. Given are a general description, including number and type of items; population sample on which the scale was developed; the response mode; scoring method; reliability and validity information; and general comments, which may include references to work using the scale, advantages and disadvantages, and a brief critical judgment. Then an exhibit of the instrument itself is provided, with title, source, the actual items, directions, and response mode shown.

Shaw and Wright do not specify the time period covered in their search; 1930 seems the earliest reference. They chose attitude measures with "at least minimal reliability and validity," and considered also "the method of construction, the population of subjects . . . for the development and evaluation, and the appropriateness of the items to the current *Zeitgeist*."

Each subsection of each chapter (e.g., scales measuring attitudes to heterosexual practices) begins with a brief overview of the instruments to be covered, and concludes with a general summary comment on the section and the issues involved in measuring attitudes covered in it.

Two preliminary chapters deal very thoughtfully with the nature of attitudes as such, and with methods of scale construction. A final chapter draws some general critical conclusions, rather gloomy ones (e.g., that most of the scales presented are of uncertain validity, are not unidimensional, do not have equality of units, and no zero points—though they are minimally reliable), and makes suggestions for improvement in item formulation, validation, and scale selection.

CRITIQUE.   Shaw and Wright have performed a distinctly-needed service very thoroughly and competently. The entries are reasonably complete, and the authors have not stinted in criticism of the adequacy of the scales presented. Almost alone among the compendia reviewed in this volume, they remind the reader that, "The attitude scales in this book are recommended for research purposes and for group testing. We believe that the available information and supporting research does not warrant the application of many of these scales as measures of individual attitude for the purpose of diagnosis or personnel selection or for any other individual assessment process." This notice appears prominently displayed at the end of the Preface.

The bibliography of 600 or so items is probably exhaustive of important work in the domain of attitude conceptualization and measurement, and must be counted a useful contribution itself.

GENERAL COMMENT.   All in all, *Scales for the Measurement of Attitudes* is a model of good compendia of instruments. It is a basic tool for anyone interested in attitude research, and should do a good deal, hopefully, to reduce the scattered, uneven, unstandardized quality of attitude measurement, and the wasteful duplication of effort which led them to produce the volume in the first place.

—M. B. M.

M
SCALES/RIQS: An Inventory of Research Instruments

AUTHOR.   Daniel L. Kegan

AVAILABILITY.   Department of Industrial Engineering and Management Sciences, The Technological Institute, Northwestern University, Evanston, Illinois 60201. Manual, Document 70/24 (rev.), September, 1970.

TESTING AREAS COVERED.   (partial listing) Absenteeism; achievement; activity; administration; adoption; affect; alienation; altruism; ambiguity; anger; anomia; anxiety; arousal; aspirations; atmosphere; attitude; authenticity; authoritarianism; autonomy; avoidance; awareness; Background; behavior; belief; belligerence; birth control; bureaucratization; business; Career; change; child; civil rights; client relations; climate; cooperation; cohesiveness; collaboration; commitment; communication; competence, complexity; concern; conflict; conformity; consensus; control; cosmopolitanism; creativity; critical incidents; cynicism; Decision-making; defensiveness; delegation; dependency; depression; development; dissatisfaction; dogmatism; Education; effectiveness; efficiency; effort; ego strength; employee; environment; esteem; evaluation; expectations; experience; external control; Fate; fear; flexibility; formal; freedom; friendship; Goals; group; Happiness; Idea evaluation; idea flow; ideal; identification; importance; inclusion; independence; influence; informal; information; innovation; innovativeness; integration; intergroup relations; interaction; interest; internal control; interpersonal; intimacy; intolerance of ambiguity; intuition; involvement; Job; job satisfaction; Leadership; legitimacy; liberalism; life goals; listening; local; loyalty; Machiavellianism; management; membership; morale; motivation; Need; network; norms; nurturance; Occupational; openness; organization; orientation; Parent; participation; perception; performance; permissiveness; personality; personnel; political; position; power; powerlessness; problem-solving; process; product; productivity; professional; project; Race; responsibility; reward; risk-taking; role; Sanctions; satisfaction; school; self-actualization; self-description; self-disclosure; self-esteem; sensitivity; sexual permissiveness; size; sociability; social; social mobility; social participation; social perception; socio-economic class; span of control; status; strain; stress; structure; subordinate; superior; supervision; support; suspiciousness; T-group; task; teacher; training; trust; Value; verbal; Warmth; work.

DESCRIPTION.   The SCALES/RIQS Inventory contains (as of June 1971) 360 instruments measuring variables relevant to organization theory.* Those which have been used for assessment of human relations training or organization development programs are of special interest. The information is fully computer-stored and retrievable; simple access requests from users can be handled without charge or at minimum cost.

For each instrument, the following information is stored: author; reference; date; where instrument was used (subjects, research site); reliability and validity; variables measured; comments by author or person depositing the item in SCALES/RIQS. The total length of entries is usually 100 to 150 words.

Retrieval from the file can be done by author, name of instrument, variable, or any desired key word.

An associated computer file, PROPS/RIQS, is used for storage and retrieval of particular empirical studies (presumably in the organizational theory domain), resulting in a propositional inventory. The entries include author, reference, date, abstract of findings, instruments used, major variables, comments, depositor's name, and the proposition derived from the study.

CRITIQUE.   It is not clear how systematic, and over what range of sources, the original search conducted for the SCALES/RIQS Inventory was. It was launched by a graduate student seminar, and is felt by Kegan (personal correspondence) to be in need of updating, expansion, and evaluation (as of June 1971).

The brevity of entries necessary in this sort of system places a considerable premium on the quality of initial review and analysis of instruments. One guesses that entries are typically made on the basis of a single study or report, rather than on the multiple sources usually

---

* The reader with interest in the domain of organizational behavior is also referred to Indik, B. P., Hockmeyer, M., and Castore, C. *A compendium of measures of individuals, groups, and organizations relevant to the study of organizational behavior.* (Technical Report 16, Nonr – 404 (10), New Brunswick, N.J.: Rutgers, The State University, 1968.) This file of several hundred measures can be accessed by writing Dr. Bernard P. Indik, Graduate School of Social Work, Rutgers University, New Brunswick, N.J. 08903. A nominal fee is charged to cover Xeroxing and other costs.

The variables covered are reviewed in Indik, B. P. and Berrien, F. K. (Eds.) *People, groups and organizations* (New York: Teachers College Press, 1968), Chapter 1. Each scale, index, or instrument in the compendium is described very briefly; reliability and validity data are largely unavailable; where available, sample and organizational setting are usually described.

relied on in the present volume. The user will naturally have to consult original sources, or other compendia, to make his final decision.

GENERAL COMMENT.   All in all, SCALES/RIQS is a useful tool, especially as new instruments, many unstandardized, and unavailable through publishers or the general research literature, burgeon. Computer storage and retrieval of such measures is an extremely attractive feature; users are encouraged to add items to SCALES/RIQS in the broad domain it covers. SCALES/RIQS is a useful and adequate working tool for researchers prepared to make their own careful judgments of instrument adequacy.

—M. B. M.

N

The Sixth Mental Measurements Yearbook

EDITOR.　Oscar Krisen Buros

AVAILABILITY.　The Gryphon Press, 220 Montgomery Street, Highland Park, New Jersey 08904. Copyright 1965.

TESTING AREAS COVERED.　Achievement batteries; agriculture; Business education: bookkeeping, shorthand, typing, and miscellaneous; Character and personality: projective and non-projective; computational and scoring devices; courtship and marriage; Driving and safety education; Education; English: composition, literature, speech, spelling, and vocabulary; etiquette; Fine arts: art and music; foreign languages: English, French, German, Greek, Hebrew, Italian, Latin, Russian, and Spanish; Handwriting; health and physical education; home economics; Industrial arts; intelligence: group, individual, and specific; Listening comprehension; Mathematics: algebra, arithmetic, geometry, trigonometry, and miscellaneous; mental ability; multi-aptitude batteries; Personality; philosophy; psychology; Reading: diagnostic, oral, readiness, special fields, speed, study skills, and miscellaneous; record and report forms; religious education; Science: biology, chemistry, physics, and miscellaneous; sensory-motor functions; auditory, motor, and visual; social studies: contemporary affairs, economics, geography, history, political science, and sociology; socio-economic status; Test programs; Vocations: accounting, clerical, dentistry, engineering, interests, law, manual dexterity, mechanical ability, medicine, nursing, research, selection and rating forms, selling, skilled trades, supervision, transportation, and miscellaneous.

DESCRIPTION.　The Buros series of *Mental Measurements Yearbooks* dates from 1938 and has become *the* reference work in the field. The current, sixth, edition reviews 1,219 tests (in its 1,714 pages) of which 628 are reviewed for the first time. The remaining 445 tests have revised or supplemented reviews.* Together they represent all tests

---

* The reader with particular interest in personality measures should also consult the comprehensive and convenient *Personality Tests and Reviews* (1970, also from Gryphon Press). It includes 513 personality measures (both projective and non-projective), drawn from all of the six *Mental Measurements Yearbooks* since 1938. Each test is briefly described, with a complete bibliography (18,330 references, all told), then all previous reviews are reprinted. In many cases new material is added, including a total of 7,116

known to have been published in the English-speaking world between 1959 and mid-1964, plus those published before 1959 but not previously reviewed, and others reviewed in earlier editions for which at least seven new references were found. Three hundred ninety-six reviewers contributed to *The Sixth Yearbook;* 246 of them are college teachers in education or psychology. In addition to the tests, 527 books or reviews are critiqued.

Each test review is preceded by the following information: test title; groups for intended use; date of copyright or publication; number and significance of part scores; whether individual or group test; machine scorability; available forms, parts, and levels; number of pages; complete absence of reliability and/or validity data in the manual (if appropriate); cost; administration time; author; publisher; and subdivisions or editions of the test, if any. All known references, including books, reviews, and unpublished doctoral theses, follow this descriptive information. Then come the reviews themselves, original reviews first, then excerpted test reviews and references to other test reviews, both from earlier *Yearbooks* and from elsewhere in the same volume.

CRITIQUE.   In his "Suggestions to Reviewers" Buros writes:

> Reviews should be frankly critical, with both strengths and weaknesses pointed out in a judicious manner. . . . Criticism should be as specific as possible; implied criticisms meaningful only to testing specialists should be avoided. Reviews should be written primarily for the rank and file of test users. An indication of the relative importance and value of a test with respect to competing tests should be presented wherever possible. . . . If a test manual gives insufficient, contradictory, or ambiguous information regarding the construction, validity, and use of a test, reviewers are urged to write directly to authors and publishers for further information. Test authors and publishers should, however, be held responsible for presenting adequate data in test manuals—failure to do so should be pointed out. . . .

---

new references. Chapter 3 contains a complete, classified list of all 2,802 instruments which have appeared in one or more of the *Mental Measurements Yearbooks*. A variety of supporting indexes makes the user's task easy. Some interesting historical trend data are provided showing numbers of published references for each test over the past thirty years.

This monograph is one of a series, *Reading Tests and Reviews,* and appeared in 1968; volumes on intelligence and on vocational aptitudes will appear soon after the *Seventh Mental Measurements Yearbook*, scheduled for late 1971.

It is the outstanding strength of the Buros *Mental Measurements Year-books* that both editor and reviewers have adhered strictly to these guidelines. The reviews are exacting, but no more so than the testing profession deserves, if it is to earn respect for its labors. Test users who have relied in the past upon test publishers' promotional literature or local tradition to guide their selection of instruments and who now consult the Buros series should be prepared to find strong, valid criticism of many of their favorite instruments.

GENERAL COMMENT.   Buros' series is the product of thirty years of his attempting to improve the quality of published tests through independent, competent, professional criticism. The scant progress toward finer discrimination in test selection that has occurred in these three decades has undoubtedly discouraged him, but its slowness has occurred only in defiance of Buros' well-conceived and dedicatedly-executed *Mental Measurements Yearbooks*.

R. B. E.

O

Sociological Measurement: An Inventory of Scales and Indices

AUTHORS.   Charles N. Bonjean, Richard J. Hill, and S. Dale McLemore

AVAILABILITY.   Chandler Publishing Company, 124 Spear Street, San Francisco, California 94105. Copyright 1967.

TESTING AREAS COVERED.   Achievement; achievement motivation; anomie and alienation; aspirations; assimilation; authoritarianism; authority, attitudes toward and characteristics of; Class consciousness; cohesion; community, attitudes toward and characteristics of; complex organizations, attitudes toward and perceptions of, characteristics of, and informal relations in; conformity and deviance; consensus; crime and delinquency; Education, attitude toward and perceptions of, and behavior in and characteristics of; Family, interpersonal relations and authority in, and perceptions of and attitudes toward; family cohesion; Health, individual; Innovation and diffusion; interests; intergroup relations, ethnocentrism in, nonracial and nonethnic, racial and ethnic characteristics, racial and ethnic discrimination, racial and ethnic group belongingness, racial and ethnic prejudice and social distance, and racial and ethnic stereotypes; interpersonal relations, attitudes toward, and characteristics of; Job satisfaction, morale, and related measures; Leadership, behavior and characteristics of community and organizational, identification of community and organizational, behavior and characteristics of small groups, and identification of small groups; Marital adjustment and courtship; marital and family roles; medicine and health, attitudes toward, and behavior in and characteristics of; mental ability; Neighborhood, attitudes toward and characteristics of; norms; Occupational roles; Personal adjustment; personality, general; personality traits: creativity, dominance, masculinity/femininity, motives and needs, sociability/withdrawal, and various categories; political attitudes; political behavior; Religion, attitude toward, participation in, and characteristics of; Self-image, self-concept, and related measures; small groups, attitudes toward, identification with and perceptions of, behavior and interaction in, and status relations in; social mobility and related measures; social participation; societal characteristics; socio-economic status: composite and objective, composite (subjective and objective), occupational, and reputational; status concern; status consistency and related measures; Urban areas, metropolitan areas and dominance, segregation, socio-economic status,

375

urbanization (family status), and various categories; Values; Work/ value orientations.

DESCRIPTION.   *Sociological Measurement* is essentially an extensive bibliography which references 3,609 uses of citations of 2,080 separate scales or indexes. For a data base, the authors used all the articles and research notes appearing from January 1954 through December 1965 in four journals: *American Journal of Sociology*, *American Sociological Review*, *Social Forces*, and *Sociometry*. The resulting references (which are not limited to these four journals) are listed chronologically under the Testing Area headings listed above; under each heading are approximately 20 subheadings. In addition, as part of their study of continuity in social research, Bonjean, Hill, and Mc-Lemore identified the 47 measures used or cited more than five times. These 47 are specially noted in the table of contents under their appropriate headings, and are the subjects of brief, one or two page descriptions. For the 2,033 measures not described, the user must consult the reference to determine the instrument's relevance. A short introduction explaining the methods used and summarizing the results of the continuity research completes the 580-page book.

CRITIQUE.   *Sociological Measurement* covers well over 1600 specific subject areas. The book is clearly an exhaustive review of the sociological literature for the eleven-year period of its concern. The descriptions of the 47 most frequently cited instruments are not thorough or consistent from instrument to instrument. Roughly half the descriptions include some psychometric data, but the data reported are generally limited to coefficients of reproducibility or unelaborated coefficients of "reliability." No assessments of validity, for example, are made. As far as they go, the descriptions are accurate representations of the instruments.

GENERAL COMMENT.   Bonjean, Hill, and McLemore have compiled a volume of pointers, which appears thorough and accurate; it covers a large percentage of the recent history of scale development and use in sociologically-oriented studies. That is all they claim to have done; as they have succeeded, *Sociological Measurement* is a valuable and easily-used reference.

—R. B. E.

P

Test Collection Bulletin

EDITOR.   Eleanor V. Horne

AVAILABILITY.   Educational Testing Service, Princeton, New Jersey 08540. Subscription: $2.00 U.S.A., $2.50 foreign.

TESTING AREAS COVERED.   Achievement; aptitude; attitude; Child; Interest; Opinions; Personality; Sensory-motor.

DESCRIPTION.   The Test Collection Bulletin is not a book, but a periodical issued bimonthly since 1968. Each issue lists acquisitions to the Educational Testing Service Test Collection, "an extensive library of standardized tests, record and report forms, and assessment devices. It also includes publishers' catalogs and descriptive materials, information on scoring services and systems, test reviews, and reference volumes on measurement and evaluation." Also included is a special Head Start Test Collection, with information on assessment instruments useful with young children.

The Test Collection Bulletin is essentially an updating report on the Test Collection, to which qualified users (subject to publishers' restrictions) may have on-site access.* Each issue, in addition to listing acquisitions, each with a descriptive sentence or two, lists: announcements of new books and instruments; testing programs; scoring services; changes in test distributors; citations of instrument reviews; tests no longer available; and new references in the testing field. Publishers mentioned in each issue have addresses given. New publishers, new addresses, and occasional news notes concerning conferences and testing developments are included. Readers are asked to write directly to publishers for additional information.

---

* It should be noted that Educational Testing Service, in collaboration with Rutgers University Graduate School of Education, operates an ERIC Clearinghouse on Tests, Measurement and Evaluation (since Fall 1970). Access is through usual ERIC channels. It is responsible for "all documents whose major emphasis is on tests or other measurement devices; for those whose content is limited to evaluation procedures and techniques, and for those documents that describe the materials, procedures, and techniques of a specific program or project, regardless of the population, level, or content of the study as a whole." (*Test Collection Bulletin,* 1970, *4* (4).)

CRITIQUE.   Though the Test Collection Bulletin is indexed yearly, the user naturally cannot form any idea of the entire holdings of the Test Collection from it, even if he lives near enough to Princeton to visit it conveniently. The *Bulletin* does, however, provide an excellent register of current changes in the products and services in the testing field.

GENERAL COMMENT.   The *Bulletin* is well worth $2.00 for researchers who wish to stay current in the domain of commercially-published tests (and some non-commercial ones).

—M. B. M.

Q
Tests and Measurements in Child
Development: A Handbook

AUTHORS.   Orval G. Johnson and James W. Bommarito

AVAILABILITY.   Jossey-Bass Inc., Publishers, 615 Montgomery Street, San Francisco, California 94111. Copyright 1971.

TESTING AREAS COVERED.   (partial list) Abstraction; acceptance; achievement; activity; adjustment; adults, attitude toward; affectionateness; affectivity; aggression; ambiguity, intolerance of; anxiety; ascendancy; attitude; authority, attitudes toward; Behavior; body image; boredom; brain injury; Child-rearing; classroom; cognitive processes; cognitive style; communication; competence; control; creativity; Defensiveness; dependence; development; discipline; discrimination (cognitive); divergent thinking; dominance; Education; empathy; ethnic groups, attitudes toward; ethnocentrism; expectancy; Family; fear; flexibility; friendship; frustration; Goals; gratification; guilt; Health care; home atmosphere; hostility; hypnotizability; Identification; ideology; imagery; impulsivity; independence; insight; intelligence; interest; interracial feelings; Language skills; leadership; learning; life space; locus of control; love; Maternal behavior; memory; mental retardation; morale; motor skills; music; National identity; need gratification; nervousness; number skills; nurturance; Occupations; opinionation; opposition; Parents; peers; perception; personality; physical attributes; playfulness; popularity; prejudice; problem-solving; psychotherapy; punitiveness; Race; reading; reasoning; reciprocity; religious identity; responsibility; rigidity; School; security; self-concept; sensory-motor skills; sex role; social desirability; social distance; social perception; socio-economic status; space, perception of; status; suggestibility; Teacher; thinking; tolerance; Values; verbal ability; Wishes; worries.

DESCRIPTION.   The authors have collected 316 instruments, not commercially published, measuring aspects of the behavior of children from birth to twelve years old.

The instruments are organized into ten major categories: cognition (including intelligence and school readiness, language and number skills, and specific achievements; cognitive style and processes; and miscellaneous); personality and emotional characteristics (including general and specific variables, adjustment and anxiety); perceptions of environment (including attitudes toward adults, toward peers, and

other factors); self-concept; environment (including quality of mother-
ing, child-rearing practices, and attitudes toward school); physical
attributes; attitudes and interests; social behavior; and unclassified.

To be included, an instrument had to be available to professionals;
have enough information available on scoring and administration for
easy use; be long enough so that meaningful norms, and reliability and
validity data (if absent) could be developed by the user; and be reasonably easy to use (e.g., heavy equipment unnecessary). Originally,
a total of about 1,000 instruments was culled from a search covering the
1956–1965 period of professional journals (in psychology, psychiatry,
and education), books, research reports, and unpublished papers.

For each instrument, the authors include: title; authors; age for
which appropriate; variables measured (it is of interest that many
measures examined were vague as to this); type of measure (e.g.,
projective test, situational interview, etc.); availability; description of
the measure, including if possible more specification of variables,
administration, scoring, length, sample items, special considerations
involved, and comments from the author or other users; reliability and
validity; and bibliography, usually a brief sample of references supplied by the author. The typical write-up of an instrument is slightly
over one page in length, about 500 words.

An Appendix lists journals in which the measures appear, and indexes are provided for authors, measures, and subjects; a general index
is also provided.

CRITIQUE.   The authors are to be congratulated not only for their
heroic effort to bring together hundreds of scattered measures in child
development, but for the uncommonly well-produced book itself,
which is a pleasure to see and use.

The authors chose not to append any judgments, and by and large
to refrain from commenting on the instruments. This undoubtedly
simplified their work, but deprives the reader of comparative help
that can be useful to searchers.

Relying on author-provided references and materials undoubtedly
shortened a long and difficult task; again we must point out that
authors and test-constructors are not always the most objective sources
of information about measures.

Finally, Johnson and Bommarito indicate that "data on norms, reliability and validity were considered desirable but not crucial"; they
also indicate that reliability figures were "infrequently provided by the
originators of the measure." Norms are almost never mentioned for
the measures included; this is perhaps understandable for many non-
commercial instruments, but seems a serious oversight. Users need at

least to know means and standard deviations in roughly-specified populations; or, lacking this, that such material does or does not exist. Reliability and validity figures are not infrequently missing (e.g., for 7 of 21 measures of intelligence and school readiness, and for 4 of 26 measures of social behavior). Given such psychometric incompleteness, the authors must have had to tread a fine line between dissemination of possibly worthless instruments, and the stimulation of use for promising but relatively untried measures. By and large, they appear to have moved toward the latter pole in uncertain cases, but the user needs to read the descriptions carefully, and seek adidtional information before making a decision about use.

GENERAL COMMENT.   This compendium shows the results of hard work, and provides a distinctly-needed service. Users do need to be discriminating about the instruments included, and in many cases should plan to collect reliability and validity data as part of their studies. The book will undoubtedly accelerate the use of many of these instruments, which will in turn deepen knowledge about their properties. To this end, the authors' willingness to update the book at five-year intervals is commendable.

—M. B. M.

R
Tests in Print

EDITOR.   Oscar Krisen Buros

AVAILABILITY.   The Gryphon Press, 220 Montgomery Street, Highland Park, New Jersey 08904. Copyright 1961.

TESTING AREAS COVERED.   *Tests in Print* covers the same areas as do the Buros *Mental Measurements Yearbooks* (which see).

DESCRIPTION.   The bulk of this 479-page volume consists of two bibliographies, one of published, available (as of 1961) tests and one of tests no longer in print, but previously reviewed in the Buros series. Each of the 2,126 entries which are in print contains the test's title, the groups for which it is intended, publication dates, special comments, the number of scores produced, author(s), publisher, and foreign adaptation, if any. All of the tests which are in print are the subjects of reviews in the Buros' *Mental Measurements Yearbooks*.

The entries in the "Out of Print" section are limited to titles, and references to reviews in the Buros series. These two bibliographies are followed by two sets of technical recommendations, one for psychological tests and diagnostic techniques and one for achievement tests, which were prepared by joint committees of the American Psychological Association, the American Educational Research Association, and the National Council on Measurements Used in Education in March 1954 and January 1955. These recommendations focus on the information which test manuals should contain, and the manner in which they should present that information. The specific areas the recommendations cover are: tests to which the recommendations apply; the levels of importance of the recommendations; the intended audience for the recommendations; interpretation of the test; validity; reliability; administration and scoring; and scales and norms. The remainder of *Tests in Print* contains a publishers' directory and index, a distributors' directory and index, and title and name indexes.

GENERAL COMMENT.   Without access to the Buros volumes of reviews, the bibliographies in *Tests in Print* are minimally useful; they can only advise as to the existence and availability of instruments. The technical recommendations sections, however, should be read and retained by all in the testing profession, test users as well as test authors. And the publisher and distributor indexes are quite handy. A new volume of *Tests in Print* is scheduled for 1972.

—R. B. E.

S

The Self Concept: A Critical Survey of Pertinent Research Literature

AUTHOR. Ruth C. Wylie

AVAILABILITY. University of Nebraska Press, 901 N. 17 Street, Lincoln, Nebraska 68508. Copyright 1961.

TESTING AREAS COVERED. Achievement; adjustment; affiliation; aggression; anxiety; aspiration; Body image; Construct; Defensiveness; delinquency; dependency; depression; Ego strength; Friendship; Happiness; health; hostility; Ideal; identification; insight; Leadership; learning; Neurosis; Projective; protocol analysis; Q-sort; Self; self-acceptance; self-approval; self-awareness; self-concept; self-ideal; self-regard; semantic differential; social desirability; sociometric.

DESCRIPTION. *The Self Concept* is far more than a compendium of measures. In it Wylie reviews the history of interest in self-relevant constructs, discusses phenomenological theories and the problems they present for measurement and research design, and makes an exhaustive and critical review of empirical studies which "relate the phenomenal self to other variables, and/or . . . test some aspect of self-concept theory." Thus her concern is strongly substantive, not only technical.

Wylie also lists, and discusses a substantial fraction of, a large number of research instruments dealing with the following domains: measures of phenomenal *self-regard* (that is, self-esteem or self-acceptance) including 29 Q-sorts, 90 questionnaires, rating scales, adjective checklists, and 7 coding schemes for the analysis of interview protocols; 5 measures of *configurational aspects* of the phenomenal self; 14 scales measuring *self-evaluation* of some specific ability or performance; 29 measures of various aspects of the *non-phenomenal* (unconscious) *self*, such as body image; and a substantial series of studies concerned with the *"insightfulness"* of the self-concept (often, minimal discrepancy between self's and others' views of self). Over 900 references are included.

In general, those instruments for which reliability and validity data are minimal are simply listed and referenced. Measures which have been used widely, and have seen more developmental effort, are discussed in some detail. No standard format is used, but the form of the instrument, how it is administered and scored, its underlying assumptions, and evidence on its reliability and construct validity are all usually discussed. The general tone is not that of an annotator or abstracter, but that of an interested scholar weighing the claims of researchers, and clarifying crucial issues in what must surely be one of the most deceptively simple and actually difficult measurement domains conceivable.

CRITIQUE.   The information provided on specific measures is quite uneven, so that it is usually not possible for a user to proceed through the book until he has found what he wants. Rather (and this is undoubtedly the course which researchers *should* take in this domain), he is led to think, reconceptualize, and face underlying issues which various specific instruments embody. In short, the user of the book, if he is not knowledgeable about the self concept from the start, shortly becomes so. Cookbookism is fortunately very difficult with this volume.

Work in the self area has not stood still in the last decade, so researchers looking for instruments, or further information on instruments assessed here, would do well to examine more recent compendia, and the recent literature.

GENERAL COMMENT.   *The Self Concept* stands as a substantial scholarly achievement, and a model which more compendia could well follow. The technical compendium, in which specific instruments are discussed atomistically, or compared briefly with alternate measures of the same variable, tends to promote arbitrary, insightless use of instruments. What Wylie's book says implicitly to the user is: "Think about the issues you are considering. Here is my best effort at a coherent organization of what has been thought and attempted in this field so far. Now go and build on this." This, not the arbitrary plugging of gaps in a research design with a convenient instrument, is the essence of science.

—M. B. M.

T
Unobtrusive Measures

AUTHORS.　　Eugene J. Webb, Donald T. Campbell, Richard D. Schwartz, and Lee Sechrest

AVAILABILITY.　　Rand McNally Company, P.O. Box 7600, Chicago, Illinois 60680. Copyright 1965.

TESTING AREAS COVERED.　　Accretion; archives; audiotape; Body movement; Content; conversation; Erosion; expressive movement; Facial expression; film; Honesty; Inclination; interaction; Noise level; Observation; Physical traces; pupil dilation; Role; Time duration; Videotape; Wiggle.

DESCRIPTION.　　This novel and interesting book examines the nature of measuring instruments or techniques, other than interviews or questionnaires, which are non-reactive—that is, influence the phenomena they are designed to measure very little or not at all. Most of the other compendia we have reviewed do not face this issue, or deal with it only tangentially through discussions of "fakeability," "item transparency," and so on. Yet the very act, in a context, of filling out a questionnaire, being knowingly observed or interviewed usually changes the respondent's behavior in ways which are relevant to the variable being measured. For example, if many people in an organization fill out a questionnaire on "trust," their views of trust, and the actual trust level in the organization may be substantially lowered (or raised).

Chapter 1 provides a thoughtful overview of the problems of reaching "approximations to knowledge," and discusses sources of error such as "guinea pig" effects, distortions arising from persons taking roles such as "respondent" or "interviewee," and change effects arising from the experience of responding to the instrument itself, as well as many other error sources stemming from the investigator, the sampling methods, and the content domains being studied.

Webb et al. discuss specific unobtrusive measures—which are only described briefly or in passing—under six major headings: physical traces (erosion and accretion of various sorts, such as "noseprints" on glass display cases in a museum); running-record archives (e.g., city directories, newspapers, voting records); episodic and private records (e.g., peanut sales at baseball games, suicide notes); simple observation (e.g., counting of tattoos); and contrived observation, involving "hidden hardware and control" (e.g., measures of pupil dilation).

Reliability and validity (except face validity) are not discussed; the reader interested in a particular technique will have to go to the original reference, if one is given, or simply construct his own adaptation of the technique involved, and assess its reliability and validity himself. Brief evaluative comments are occasionally included. Essentially, the authors are less interested in any particular measure, and more interested in elucidating the general problems involved in collecting data by unobtrusive means; specific measures are primarily alluded to as examples.

Each chapter concludes with over-all commentary on the problems of its domain, and there are some useful final reflections on advantages of non-verbal, non-reactive methods in moving "from symbols and shadows to the truth" (Cardinal Newman's epitaph, printed here as "Chapter 9" of the book). Over 500 references are included.

CRITIQUE.   Webb and his co-authors did not set out to produce a compendium in the usual sense, but simply to locate and describe a range of techniques which do not suffer from reactivity, and to do so in a heuristic way. This objective has been achieved; the reader of this book will never again quite be able to use any measure without considering the degree to which its very use may be altering the phenomena in which he is interested. And he will have a variety of ideas at hand for measuring social behavior unobtrusively and simply.

However, the validity issues involved are not minor. For example, one measure used to study the effect of introduction of television into a community was rate of library withdrawals. Webb et al. say, "Fiction titles dropped, nonfiction titles were unaffected"—as if the measure were sound and causality had been demonstrated. Yet studies also exist which show that amount of reading, for children, is *greater* for frequent TV watchers. Face validity is not empirical validity. In most cases, the authors do discuss alternate interpretations to be drawn from a given measure.

The authors acknowledge that they have not dealt at all with the ethical issues involved in the use of many of these techniques, which are basically devoted to the collection of information without the awareness of individual "respondents." Such methods as eavesdropping, the use of concealed cameras, and the examination of governmental documents do involve the invasion of privacy, and the provision of data without "informed consent." On the other hand, counting "noseprints" on a glass display case as a measure of interest in its contents would not seem to invade privacy, or identify a component of the aggregate measure derived. In general, the ethical issues surrounding the collection of data from human subjects have seen sharply increased concern since 1966, when this book was written. It is encouraging that the general political climate has placed increasing restrictions on collection of privileged or covert information for research purposes. Persons are not objects, and should not be tacitly treated as such by researchers.* Anyone considering using methods in this book should carefully consider the ethical implications of what he would like to do. In most cases, funding agencies, especially governmental ones, now insist on informed consent of subjects, thus ruling out many measures described here.† However, many useful and ethically inoffensive measures remain, and their range and variety will stimulate and delight the reader.

* Cf. the thoughtful discussion by H. C. Kelman of the human use of human subjects, in *A time to speak,* San Francisco: Jossey-Bass, 1968; and B. Barber, Experimenting with humans, *The Public Interest,* 1967, 6, 91–102. Also G. Sjoberg, *The ethics and politics of social research,* Cambridge, Massachusetts: Schenkman Publishing Co., 1967.

† See Department of Health, Education and Welfare, Grants Administration Manual, Ch. 1–40, Protection of human subjects. Washington, D.C., 1970. Also United States Public Health Service, Surgeon General's directives on human experimentation, *American Psychologist,* 1967, 22, 350–355.

Uniterm Index

UNITERM INDEX

This index enables the reader who is interested in a particular *variable* to find tests (or compendia of tests) concerned with that variable. Additionally, if a given instrument employs a *method* other than the usual pencil-and-paper test format (true–false, checklist, ratings, Likert or Guttman scales, or the like), a Uniterm for the method is also assigned. Methods so indexed include content analysis, graphic, observation, performance test, projective, protocol analysis, Q-sort, and semantic differential.

The *numbers* after each Uniterm (which is essentially a keyword or tag) refer to the number of each instrument which is referenced by that Uniterm. Instruments are arranged in Section I of the book alphabetically by title and sequentially by number.

Letters appearing after a given Uniterm refer to compendia published elsewhere, in which one or more instruments referenced by that Uniterm appear. These compendia are found in Section II of the book, arranged alphabetically by title and sequentially by letter.

Liberal use of synonyms or possibly-associated Uniterms will aid the reader in his search. No effort was made to make the present set of Uniterms completely systematic and exhaustive.

Uniterm Index

Uniterms	*References*
aloofness	52
altruism	3, 17, 48, B, M
ambiguity	H, M, Q
ambition	B
American	15
amorality	36
anal character	D
anger	46, B, M
anomia	C, M
anomie	52, H, O
antagonism	29, 31
anti-Semitism	32, H
anxiety	4, 6, 7, 39, 44, 46, 48, 72, B, D, J, M, Q, S
apathy	J
approach-avoidance	72
approval	8, 27, 41, B
aptitude	P
aquaintanceship	G
archives	T
arithmetic operations and concepts	A, K
arousal	M
articulation	D
arts and crafts	A
ascendency	40, Q
aspiration	48, 60, M, O, S
assertion	28
assimilation	O
association	71
assurance	J
atmosphere	M
attainment	83
attention	D
attitude	5, 15, 16, 22, 26, 43, 64, 68, C, F, G, H, L, M, P, Q
audacity	1
audience	6
audiotape	T
authenticity	17, 52, M
authoritarian	B
authoritarianism	18, 22, 41, 43, 48, C, M, O
authoritative	67
authority	18, 22, 39, 42, 56, 62, 73, O, Q
autocracy	53
autocratic	30

Uniterm Index

Uniterms	References
automation	F
autonomic nervous system	7
autonomy	2, 19, 24, 32, 49, 52, B, M
avoidance	8, 69, B, M
awareness	16, 17, 50, M
background	B, M
behavior	8, 9, 14, 23, 25, 28, 29, 31, 34, 38, 39, 50, 52, 55, 57, 64, 76, 78, M, Q
behavior, classroom	D
being	12
belief	5, 15, 18, M
belligerence	M
belonging	B
Bible	H
biological characteristics	L
birth control	M
blame	63
blunt	30
body image	Q, S
body movement	T
boldness	A
boredom	Q
boss	62
brain injury	Q
breast feeding	B
bureaucratization	M
bureaucracy	66
business	G, M
business education	N
capitalization	A
career	M
career orientation	F
caring	12
categorizing	13, 74
change	1, 2, 5, 19, 50, 70, M
changefulness	17
character and personality	N, R
chart	56
child	6, 9, 45, 57, 76, 80, B, M, P
child-rearing	B, D, Q
church	H
citizen duty	G
citizenship	A
civic competence	G
civics	A

Uniterms	*References*
civil liberties	G
civil rights	M
class	15
class consciousness	O
class identification	F
classroom	57, 76, 81, I, Q
client relations	M
climate	52, M
climate, classroom	D
clinical	74, 82
cognition	13, 18, 20, 37, 58, 80, 82
cognitive	74, I
cognitive dissonance	5
cognitive processes	Q
cognitive style	Q
cohesion	O
cohesiveness	B, C, M
collaboration	17, M
comfort	50
comention	J
commitment	38, H, M
communication	32, 40, 50, 65, B, M, Q
communists	G
community	B, O
community attitude	C
companionship	B
company policies and practices	42
compatibility	21, 23, B
compensation	42
competence	17, 25, 31, 39, 51, 54, 55, 63, B, G, H, M, Q
competition	3, 48
competitive	30
competitiveness	B
complexity	49, M
complex organizations	O
compliance	66, B
computational and scoring devices	N, R
concentration	44
concept	5
concern	31, M
confidence	77, 81, B
conflict	8, 62, 66, B, L, M
conformity	10, 15, 17, 28, 31, B, M, O
confrontation	28

Uniterms	*References*
delinquency proneness	D
democracy	53, B
democratic attitudes	G
denial	14
dependability	63
dependence	39, 40, 51, 78, A, Q
dependency	69, B, M, S
dependent	30
depression	39, 46, B, M, S
deprivation	B
development	57, 80, B, M, Q
deviance	B, D, O
deviation	17
diagnosis	38, 82
diagnostic	74
disagreement	29
disapproval	41
discipline	76, B, Q
discrimination (race)	26
discrimination (cognitive)	58, Q
discussion skill	76
dismay	J
dissatisfaction	D, M
dissimilarity	35, 72
dissofrustance	J
distance	35
distrustful	30
divergent thinking	Q
divorce	B
docile	30
dogmatism	18, H, M
dominance	2, 10, 19, 23, 30, 40, 51, B, Q
driving and safety education	N, R
drug abuse	E
drug effects	E
drug information	E
drug use	E
dyad	12, 29, 32, 70, I
echelon	56
economic	B
economic practices	L
economic systems	L
education	B, D, L, M, N, O, Q, R
educational institutions	L
educational workers	L

Uniterm Index

Uniterms	References
generous	30
geography	A
geometry	A
Gestalt	20
goal	24, 40, 48, 83, B, M, Q
good impression	10
Gottschaldt figures	20
government	F, G, K
grade point average	60
grammar	A
graph	53
graphic	20, 37, 40, 41, 48
gratification	Q
gratification, delay of	D
group	25, 28, 29, 35, 38, 40, 50, 55, 57, 61, 69, 76, 78, 83, C, I, M
group dimensions	24, C
group dynamics	C
growth	59, B
guidance	D
guilt	B, Q
handicapping, conditions	D
handwriting	N, R
happiness	B, M, S
harm	4
health	59, B, K, L, O, S
health and physical education	N, R
health and safety	A
health care	Q
hedonic tone	24
helplessness	H
heterosexual practices	L
heterosexuality	2, 19
history	A, K
home	9, B
home atmosphere	Q
home economics	N, R
homemaking	B, J
homespunness	J
homogeneity	24
honesty	33, T
hostility	39, 46, 72, 75, A, B, Q, S
human-heartedness	26, 68
human nature	D
human relations training	31, 39, 50, 51, 58, 63, 69

Uniterm Index

Uniterms	*References*
occupational mobility	F
occupational ratings	F
occupational roles	O
occupational status	F
occupational values	F
occupations	Q
oedipal	B
older persons	F
openness	18, 52, 58, 63, M
opinion	29, P
opinionation	18, Q
opinion leadership	G, H
opportunism	36
opposition	Q
order	2, 19
orderliness	1
organization	34, 35, 51, 52, 53, 56, 62, 63, 66, 67, M
organizational	73
organizational characteristics	F
organizational control	F
orientation	29, 54, M
originality	77
others	27, 63
overindulgence	45
overprotection	45, B
pacifism	G
pairing	69, 78
parents	B, M, Q
participation	24, 25, 38, 40, 62, C, G, M
participative	53, 67
partisanship	G
party image	G
passiveness	J
passivity	B
pathemia	J
patriotism	G
peer	51, 52, 56, 60, 62, 77, Q
peer group	B
peer status	D
penmanship	A
perception	13, 32, 35, 37, 47, 56, 58, 60, 79, M, Q
performance	83, B, M
performance test	76, 82

Uniterms	*References*
permeability	24
permissiveness	58, B, M
persistence	75
person	58
personage admiration	G
personal adjustment	2, O
personality	10, 11, 19, 22, 27, 46, 47, 49, 59, 61, 72, 74, B, C, D, E, M, N, O, P, Q, R
personality traits	O
personnel	M
perspective	32
philosophical issues	L
philosophy	B, N, R
physical attributes	Q
physical development	33
physical education	A
physical environment	I
physical skills	A
physical traces	T
planning	60, 62, 73, 76
play	B
playfulness	Q
polarization	24
political	18, 22, M
political attitudes	G, O
political behavior	O
political issues	L
political participation	C
political system	G, L
polyarchy	53
popularity	Q
position	66, M
positive regard	D
potency	24
power	17, 53, 67, 73, B, G, H, M
powerlessness	C, H, M
practicality	49
practicalness	J
praise	B
prejudice	5, 18, 26, 68, B, G, Q
premarital	B
prestige	B
principal	52
problems	64, 65

Uniterm Index

Uniterms	*References*
skepticism	44
small groups	O
sociability	10, B, M
social	61, 79, M
social attitudes	G
social competency	D
social desirability	41, 49, H, Q, S
social distance	58, C, D, G, Q
social institutions	L
social intelligence	37
socialism	G
social issues	L
socialization	10, 80, A
social mobility	M, O
social organization	A
social participation	C, M, O
social perception	M, Q
social practices	L
social problems	L
social responsibility	H
social service	42
social skills	33, 37, K
social status	42
social studies	N, R
social systems	L
social welfare	G
societal	15
societal characteristics	O
society	16
socio-economic status	15, 60, B, C, F, M, N, O, Q, R
socio-emotional	25, 29, 34, 52, B
sociology	A
sociometric	25, 35, C, S
solidarity	29, C
Soviet Union	G
space	Q
span of control	M
spatial ability	K
speaking	A
spelling	A
spontaneity	10, 59
sportsmanship	A
spouse	B
stability	24, B
standards	B

Uniterm Index

Uniterms	References
statistics	A
status	10, 24, 33, 63, 66, B, L, M, Q
status-concern	H, O
status consistency	O
status inconsistency	F
stolidness	J
stolparsomonia	J
strain	B, M
stratification	24
stress	M
strictness	B
striving	48
structure	40, 52, 56, C, I, M
student	57, 77, 82, I
study skills	K
subduedness	J
subgroup	78
submission	40, B
subordinate	34, 51, 56, 62, M
success	48, 83, B
succorance	1, 2, 19
suggestibility	Q
suggestion	29
summarizing	38
super ego	75
superego asthenia	J
superior	34, 51, 52, 56, 62, M
supervision	42, 52, B, C, F, I, K, M
supervisor	73
support	32, 51, 83, B, M
suppressibility	J
suppression	49
surgency	44
suspiciousness	M
sympathy	26, B
system	67
T group	31, 39, 50, 51, 58, 63, 69, I, M
task	29, 34, 40, 52, 54, 58, 63, 76, B, M
teacher	43, 52, 57, 66, 77, 81, I, M, Q
teacher behavior	D
teacher performance	D
teacher-pupil relationship	43
teaching	D, K
temperament	A
tempo	40

Uniterms	*References*
tensinflexia	J
tension	29, 40, B, F
test anxiety	4, 46
test programs	N, R
tests	D
theoretical	49
Theory Y	67
therapeutic community	61
therapy	28
thinking	47, 82, Q
threat	72, 83, B
time duration	T
time perspective	18, 59
timidity	1
tobacco	E
toilet training	B
tolerance	10, 50, B, G, Q
toughmindedness	H
traditionalist	43, B
training	M
trust	17, 31, B, H, M
trustingness	J
unassertiveness	J
unconditionality of regard	70
underdog	G
understanding	32, B
undisciplined students, identification of	D
union and management	F
urban areas	O
value	15, 16, 27, 33, 49, 58, 59, 60, 84, B, D, H, M, O, Q
variability	J
variety	42
verbal	M
verbal ability	71, K, Q
verbal behavior	I
verbalization	B
videotape	T
Vietnam	G
vigor	44
viscidity	24
vocabulary	71
vocational interest	F, K
vocations	N, R

Uniterm Index

Author Index

Test and compendia authors, and their numbers and letters,
respectively, are shown in boldface.

Adorno, Theodor W., **22**, 65, 67, 80, 81, 82, 83, 84
Alexander, Sheldon, **4**, 14, 15, 16, 17
Alfert, E., 284, 286
Allen, V. L., 87
Allport, G. W., 101, 103
Altrocchi, John, **72**, 281, 282, 283, 285
Amidon, E., 67, 323
Anderson, D. P., 211, 212
Anderson, Lois L., **42**, 165
Andrews, F., 279, 280
Andrews, J. H. M., 130, 131, 209, 210, 211, 212
Applezweig, Mortimer H., **8**, 28, 29, 30, 31, 32, 193, 195
Argyris, Chris, **31**, 119, 120, 121, 122, 205, 208, 360
Ari, O. N., 215, 216
Athanasiou, Robert, **F**, 354, 355, 359
Atkinson, John W., **48**, 191, 192, 193, 194, 195, 329
Ayers, E. G., 77, 78
Baldwin, J. M., 317, 318
Bales, Robert F., **29**, 107, 109, 110, 111, 112, 153, 154, 348, 361
Bannister, D., 292, 293, 294
Barber, B., 387
Barratt, Ernest S., **7**, 24, 25, 26
Barrett-Lennard, G. T., **70**, 272, 273, 274, 275
Barry, J., 281, 283, 285
Bass, Bernard M., **54**, **62**, 81, 159, 162, 163, 217, 218, 219, 245
Baum, B. H., 216
Beatty, Walcott H., **D**, 350, 351
Bell, H. M., 307, 308
Bendig, A. W., 245, 246, 247
Benedict, B., 62
Berger, E. M., 64, 67, 102, 103
Berkum, M., 176, 177
Berrien, F. K., 370
Berzon, B., 274, 275

Biase, D. V., 183, 185
Bills, Robert E., **27**, 100, 102, 103
Bion, W. R., 268, 270
Birney, R., 193, 195
Blakely, L. S., 172
Block, Jack, **11**, 42, 43
Blumberg, A., 264
Bommarito, James W., **Q**, 345, 379, 380
Bonjean, Charles N., **O**, 347, 357, 375, 376
Borgatta, E. F., 111, 112, 176, 177, 298, 299
Boyd, P. R., 293, 294
Boyer, E. Gil, **I**, 360, 361
Bowers, N. D., 304
Brady, J. P., 182, 184
Brannon, C., 142, 143
Braun, J. R., 218, 219
Briggs, Katherine C., **47**, 186, 197
Brookover, W. B., 307, 308
Brown, A. F., 212, 213
Brown, R. J., 211, 212
Brunswick, E., 228, 230
Buchanan, P. C., 202, 204
Budd, W. C., 172
Budner, S., 142, 143
Buhler, C., 234, 236
Bunker, Douglas R., **50**, 200, 202, 203, 204, 211
Burdick, H., 193
Buros, Oscar K., **N**, **R**, 39, 40, 365, 366, 372, 373, 374, 382
Byrne Donn, **72**, 281, 282, 283, 284, 285, 286
Callahan, D. M., 61, 62
Callis, Robert, **43**, 170, 171, 172
Campbell, Donald T., **T**, 81, 84, 130, 131, 385, 386
Carlson, Robert E., 165
Cartwright, D. A., 157, 158
Castore, C., 370
Cattell, Raymond B., **J**, 7, 9, 26, 362, 363